D0874989

Burma
The State of Myanmar

David I. Steinberg

GEORGETOWN UNIVERSITY PRESS
Washington, D.C.

Dedicated

to the

diverse Burmese peoples

who have suffered too much

in a state

yet to fulfill its promise

Georgetown University Press, Washington, D.C.
© 2001 by Georgetown University Press. All rights reserverd.
Printed in the United States of America

10   9   8   7   6   5   4   3   2   1

This volume is printed on acid-free offset book paper.

Library of Congress Cataloging-in-Publication Data

Steinberg, David I., 1928–
Burma, the state of Myanmar/David I. Steinberg.
   p. cm.
Includes bibliographical references and index.
ISBN 0-87840-842-8 (cloth : alk. paper)
1. Burma—Politics and government—1988–   I. Title

DS530.65 .S74 2001
959.105—dc21   00-061037

Contents

Preface and Acknowledgments

Preface

The past lies before us and the future behind, the ancient Greeks believed. We can see the past, but since we cannot view the future, it must be hidden in back of us. But if we look to the past and understand it, perhaps it will give us a mirror with which to peer over our shoulder and anticipate the future.

If we live long enough and retain a modicum of memory, we may accrue what may be called "longitudinal knowledge," sometimes accurate or possibly fanciful. Such knowledge built over time may help provide perspective on events of the past and their relation to the present and even the future. In writing this manuscript, I have brought together in more coherent and coordinated form experience over a number of decades that I have tried to express in various fora. In doing so, I have drawn upon my memories and the myriad intellectual and social debts that I have accrued over the years, even though some who have contributed to this effort are, as they say, unindicted co-conspirators. To identify such people would be impossible because of their numbers and indiscrete because some who have held high positions in a variety of governments might be placed in intellectual, if not physical, jeopardy. Some have passed on to their karmic rewards, and others must be repaid in future incarnations, since I know there is no way for me to recompense what they have taught me. The mistakes that are included herein are a product of my own ignorance, and no institution or other individual should be held responsible for these errors.

The reader should know that I have been following Burma since 1956, when, to broaden the base of my interest in the Chinese management of the non-Han areas of Southwest China, I attended the School of Oriental and

African Studies of the University of London to study Burmese and Southeast Asia. I spent four years in Burma, from 1958 to 1962, as the assistant representative of The Asia Foundation, and in that role I was privileged to travel widely throughout the country and to meet diverse peoples of all levels and all nationalities. Much later, as the director of the Office of Philippines, Thailand, and (residual) Burma Affairs in the Agency for International Development, Department of State, I led a team in 1978 that negotiated the re-entry of the USAID assistance program to Burma. Since that time, I have written extensively on that country and revisited it on numerous occasions.

The chapters of this volume represent both new efforts and ones reconsidered, restructured, regrouped, and updated to reflect events at the time this volume went to press. Events in any work on contemporary issues may overtake publication. But I have attempted to deal with broad trends that I feel will stand scrutiny over time.

The reader will recognize that there are very few people who continuously follow and attempt to write seriously about the political economy of the country called either Burma or Myanmar. One irony of this relative isolation, reflecting much of the isolation of Burmese history, is that it increases the relative importance of any serious work while at the same time lowering its quality because of a lack of competition and dialogue. The marketplace of ideas on contemporary Myanmar tends to be oligopolistic.

Although I have tried to be balanced in my approach to the complex and highly emotional political and social issues of this state, my predilections will no doubt surface, but I hope they will be marked by openness and transparency. I have tried to deal objectively with events, and although my interpretations of patterns and trends must necessarily be subjective, I have attempted to keep my analytical gyroscope level. Only my readers will be able to judge whether this has been accomplished.

I would like to thank those who have encouraged me in this work and those who have been kind enough to read the manuscript and offer detailed suggestions that have immeasurably improved the quality of this volume. I am especially indebted to David Chandler, formerly of Monash University and now adjunct professor at Georgetown University; John Brandon of The Asia Foundation; and Bradley Babson, formerly of the World Bank, all of whom made numerous substantive and editorial corrections and suggestions. The errors of fact or interpretation, of course, are the responsibility of the writer alone. I would also like to thank Ms. Deborah Weiner of Georgetown University Press for assistance, encouragement, and efficiency in bringing this volume to fruition, and Ms. Bojana Ristich for copyediting that has sharpened my prose and focused my writing.

My wife, Ann Myongsook Lee, accompanied me on several trips to Burma and bore up under the strain of my preoccupation with finishing this work, and to her I apologize for my immersion and preoccupation in this effort.

Acknowledgments

The author wishes to thank the following publishers and publications for their approvals to use materials written by the author and earlier published or written under their auspices. All previous publications have been edited, updated, and often amalgamated with other new and older materials and selectively mined for data and interpretations. It would be inappropriate, however, not to mention the assistance in this endeavor.

Asian Survey
"Burma 1992: Plus Ça Change . . . ," 1992
"Burma 1991: The Miasma in Myanmar," 1991

Brookings Institution
"The Road to Political Recovery: The Salience of Politics in Economics." In *Burma: Prospects for a Democratic Future,* ed. Robert Rotberg, 1998

Burma Debate
"Myanmar and the Requirements of Mobilization and Orthodoxy," 1992

Crawford House Publishing, Adelaide, Australia
In *Burma/Myanmar: Strong Regime—Weak State?* eds. Morten Pedersen, Emily Rudland, and R.J. May, 1999

Forum of Democratic Leaders in the Asia Pacific (Seoul)
"NGOs and the Building of Civil Society in Burma/Myanmar," 1999

Institute for Security and International Studies, Chulalongkorn University, Bangkok, Thailand

Crisis in Burma: Stasis and Change in Political Economy in Turmoil. Working Paper No. 5, 1989

Institute for Southeast Asian Studies, Singapore
"Burma: Liberalization in Myanmar: How Real Are the Changes?" *Contemporary Southeast Asia,* 1993
"Burma/Myanmar and the Dilemmas of U.S. Foreign Policy," *Contemporary Southeast Asia,* August 1999
"Myanmar: Regional Relationships and Internal Concerns," *Southeast Asian Affairs,* 1998
"Constitutional and Political Bases of Minority Insurrections in Burma." In *Armed Separatism in Southeast Asia*, ed. Lim Joo-Jock and Vani S., 1984

Library of Congress
A chapter on economics, written and approved for publication in the planned 1994 Burma country study. The work was never published because of a budget shortage.

M.E. Sharpe
"Myanmar: The Anomalies of Politics and Economics." In *Driven by Growth: Political Change in the Asia-Pacific Region,* 2d ed., ed. J. Morley, 1997

Silkworm Books
"A Void in Myanmar: Civil Society in Burma." In *Burma Central Netherlands and Transnational Institute,* 1999.

Studies in Conflict and Terrorism
"Myanmar as Nexus: Sino–Indian Rivalries on the Frontier," 1993

Westview Press
"Japanese Economic Assistance to Burma: Aid in the 'Tarenagashi Manner'?" In *Managing Japan's Foreign Aid: Power and Policy in a New Era*, ed. Bruce Koppel and Robert Orr, 1993

World Bank
Chapter 5, Appendix B, "Myanmar: An Economic and Social Assessment," by Bradley Babson. Duplicated 2000.

I would also like to thank and acknowledge the approval of Martin Smith and Zed Books for permission to publish Appendices C and D to chapter 4.

Notes

On Names—National, Personal, and Geographic

In 1989, the military government of the Union of Burma changed the name of the country to the Union of Myanmar. Myanmar is the spelling of the official name of the country in Burmese script, the full term of which is Myanmar Naingandaw (lit., "the Royal Country of Myanmar"). The military claimed that this was ethnically a more neutral term and would lead to greater harmony among the state's diverse peoples and "provide a feeling of release from the British colonial past and . . . give a previously divided and fractious country a sense of national unity under a new banner of 'The Union of Myanmar.'" The term was applied with rigidity (sometimes spelled as Myanma), and applied to the total history of the country.[1] The major ethnic group in the country was termed the "Bamars." Many of the geographic names used in English were changed to conform to indigenous spelling. For example, Rangoon became Yangon. Some streets and other designations that had been named during the colonial period were also changed.[2]

Because these changes were imposed by a government that the opposition felt was illegitimate—and there is considerable dispute over the historical uses of either "Burma" or "Myanmar"—the opposition refused to acquiesce to them. Although the United Nations and most countries accepted the changes as the prerogative of a government in power, the United States did not. As this is written, the use of either term is a surrogate indicator of political persuasion, and perhaps Burma/Myanmar is the only state in which this dichotomy of national name is such an indicator.

In this volume, I have tried to use the terms without political implications— a daunting task. Thus both terms are used in the title to this work. In the text, "Myanmar" will generally be used for the period since the military coup of 1988, but "Burma" will be applied to the rest of that country's history.

At times, both terms will be used to demonstrate that they are adopted with political neutrality and to reflect the flow of history. "Burman," the traditional term for the major ethnic group, is also employed here, while "Burmese" is used for any citizen of that country. "Burmese" is also applied for the language of the Burman ethnic group and as an adjective.

The Myanmar government rejects the use of the term "opposition" in reference to the National League for Democracy (NLD). It notes:

> The NLD is constantly and erroneously referred to as an opposition party. In fact, the Government of Myanmar does not regard the NLD or any other 9 legally existing parties as opposition parties since the Government regards itself not as a political party but as a transitional government (a national institution) taking the responsibility of discarding the Socialist One-Party System practicing a Socialist Economy and paving the way for a Multi-Party Democracy by introducing a Market-Oriented Economy.[3]

For the sake of clarity, however, the NLD will often be referred to as the opposition, for whatever its legal status, it is clearly opposed to the present military regime.

The Burmese have no surnames. Each person, including children in the same family, will have a personal name. Names are normally of one to four syllables, and often the first letter is chosen after the birth day of the week. The term "U" (pronounced "oo") is a designation of respect and means "uncle" (thus U Nu's name is really "Nu") and is roughly equivalent to "Mr."; "Daw" (aunt) is the female equivalent. Other familial terms are also employed; *ko* for elder brother, *maung* for younger brother, *ma* for younger sister. But the reader is warned that these terms may also be integral parts of names and not familial appellations. Titles are normally eliminated in the volume after first use.

Political leader Aung San Suu Kyi has attached her illustrious father's name, Aung San, to her personal name, Suu Kyi, to benefit from the political aura associated with it.

Geographic Names

Traditional Spelling/Name	Military Revised Spelling/Name
Union of Burma	Union of Myanmar
Burma	Myanmar; sometimes Myanma

Rangoon	Yangon
Burman	Bamar
Pegu	Bago
Pagan	Bagan
Irrawaddy	Ayeyarwady
Tenasserim	Tanintharyi
Arakan	Rakhine
Akyab	Sittwe
Moulmein	Mawlamyaing
Magwe	Magway
Karen	Kayin
Bassein	Bathein
Paan	Hpa-an
Salween (river)	Thanlwin
Sittang (river)	Sittoung
Chindwin (river)	Chindwinn[4]

Dramatis Personae

Aung Gyi	B. 1918. Brigadier (retired), former close associate of Ne Win, 4th Burma Rifles; heir apparent to Ne Win, 1962–63; later jailed and then released; founded Union Nationals Democratic Party, 1988.
Aung Min	Colonel, Minister of Cooperatives under State Law and Order Restoration Council (SLORC) and Secretary General, Union Solidarity and Development Association (USDA).
Aung San	1916–47. Generalissimo; commander of army in World War II; founder of independent Burma; assassinated July 19, 1947, before independence.
Aung San Suu Kyi	B. 1945. Daughter of Aung San; educated abroad; married to an Englishman (Michael Aris, who died in March 1999); leader of opposition NLD, 1988 to present; under house arrest 1989–95; Nobel Laureate, 1991; often referred to by the military as "the Lady."

Aye Ko	B. 1921. General, 4th Burma Rifles; Joint Secretary, Burma Socialist Programme Party (BSPP) until his resignation in July 1988.
Ba Swe	1915–78. Member Anti-Fascist People's Freedom League (AFPFL); sometime Deputy Prime Minister; socialist leader; split with U Nu in 1958; with Kyaw Nyein founded the Stable AFPFL political party.
Bo Mya	B. 1927. General; leader of the Karen National Defense Organization (KNDO); Chair, Democratic Alliance for Burma (DAB); replaced as leader in February 2000 by Ba Thin Sein.
Khin Nyunt	B. 1939. General; Director, Directorate of Defense Security and Intelligence (DDSI); Secretary-1, SLORC, State Peace and Development Council (SPDC).
Khun Sa	B. 1933–34. Former Commander, Mong Tai Army; drug lord; also known as Chang Chi-fu.
Kyaw Nyein	1915–87. Founding member, Burma Socialist Party; member AFPFL; joined with Ba Swe in 1958 to form Stable AFPFL.
Kyaw Tun	Member, AFPFL.
Kyi Maung	B. 1920. Colonel (retired); member, Revolutionary Council, 1958–60; jailed; then spokesman, NLD.
Maung Aye	B. 1940. General, Commander, Burma Army; member, SLORC, SPDC.
Maung Maung	1925–94. Newspaper publisher; law scholar; President and Chair, BSPP, August–September 1988.
Ne Win	B. 1911. General (retired); Commander, 4th Burma Rifles; Deputy Commander, Burma Army, 1948, and Commander, beginning 1949; Prime Minister, 1958–60; Defense Minister; Chairman, Revolutionary Council, 1962–74; President, 1974–81; Chairman, BSPP, 1962–88.
Nu	1907–95. Prime Minister, 1948–56, 1957–58, 1960–62; jailed, then in rebellion in Thailand; later returned to Burma and spent remaining days editing Buddhist scriptures.

San Yu	B. 1918. General, 4th Burma Rifles; President under BSPP, 1981–88.
Saw Maung	1928–97. General; Chairman, SLORC, 1988–95.
Sein Lwin	B. 1924. General, 4th Burma Rifles; President, July–August 1988.
Sein Win	Prime Minister, NCGUB, cousin of Aung San Suu Kyi.
Shu Maung	Original name of Ne Win.
Smith Dun	General, Karen Commander, Burma Army, 1948–49.
Suu Kyi	See Aung San Suu Kyi.
Than Shwe	B. 1933. General; Chairman, SLORC, SPDC, 1995–.
Thant	1909–74. Secretary to U Nu; Ambassador to United Nations, 1957; Secretary General, United Nations, 1961–71.
Tin Oo	B. 1927. General; in 1976 appeared to be successor to Ne Win and was jailed; leader, NLD.
Tin Oo	B. 1940. General; Secretary-2, SLORC, SPDC.
Tin Pe	B. 1913. Brigadier, 4th Burma Rifles; architect of 1963 nationalization program and considered Ne Win's heir; dismissed before first BSPP congress in 1971.
Tin, Thakin	AFPFL leader. ("Thakin" means "master" and was used by the Burmese as part of the nationalist movement in the 1930s, as the British were called by that term.)

Notes

1. The use of the final "r" or its absence in "Myanma[r]" relates to the tonal structure of Burmese.
2. Government Information Sheet, No. B-1177 (I) (Yangon, Myanmar, December 9, 1999). This is disputed by many observers.
3. Government Information Sheet, No. B-1173 (I) (Yangon, Myanmar, December 6, 1999).
4. Partial listing.

Political Divisions of Burma/Myanmar.

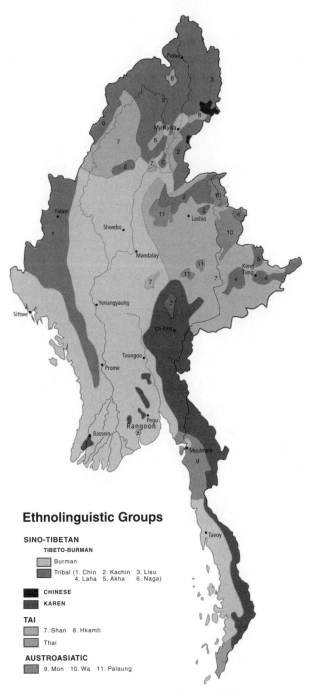

Ethnolinguistic Groups

SINO-TIBETAN

    TIBETO-BURMAN

    Burman

    Tribal (1. Chin 2. Kachin 3. Lisu
            4. Laha 5. Akha 6. Naga)

    CHINESE

    KAREN

TAI

    7. Shan 8. Hkamti

    Thai

AUSTROASIATIC

    9. Mon 10. Wa 11. Palaung

Ethnolinguistic Groups of Burma/Myanmar.

Statistical Profile

Land Area: 676,577 sq. kilometers

Population (1998 est.):   47,255,000

Kachin State	1,225,000
Kayah State	253,000
Kayin State	1,431,000
Chin State	465,000
Sagaing Division	5,280,000
Tanintharyi Division	1,298,000
Bago Division	4,930,000
Magway Division	4,382,000
Mandalay Division	6,314,000
Mon State	2,391,000
Rakhine State	2,654,000
Yangon Division	5,382,000
Shan State	4,702,000
Ayeyarwady Division	6,548,000

Annual growth rate: 1.84%

Urban population: 26.6%

Religion (in percent):

89.4	Buddhist
3.0	Christian
3.9	Muslim
0.5	Hindu

Poverty: 22.9% (1992–97); 30–40%[1]

Infant Mortality (000 live births): 79 (1992–97)

Childhood Mortality (under 5): 131

Life Expectancy:

Average	60 years
Male	59 years
Female	62 years

State Expenditures, 1997/98 (% of GDP):

Health	0.3
Education	0.9
Military	1.5–4.5[2]

Per Capita Income: K.1,670 (1998) = $278 (at official exchange rates)[3]

GDP (1998/99): $14.2 billion

Exchange Rate: Official—K.6.2 = $1.00

Curb market rate (approximate, 11/2000)—K.390 = $1.00

Fiscal Year: April 1–March 31 (before 1974, October 1–September 30); e.g. 1998–99, April 1, 1998–March 31,1999.

Ethnicity (in percent; from 1983 census; note: unofficial figures may vary; "other indigenous races" category is clearly understated)

Burman	69.0
Shan	8.5
Karen	6.2
Arakanese	4.5
Mon	2.4
Chin	2.2
Kachin	1.4
Kayah	0.4
Other indigenous races [sic]	0.1
Foreigners, including mixed races [sic]	5.3

Sources: Myanmar government; World Bank; various publications. The *CIA World Factbook 2000* lists Chinese at 5 percent and Indians at 2 percent. Other statistics vary marginally.

Notes

1. This figure is based on a World Bank nationally determined poverty line but is likely to be understated. The IMF Staff Report, May 22, 1998, indicated the 30–40 percent rate.

2. Approximately $300 in 1999. *U.S. Commercial Guide for Fiscal Year 1999* (Rangoon, September 1998). Figures are for 1997/98. Other estimates are 2.8 percent and 4.5 percent. The U.S. Embassy guide cites health expenditures at 0.1 percent and educational expenditures at 0.5 percent that same year.

3. "At market exchange rate and after adjustments to take into account unrecorded transactions" (*IMF Report* 99/134, November 1999).

State Peace and Development Council (SPDC)

(As of October 2000)

Senior Gen. Than Shwe, Chairman
Gen. Maung Aye (Army, Commander in Chief)
Lt. Gen. Khin Nyunt, Secretary-1
Lt. Gen. Tin Oo, Secretary-2
Lt. Gen. Win Myint, Secretary-3
Rear Adm. Nyunt Thein (Navy, Commander in Chief)[1]
Brig. Gen. Kyaw Than (Air Force, Commander in Chief)

Regional Commanders

Maj. Gen. Aung Htwe (Western)
Maj. Gen. Yi Myint (Central)
Maj. Gen. Khin Maung Than (Rangoon)
Maj. Gen. Kyaw Win (Northern)
Maj. Gen. Thein Sein (Golden Triangle Area)
Maj. Gen. Sitt Maung (Coastal Command, Tenasserim)
Brig. Gen. Shwe Mann (Southwest)
Brig. Gen. Myint Aung (Southeast)[2]
Brig. Gen. Maung Bo (Eastern)
Brig. Gen. Tin Aung Myint Oo (Northeast)
Brig. Gen. Soe Win (Northwest)
Brig. Gen. Tin Aye (Southern)

Notes

1. Resigned for health reasons.
2. Resigned because of ill health, October 2000. To be replaced by Maj. Gen. Aye Kyawe.

Glossary

ADB	Asian Development Bank
AFPFL	Anti-Fascist People's Freedom League
AIR	All India Radio
Ana	Power, Authority
Awza	Influence
BCP	Burma Communist Party; also CPB
Bogyoke	Generalissimo
BSPP	Burma Socialist Programme Party
Burman	Majority ethnic group
Cetana	Goodwill, kindness
CPB	Communist Party, Burma; also BCP
CRPP	Committee Representing People's Parliament; NLD group of ten established in 1998 to represent parliamentary majority elected in May 1990 but ignored
DAB	Democratic Alliance of Burma; set up November 1988 by twenty-three dissident ethnic and other opponents of military rule
DDSI	Directorate of Defence Services Intelligence
Dharma	Buddhist law
DSI	Defence Services Institute; military-run conglomerate set up in 1951
GDP	Gross Domestic Product
GNP	Gross National Product
ICRC	International Committee of the Red Cross
IMF	International Monetary Fund
KNDO	Karen National Defense Organization

KNU	Karen National Union
Kyat	Unit of state currency; noted as K.
Lon htein	Riot or security police
LORC	Law and Order Restoration Council; local equivalents of SLORC; military controlled
MEC	Myanmar Economic Corporation, a military-dominated economic conglomerate
MEHL	Myanmar Economic Holdings, Ltd., a military-dominated economic conglomerate and investment company
NCGUB	National Coalition Government of the Union of Burma; opposition group set up December 1990; now located in Washington, D.C.
NLD	National League for Democracy, 1989–
NUP	National Unity Party, 1989–
PSB	Press Scrutiny Board
Pyithu Hluttaw	National Assembly, or Parliament
Sangha	Buddhist monkhood
Sawbwa	Shan hereditary rulers; maharajahs
SDR	Special Drawing Rights; IMF designation of currency valuations
SEE	State Economic Enterprises, public sector
SLORC	State Law and Order Restoration Council, 1988–97
SPDC	State Peace and Development Council, 1997–
Tatmadaw	The military forces of the state
UNHCR	UN High Commissioner for Refugees
USDA	Union Solidarity and Development Association, 1992–
WTO	World Trade Organization

Introduction

B urma or Myanmar is a country in which access is limited, field work generally prohibited, information hoarded, statistics often whimsical, visitors discouraged until recently, and data often interpreted and released through myopic and controlled political lenses. Myanmar presents problems—problems of analysis and even data. Statistics are often whimsical, events are sometimes opaque, the complexity of the past clouds our thinking, information is filtered through skewed political lenses, propaganda is rife, and the future presents conundrums even for participants in the drama, let alone observers on the periphery.

Myanmar is still basically closed and secretive, knowledge and information are power and are not readily shared, and to understand these dynamics expatriate Burmese and foreigners often resort to reading the Rangoon tea leaves, much as old China watchers in Hong Kong or Kremlinologists of yore were reduced to doing on those societies. Thus to write on contemporary issues about such a country requires a degree of hubris as well as an act of faith. Writing on this state becomes an art, not a scientific inquiry, and in art we all know what we like, although objective criteria escape us. However murky our crystal balls may be, the importance of attempting to predict the future becomes critical so that present policies may deal with future realities. Dante Alighieri in *The Divine Comedy,* however, consigns soothsayers and their ilk to one of the lower circles of hell, although political predictions today are a growth industry. The future of Myanmar may not equate to the present, but the present will endow the future with detritus that the poor, damned prognosticator ignores at his or her peril. History may not repeat itself, but it often rhymes, as Mark Twain quipped.

Here is a society important in itself, strategically situated, possessing rich and varied cultural traditions over a millennium, with extensive natural resources, one from which important lessons may be learned, and yet it is one of the least known of significantly sized states in the contemporary world. Long isolated and ignored, Burma/Myanmar has struck the imagination of a growing number of people concerned not only with geopolitical or trade considerations, but also with poverty, health, and human rights interests. It remains exotic because of its isolation, and because few foreigners can find employment in its pursuit, it remains to the outside world a virtual *terra incognita.*

Although the pre-Burman history of what is now Burma or Myanmar dates back millennia, the thousand years of Burman recorded history provide ample evidence of the greatness to which the culture grew and even some clues to the contemporary Burmese scene.

But those who write about this sorry yet potentially wealthy state tend to be polarized, much like its inhabitants. One person's use of the term "Burma" or "Myanmar" indicates political preferences and indicts one in the eyes of another. Writing on Burma subjects one to the stresses of confrontation; balanced and nuanced analyses are difficult to formulate. The data available, moreover, are unbalanced and lacking nuance.

The appropriateness of foreigners in reviewing, commenting on, and attempting to influence events in Myanmar, as this volume purports to do, is thus subject to debate; one may well ask: what are their proper functions and roles, and when and how should they be expressed?

Many would argue that change for the better in Myanmar can be accomplished only by the Burmese themselves; they are the actors on the stage. One eminent Burman in 1988, commenting to the author on the dire conditions of continued, enforced military rule in Burma, said, "The play is over, the audience is forced to remain in their seats, and the actors refuse to leave the stage." To continue the analogy, some foreigners might contend that they can be stagehands behind the scenes, assisting the production but remaining obscure. Perhaps they are like the Japanese *kurogo,* those individuals dressed in black who squat at the back of the kabuki stage and manipulate the props while being socially invisible. The military authorities might insist that foreigners are the audience, divorced from the action, who should view the scene through the lenses prescribed by the playwright and the director. The ruling junta also might hope that foreigners might play the role of the financiers of the production, allowing the directors the freedom to stage the drama according to their "artistic" (political) preferences. Still others might maintain that the foreigners' roles are those of drama critics who assess the performance. It is significant in this analogy that Aung San Suu Kyi is essentially portrayed by the state as a foreigner and thus unworthy in their eyes to be a potential actor on the Burmese stage.

In what follows, I will contend that the solutions, insofar as there are any, to the problems facing Myanmar must be resolved by the Burmese through their own actions. This does not deny a role—in fact multiple roles—for foreigners, ones far more active than simply viewing the unfolding drama of Burmese events.

One essential role, in a sense, is forced on foreigners who have the interests of the Burmese people in mind. This is due to an inherent inability and unwillingness of those within the internal political processes in Myanmar to assume the function of internal observers and potentially constructive critics. This function stems from the isolation or lack of willingness of the leadership of the *tatmadaw* (armed forces), successively of the Burma Socialist Programme Party (BSPP) or the State Law and Order Restoration Council (SLORC) or the later State Peace and Development Council (SPDC), to ascertain from the bottom of the hierarchy the actual conditions and problems affecting ordinary people within its state. There is a pervasive reluctance to bring issues to the attention of the highest authorities when such issues may conflict with reality as propagandized from above or as perceived from below as "politically correct." Further, the military evidently does not trust most of the civilian professional Burmese bureaucracy (of whatever ethnicity); their views are generally not sought. The leadership thus cannot effectively plan to alleviate problems and their causes, even if it views political conditions as warranting change.

This situation seems an anomaly in a state in which the government, through all its organs (including intelligence agencies, mass mobilization efforts, and the ubiquitous parastatal cooperative network) reaches down into the bowels of society. Yet a milieu of fear so pervades the polity and distrust is so prevalent that problems, some quite obvious to outside observers, cannot surface to the top of the intensely hierarchical, command-driven military structure from the lower rungs of the social, political, or economic ladder. This has been evident since the military coup of 1962 and is even more pronounced today. This fear also means that foreign negotiations carried out at a lower level may not be reported up the hierarchy with the same emphasis intended by those outside. The BSPP had designed an elaborate feedback mechanism in which

BSPP officials would report back to the constituencies from which they were "elected" (under a single-party mobilization system) to the legislature and learn about local problems, which they would in turn bring to the attention of the party's leadership, thus prompting reform. This system failed, and the leaders were unaware until too late of the problems of the periphery.[1] The present government has no such system and seems to rely on the reporting of the intelligence agencies, which have their own interests in mind.

The issue is even more pervasive, and not confined to the BSPP, but is apparent over more than three decades of military rule. General Ne Win in 1987, before his retirement in 1988, finally recognized it and stated that it was time to stop lying about increased production with imagined and politically correct statistics. Yet such falsehoods were in effect politically required, and this requirement was prompted not only by fears of the military throughout the country, but also by Ne Win's own mercurial personality, which brooked no disagreement from below. The evidence that the *tatmadaw* has been out of touch with the populace is demonstrated by its failure to understand the dynamics of popular sentiment and predict the results of the elections of 1960 or 1990.

A foreigner is thus able to perform the functions of the traditional Imperial Chinese Censorate, which had access to the emperor and told him what was going wrong and the mistakes he was making. In democracies, the media often provide this essential service; in Myanmar there is no censorate and no independent media. One role of foreigners, then, is to help bring transparency to a state that is opaque; where power is personalized, fear is endemic, and statistics whimsical; and where politics and power are the driving forces to which all else is subordinated.

There are also external roles for the foreign observer; all of them seem anathema to the SLORC/SPDC. The first is that of analyst—the assessor of events, internal and external, and the predictor of future trends and needs. As the Koreans say, it is dark under the lamp (because one is too close to the subject), so stepping back may throw more light on the issues. A second function is that of information sharer and dispenser. In Myanmar, information is viewed as power, the media vigorously controlled, and an image presented both internally and to the outside world that sifts and winnows only those data that the government wishes to present and colors such information to attempt to shape public opinion. In a sense, the role of the foreigner (and foreign institution) in this regard is not only to provide other data to a broad audience, but also to counter the official views with different perspectives because one of the most dangerous of circumstances is a regime that believes its own propaganda, as seems to be the case in Myanmar. Foreigners may dismiss many of the pronouncements of the *tatmadaw* as cant or simply campaign slogans, but they may instead represent the leadership's ardent and strongly held, if parochial and insular, beliefs. Thus the charge that foreigners are out to break up the country and that only the *tatmadaw* can protect the unity of the state are views that are tenaciously believed by the military itself. Since foreign intervention has had historical bases in fact, the acceptance of such attitudes today becomes all the easier in spite of a complete change in the attitudes of both internal groups and external powers.

It is also important to place opposition comments in perspective, separating wish from reality and advocacy from fact. The political agendas of any group, no matter how sympathetic one might be to the group's goals, should be given the scrutiny and critical attention they deserve. This has become exceedingly difficult in contemporary Burma/Myanmar because of the polarization of opinion, to which selective facts are marshaled in support.

More proactive roles that the foreign community can play are those of advocates of reform. These can be both institutional and personal roles. It is important, for example, that both past and potential multilateral and bilateral donors continue to analyze and press for economic reforms, as well as for those related to what are called "good governance" and human rights. The conducting of sectoral and other surveys of needs in the society before conditions permit action should be on the potential donors' agendas, if the authorities would agree to such studies. This has a dual function: it allows quick action by donors if and when general conditions prompt the resumption of lending and assistance, and it offers a potential incentive for reform even if left unimplemented.[2] The negative implications are modest—namely, that such actions would be used to add legitimacy to the regime and that the fact of such studies might encourage action. These are perhaps less important than the overall potentially positive impacts. But it is equally important to review the content of opposition agendas and policies to consider if and when these offer the most sound and practical means for positive change.

Another foreign function is that of support to those affected by the internal events—political dissidents, students, refugees, women, and migratory workers as prey of unscrupulous exploiters. Neighboring states, such as Thailand, view such persons as threats to their perceived national interests. It is here that the nongovernmental community has an especially important role. Its functions also include advocacy, support, and development of action programs insofar as the state allows them to take place.

Contrary to what the military may believe, there are, then, multiple and legitimate roles for the foreign observer of the Burmese scene—or indeed the observers of any government and its political and economic processes.

The foreign observer, or the expatriate Burmese, must determine how these functions are to be performed. Is it essentially to rally the opposition supporters or influence policy changes? Although these positions are not necessarily contradictory, different emphases could produce different effects. How public or private should these observations be? The dilemma is not easily resolved and has plagued government observers and academicians widely in the contemporary world. Public criticism of any regime often creates a backlash of nationalism that will make adoption of foreign suggestions even more difficult. This is especially true in Myanmar, where we have witnessed xenophobia, as expressed through the controlled press, that is among the world's most vitriolic. This is particularly prevalent in response to foreign media. Academic articles and advice, on the other hand, receive more muted negative responses simply because they have far less circulation. Public critical statements, however, may be effective in exhorting believers to rally around opposition organizations. At the same time, private advice can be easily ignored. Whatever private conversations the Association of Southeast Asian Nations (ASEAN) authorities may have held with the SLORC/SPDC under the guise of "constructive engagement," they seem to have had little, if any, impact.

A quite different set of functions occurs in the foreign business community and its engagement with Myanmar. The limited openings to the private sector that the SLORC has encouraged would under normal political circumstances have been viewed by the world community as the most important progress that Burma has made in several decades. Political factors, however, retard the acceptance of these changes as an unlimited good. All internal political parties, including the National League for Democracy (NLD), encourage the private sector, but the NLD says that the time is not politically appropriate for foreign investment. Political reform must precede economic reform, they argue, or the present, illegitimate government will be strengthened and be even more unwilling to sponsor political change. The SLORC/SPDC and some foreign businesses claim that private sector investment will improve the lives of the people, even though the process is one of "trickle down," which has proven less than efficacious in many societies. There is no question that unemployment, at least in Rangoon and Mandalay, has been down compared to the pre-1988 period, and that wages for workers in the private sector have risen, although not sufficiently to keep up with inflation. The economic impact of foreign investment so far has been concentrated geographically and socially, and has not reached the society as a whole.

Some would argue that economic growth through foreign involvement in the private sector will lead to political reform and democracy. This is perhaps the most questionable assumption. Although the demands of a vigorous private sector do increase the need for timely economic information, and create strains with which governments have to cope as businesses try to limit state interference in economic matters, their effect on politics is over a very long period. Korea and Taiwan, for example, show that economic development had an impact on the political power structure only after several decades, and growth in Singapore, China, Indonesia, and other states indicates that there is as yet no necessary shorter-term correlation among economic development, growth, economic diversity, and the development of political pluralism. Those who rationalize that investing in Myanmar will force political changes that they will witness had better be young enough to wait out the probable protracted impact of such investment, for it would be unlikely to happen in my lifetime or that of any in the older generation.

Foreigners have yet another role in which they may be able to assess the implications of foreign relations in a more dispassionate approach than those living under the stress of international pressures.

This volume is not a comprehensive history or a political economy volume on Burma/Myanmar and should not be so interpreted. Such a volume would have to include balanced coverage of a broad spectrum of society, and this is not attempted here. Rather, this is a study of contending authorities and issues of legitimacy essentially since 1988 but in historical context. This volume explores a society through its politics, economics, social structure, and culture, and as such necessarily suffers in the depth to which these elements are treated. I hope, however, that the breadth compensates for omissions that some readers will find obvious and disconcerting. The paucity of materials on Burma may justify my approach because the ability to do requisite field work to supplement bibliographic research is lacking. Culture, contrary to the opinion of many so-cial scientists, is not in this case the last residual element to which, if there are no other plausible explanations, all else is relegated. Rather, it is integral to attempting to understand this complex society.

One may study Burma/Myanmar for its own sake and because of a fasci-nation with a unique culture, but also for the lessons, if we are astute enough to recognize them, that we may draw from this experience. We may learn a good deal from the Burmese vicissitudes of the management and problems of multiethnic states, the role of the military, the efficacy of sanctions, the transi-tion from centrally planned economies to more open market systems, the plight of the peasant, various economic policies or the dangers of lack of reform, the relations between small and larger powers, and even geopolitical placements, as well as a vast variety of other issues, all of which this state has encountered and with which it has dealt, usually with less than satisfactory results to date.

In 1978, I wrote the following, much of which still remains valid:

> Burma is an anomaly—a unique nation dominated by a highly centralized single-party dictatorship, yet composed of over sixty-five thousand village economies only loosely tied to the central government. Burma's political ide-ology ostensibly enforces a rigid socialist system, but economically it openly tolerates, and indeed is dependent on, an informal, and often illegal, parallel market. It preaches the harmonious equal union of diverse ethnic groups, yet it has been internally domineering toward these groups and in consequence is plagued by minority dissension and rebellion. The Government espouses Marx-ism, but the Burma Communist Party is in active revolt; while it blends doctri-naire socialism with the Buddhist concept of the impermanence of things, it rejects historical determinism. . . . Burma could be considered *terra incognita* in the contemporary sense, where crucial statistics are often lacking, where available data are often contradictory, and where public distribution of material is controlled.[3]

It is my hope that this eclectic work will add to the dialogue, both specific to and abstracted from the Burmese experience. If this volume adds to the intelligent debate on these questions, it will have succeeded.

Notes on Data

Since the statistical base in Myanmar is relatively undeveloped, opaque, and subject to political manipulation and because even foreign professional economists must rely on local sources for much of their information, there are major discrepancies in many of the data presented in this volume. Some also may be traced to differing exchange rates used. The basic economic and social figures are taken from a variety of sources unless otherwise indicated, including the following: Union of Myanmar, Ministry of National Planning and Economic Development, annual reports on economic and social conditions for various years; World Bank studies; International Monetary Fund (IMF) reporting; Asian Development Bank (ADB) appraisals; U.S. Embassy (Rangoon) unclassified economic reporting; and the quarterly reports of the Economist Intelligence Unit. In addition, the government has stopped publishing some statistics.

Australian reports set the problem of statistics nicely:

> Neither official nor unofficial economic statistics for Burma are reliable. Official statistics are distorted by the use of an overvalued exchange rate and an undervalued rate of inflation; both of which make the economy appear larger than it is. In addition, agricultural statistics have in the past been over-reported, although there are signs in recent statistics that this is being addressed. . . . Provisional figures are often based on projections using data for the first 6–9 months of the fiscal year. But the statistics are also incomplete: the large black market—which includes unregulated border trade, drug-related commerce and informal economic activity—is often not taken into account. This incompleteness makes the economy look smaller than it is.[4]

This selective use of data results in widespread erroneous conceptions of the economy.

Notes

1. Personal communication from one of the members of the Central Committee of the BSPP, 1988. The issue, he said, was not socialism but feedback.
2. See David I. Steinberg, op-ed, *International Herald Tribune,* November 15, 1999.
3. David I. Steinberg, "Development Strategy for Burma" (Washington, D.C.: USAID, 1978).
4. Australia, Department of Foreign Affairs and Trade, p. 8.

CHAPTER 1

Setting the Stage:
The Crisis of 1988
and Its Origins

We in Myanmar were not prepared for the force and fury of the storm [1988 revolution]. As the years rolled by, we had started to equate lethargy and lack of change with stability; speeches and notions with progress; excuses with reason; and manipulated statistics with the real facts.

—Maung Maung[1]

The Coup of September 18, 1988

Coups may be commonplace in the third world, but a military coup designed to shore up another military regime is unusual, although it has also occurred in Thailand.[2] Although the Burmese coup of 1988 replaced the previous leadership with a new group of officers, it was not intended to shift power even among the military or between military factions. Rather, it was designed to continue military rule by other means. It took place with the acquiescence of the authorities.

On September 18, 1988, General Saw Maung, commander of the Burma Army, carried out a coup in support of a tottering military government that probably could have continued for only a few more days. Battered by widespread popular riots that had evolved over the previous months into a people's revolution, the government was under popular siege. Perhaps at its height a million people had demonstrated in Rangoon, the capital, with a population of about 2 million at that time, and Mandalay, the seat of Burman culture, about half that size. Demonstrations had been accompanied by widespread looting, for the causes of the popular malaise were a mixture of both political and economic frustration and hatred.

Brutal suppression of popular discontent followed the coup. Dissenters were sought out, jailed, or killed, and although the authorities admitted to the deaths of a few looters and malcontents, observers estimated that over a thousand died in those few days; in 1988 and the events leading up to the coup perhaps four or five times that number had been killed. Based on photographs taken at the demonstrations, the military conducted house-to-house searches to seek out those who had participated. Some 10,000 students and young people fled to the periphery, some to the Indian border, others to the China frontier, but most to Thailand, where many sought refuge. Some later returned to Burma under government auspices, but many others joined the ethnic insurgents, who controlled a substantial part of the Thai littoral at that time, and received military training to continue the struggle against the military.[3]

Whether the coup was the result of an earlier planned scenario is unclear, but the apparent demoralization of several dozen soldiers holed up on September 17 in the Ministry of Trade building, where they were surrounded by demonstrators and a mob demanding their heads, probably prompted the army to act when it did, even if it had earlier expected that it would have to move at some point to support the regime. On September 15, the crowd had been on the verge of storming the Ministry of Defense and was dissuaded only by the respected dissident, retired brigadier Aung Gyi. It was widely believed that General Ne Win, former national leader, recently retired, had ordered the coup. Saw Maung was said to have visited him at Ne Win's palatial home on Inya Lake in Rangoon on the evening of September 17 and again on the morning of the following day. President Maung Maung, a civilian installed only a month earlier to placate the populace following earlier demonstrations and massacres, only met with Ne Win at about 3:00 P.M. that day, and the coup was instituted shortly thereafter—between 3:30 and 4:00 P.M.[4] He may have been only belatedly informed.

The military instituted a new government, called the State Law and Order Restoration Council (SLORC). The cabinet was completely composed of active-duty military officers, with the exception of the minister of health, who had close ties with the *tatmadaw* (armed forces). It reinstituted the old name of the state, the "Union of Burma," dropping its previous socialist appellation, "the Socialist Republic of the Union of Burma." It dissolved the previous single legal party—the Burma Socialist Programme Party (BSPP)—and reconstituted a smaller National Unity Party (NUP), withdrawing overt (but not covert) government support from any political group. It made many changes in the government's institutional framework and presented an image of a taut, authoritarian administration bent on change.

The people's revolution that prompted this action burst forth after a generation of simmering discontent, which merits explication.

The Origins of the People's Revolution

> The people of the country have lost confidence in the monetary system; they cannot accept reports on the economic situations [*sic*] as correct appraisals, correct economic situations in the country are withheld so that the people may not know the truth, data and statistics are falsified and presented, and the suggestions and advice given by economic experts are ignored.[5]

The people's revolution and the taut response to it by the *tatmadaw* were the cumulative product of a series of policies and events that had their origins early in the military administration following the coup of 1962 and its political and economic rigidities, but the immediate precipitating factors are to be found in 1987.

In August 1987, in a statement remarkable in the Burmese context, Ne Win, then chairman of the BSPP, publicly noted that there was a need for change in the political, economic, and even the constitutional arenas to respond to deteriorating conditions in Burma. He said that the government could not continue to lie with statistics.[6] He called for suggestions on improvements. This confession was unusual in that it was the first official recognition since 1971—and obviously authoritative—that conditions in Burma were not as rosy as officially portrayed. Ne Win reiterated the call in October of that year, with little public effect.

Two events in September 1987, however, occurred that were to have contradictory influences on the economy and the society and contributed to the trauma of 1988. On September 1, the government announced the liberalization of trade in the nine grains, most importantly in rice. In what was the most widespread single gesture of reform since the military coup of 1962, and one that affected about 80 percent of the population, peasants were freely allowed to buy and sell rice to traders at whatever price was appropriate and wherever they wished to sell it. Since producer prices had been artificially kept low (and indeed the revenue of the central government was in large part dependent on ensuring that the gap between the prices paid to farmers and the export price remained as wide as possible), this immediately raised farm income. Farmers could cross township and provincial boundaries to sell their produce, as prices varied by locality and scarcity; this had been previously prohibited as well.

This edict was badly timed, however, if it had been economically motivated, because it came at the close of the growing season and thus could not affect immediate production. This change was followed by another in February 1988 allowing private traders to export rice (but not allowing them to hold foreign currency); this previously had been a government monopoly. This regulation was totally ineffective because of an unrealistic exchange that forced traders into losses if they had to redeem foreign exchange for kyat (K.), the local currency, at official rates. Few registered as exporters, and no private trading took place. Foreign observers, noting the widespread changes that had characterized the Chinese centrally planned economy in the 1980s, were quick to point out the potential for these reforms if they were carefully planned. They hoped that these were harbingers of a new and needed economic pragmatism in Burma. In fact, these changes were poorly planned, but the first was a rather shrewd political move designed to alleviate pressure on the government from the rural sector, which contained the bulk of the population. But many foreigners expected further reforms to take place to support economic liberalization. Such efforts did not follow because this was more a political than an economic statement.

Yet only five days later, the regime announced a devastating change—perhaps the most sweeping demonetization in the contemporary world and the third since the military took over in 1962. Under it, all bank notes over K.15 ($2.50 at the official rate) were declared illegal, and no compensation was to be paid for them. The motivations behind this scheme were probably complex;

it was ostensibly to eliminate the black market, a quixotic gesture since in fact the government depended on it for its existence, but it may also have been promulgated to cut inflation and the expansion of the money supply, and—some say—for abstruse astrological calculations that would enable Ne Win to live to be ninety. (Nines were said to be lucky for him. He had some years earlier had all the currency bills changed to add up to nines for the same reason; thus K.45 and K.15 bank bills were introduced and K.50 and K.100 bills, among others, withdrawn.) In any case, the BSPP Central Executive Committee was not informed in advance and was simply ordered to vote for the demonetization; it had no choice. Some modest financial modifications were later announced to select groups; after student demonstrations, some small financial conversions (K.100) were allowed so that the students could return to their homes, and rumors abounded that some members of the military bought at discounts or commandeered discredited kyat and were able to have them surreptitiously converted into legal currency.

The result was a pervasive atmosphere of economic fear as further demonetizations were expected. Since all such currency "reforms" had occurred over weekends, businesses bribed banks to accept sealed bags of uncounted currency on Friday afternoons, to be redeemed on Monday mornings if there had been no further demonetizations. (Such funds "deposited" thus would not count as banknotes under this arcane economic equation.) Urban dwellers and farmers at those uncertain times acted with pristine economic logic. The former bought any commodity rather than hold cash, and the latter held their only asset—paddy (unhusked rice). The former fueled inflation and created an intensified demand for increased smuggling since Burmese industry was operating far below capacity levels. At that time, smuggling greatly benefited China, while the price of now uncontrolled rice rapidly rose. These factors most adversely affected the urban dweller on a fixed income. As one Burmese observer noted, "The spear landed at the lowest point"—the common people were mostly affected because the military and civil servants had access to commodities and rice through government procurement mechanisms.[7] The poor were most adversely affected by inflation.

At the same time, internal debt had risen to dangerous levels. Many of the State Economic Enterprises (SEEs), the public sector that had been the economic symbol of modernity, had effectively failed, borrowing from the government without the possibility of repayment as their production faltered and smuggled goods increased, replacing the modest production that did exist. The SEEs had been designed to be the fruition of the economic manifesto, *The Burmese Way to Socialism,* which the military had propounded to provide the nonreligious, nonethnic articulated basis for nationhood and a national ideology, as well as to enhance its own legitimacy.

Even more important, external debt had exploded. At that time, Burma owed about three-quarters of its GNP (at official rates of exchange), foreign exchange reserves were about $28 million, and its debt service ratio was calculated by various groups as between 55 and 91 percent of exports.[8]

As important as were these economic indicators of malaise that contributed to the subsequent unrest, the events that triggered the overtly political crisis were ironically apolitical.[9] Students had been in the forefront of the nationalistic and independence movements (along with monks), and most of the leaders of modern Burma have come from those movements. In mid-March 1988, students at the Rangoon Institute of Technology got into a fight with the owner and patrons of a local tea shop. The resulting riots quickly spread, and the *lon htein* (security or riot police) were called in to put them down, which they did with unprecedented brutality and an unknown number of deaths. The riots spread from the outskirts to downtown Rangoon. Female students were beaten up, some say raped, and forty-one young people suffocated in a police van into which they had been stuffed to be taken to jail. It was only after four months that the government was forced to admit after a formal inquiry into the affair that this had happened. Ne Win was out of the country at the time. When he returned, he is said to have called in the BSPP Central Executive Committee and the People's Inspectors (auditors). All were standing, and he appeared to be visibly upset. He asked whether the reports on the suffocations were true, expecting to hear that they were exaggerated. He was informed that indeed they were accurate. He could not respond at first, he was so agitated. He then indicated that the committee had let the country down, and the meeting ended. When Ne Win resigned his position as party chairman in July, he took partial responsibility for the action. Others were fired and had their pensions cut. As one Burmese privately said, "Not since King Thibaw murdered his princes to secure his succession to the throne in the nineteenth century was such brutality evident in Burma." [10] Overall, the deaths were in the hundreds. Schools were closed and the atmosphere was tense. On May 30, schools were reopened, and since the government continued to impose a rigid, frustrating control of all media, the students gathered to ascertain who was killed, who was arrested or missing, and who simply had not returned from their homes.

Rice prices had exploded to about three times their value a few months before the students began to organize, and urban discontent became widespread.[11] Burma had begun to fall in arrears in its debt repayments, an event unique since Burmese independence and an important indicator of the extent of the economic debacle. On June 16, demonstrations began again and spread throughout Rangoon.

The overwhelming popular outburst in the capital indicated that the motives behind the demonstrations were far more intense and the population affected far more broadly than the government was prepared to admit. The dissatisfaction was so widespread and so evident that Ne Win on July 7 called for a special congress of the BSPP, one year in advance of its normal gathering. This did not satisfy Burma's urban population: demonstrations spread to Prome, where martial law was declared over an ostensibly communal dispute,[12] and to Taunggyi, as well as to other urban centers.

On July 23, the special party congress was convened. Ne Win and four of his close associates offered their resignations from official positions.[13] Ne Win wanted to resign from the party as well. He also suggested that political and constitutional changes might be needed, and he called for a plebiscite on amending the single-party, mass-mobilization constitution of 1974 to allow for a multiparty political system. Observers said that it was an emotional presentation that someone else finished reading, after which, contrary to his normal practice, Ne Win left the assembly. The secretary of the BSPP presented a catalogue of the economic ills, quite similar to those enunciated in 1971 at the first BSPP congress, and called for economic reforms, including encouragement of the private sector and foreign investment by both public and private firms with state, cooperative, or private enterprises in Burma. Certain sectors, however, were to be reserved to the Burmese: onshore oil, gems, teak, and banking. The economic reforms were supported by the party, and authority was given to the Central Executive Committee to work out the details. The socialist basis of the economy, however, was never brought into question. It seems evident that the BSPP regarded these as tactical shifts rather than strategic restructuring.

The resignations of Ne Win and his colleagues from official party positions were accepted, but not from the party itself, as this was against the rules of the party, in which membership was for life. This demonstrated that since its inception in 1962, the BSPP, and thus the military, was to have perpetual control over the society. In a move that may have been prompted personally by Ne Win, but in any case in a decision made and endorsed by those insulated from public opinion (including Ne Win himself), Sein Lwin was chosen as successor to Ne Win as BSPP chairman.

In the session following Ne Win's presentation, speaker after speaker argued against the multiparty concept. As the afternoon wore on, the trend became obvious, and some observers believe a messenger was sent to Ne Win's home to ascertain his views. He is said to have agreed to let the majority rule, and thus the multiparty option was defeated.

The motivations of individuals and groups at that time must still remain conjectural, but the best evidence available indicates that Ne Win was probably serious in his suggestion of a multiparty election, but perhaps solely to shake up the lethargy and bureaucracy of the party itself, with which he had become disillusioned, perhaps by the economic problems exacerbated by the suffocation deaths, and fully expecting that a vote would return a reformed BSPP to power. Some speculate he may have been trying to distance himself from the debacle of regime disintegration. Perhaps Sein Lwin, who was said to have been against the referendum, expected that the party would lose. Ideology was said to have played no role; continued party control was designed to protect the party's own extensive interests.

A few days later Sein Lwin was chosen as president by the Pyithu Hluttaw (National Assembly). There are strong rumors that the Central Executive Committee had been prepared to pick Dr. Maung Maung (the civilian closest to Ne Win and his biographer—perhaps hagiographer) as president but that Ne Win again made the ultimate decision. Deputy Prime Minister Tun Tin became prime minister.

No move could have been better calculated to enrage the students, for Sein Lwin, who had only a modicum of formal education but who had been a close associate of Ne Win when the latter commanded the 4th Burma Rifles (and from which he had chosen his most intimate colleagues—the ultimate faction in Burma at that time), had been in command of the *lon htein* in March and thus was immediately responsible for the deaths in the spring. (Observers said that his telephone orders to this effect were overheard.) His record of antistudent violence, indeed, went back a quarter of a century, for he had been responsible for the student killings at the hands of the military and the dynamiting of the Rangoon University student union building in 1962, shortly after the coup (see chapter 7), as well as suppressing the student demonstrations in 1974 against the military's inappropriate treatment of the funeral and burial of former UN Secretary General U Thant. The students had wanted Sein Lwin tried, not promoted.[14] Even Maung Maung rather poignantly wrote:

> U Sein Lwin's elevation did not seem to please the people and the students. It had been his misfortune that whenever there was a confrontation with students and demonstrators he had been there at the front, very visible, very audible. . . . In 1962, he was acting on orders. In 1988, he was giving them.[15]

As the students gathered in the shadow of the Shwedagon Pagoda, the premier national religious site, shrine, and symbol of Burmese nationalism, Sein Lwin arrested Aung Gyi and ten of his associates. The former heir apparent to Ne Win some twenty-five years earlier, Aung Gyi had been the regime's (if not Ne Win's) most vocal public critic in the spring through a series of quasi-publicly released letters.[16] Demonstrations spread, and martial law was declared in Rangoon on August 3, but the pent-up economic and political frustrations that had built up exploded nationwide, with demonstrations, rioting, and looting that were suppressed with great loss of life.

August 8, 1988, was a significant day. (Eights were said to be lucky for the opposition, and this was 8-8-88.) It was, symbolically, also the date of the fall of the Ava Dynasty (1526 A.D.; 888 according to the Burmese era). At 8:08 A.M., it is believed, a strike began that gathered momentum in the following days. In the next five days in the suppression of the demonstrations, some 3,000 people were estimated to have been killed. By August 12, if not earlier, it had become apparent that Sein Lwin was a liability.[17]

Dr. Maung Maung was chosen as president. The first civilian to head the state since Ne Win overthrew U Nu in 1962, he had been a respected legal scholar and was the author of several books on contemporary Burma. He had for three decades been the closest civilian associate of Ne Win. He had also been the author of the notorious citizenship law of 1982 that had forced residents of foreign ethnic origin who could not prove that their ancestors had come to Burma before 1824 into second-class status.

Political turmoil, economic decay, and rising prices, together with the heady atmosphere of soaring mass aspirations, could not be contained by this choice, although had it occurred instead of Sein Lwin, it might have subdued popular unrest.[18] The government announced a wide range of conciliatory gestures, including an advisory committee to gauge public opinion; a party congress and (and if approved by the BSPP) a national referendum on multiparty elections, which would involve constitutional changes; the lifting of martial law on August 24; and a promise to rebuild the Rangoon University student union building, which had been demolished by the military in 1962. None of these stopped the demonstrations, which had become the most widespread urban manifestation of popular discontent in recorded Burmese history. These demonstrations took place in at least 250 towns, and town dwellers were sometimes joined by farmers who came into the urban areas. A million people turned out on one day in Rangoon, but cumulatively during this period many millions had demonstrated. The populace was well organized, with students playing a critical role and monks in Mandalay maintaining order. Opposition groups called for political changes, banners equated Ne Win with Marcos (who had been forced to resign in 1986), and "people power" seemed to have come to Burma. The press, previously rigidly controlled, became unrestrained, with ephemeral publications mushrooming and chronicling the changes and rumors. Many argued that a plebiscite on a new multiparty system was not needed, as the people had voted for it in the streets.

Opposition groups proliferated. Nu, on September 8, almost nostalgically reconstituted a shadow government, with figures out of the 1950s. Aung San Suu Kyi, the daughter of Aung San, the leader of Burmese independence who was widely revered but was assassinated in July 1947 prior to independence, joined with General (retired) Tin Oo and Aung Gyi to demand political reforms. Aung San Suu Kyi, in Burma from England to minister to her mother, who subsequently died in December, was said to have anticipated some undefined future political role for a number of years while still a student. Student organizations, previously illegal, were reconstituted. Civil servants, professional staff, monks, and even some junior members of the military joined in the demonstrations. On September 10, the BSPP Central Executive Committee rescinded its cry for a plebiscite on a multiparty system, agreeing to it as the government collapsed in many urban areas. Monks and political notables took control of local administration to contain the looting, which was a reflection of the cumulative economic hardships and antistate sentiment. Many called for an interim government to safeguard free elections, and there were rumors that this, or a coalition government, was in the process of surreptitious negotiations through intermediaries, with Aung Gyi playing a critical role. There were cries for private sector economic freedom. Both the Burma Communist Party (BCP) and the ethnic rebel groups on the periphery demanded the government step down. Security collapsed, and foreign embassies evacuated their nonessential personnel and dependents. It was during this period that reports of a U.S. aircraft carrier in the Bay of Bengal for such evacuations gave rise to military fears of a U.S. intervention into the political process—fears that have continuously resurfaced and have been given greater credence after Haiti and Kosovo.

It was in this atmosphere, when expectations were rampant that the government could not last more than a few days, that two events took place traumatic to the military. On September 15, at the Ministry of Defense, Aung Gyi quieted a crowd bent on a confrontation and on storming the ministry, virtually promising an interim government, as the public wanted. The implicit assumption was that he would lead it or figure prominently in it. This move later cost him much political support from the student community, which felt that this confrontation might have overthrown the regime. The last straw was the failure of the troops in the Ministry of Trade on September 17 to defend themselves. (Whether they were ordered by the military to refrain from firing on the demonstrators or whether they surrendered to the civilian mob is disputed, the government claiming the former and many in the opposition the latter.) In any case, they are said to have been well supplied with arms and ammunition. The military may have feared its own disintegration and thus acted to prevent it from happening.

Burma would never be quite the same. This was a failed revolution, at least in this, perhaps interim, period. Yet revolution it was, perhaps resembling the Paris Commune of 1870. Although many of all social levels participated in the demonstrations, the monied groups were concerned, for elements they considered young and radical, heretofore kept in check by the repressive intelligence services, were the best organized and began to take leadership roles. The specter of a renewed communist party influencing events continued to be a danger in military perceptions. Since that time, the *tatmadaw* has constantly proclaimed that it acted as it did to prevent social chaos and the disintegration of the state. This is disputed by the opposition.

During this period, there were persistent reports of daily visits by senior military members of the SLORC, especially General Khin Nyunt, the chief of the vast military intelligence network, to Ne Win's home, and close contact between Khin Nyunt and Ne Win's daughter Sanda, who is said to have been the protector of her father and an important influence over him. But no discussion of the condition of Burma/Myanmar can ignore the role of "Number One" or "the Old Man"—Ne Win.

Ne Win—From Sun King to Cardinal Richelieu?

In explicit recognition of his own mortality, Ne Win in August 1981 announced that he was retiring from the position of chairman of the Council of State of the Socialist Republic of the Union of Burma, a position that also equated with the presidency of the republic. This was seen as a momentous event. He had indeed founded the transformation of the Union of Burma into its socialist republic chrysalis and had been the founder of the BSPP.

Ne Win had been, and remains at the turn of the millennium, the most important, if not the most efficacious, figure in post-independence Burma/ Myanmar. He has been close to or at the pinnacle of power in that country since independence, and although others in the post–World War II era may have outdistanced him in terms of the longevity of official top position (e.g., Kim Il Sung in North Korea, Fidel Castro in Cuba), he is probably the world figure with the longest continuous influence in his own society. "A leading Burmese military officer remarked in 1988 that as King Anawrahta first unified Burma in the 11th century and his son King Kyanzittha solidified the kingdom, so in the 20th century *Bogyoke* [Generalissimo] Aung San founded independent Burma and *Bogyoke* Ne Win solidified it." [19]

In 1978 I commented as follows:

> At the highest level, power is centralized in the hands of one person—Ne Win. It is Ne Win alone who makes decisions on a wide variety of policy, and, indeed, mundane issues. No other leader in Burma can approach him in charismatic appeal, nor has any other person the same capacity to manipulate the power structure. In much the same way that power is centralized in Ne Win as the national leader, power is also centralized in the leadership of individual ministries, corporations, or other bureaucratic entities. Since the vast majority of the

bureaucratic and military hierarchy are from the army, they are a part of the clique of military comrades who can relate to each other as members of the same club, chaired by Ne Win.[20]

Since 1940, when he was trained by the Japanese in anti-British activities as one of the now legendary "Thirty Comrades," Ne Win has been a major influence in Burma. He was commander of the 4th Burma Rifles before independence, and he has employed those he knew from that period in subordinate positions of power, so that the web of the factional entourage that Ne Win created permeated the state organs of power until the close of the twentieth century.[21] On independence in 1948, he was the deputy commander of the Burma Army, but with the rise of the Karen insurrection shortly thereafter, Prime Minister U Nu dismissed the loyal Karen commander of the army, General Smith Dun, and replaced him with Ne Win. He remained in that position for two decades, while at the same time and at varying periods he was minister of defense and deputy prime minister. Since independence, his influence in Burma in all fields has been profound, and, representing the military, he had virtual veto power over vital decisions in that society.

Ne Win assumed the role of prime minister during the "Caretaker Government," a military coup constitutionally undertaken with the consent of the civilian government when factional civil war loomed in 1958 as a result of a personal split within the ruling party, the Anti-Fascist People's Freedom League (AFPFL), a broad coalition of disparate elements. The military ruled for eighteen months under Ne Win in a period that turned out to be salient in the development of military attitudes toward society and military exercise of power. In 1960, the military voluntarily relinquished power, turning the government over once again to Nu and his Pyidaungsu (Union) Party, which had won a free election that had been supervised by the military but which the military had hoped would be defeated.

From 1960 until the coup in 1962, the civilian government seemed ill equipped to deal with the economic and political problems facing the state. Nu could order the building of 70,000 sand pagodas to ward off the dangers facing the country, but drift was evident, and to the military, the dissolution of the Union seemed possible.

From the military coup of March 2, 1962, Ne Win ran the state. First he was chairman of the Revolutionary Council, a group of military officers who ruled by fiat until the new constitution was implemented in 1974. Thereafter,

he was president, but he was also the chairman of the BSPP, which he transformed in the early 1970s from a very small coterie of military officers to a
mass organization that had millions of members.

Ne Win explicitly recognized that he was retiring from the presidency of
the party in 1981 to ensure a smooth transition to new leadership because implicitly he recognized that on his demise a struggle for power could erupt. He
said, however, he would retain his role as chairman of the party for the time
being to provide continuity. Since the party was stipulated under the constitution of 1974 to lead the state as the only legal political entity, there was no
question institutionally (or personally) where real authority would remain. In
1981, Ne Win did indeed control the state. Many felt that as long as he was
alive, well, and in the country, he would effectively retain power as he had for
so many years. His commands, even his whims or offhand remarks, were tantamount to law. His was a role beyond the common, dominant influence of
military leaders and elites in the third world.[22]

Ne Win's decision to resign as chairman of the BSPP on July 23, 1988, was
therefore a major event.[23] But his disappearance from the official scene did not
necessarily mean that his influence was over. Even after retirement, rumors
persisted that he was the master puppeteer pulling the strings of power in that
society. As time elapsed, he was said not to be involved in daily decisions but
that his views on key changes in policy were critical. Changes in leadership
among the SLORC and other vital decisions were said to have had his approval
or to have even been his initiative.[24]

Some Burmese seem ambivalent about Ne Win's continuing influence.
Some regard him as the *éminence grise* manipulating events behind the scene,
or the deus ex machina who controls all for his inscrutable ends. Others believe
he has truly retired. Whichever may be the case, he is treated with great respect,
and among some of the older army officers, even with veneration. But as one
classically educated Burmese dissident said in 1988, paraphrasing Henry II
about Thomas à Becket, "Who will rid me of this man?"

As a devout Buddhist, Ne Win has achieved the pinnacle of this worldly
realm: he has constructed a pagoda of importance, the Maha Vizaya (Great
Victory), located close to the venerated Shwedagon, thus ensuring his future
good *karma*. In doing so, he has been in the tradition of the Burmese monarchs
from the beginning of Burman recorded history in the eleventh century. He has

been treated as a king and the fifth great unifier of the Burman state, and perhaps because the mechanisms of power and control have increased since imperial times, he was even more powerful than they were, even if he did not go off to try to conquer adjacent lands. Maung Maung, Ne Win's closest civilian associate, wrote, "[Ne Win] knew he was being used and deceived left and right. But he was attached too much and continued to allow himself to be used and deceived, partly because he did not know and would be uncomfortable in the company of the younger generations." [25]

Ne Win, in 2000, was eighty-nine years old (he was born in 1911), and (as noted) numerologists had predicted that he would live to be ninety if he followed their suggestions, which he seems to have done.[26] Whether he succeeds or not, he is nearing the end of this incarnation. The implications of his demise are likely to be profound. He was mercurial as a person, controversial as a leader, and an officer who exuded charisma and generated the loyalty of the military close to him, but his influence over the lives of all citizens in Burmese society must be considered to have been detrimental. His legacy will be controversial, even negative, but his passing may bring even more profound changes.

The Inherited Economic Miasma

Returning economic power to Burman control and ensuring that it remained there has been the guiding leitmotif of Burmese economics of the past half century. The modernization of the Burmese economy in the colonial period produced a dual society, in which the modern sectors were essentially under foreign ownership and traditional trade was in local hands. But even indigenous control over the traditionally based rural sector had been severely eroded through foreign (Indian) investments in credit that mortgaged and alienated much of the best land to foreigners as a result of the Great Depression of 1929 and its aftermath, which devastated the Burmese economy.

Thus foreign domination was pervasive. The Europeans controlled international trade and industry, while immigrants from the subcontinent had extensive interests in credit, retail trade, and a variety of intermediate industries. The overseas Chinese community of some several hundred thousand also had important urban retail businesses. It was only in the petty trading in the bazaars that the Burmese prevailed.

From the late 1930s, then, the politically correct Burmese economic slogan was socialism, as in politics it was nationalism. With independence, for which there was widespread demand among the Burman ethnic majority, it was assumed that the economy must revert to Burman hands, which meant state control in the Burmese context. This seemed to be the wave of the future, led by such distinguished proponents as those at the London School of Economics. It was a wave that also supported Buddhist antipathies against what were considered the capitalist values of greed and private accumulations of wealth. On independence in 1948, the economic hallmark of political legitimacy was socialism; the only question was its degree and the rapidity with which various political groups wished to see it introduced.

Nationalism thus became the overarching rationale that influenced all policies, while social concerns for the poor guided economic and growth patterns. The economic decision-making process was motivated by political expediency, together with a genuine concern for the society. Nu, prime minister for most of the civilian period (1948–58, 1960–62), promulgated a Buddhist-oriented welfare state under what became known as the Pyidawtha Plan (lit., "happy land"). Pricing policies for state industries were geared more to the consumer's buying power than to the costs of production. When E. F. Schumacher wrote his influential, Buddhist-oriented volume, *Small Is Beautiful: Economics As If People Mattered,* Burma was the incipient model.[27]

If internal politics helped dictate economic policies to a major degree, Burma's international reputation also influenced the economic donor community to support development there. The various power blocs vied with each other for influence in the quintessential neutral country. The Soviet Union, together with the Eastern bloc, and the West (the United States and the Colombo Plan, which included much of the former British Empire) sought influence there against each other through provisions of foreign aid, while China was viewed by all of the above as a major geopolitical and security threat and also was a donor. Japan, to regain influence and because of a strong sense of war guilt, in 1956 began its reparations program, which was designed in part to ensure influence and thus access to the natural resources of Burma; this was followed by more traditional foreign aid in both loans and grants that by 1988 totaled $2.2 billion in foreign assistance.[28] Japan was the major foreign support to all Burmese regimes, and without its assistance in the 1960s they might well have collapsed. The Federal Republic of Germany as well became a significant bilateral donor, while the World Bank and the Asian Development Bank (ADB) were even more important.[29]

The Military as Caretakers

The Caretaker experience (1958–60) may well have been the defining period for the military in Burma. It had absolute power, was generally popular, and had a limited time horizon (extended from six to eighteen months), during which it could make unilateral changes. The economic and security situation started from a low base, as the overall standard of living in the country had not yet been restored to pre–World War II levels, and insurgencies continued. (It was not until the Burmese fiscal year 1975/76 that per capita GDP reached pre–World War II levels.)[30] There was, in a sense, no where to go but up.

A wide variety of decisions, some ephemeral, some relatively permanent, were made in that period. Prices were temporarily lowered in the bazaars on military orders. The "magic" of the marketplace did not matter. Over 160,000 squatters were forcibly removed from downtown Rangoon to the rice paddies on the periphery of the city where they were given plots of land but few services (a pattern that the SLORC was to repeat on a larger, nationwide basis following the coup of 1988). A border agreement was signed with China, the Shan *sawbwas* (maharajahs) were stripped of their administrative (if not social) authority, and a universal military conscription bill passed (for both men and women, on an Israeli model) that was never implemented because at that time volunteers were in excess of need.

Important for future economic policies and performance was the expansion of the Defence Services Institute (DSI), the military-run state economic sector. Starting as a type of post exchange for the military in 1951, it expanded during the Caretaker Government to include fourteen Boards of Management. In addition to extensive networks in international trade, the military established the Five Star Shipping Line, the Ava Bank, department stores, hotels, and an electronics workshop. The effective running of such a broad range of economic activities gave the military confidence that it could, in fact, run the country's economy as well.

In addition to the military's own economic activities, military personnel were placed in all ministries and at all levels of administration. They brought with them enthusiasm and a disdain for the bureaucracy, which was regarded as corrupt, politicized, or incompetent. Both because they were making shorter-term decisions within the administration and because they operated under a tight command structure, they appeared to be efficient as well as forceful. When they were (relatively) permanently ensconced, however, the very factors that enabled them to perform so well over the short term were a detriment over the longer period. Enthusiasm and loyalty were more important than knowledge, and the command system brooked no deviation from policies set at the top of the hierarchy. Thus necessary policy and administrative adjustments were exceedingly difficult to make as information and data were controlled.

Most important, beyond individual military decisions was a pervasive sense of pride in military accomplishments that was widely shared and that, in retrospect, was the basis on which future military rule was built. This emotion was propagated and epitomized in the publishing of the summary of military rule, *Is Trust Vindicated?*, the paean to past accomplishments.[31] The military's self-perception of its role was graphically illustrated on that volume's dust jacket, which pictured Hercules cleaning out the Augean stables.

On assuming power, the military stated it had three goals: to restore law and order, to implement democracy, and to establish a socialist economy. These goals were later modified and democracy eliminated in the military's next incarnation after 1962.

What caused the legalized military coup of 1958 and indeed the coup of 1962 as well? It was not only the threat of civil war and the growing confidence and capacity of the military itself. It was the failure of the civilian political process.

The armed left wing, represented by two underground communist parties— the "red flag" (some call it Trotskyite) and the "white flag" Stalinist (later Maoist)—was in revolt. The aboveground, legalized left was represented by the National Unity Front (NUF), which had surreptitious links to the Stalinist party. The NUF wanted more stringent socialism, and it received a significant share of the votes in the elections. The military, however, looked on the communists as a major threat, as it had been fighting the underground parties since independence. When it came to power, it engaged in a major psychological warfare campaign against them, publishing materials indicating that the communists were out to destroy Buddhism (*"Dharma* [Buddhist law] in Danger"). Thus, as Nu had used Buddhism, so did the military, and that emphasis still continues. The fear of the communists was real and continuing; even after the destruction of two internal communist rebellions and the collapse of communism virtually worldwide in the late 1980s, that enmity remains. The communist menace is still invoked against the National League for Democracy (NLD), and the army emphasizes that Aung San Suu Kyi does not have the sophistication to deal with these internal divisive forces. Aung Gyi left the NLD before the 1990 elections, forming his own party, also claiming that the communists were infiltrating the NLD. This helped solidify the military's antipathy toward the NLD and Aung San Suu Kyi as well, or at least gave it a public excuse to take such a position.

The failure of the civilian political processes may also be traced to the tensions between traditional concepts of power and authority operating within a modern parliamentary system. Parliamentary government depends on compromise and accommodation to succeed, but traditional concepts conceive of power as finite and personalized, and political parties of even an ideological nature are constructed as entourages (see chapter 2). Factionalism thus becomes endemic, and there are tendencies for fissures to develop. At the stage of the 1958 coup, ethnicity was not a major factor, although it rapidly became one four years later.

The Caretaker Government thus set the stage for the second coup of 1962, which eventually led to the third in 1988, which was designed to shore up the second.[32]

The Military as Socialists

The ostensible rationale for the 1962 coup was the potential breakup of the Union of Burma through a meeting of minority leaders held in Rangoon at that time.[33] If not the fundamental reason, it was a convenient excuse, for it led to the easy arrest and imprisonment of the leaders. The motivations went beyond the minority problems, which were severe. The military seemed to have wanted to resume power and probably assumed (with some reason at that time) it was the most competent group in the country. There had been rumors of an earlier coup plan, which had been postponed by Ne Win.

In a short period, the intellectual and institutional underpinnings of the society were established. Within a month, *The Burmese Way to Socialism* was published; it was an eclectic mixture of heterogeneous elements of Buddhism, humanism, and Marxism. As Dr. Ba Maw, veteran political wartime leader of the Japanese puppet regime, said, because it was socialist, it was good, but because it was Burmese, it was better.

In July 1962, the BSPP was founded. As noted, it remained a cadre organization within the ruling Revolutionary Council, but it was to expand into a mass mobilization system within ten years. In 1963, *The System of Correlation of Man and His Environment* was published. It was the muddled, but influential, intellectual and philosophical basis of the Burmese approach to socialism and society. The organizational, operational, and philosophical bases for the regime were thus in place, and for years these documents were taught in indoctrination courses required for the military, academicians, and other civil servants. But how seriously should these be taken as reflecting reality? Some have argued that it was power, not philosophy, that drove the military and that socialism was a means to that end. The search for a secular ideological rallying focus could have contributed to this choice. When asked whether Ne Win was a socialist, a leader of the Revolutionary Council (later jailed) said that Ne Win would be a socialist when Mao Tse-tung learned how to play golf.[34]

Following the coup, xenophobia became manifest when all private foreign aid organizations and the public information libraries of embassies were forced to leave. Some hundreds of thousands of residents from the Indian subcontinent were repatriated to their homes, even though some had lived in Burma for generations. The civil service was purged of its highly professional, competent, and apolitical senior staff, who had been members of the Indian Civil Service, and then the Burma Civil Service. Thus when socialism became a reality, there were few experienced within the state bureaucracy who could manage such a complex undertaking.

In 1963, the major nationalization campaign began after Aung Gyi was dismissed and Brigadier Tin Pe took over as virtual heir apparent to Ne Win. The country turned inward, and a rigid socialist system was instituted. Some 15,000 firms and businesses were nationalized. The country was cut off from the outside in a military-imposed cocoon. Few Burmese were allowed to leave legally, while visas for foreigners were severely restricted—to twenty-four hours for a period. Outside information was obstructed through controlled imports of news and a state-dominated press, while there were few short-wave radios at that time. With this autarky, the minority rebellions increased because even the modicum of local authority that the states (ethnic provinces) had was eliminated. All power emanated from the center. Burma also seemed intent on creating an industrial proletariat in a country that had little industry.

The rigid economic system collapsed within five years. Even the leadership recognized its failings. It was during this period that the BSPP expanded from a cadre party to a mass base. At the first BSPP congress reflecting this expansion, in June–July 1971, the government openly catalogued its failures and made a series of tentative reforms. It noted that although it had good diplomatic relations with the world, its economic relations were deplorable. It thus asked the World Bank back into Burma (Burma had joined in 1952), entered the ADB, and sought more bilateral foreign assistance.[35]

At the same time, the military developed new economic priorities and formulated a Twenty-Year Plan, to be implemented through five four-year plans. Priority was now to be placed on the development of Burma's natural resources—agriculture, forestry, and mining (especially oil and natural gas). The state sector was to grow, the private sector to shrink, and the cooperatives, a parastatal organization under ministerial control, to expand from 3 percent of the economy to 26 percent. None of these goals could be realized.

In the 1970s, after these reforms were introduced, Burma again began to grow, and by 1976 it had finally reached its pre–World War II living standards. A variety of factors were involved in this spurt of growth. Probably the most important for the Twenty-Year Plan was the serendipitous introduction of the high-yielding varieties of rice that were brought in the early 1970s from the Philippines. It was only in 1964 that paddy production per acre reached pre–World War II levels. This resulted in extensive increases in production (even though the surpluses had to be sold to the state at extremely low prices) and a rise in exports, although never to prewar levels. The effort offered such promise, if coupled with extensive fertilizer use and effective water management, that whole townships were given over to the production of these varieties, often over the objections of some farmers who preferred the taste of the traditional rice. Seventy-two of the most productive townships were targeted for these varieties and production was enforced, as the state owned all land and threatened those who disobeyed with expropriation. Incomes did rise, however.

A second factor was the exploitation of onshore oil, which had been a traditional industry from the precolonial period. In colonial times (1940), oil exports totaled $35 million. Increases were apparent, and hopes were raised for much greater production. By 1978, annual oil production was 9.55 million barrels. By fiscal year 1995/96, production had declined to only 4.28 million barrels. Natural gas was found and began to be produced in 1974. The World Bank, in addition to funding a variety of projects, became involved in supporting the expansion of teak exports. With World Bank advice, certain administrative reforms were also undertaken that increased government revenues. For a period, then, there was considerable optimism about the economy on the part of the government and among some donors as well. The planning process, although not integrated, projected increases in most fields of production. Yet political stasis under the military-dominated BSPP remained. Human rights did not enter into the donors' equations at that time.

Administrative and modest economic reforms were not accompanied by or translated into political change. Civil society continued to be suppressed, and the new constitution inaugurated in 1974 mandated a highly centralized state with a single-party mobilization system (apparently on the model of East European constitutions) under the authority of the party, which in turn was thoroughly controlled by the military. The military continued to dominate the bureaucracy, and all internal public expressions of opinion—from newspapers and magazines to novels, poetry, and drama— were subject to rigid censorship. Imported books were screened for political, and thus economic, content. No opposition was tolerated.

As the 1980s began, the economic situation began to change. As a result of the increases in foreign assistance, imports rose dramatically, and with them foreign debt increased (most Japanese assistance was in the form of loans). As the Japanese yen was revalued, this debt exploded, and at the time of the coup in 1988 it was about three-quarters of GNP. At the same time that both imports and exports expanded, the value of export commodities dropped while the costs of imports rose. The SEEs were a major drain on the national budget as most operated at losses. Major deficits began to be apparent.

Internally, the natural limits, given rural infrastructure, seed, fertilizer, and credit availabilities, had been reached in the rural economy and the expansion of the new varieties of rice. Fertilizer was in limited supply; irrigation covered only about 11 percent of the land, and much of that was limited to preventing a failure of the monsoon. Teak production peaked, and oil, in contrast to the projected increases, began to falter as production limits were encountered at the level of technology available to the state, which did not want onshore foreign intervention at that time. Although considerable arable land was still unexploited, it was generally in minority areas or other regions that were considered inhospitable to the Burman majority.

The government became less and less aware of the actual situation in the country because of a pervasive atmosphere of political fear and a rigid command system, which did not allow for bad news to filter up to the top of the hierarchy. So politically correct production figures were invented, and production seemed to rise because it was mandated that it do so. Of course, there were increases in production, but even in the official annual accounts that were publicly available, the projections estimated in the past year rarely seemed to equal the actual production figures reported the following year. Eventually, even the leadership began to realize that something was wrong. By that time, August 1987, when Ne Win publicly noted the problem, it may have been too late simply to tinker with a system that needed major reformation. The military had inherited a country both ethnically diverse but in which minorities could play important roles as long as they played by Burman rules, and one that was (in Burman areas) socially mobile. In the course of its rule it changed the nature of the sociopolitical process, thereby increasing latent societal discontent.

Burma was a "union," in the sense that a number of provisions allowed minority areas to have some local autonomy, and minority figures in the central government were important. (The presidency, for example, rotated among ethnic groups as long as the incumbent was Buddhist.) The 1974 constitution created a highly centralized state that destroyed the fig leaf of local authority. The military had been an important occupation for some minorities, but they eventually were virtually excluded from the higher command positions. The minorities were, then, effectively marginalized.

Burman society since independence was noted for its social mobility. It may have been the only area in Asia in which the precolonial elites did not resume positions of some authority in the postcolonial period.[36] The very fact that the precolonial elites did not reemerge may be an indication of the highly personalized basis of authority and power in the traditional period, in spite of a hereditary class structure among some elements of the population. Social mobility was through four channels. Education was free, and many from poor, rural backgrounds attended university. The military was an attractive channel, for the poor could get a university education through it, and it was prestigious. The Buddhist *sangha* (monkhood) was an important means for the poor to receive an education and attain high social status. Finally, the mass mobilization organizations, such as those for peasants or workers, allowed even uneducated persons national stature. The military destroyed this system. It eliminated mass organizations except those created under its control. It registered and dominated the Buddhist clergy. It limited access to education except for those approved. Thus social mobility under the Burmese military government was through the military and its rigidly controlled groups. They were the arbiters of social standing, resulting in both increasing frustration and discontent.

By eliminating any legal expression of political differences, the military had ostensibly exterminated its opposition. It prevented organized dissent but created the frustration that became more intense because there were no legal means of its expression; thus any spark could set off a conflagration. By concentrating power at the center, it increased minority frustration as well, thus encouraging the revolts that it had attempted to dispel through political uniformity.

This frustration was exacerbated by dire economic conditions—incessant inflation and increases in the price of the staples of rice and cooking oil, on which all families depended. Those in the military and bureaucracy were insulated from these problems through special shops and rations, as well as corruption from below, perquisites that common people and casual workers in state enterprises, who received far fewer benefits, did not possess. Thus the 1988 revolution was a generalized and widespread mass movement against a military that had become out of touch with the people. As one very high ranking but older officer said, "We in the military were taught: 'This bowl of rice comes from the people; this uniform comes from the people; this rifle is paid for by the people.' The present [SLORC] military have forgotten this."[37]

One highly placed military officer of the BSPP period, a believer in socialism and the role of the military, summed up that period and effectively articulated its epitaph:

> After 26 years, we have become corrupt, stratified, and generally stupid. What
> we have had [in 1988] is not a political uprising, but a social upheaval. After the
> 3rd Party Congress [BSPP in 1976], intelligence chief Tin Oo and Sein Lwin
> managed to get rid of all those who at all questioned the system and whom they
> did not want. The result was that military rule became absolute as socialists,
> even communists, were pushed out. From then on, the party was more form and
> not content. Even at the Central Committee, discussions of papers were dis-
> couraged; things were viewed as "foreordained." Even the *longyis* [sarongs]
> and shirts became a kind of uniform, reflecting the unanimity of ideas. This
> percolated down to the township level, where papers were read and votes cast,
> virtually automatically. I see a lot of damage done as party functionaries were
> appointed from above, beholden to the appointer, not to the membership. In the
> early days, when I reported back to my constituency, there were real questions
> asked. Later there were few or none. All actions were directed from the center,
> but the centralization became even more intensified at the local level. Thus the
> sense of having elected officials lost all meaning. This was a major source
> of corruption. I like our 1974 constitution, but we ourselves have wrecked it.
> Aliens to their neighborhoods had to be elected, and were not responsible to the
> people. . . . Part of the frustration [of 1988] was because of the stratification.
> We have these special shops, black sedans were given, telephones, building ma-
> terials, electricity allocated, travel privileges, and this system slowly divided
> those who got these things from those who did not. Ne Win was at the apex,
> and slowly these layers were built up, and solidified, when Burma had once been
> an open society.[38]

International Reactions to a Reclusive State

Burma was the quintessential neutralist nation. It refrained from joining the
British Commonwealth to ensure its autonomy. Hemmed in by the largest populations in the world and caught in the maw of the Cold War that spilled over into
its territory when Chinese Nationalist troops fled from the Chinese communists
in 1949–50, Burma had no other solution to its continued independence.
Plagued by two communist insurrections, as well as major ethnic revolts, it concentrated on survival and political balance between leftists and more moderate

political forces. Although berated by John Foster Dulles, the American secretary of state who considered all neutral nations immoral, Burma maintained its position with great care and attention. It was the object of much foreign aid, partly designed to win friends, and from an American vantage point to deny communist China and the Soviet Union a foothold in Southeast Asia. But Burma expelled the U.S. aid program over the incursion of Chinese Nationalist forces in the Shan State that were surreptitiously backed by the American CIA, and it paid for Russian assistance with rice rather than be in the Soviets' debt. It was for these reasons that U Thant, who became the most internationally famous of all Burmese (at least until Aung San Suu Kyi), was chosen to become secretary general of the United Nations. He was Burmese ambassador to the United Nations and had he been resident in Burma at the time of the 1962 coup, he could have been arrested along with other civilian leaders, as he had been U Nu's secretary and was close to him.

The Burmese felt insecure. They believed foreigners were unsympathetic, and their views antithetical to the goals of the society, which were both Buddhist and socialist and therefore outside of the Western mainstream.

Following the coup of 1962, contacts were not encouraged. Within about a year, the government began to restrict the entry of foreigners and the exit of Burmese, except those especially approved. Internal travel was greatly reduced. Since the media were completely controlled by the state, Ne Win was able virtually to cut the country off from the outside world. As the private sector, internal or external, was anathema, Burma entered into a period of isolation. Internal insurgencies increased, and the international media, with virtually no access to the country, let Burma slip off the news radar screen.

As the Burman regime at the center became more isolated, the minorities on the periphery came in closer contact with the outside world. Of all the major ethnic groups in that country, only the majority Burmans were completely physically located within the state boundaries. Chin, Kachin, Shan, Karen, and Mon peoples all had ethnic and linguistic relatives across the arbitrary frontiers created through the happenstance of colonial interests.[39] Further, some of the minorities were significantly Christian and were in touch with international Christian movements. All these factors increased both the isolation of the Burmans and the sense of anxiety that the state was ringed with potential enemies designing to destroy the unity of the Union, which had so laboriously been built and which the military regarded as its sacred duty to protect. The heritages of the past were perceived as salient even when much had changed: elements of the British had supported the Karen insurrection, the U.S. CIA, the Chinese Nationalist Kuomintang, the Chinese communists, the BCP, the Thai, a variety of rebellions along its western littoral trying to create buffer zones against a radical regime in Rangoon, Nagas in revolt in India, and Muslims in rebellion in the Arakan on the East Pakistan (later Bangladesh) frontier. National unity and the threat of both minorities and foreigners were a central concern of the state.

Although the official reassessment by the BSPP of the economy in the early 1970s resulted in a reinfusion of foreign assistance, little foreign exposure was allowed. As Burma became isolated and as imports of consumer goods were restricted and as the state took over the marketing of exports, smuggling increased; Thailand became a major conduit and supplier of all kinds of consumer products. China was still on the threshold of its economic liberalization; neither India nor China viewed a somnambulant Burma as of any particular interest.

This heritage both remained and changed after 1988. The military's employment of xenophobia to pursue its own purposes could be based on previous attitudes honed under the BSPP. After 1988, however, Burma's isolation ended, and foreign interest mushroomed when Burma was perceived to open to the private sector and needed foreign investment and when China internally liberalized its economy and began vigorously to seek foreign markets and expressed more openly its security interests in Burma. As Indian–Chinese rivalries began to be formulated, Burma moved to become the regional nexus of rivalry, even as relations with the minorities continued to be a grave concern.

Notes

1. Maung Maung, *The 1988 Uprising in Burma* (New Haven: Yale University, Southeast Asian Studies, 1999), p. 1. Monograph 49. This volume, Dr. Maung Maung's personal account of the period, was published posthumously. Maung Maung died in 1994.

2. Part of this chapter appeared in the author's "Crisis in Burma: Stasis and Change in a Political Economy in Turmoil," published by Chulalongkorn University, Bangkok, 1989 (see acknowledgments). For a study of the coup, see Bertil Lintner, *Outrage: Burma's Struggle for Democracy* (Hong Kong: Review Publishing, 1989).

3. The number of students along the borders in the first quarter of 1989 was estimated as follows: Thailand, 4,000; India, 800; China, 1,500; underground in Burma, 1,500.

4. There were persistent rumors in Burma and Thailand that before the coup, Saw Maung flew to Chiangmai and met with General Chavalit Yungchaiyudh, Thai supreme commander. At that time, Saw Maung is said to have informed Chavalit that a coup would be forthcoming that was necessary; otherwise anarchy would prevail and the communists would take over, and this would be a danger to Thailand. If true, it would not preclude the possibility that the timing was determined by conditions in Burma, such as those on September 15 at the Ministry of Defense and the September 17 siege at the Ministry of Trade. These rumors are given further credence by the fact that in February 1991, General Suchinda Kraiprayoon, the Thai commander at that time, was in Rangoon meeting with the Burmese military hierarchy, and the day following his return to Bangkok there was a coup against the Thai government. The speculation is that the Thai reciprocated the Burmese courtesy of giving early warning.

5. Statement issued by the Institute of Economics Teachers Union, August 2, 1988.

6. One district agricultural officer admitted that it was politically required that he report that agricultural production increased 10 percent a year, whatever may have been reality. Personal interview, 1989.

7. Personal interview, Rangoon, 1989.

8. At the end of September 1987, official Burmese figures show foreign exchange holdings at K.157 million, or about $26 million, plus $12.4 million in gold (*Report to the Pyithu Hluttaw, 1988/89*). The International Monetary Fund (IMF) notes that in December 1987 Burma held Special Drawing Rights (SDR) 27.2 million, or about $29 million (*International Financial Statistics*). In either case, the figures were the lowest in Burmese history.

9. At this time too (in 1987) Burma was designated a "least developed country" (LDC) by the United Nations. For details, see chapter 5 below.

10. Personal interview, Rangoon, 1989. Maung Maung characterized the incident of the deaths in the van as those of "street-dwellers or troublemakers who somehow lived off the city's population. But they were people all the same, human lives, that had been so casually and callously lost" (Maung Maung, p. 62).

11. A well-placed Burmese in Rangoon in May 1988 suggested that the most volatile group in Rangoon was the casual labor—those tens of thousands who were employed in any position by government but who had no tenure and few of the perquisites of office. They had less to lose and were massive in numbers. They joined the demonstrations and were critical elements in swelling the crowds.

12. Often in the past the state fomented protests designed to redirect dissent away from government and onto others, especially minorities.

13. In addition to Ne Win, these were San Yu, president; Aye Ko, joint secretary; Sein Lwin, general; and Kyaw Tun.

14. The following is a paragraph from a report by the author to the World Bank, dated August 1, 1988:

    "Party Leadership has passed to General Sein Lwin. A Burman Buddhist born in 1924, he has had a limited education, and was an associate of Ne Win's during World War II, and in Ne Win's regiment (the 4th Burma Rifles) as an enlisted man. He is said to be close to and trusted by Ne Win. Following the ouster of Tin Oo as intelligence chief in 1983, it was Sein Lwin who led the purge of Tin Oo's former associates, and then was placed in command of it. Sein Lwin has held various ministerial posts (Cooperatives 1974–75, Transportation 1975–77, Home and Religious Affairs 1977–81, after he retired from the military). He is essentially known as a hard line, even brutal, commander. Sein Lwin was responsible for the deaths of the Rangoon University students in 1962, and the student and monk casualties in 1974 in connection with U Thant's funeral, and most recently with the deaths associated with the student riots in the spring of 1988, when he gave the orders for the riot police to open fire. He is also said to be suspicious of the business community and distrusts traders. He has been ambitious. Last year he was reported to travel to various sites giving 'essential guidance,' a term usually reserved in the press only for Ne Win. He is said to be hated by the students, and in a sense the worst possible choice at this critical juncture for rallying the populace and dealing effectively with the economy. Demonstrations against him are likely. He may further have been chosen because of his loyalty to Ne Win, which gives further credence to the possibility that Ne Win will continue to remain in command behind the scenes. No one, however, can replace Ne Win in terms of his historical role and cumulative military loyalties."

15. Maung Maung, p. 61.

16. These may have been written with the expressed approval of Ne Win, who met with Aung Gyi.

17. The doggerel in Rangoon, in the form of a children's rhyme, was:

    One pyi of rice, sixteen kyat
    Cut off Sein Lwin's head.
    One egg, two and a half kyat
    Smash Sein Lwin's head.

18. It is said that Ne Win, perhaps influenced by the March massacre, instructed military units not to fire on civilians, but this was changed or countermanded in August.

19. David I. Steinberg, *The Future of Burma: Crisis and Choice in Myanmar* (Lanham: University Press of America and The Asia Society, 1990), p. 9; Asian Agenda Report 14. This work was intentionally written before the May 1990 elections to deal with broad trends in the society.

20. David I. Steinberg, "Report on the Resumption of Bilateral Assistance to Burma" (Washington, D.C.: Agency for International Development, Department of State), May 17–27, 1978, p. 17.

21. Those key figures from the 4th Burma Rifles include (among others) Aung Gyi, Tin Pe, San Yu, Sein Lwin, Aye Ko, Kyaw Tun, Tun Tin, Tha Kyaw, and Saw Maung. When asked whether he had been in the 4th Burma Rifles, a Burmese military attache replied, "If I had been in the 4th Burma Rifles, I would be a minister by now." He was probably right. Personal interview. Robert H. Taylor notes: "General Ne Win's ability to dominate the armed forces, and hence the government, through-out the 1960s, 1970s and 1980s, was a consequence of the fact that almost all of the key officers around him had been brought into the armed forces in the late 1940s and early 1950s, when the military was most heavily involved in combating the Communist KNU and KMT forces. They looked to Ne Win as the founder of the armed forces and the legitimate successor to the assassinated General Aung San. Many of the officers, who were not as well educated or widely traveled as their predecessors in the prewar generation or nationalist politicians turned soldiers, were devoted to General Ne Win, despite one or two serious attempts to oust him in the 1970s. His word became law ("Myanmar: Military Politics and the Prospects for Democratization," *Asian Affairs* [London] 85, 1 [February 1998]).

22. There seems to have been a reluctance to use his name in conversation. It is remi-niscent of the taboo against using the given name of the Chinese emperor.

23. Some maintain that his resignation encouraged the demonstrations that followed.

24. In 1989, a knowledgeable Burman said that you could tell whether Ne Win retained influence by noting whether there was an official devaluation of the kyat, as Ne Win had sworn he would never do that. Since that time, the currency has not been officially devalued, but accommodation rates have been approved and have replaced the offi-cial exchange rate in most cases. Personal interview. This anecdotal evidence should be treated with care but is indicative of how many Burmese felt about Ne Win.

25. Maung Maung, p. 266.

26. Numerous stories abound about the symbolic use of numbers and other incanta-tions. Since nine is Ne Win's lucky number, elections (May 27, 1990: $2 + 7 = 9$) and other important events take place when the sums of the dates add up to nine. In the 1970s, Ne Win changed driving on the left-hand side of the road to the right-hand side because it was said to help beat the insurgents. It should be remembered that the time and date of Burmese independence in 1948 were chosen after consul-tation with astrologers.

27. London: Blond and Briggs, 1973.

28. See chapter 9 and David I. Steinberg, "Japanese Economic Assistance to Burma: Aid in the *Tarenagashi* Manner?" in *Managing Japan's Foreign Aid: Power and Policy in a New Era*, ed. Bruce Koppel and Robert Orr (Boulder: Westview Press, 1993); also in *Crossroads* 5, 2 (1990).

29. See chapter 9.

30. David I. Steinberg, *Burma's Road toward Development: Growth and Ideology un-der Military Rule* (Boulder: Westview Press, 1980), pp. 78–79.

31. Director of Information, *Is Trust Vindicated? The Chronicle of a Trust, Striving*

and Triumph, Being an Account of the Accomplishments of the Government of the Union of Burma: November 1, 1958–February 6, 1960 (Rangoon, 1960).

32. For a discussion of the Caretaker period, see Steinberg, *Burma's Road toward Development,* pp. 14–18.

33. Provisions in the 1947 constitution allowed the Shan and Kayah States to opt for succession after ten years and following a plebiscite, but few believed that such an option was realistic.

34. Personal communication.

35. It was only after the end of the Vietnam War in 1975, and perhaps with Chinese acquiescence, that the United States was informally asked to restart its foreign aid program. Total foreign economic assistance rose from about $25 million in 1970 to approximately $400 million a decade later.

36. The Burman areas should be distinguished from other regions of Burma, such as the Shan and Kayah States, where traditional, hereditary, precolonial elites retained power.

37. Personal communication.

38. From David I. Steinberg, "Desultory Field Notes: Burma. February–March 1989." Personal interview.

39. There were more Kachin in China than in Burma, the Shan were linguistic cousins of the Thai, and there was a Shan autonomous region in Yunnan Province; the early Mon had developed the civilizations of southern Burma and Thailand, and the Karen straddled the Burma–Thai border. The Chin were related to the Zo of India's Mizoram State.

CHAPTER 2

The Social and Political
Backdrop to the Crisis:
Myanmar's Modern Heritage

Unrealized Potential

If an allegedly prescient observer of the Asian scene in about 1955 were to have attempted to predict the economic and political future of several Asian states a generation hence, that observer might well have chosen three countries for comparison.[1] Burma, Thailand, and South Korea seemed quite diverse, but they had populations within about 10 percent of each other and per capita GNPs around $50–$70, and they thus invited parallel consideration.

Each had problems. Burma had been devastated by World War II, and then the center's hold over the country had been circumscribed by multiple insurgencies of various political colorations and diverse ethnicities following independence in 1948. Thailand came out of World War II unscathed, but its administrative control, if not sovereignty, was tenuous over some of its frontier areas. South Korea had been virtually destroyed by the Korean War.

Political comparisons were less clear. South Korea suffered from an authoritarian state in the guise of a democracy. Thailand was dominated by the military in fact, if not in law. But Burma, operating a fragile parliamentary system, seemed more responsive to democratic forms than either of the other two states.

That observer with reasonable confidence would have pointed to Burma as the potential economic and political leader of the three. It was perhaps the only developing country (although that term came into prominence later) that was an exporter of food and fuel, having been the world's largest exporter of rice before World War II, and a supplier of oil (the Burmah Oil Company), especially to India. It had untapped, even unexplored, natural resources. It contained about 75 percent of the world's teak reserves and had vast other timber potential. Its population in relation to its land base was the most favorable of any continental Southeast Asian country. It contained a natural communications network through the Irrawaddy River (Kipling's "Road to Mandalay"), and its tributaries extended from close to the China border to the Bay of Bengal. Literacy was high; the use of English was widespread: thus international communications were relatively easy. *The Economist* years later pointed out that Rangoon, along with Manila, in that period would have been considered to be one of the model urban areas of Asia's future. The Burmese seemed to have absorbed a good bit of the British parliamentary experience of the colonial era, with reasonably good results. A modern legal system was in evidence, lawyers were well trained (many in London), and the courts were more autonomous than in the other states.

Thailand undoubtedly would have been second choice. It was a large rice exporter but lacked other natural resources. It had early squandered its teak stands, but it too had untapped land. Its politics were less clear and the future of representative government dubious, even though the absolute monarchy had been overthrown in 1932.

South Korea (hereafter Korea) would not have been a contender in anyone's imagination. Not only had it been devastated by the Korean War, but also its population to land ratio was one of the highest in the world, and only 20 percent of that mountainous country was arable. Korea lacked all natural resources, its industrial base was very modest (and then in light industry alone), and its educational infrastructure was weak, although it was growing. Its politics were a travesty of the slogan it and the United States purveyed internationally of Korea in the "free world." Although known as a Confucian society, which has considerable developmental cachet today, in that era Confucianism was considered to be an impediment to growth and the development process, as well as to democracy. It was considered then to exalt the past rather than strive toward the future.

Yet thirty years later, in the 1995–96 period, Korea's per capita GNP was over $10,000, Thailand's was about $2,500, and Myanmar's about $230.[2] Myanmar, instead of becoming the richest country of the three, was one of the world's poorest, or in UN terms, "least developed." Only a few such countries were so designated in Asia; most were in sub-Saharan Africa.

Politically, in the contemporary period Korea has embarked on a stable form of procedural democracy (although traditional attitudes toward power were still prevalent), and the military had been retired to the barracks without bloodshed or even incident in a feat that excited world admiration. Thailand has cautiously moved toward democratic forms, although the role of the military was still pervasive in mufti and occasionally in uniform. Burma, on the other hand, has settled into a period of military authoritarianism that seems likely to continue, first in uniform and then civilianized into the future for an extended, if unknown, period.

What caused these quite logical and informed predictions to go wrong? Conversely, what prompted the other countries to succeed economically or to move toward, at different periods, or away from political reform and pluralism?

Transformational Events and the Military

In each of these three countries decisions were made that had profound influences on the future economic and political directions. Within the space of a few years from each other, and from our imaginary prescient observer's speculations, these three states underwent important events that have helped shape, and even determine, the developments, both positive and negative, we have witnessed since that period.

In Thailand, the World Bank conducted a major policy review of the economy and in about 1959 presented a report to the Thai government, then controlled by the military following a 1958 coup. It suggested that the Thai plan to expand the state's economic control through public sector development would be in error and instead recommended a more open market economy and the encouragement of foreign investment. This study was backed by the U.S.

foreign assistance program and was later adopted as policy by the Thai bureaucracy. The implications of this policy went far beyond economics into the social composition of the state and its elites and seem to have been understood, if unarticulated, by the Thai leadership. They were: to achieve a market economy in Thailand, the Chinese minority, with entrepreneurial talents, access to capital, and a commanding influence in the economy, must be integrated into the fabric of Thai society, and foreign investment must be encouraged. As a result, Chinese integration has taken place to a degree not achieved in any other Southeast Asian nation in which the Chinese have been a minority.[3] Coincidentally with this decision, made essentially by the Thai military, which itself was expanding its direct economic interests, was the effort to build up the role of the Thai monarch as the unifying force in Thai society.

The Korean change came with a May 16, 1961, military coup that brought General Park Chung Hee to power. Lacking any traditional attributes of political legitimacy and having once been in the Japanese army and thus without nationalist credentials, Park turned to an export-led growth strategy as the means to alleviate the poverty of the state. This strategy also was his key to political control and eventually to political legitimacy. His successes were already evident before he introduced the most stringent authoritarian rule Korea had yet seen under the Yushin Constitution of 1972, which ensured his perpetual presidency, if not his perpetuity—he was assassinated in 1979.

In Burma, there were two seminal and related events, both also involving the military: one in 1958 and the other in 1962. The first was the "constitutional" military coup, under which the civilian government of U Nu "invited" Ne Win and the armed forces to run the government for an interim period to avoid a brewing civil war between factions within the ruling civilian AFPFL. This experience, known as the "Caretaker Government," was a heady one for the military, for it gave it administrative experience, a prominent political mobilization role, confidence in its modernity and vision, and placed it at the center of various economic activities (examined below).

After returning control to a newly elected civilian government in 1960, in an election the results of which the military did not anticipate (a precursor to the situation in 1990) and in which the military-backed party lost, and watching the country further deteriorate in economic and ethnic terms, the military launched its coup of March 2, 1962, which was designed to be permanent. It was this event that set into play the "Burmese Way to Socialism," which was to be the dominant ideological theme of the society for a quarter of a century.

In all of these three countries, the critical events had been products of the military. All three were rooted in authoritarian control of power. All were explicitly antidemocratic in any sense of the term that is understandable today. Yet the road toward democracy, however defined and lengthy, is routed in strikingly different manners in each of these societies. Although none of these three states today can be termed a "democracy" in a sense comparable to democracies in Western Europe and North America, the process of democratization is apparent in both Korea and Thailand, but has yet to surface in Myanmar.

As these three states evolved, the military's direct role in economics dramatically differed among them, although in all three it was the ultimate source of economic decision-making. The Korean military, although maintaining control over the economic policymaking, became directly involved in neither the production process nor the distribution of matériel. In Thailand, the military made direct, legal investments in a wide variety of economic activities from banking to the media. In Burma, as we will note below, the military also became directly involved in the control of a substantial portion of the economy.

Also significant were the differences in the military's use of civilian experts, especially economists. In Korea, the military regime sought out the most talented civilian specialists, especially economists and scientists, and established institutional means by which they had direct and critical access to the leadership. The Thai also employed expert civilians. But the Burmese military was suspicious of civilian experts and never gave them influential policy roles, relying instead on the enthusiasm, vitality, and loyalty of the officer corps, which could not perform adequately. Thus in Burma civil administration was stunted.

It was in this period that a considerable body of international academic literature was developed on the positive role of the military as a rational, future-looking, and goal-oriented body that worldwide was the great hope for progress in many societies. Decisions in these three countries alone indicate that although the military became an important force for change, its internal orientation or other factors influenced the roles that it would play in those societies. In Burma, in spite of an early period during the Caretaker Government when many of the military's accomplishments were widely applauded by local and foreign observers, the euphoria rapidly changed to concern as a strong strain of xenophobia became paramount. Burma's options seemed open. In the early developmental literature, Burma had many positive elements in its favor:

> Burma was first attractive, then, because of the newness of the nationhood and because it had, and has, a commitment to the building of a modern, welfare, and democratic state capable of generating continual economic growth and adapting to a changing world. The changes of Burma building or making of itself what its plans and aspirations called for were not hampered by that virtually omnipresent barrier or impediment in Asia: a dense, heavy population eking by on meager land and other national resources. Burma has the option of living at a level of primitive self-sufficiency or trying to build a modern economy. It was not locked into a set of vicious circles keeping the economy at a low-level equilibrium.[4]

State and Society in Burma

The traditional origins of state authority and the role of the leader in Burma, as in much of Southeast Asia, have been set forth persuasively by scholars for at least a generation. The Indian origins of the nature of the state and the role of its ruler were described in Southeast Asia much as the Confucian conceptual origins of statecraft based on the familial analogy have affected Northeast Asia.[5] In the absence of the modern concept of rigid, demarcated borders, authority emanated in concentric circles radiating from the center—the capital, the palace, and ultimately the throne and its occupant. Power became weaker as the distance from its core grew and could, and did, overlap in the peripheral areas with other waves of concentric power emanating from other, similar capitals of greater or lesser strength. This traditional pattern, maintained until the European colonization of Southeast Asia, seemed to offer no intellectual inconsistencies.

It seems evident that the magical nature of the ruler (the Burmese king was sometimes known as an "embryo Buddha") produced highly personalized rule and concepts of authority. Loyalty was personal: it centered on the king of the moment, not on the concept of kingship or governance or principles themselves. It was not ideologically based, although in the Burmese case rule was legitimated through the proper promulgation of, and relationships with, the Buddhist sangha and the symbols associated with that religion.

That loyalty was personal misses the point, although it accurately describes the phenomenon. The question is why was it personal, and what were the implications of this for governance in Burma/Myanmar?

There is a set of essential concepts that help explain the persistent patterns of governance that have evolved over Burmese history. Seven are discussed here; five are general and two are specifically Burmese. Most fundamental is the concept of finite power and evolving from that, the distance, or space, between the state and the individual and civil society. The two Burmese concepts that are important are those of *ana* (authority) and *awza* (influence). The role of political parties is also relevant, as are those of political legitimacy and ethnicity. As Lucian Pye has pointed out, "There are few cultures that attach greater importance to power as a value than the Burmese. Considerations of power and status so permeate even social relationships that life tends to become highly politicized. The fact that Buddhism is a central feature of Burmese life makes the quest for power more subtle and more indirect." [6]

Power as Finite

The first essential concept is about the finite nature of power. [7] Modern societies, administrative theory tells us, consciously consider that power is infinite, so that the sharing, delegation, or distribution of power may result in greater power and benefits to all: a win-win situation. In many traditional societies, however, power is conceived as finite. [8] If power is considered finite and yet its origins are related to religious concepts and remaining traditional and residual attitudes, then the sharing of power, its delegation or devolution on an individual or institutional basis or from central to local governments, becomes far more problematic than in societies with a view of power that is infinite, no matter how unconscious these concepts may be in either society. Under such conditions, and related to earlier religious beliefs, power thus becomes highly personalized. Although such power was originally centered on the monarch, it has an important influence on contemporary leaders. Loyalty, as noted, is personally based, rather than dependent on ideological, legal, or institutional relationships. Since loyalty is personalized, factionalism becomes common, with highly developed patron–client relationships prevalent. This strengthens social hierarchy.

Personalized loyalty can result in confrontations in which compromise becomes more difficult because although one may question the validity of an idea, concept, or political theory, it becomes a matter of loyalty not to do so. A "loyal opposition" thus becomes an oxymoron, for if one is in opposition, one obviously is not loyal. Governance then becomes the province of the leaders more than the bureaucracy or the people. The Burmese did not develop the concept of a meritocratic civil service that could act as a brake on personalized authoritarianism, as did China and those countries closely associated with the Confucian tradition, although the Buddhist hierarchy was in its own way an example of a religious-based "civil" service dependent on the purity of faith and performance within that context and did mitigate many of the worst excesses of leadership. Pye has argued that the difference between Burma and Thailand in the past was that in Burma "the idea of power revolved around profound tensions between superiors and inferiors, with subordinate roles carrying deep anxieties, while in Thailand inequities were not only acceptable but a dependent relationship could offer considerable security." [9]

The second concept akin to the issue of personalized power is that of the role of the administrative mechanism used to enforce that power—the state bureaucracy. Traditionally, recruitment was based on personalism and loyalty to the head of the party or, more recently, to the military. The colonial period transformed the traditional political culture and unwittingly reinforced the centralist tendencies of the state and thus its leaders. Not only did it eliminate those diminishing concentric circles of power emanating to the borders and introduce the mechanisms of lateral state control over all territory to newly, stringently demarcated frontiers, but it also transformed local governance. The village headman, who traditionally was locally appointed and was often hereditary, was the top village official; it was his job to keep the central government (the king), one of the five traditional evils of life (the others include fire, water, thieves, and enemies), away from the village. The British administration transformed that position into the lowest level government appointee, whose function was to represent the state at the lowest level. This completely transformed local governance, no doubt making it more efficient even as it eliminated autonomy. The state thus reached to the village and could, and did, more easily intervene, as it still does today.

Social Space

One major issue in contemporary politics in Burma/Myanmar is the degree to which the state (namely, the ruler, or in the present case, the coalition of military leaders now known as the State Peace and Development Council—SPDC) believes it has the right of, and the people feel willing or are obliged to accept, intervention of the government into society. That is, what is distance, or how much space is there, between the state and the individual and civil society? How autonomous is the state willing to let the individual or groups of individuals be? Although the question is most obvious at the overtly political level, such as in elections and in petitioning the state, the issue affects all elements of the society. Thus if the private economic sector is now encouraged, how free of governmental interference will it be? How much will the government attempt to regulate individual actions, such as freedom of speech, the press, media, movement of people, privacy, freedom of association, and a whole range of human rights? Finally, to what degree will the state allow citizens to band together to pursue common interests? In other words, will it allow civil society to be formed or flourish? (A separate question is whether people willingly will bond together exclusive of the state—see below.) If the state seems reluctant to provide such space, then is this a cause or effect of a lack of social capital?

If the Confucian-oriented ruler can intervene into the most minute and private aspects of the lives and operations of the citizenry on the basis of the moral need of the father (the ruler) to care for his children (the people), the Burmese ruler, traditional or modern, rather may conceive of such interventions as his prerogative simply as ruler, based on his *ana* (authority—see below), which in turn is dependent on his karmic heritage. He may need no external moral justification because he has it based on his earlier, obviously stellar, karmic performance. He must always be cognizant of issues connected with Buddhism and be seen as supportive of the *sangha*.

The regulation of society and its control are clearly illustrated in the economic sphere. Burmese monarchs had singular theoretical control over the economy. They had monopolies on the export trade and the production of oil and teak (the "royal tree"). Although this pattern was broken during the colonial period, it was in a sense reinstituted in the moderate socialist period of civilian rule and then with rigor and disastrous consequences under the "Burmese Way to Socialism" and the BSPP after the coup of 1962. Under the SLORC and the SPDC, there has been a movement toward a more open economic system and the encouragement of both the internal private sector and external investment. Yet the same distrust of autonomous businesses persists, and the military has made its influence over the economy apparent not only through the formulation of economic policies (no matter how poorly and arbitrarily they have been administered), but also through direct ownership of significant aspects of the economy through the Myanmar Holdings Corporation, Ltd., military procurement factories, and more recently the Myanmar Economic Corporation, as well as through the state banking system and the ostensibly private (but actually state-controlled and monitored) "private" banks.

The political and emotional need for government control was exacerbated by the colonial economy, in which foreigners essentially commanded most aspects of trade and investment. Europeans, Indians, and Chinese at various levels in business and the professions were major forces in the economy, thus alienating the Burman population and guaranteeing that socialism would be viewed as a political requirement on independence.

The restrictions on the individual in the state are so well documented they need little exegesis here. The media are firmly, pervasively controlled. Travel is restricted; visitors who stay overnight are supposed to be reported to local authorities. Free speech is impossible. Arbitrary arrest is common. Law is not the protection of rights but rather an arbitrary set of regulations promulgated to support the state establishment and to prevent dissidence. Law is thus personal, not contractual, opening avenues for corruption, which, because of economic mismanagement, minuscule official salaries below subsistence, and more basic questions of personalism, is endemic and indeed necessary for survival. In provincial areas, local military commanders have virtual dictatorial powers to enforce (or ignore) regulations that serve what they regard as state (or personal) interests. There is much here that is reminiscent of traditional patterns of state authority. The implications for privacy and human rights are obvious, even under a benign administration, in which the space between the state and the individual will be restricted to some significant degree.

Ana (Authority) and *Awza* (Influence)

Burmese patterns of power are centered around two contrasting but sometimes overlapping concepts.[10] The first is *ana,* which is authority. It is an idea grounded in a centralized sense of power inherent in an individual. One has it because of one's previous deeds in other incarnations, and it is not necessarily related to a moral presence. It is this authority that the military regime in Myanmar maintains. The standard dictionary (Judson) translates this term as both "authority" and "governmental domination."

Awza, translated as "influence," is dependent on a distributed or diversified authority or awe. The dictionary expands on this usage by noting that it is "relish, richness [in food], the quality of a thing in which its richness or strength consists . . . weight, impressiveness, authority to words and influence." In other dictionaries, it is sometimes translated as "power."

> *Awza* is a function of relationships, the important thing being that in every group there is someone who has *awza.* In every family, class, community, office, organization, political party, nation, there is one person who has *awza.* . . . The components of *awza* include the characteristics we would normally associate with power, influence, and prestige—among them, respectability, wisdom and knowledge, a degree of religiosity, a commanding presence, and skill and ease in handling authority.[11]

It is obvious that although there are distinctions between these two key terms in Burmese political culture, there are overlapping usages and meanings.

While *awza* is always positive, *ana* can be either positive or negative. It is said that Aung San Suu Kyi has *awza* but not *ana,* while the military junta has *ana* but not *awza.* One of the implications of having *ana* is that when the SPDC claims, as it continuously does, that when it is taking some action or indeed is in power, it is distributing benefits with *cetana* (goodwill), an extremely important Buddhist concept that is constantly reiterated in the press and in government slogans. Under such circumstances, no one could possibly disagree or object to the actions taken, and thus social protest against the military requirements imposed on the public is completely inappropriate in this essentially Buddhist context.[12] Thus many of the premises on which negotiations between the Burmese state and foreign powers are conducted are completely different.

If this analysis is correct, then these are reinforcing concepts in the nature of Burmese political culture that affect how political leadership is viewed and how power is exercised.

Issues of Legitimacy

Political legitimacy is always a complex product of history, process, and adherence to societal norms; in the modern world it may also be related to questions of international acceptance or denigration.[13] Four elements normally compose political legitimacy in any country: shared norms and values (the normative and most fundamental element); conformity to the established means for acquiring power (procedural element); proper and effective use of power (performance); and consent of the governed (the consensual factor). These bases of legitimacy may be affected by the charisma of the leadership, a politically defining moment (such as independence or revolution), international support, and ethnicity. Legitimacy is not static; it may erode through nondelivery of promised benefits and changes in the political value system, or it may expand under other circumstances. It can obviously be reinterpreted ex post facto for earlier regimes.

The military and the NLD, as well as foreign observers, have differing interpretations of the relative weight of each of these factors in the Burmese equation. But within this broad conceptual framework, in the Burmese context five foci have been used to legitimate the various governments or pretenders to power: nationalism, Buddhism, socialism, the military, and elections. They vary over time, and the changes and different stresses and weights that apply at any specific time are part of the conceptual issues facing analysts; their diverse interpretations contribute to the crisis Myanmar faces today. Each of these elements has become the focal point, or even the ideology, of various regimes. However important ideology may be, it may also have a supplementary role. According to Pye, ideology has a broader function: "One of the cardinal principles of Burmese political culture . . . holds that statements of ideology should be used to soothe the aggressive passions of others and to convince them that one is blissfully innocent of malice toward anyone." [14]

Nationalism is the enduring element in Burmese legitimacy—the sine qua non of political life. This was quite apparent in the struggle for independence from the British, but it has been a theme that has been appealed to by every government since that time.[15] Many would argue that nationalism is essentially xenophobic. It is evident that the appeals to nationalism are powerful and pervasive. They have been even more strident under the SLORC/SPDC regime than under previous governments. Although the state wants foreign investment and needs income from tourism, the junta has consistently and in the most vituperative language denounced the evil machinations of foreigners who want to divide the country, exploit the people, destroy Burmese (read Burman) culture, are in league with the opposition, want to seduce Burmese women, and "do not love us." Nowhere is this more comprehensively shouted than against Aung San Suu Kyi because of her (now deceased) British husband, her "mixed race" children, and the foreign support that she has received. Although nationalism is a constant, varying only by the intensity of the clamor with which it is invoked, other elements have varied over time. The early economic import substitution policy after independence can be interpreted as both a response to general economic theory of the times and a facet of nationalism. Its resurgence in the late 1990s, together with a drive for rice sufficiency, may also be regarded in a similar light.

Socialism has disappeared as an element of legitimacy, although it was strong during the early civilian era. (One of the reasons the communists split was because it was not strong enough.) It was the rationale for the BSPP era, and the military portrayed itself as upholding its aims and traveling the road toward the glorious socialist future under "the Burmese Way to Socialism." Yet the fervor of capitalism has not replaced socialism as an element of legitimation because socialism could be considered, and was so by Nu, as akin to Buddhist concepts, while capitalism was based on greed—a singularly inappropriate motive under Buddhism. Nu clearly won the 1960 election on the basis of his Buddhist religiosity. Although making Buddhism the state religion may have appealed to the Burman population (98 percent of whom are Buddhist) and perhaps some other groups such as the Shan, it upset many of the minorities and helped prompt rebellions against the state. The military was also opposed to using Buddhism in this fashion, although during the Caretaker Government it was not averse to launching a major campaign against the communists, citing that the *dharma* (Buddhist law) was in danger.

The failure of socialism as a tool of legitimization has perhaps prompted the military to equate legitimacy with military rule itself. In other words, the military has gone from being the flag bearer of socialism to the deliverer of competent government (during the Caretaker period) and even beyond legitimacy focused on the delivery of economic well-being (which it obviously has not delivered at any time). It has come to a position that focuses on the military itself as an ideology. The role of the military, the motivations of the military, the good will (*cetana*) and plans of the military for the people are all in fact directed toward adulation of the military in its leadership role. To this end it has rewritten history and created a revisionist understanding of the place of the military in Burmese history, even founding a museum to this end. As the upholder of state security, it sees security threats to the state as essentially internal, rather than external, even if external elements support internal dissidents (sometimes known in the local press as the "traitorous minions").[16]

To supplement this focus, the military has used nationalism and Buddhism, the latter an essential element of legitimacy for any regime in that country. After the military "purified" the *sangha* in 1980 and registered the monks, it suppressed the demonstrations and activities of some of the monks under the SLORC, occupying some monasteries and forcing an end to monk protests in 1990, but at the same time performing all the Buddhist acts that kings and other leaders have performed from the beginning of Burmese recorded history. Since independence, U Nu, Ne Win, and Than Shwe (the chairman of SLORC/SPDC) have all built pagodas (Than Shwe has built two), as have all Burmese monarchs, and Khin Nyunt in 1999 has supervised the extensive refurbishing of the most revered of shrines, the Shwedagon. All of these actions, plus the obeisance to monks and the paying of appropriate homage, are normally front page stories in the controlled press. The bayonet alone is no match for the lotus, as the British learned in the anticolonial demonstrations, but they are used today to supplement each other.[17] Aung San Suu Kyi has not neglected her Buddhist connections, has visited a variety of monks, and on the death of her husband held a Buddhist memorial service for him in Rangoon in April 1999. Buddhism is an important force for legitimacy, and no leader can be seen to be against it.

The final element in the legitimacy equation is the role of elections—the procedural element.[18] Although elections are a critical and perhaps the most obvious of the institutions that comprise democracy, it is likely that the international popular press and some governments regard them simplistically as the single defining element in legitimacy and democratic governance. The May 27, 1990, elections are viewed by the NLD as giving it the rightful role to rule because it (along with minority parties aligned with it) won 82 percent of the National Assembly seats and received 59.9 percent of the votes cast. The United States and other countries accept this position. By international standards, the argument makes sense, but the issue is whether within Burma any election alone is sufficient to provide legitimacy. Many would argue that it is; the military, however, look to other criteria.

Elections are important, visible, and quantifiable, while the exercise of power and more subtle systems of checks and balances are often ignored in the hyperbole associated with elections. In Burma, the 1990 elections were important, and they provide international legitimacy for the NLD. Whether they provide internal legitimacy and whether, if they did, there has been attrition of that legitimacy over the past decade are issues on which no definitive answer can be given, although Aung San Suu Kyi believes the NLD is even more popular a decade after the 1990 elections. The military has played up nationalism by equating it with its own administration and charging that the NLD, with its outside moral support and even funding from the Nobel Peace Prize (although it is not used for that purpose) all indicate that the NLD has no nationalistic credentials. The dilemma for the military is that Aung San Suu Kyi has a nationalistic aura as the daughter of Aung San, so the army has assiduously attempted to downgrade Aung San's image and focus on eliminating any nationalistic identity of his daughter. Whatever legitimacy the 1990 elections may confer on the NLD, the voting may have also reflected a negative response to the military in control of state power as much as it may represent a positive force for the NLD.[19]

Ethnicity

The ethnic factor remains potentially the single most explosive element in contemporary Myanmar. Although academicians have argued about the importance of ethnicity in Burmese history, the rise of internal ethnic nationalism has been as apparent in Myanmar as in many other societies. The actual and potential sources of national power, the military and the NLD, are Burman-based. Ethnic parties did win seats in the 1990 election; there were nineteen different ethnic minority parties,[20] and some of those were aligned with the NLD. It is still evident today that to achieve power one must play by Burman rules redefined as "Myanmafication." [21]

Although in the early period of NLD activities Aung San Suu Kyi did not stress the issue of minorities, claiming that democracy would have to come first, her position has evolved over time so that it has become evident that some significant degree of ethnic political pluralism would be instituted under an

NLD-led government. An alliance with ethnic minorities, real presumably as long as the NLD remains out of power, would come in for considerable stress if the NLD were in control because of the fundamental problems of the distribution of the assets of the state and state power. It seems also apparent that in spite of offering local control of some small minority regions (in part in return for cease-fires in some areas), the central military authorities have no intention of sharing national power.

Yet the twenty-two or so cease-fires with the minorities are fragile.[22] They depend on the delivery of better education, health, and living standards to these areas if they are to persist. These the military is financially incapable of providing, and it may also be incapable in organizational and administrative terms. The minorities have not surrendered their arms and are unlikely to do so even when a new constitution is promulgated. The arrogance and distrust shown by the military and the central authorities in their dealings with minorities are concealed by the verbal and ceremonial, but essentially meaningless, public rites performed by the military. Houtman reports on a Union Day minority cultural event in which all the minorities performed the same dance, differing only in their ethnic costumes.[23]

The distrust of the minorities is not based only on the favoritism shown by the colonial authorities to them and the separate administration of some of those areas, nor is it solely based on the 1947 constitution, which had provisions for the secession of the Shan and Kayah States. It is also more recently a product of some minority calls for independence thirty or forty years earlier. Such independence is no longer advocated. That the Burmans, not the minorities, have been isolated is a strongly held belief; the minorities have ethnic cohorts across the borders in neighboring countries while the Burmans do not; some of the minorities have international Christian connections, and the outside world has been seen to support ethnic-related rebellions.

In a country that is ethnically about two-thirds Burman, to be politically legitimate today means to be Burman, although in the civilian period the ceremonial position of the presidency was rotated among major ethnic groups while real power lay with the Burman prime minister and the Burman-dominated army. The continued insistence on a unitary, centralized state will mean that tensions of the distribution of state assets will be a matter of contention into the foreseeable future.

The Role of Political Parties

In societies in which power is highly personalized and patron–client relationships are important, political parties play a secondary role to their leaders. Parties become the product of their leaders, normally do not train successors to that leadership, and become the "property" of those in command. When the AFPFL split in 1958, it divided on personality questions, not programmatic issues. Thus political parties are vehicles for their leaders to either retain power or achieve it. They are held together by those common goals, rather than by the programmatic interests of the leadership. Even the BSPP, which was built around a socialist ideology, was more a means to retain military authority by mobilizing the state around an acceptable goal than it was a commitment by the leadership to a socialist vision of the future. The two communist parties that were in revolt were each led by a single charismatic leader.

Political parties, those supported by the government or opposed to it, are likely to continue to be personality-centered and thus more a means to retain or seek authority than a unifying force in the society.[24]

Problems of Pluralism

Pluralism, a concept inherent in the functioning of democratic societies, has flourished, both internally in states and internationally in and across a wide spectrum of countries since the end of the Cold War. The spread of apparently democratic regimes since that time—the so-called third wave of democracies—has been a product of this internal shift. Externally, the end of polarization has led to more regional pluralism. Although generally considered to be a force positive for political development, pluralism has also led to sometimes virulent ethnic nationalism and its dire consequences; the Balkans offer a primary example.

Pluralism, or the diffusion of power to different and contending centers of public or private authority, has been a deterrent to the rise or continuation of autocratic rule. Such multiple centers of power may be located within government (such as those in the checks and balances of the American political system), between or among political parties, between the private sector and the state, in the media, and in the group activities of citizens pursuing their, or what they regard as national, interests. A plural society may be so delicately balanced in power terms that it leads to policy or program inertia, and it can result in some states in tribalism, but in general the mitigation of extended control by any one source of power is believed to be supportive of the democratic process—and may be considered a way station on the road toward democracy.

Although Burma was ruled through a broad political coalition, the AFPFL, from independence in 1948 until the legalized military coup of 1958 and the formation of the Caretaker Government, there were legal, contested plural centers of power beyond those connected with ethnicity. An opposition party existed (the NUF), the press was active and critical, the courts were relatively unimpeded, and there was debate in a bicameral National Assembly, in which the minority peoples were specifically represented in the Chamber of Nationalities. The minority areas, called states (or in one instance the Chin Special Division), had very limited autonomy, but their authority, however inadequate many members of the minorities regarded it, was one element of pluralism. Civil society, an aspect of this pluralism, was active and important.

Pluralism in Burma was intentionally destroyed. Military rule following the coup of 1962 brought in a regime that eliminated any legal centers of pluralism. Immediately on seizing power, the military eradicated the National Assembly, took over the legal system, abolished local ethnic governments, and declared all political parties illegal. Selected key officials of all branches of government were jailed so that there could be no challenges to military rule. Over the course of its authority, it nationalized some 15,000 private enterprises and formed the BSPP, which was the only recognized party in the state.[25] When military rule was codified under a new constitution in 1974, it legally became a single party mobilization state with the BSPP as the only legal political party. It was a unitary state, meaning that the fictive autonomy that had been allotted to minority states within Burma was withdrawn and replaced by centralized military control that brooked no local power. The model for the constitution was evidently the East European countries under Soviet influence.

Pluralism did in a sense continue to exist, but it was an underground pluralism, on the periphery essentially in revolt against the central authorities. Many of the elements of the national minorities, who felt repressed by military rule, Burman dominance, and what they considered the unequal sharing of the fruits of independence, sought solace in rebellion, some with a goal of federalism, but others for greater autonomy, even independence.

The military government of the BSPP, even if it did not want competing centers of even local authority, did theoretically understand the need for a means to learn of local conditions and change policies in response to local problems. It attempted to learn through a formalized mechanism whereby the members of the parliament would return to their districts and learn about the issues by discussing them with their constituents and then report back to the central body so that remedial action might be taken. This system, so leading proponents of it have argued ex post facto, did not work. As noted, a pervasive hierarchy of fear permeated the society, so that bad news or inappropriate questions were not brought to the attention of those in superior positions. Thus the regime and its leaders were effectively insulated from plural ideas. The effective decay and virtual collapse of the BSPP regime could be traced to this lack of pluralism of both ideas and institutions in the society.

The Culture of Power

Power in Myanmar continues to be defined in a descending hierarchy: personally, institutionally, and ethnically. In each of these categories, rigidity of control prevents pluralism and autonomy of other leaders, institutions, or ethnic groups. The critical figures in the SPDC have personal power, the military has institutional power, and the Burmans have ethnic power.

Power Personalized

Power in Burma is generally considered to be highly personalized, both historically and contemporaneously. From the days of the pagan kings in the eleventh century, personal and even bureaucratic loyalty was to the individual monarch, and the locus of power resided in the individual. Within this construct, obtaining, holding, and using the symbols and perquisites of power (regal, religious, administrative) were important for that individual's legitimacy. No one in the modern era has exemplified that factor more than Ne Win.

Although Ne Win ostensibly retired in 1988, during his various roles as president, chairman of the BSPP, chairman of the Revolutionary Council, or commander of the *tatmadaw,* his presence made the office, whether he created or inherited it. His absence from the current official scene should not be equated with a lack of influence. Indeed, in spite of (perhaps because of) repeated denials, first by President Saw Maung and later by others, that Ne Win was no longer active in government, there are still those in Rangoon who believe that his role continues to be profound, if quiet, on major questions if not pervasive on mundane matters in spite of his age. One need not subscribe to conspiratorial theories or the concept of his role as a type of deus ex machina to believe he is still important on critical issues. Conversely, should he decide to place his influence against any particular individual, his attitudes may be determining. Observers say he is intellectually active, and there is evidence that he is at least occasionally still visited by critical SPDC leaders. Although his role may be somewhat obscured, his past authority is unique in modern Burmese history. There is no one yet on the national scene whose span of control is as extensive.

Power in Burma is not based solely on command structures or titular office, however, as institutions are secondary to individuals. As indicated, personal loyalties play important roles, and these loyalties are associated with groups and entourages encircling critical figures. The most famous of these groups has been composed of the men involved in the 4th Burma Rifles, once commanded by Ne Win and from which he drew his closest associates.[26] Conversely, when Ne Win purged General Tin Oo from military intelligence in 1983 (it is said because Tin Oo was too popular with the military and was thus a threat to Ne Win's domination), he accompanied that move by eliminating from positions high and low an extensive clique of those felt to be Tin Oo associates, thus demonstrating the two-edgedness of the sword of personal loyalty, and inadvertently enabling the North Koreans to attempt to assassinate President Chun Doo Hwan of South Korea, missing him but killing seventeen high Korean officials and three Burmese.[27] The intelligence capacity of the state had been seriously compromised. Although the power of contemporary military officers is by present Burmese standards widespread and they are feared, no one has developed the entourage that Ne Win succeeded in acquiring. The instability of the state forces the conclusion that no single person from any group in the foreseeable future is likely to do so. There is also the likelihood of a rise of factionalism over time because of the continuity of the traditional attitudes toward power as personalized and information as power. Struggles for power are to be expected until one figure emerges as clearly dominant and then has the spoils with which to attract a broadened personal following. Although the

SPDC constantly claims to be united, the most heinous crimes today are activities that attempt to split the armed forces, indicating that the fear of and potential for factionalism within the military are still perceived to be strong. Conversely, this is related to the incessant preoccupation of the military with the need for national unity.

Institutional Power

The only present institution of power within the state is the military. With the elimination of the BSPP in 1988, itself a creature of the military, miltary presence and control are profound, reinforced—as the military constantly reminds Myanmar citizens—through martial law solely responsive to the leaders of the regime. Since 1962, the military has prevented the emergence of any autonomous centers of influence. Education, the *sangha,* the bureaucracy, private and voluntary organizations, professional groups, and even the political parties are fragmented, controlled, and/or rigidly restrained.

At the same time, since 1988 there has been a conspicuous effort by the military to expand its numbers, improve its equipment, and increase its actual (as opposed to public) budget. There had been rumors of military plans to double the armed forces to close to 500,000 (some say 430,000) by the end of the century from the force of about 186,000 at the time of the 1988 coup. China is reported to have sold on credit $1.2–1.6 billion in arms to Myanmar, and provided military training; jet aircraft have been supplied from a variety of sources, including China, and the state is said to have the "probable" capacity to produce chemical weapons.[28]

In spite of a modest tradition of institutional independence of the Burmese judiciary from 1948 until 1962, based on the colonial model, the discrete autonomy of the executive, legislative, and judicial elements of state governance was neither established nor considered desirable. The permeation of the military and the former BSPP into all three branches of government (even the elimination of the judicial system and replacement with People's Counsels) is an indication that the separation of powers, and thus institutional autonomy, has not existed under military rule. It is evident that the present *tatmadaw* leadership has little appreciation of the usefulness of such autonomy—indeed may fear it—and it is obvious from previous military statements that whatever form of state emerges from the fire of revolution and repression, it will bear the military imprint of monolithic power, even under the multiparty political system the SPDC says it will introduce. Institutional autonomy would be exceedingly difficult to maintain under the best of Burmese circumstances and under any regime, given historical precedents.

The conceptual model in Myanmar for authority is the family. The government, it says, is the parent; the people are the children who must obey the parents and must be punished when they do not do so. If recalcitrant children (e.g., the insurgents) repent, then as wayward sons and daughters they would be welcomed back into the fold.[29] No citizen, except the supreme leaders, has inviolable rights.

At the same time that the autonomy of branches of government has not been established, the perpetual problem in modern (and traditional) Burma has been the politicization of the administration and the formation of bureaucracies earlier based on the party, then on the military and the BSPP, but always focused on personal loyalties within these constructs. Although the SLORC/SPDC has determined that the bureaucracy and the military should remain free from political activities and membership, the independence of the executive branch from partisan and/or military-dominated direction has not occurred and is most unlikely to happen over the near term.[30]

There have been successive purges of public servants over the military years, for absolute loyalty to the regime was required over competence. After the 1988 coup Khin Nyunt indicated that 4,545 public servants had been dismissed, suspended, retired, demoted, or transferred; 2,992 of them were relieved of their positions because of opposition to the regime. This was in addition to the purges following the coup of 1988, about which Khin Nyunt noted, "Everybody will clearly remember that during the 1988 disturbances, *most* public service personnel erred by following the wrong path of their so-called leaders or officers" (emphasis added).[31] That is, they opposed the regime in power. Following the coup of 1962 (as noted), the military also purged the elite Burma Civil Service.

Thus in spite of appearing to acquiesce to more diversified and local control, the military will likely retain effective power if its plans mature. There is no evidence that concepts of power—the movement from personalization to institutionalization or to institutional autonomy—have changed. Even if there were an immediate return to democratic forms, democratic content is little understood in a young population without personal exposure to it and little attitudinal understanding of its nature. Under any circumstances, any such movement—should it occur—is likely to be slow, arduous, and painful. The institutions that would have to support democratic governance would have to be created and sustained.

The events following the election of 1990 may be considered in this light. The repression of 1990 and earlier was simply continued.[32] Opposition leaders remained harassed. That Aung San Suu Kyi was awarded the Sakharov Prize by the European Parliament in January 1991 and nominated by President Vaclav Havel of Czechoslovakia for the Nobel Peace Prize in the spring made no difference. On October 14, 1991, the Nobel Committee awarded her the Peace Prize, citing her as "one of the most extraordinary examples of civil courage in Asia in recent decades. . . . She has become an important symbol in the struggle against oppression" with her employment of "non-violent means to resist a regime characterized by brutality."

New, effective, charismatic leadership was not allowed to develop; local elected leaders were not allowed to perform any of the functions for which they were voted into office (under various contrived legalistic excuses, such as unsatisfactory accounting of campaign expenses); and more parliamentary leaders were jailed.

Ethnic Power

Power in Myanmar is also organized ethnically. Since the 1990 elections, the results of which remain ignored, there has been a growing recognition by the SLORC/SPDC of ethnicity. Indeed, ethnic issues—rephrased, however—have been in the official limelight, but with a special twist.

Since the coup of 1962, the military had downplayed ethnicity, ignoring it when it could, treating it as public relations when necessary. Under the constitution of 1974, the unitary state that was created contained the fictive balance of seven "states" (supposedly for the minorities) and seven "divisions" (or provinces, the equivalent of states, for the Burmans).[33] In fact, authority—administrative, legislative, judicial, and fiscal—rested with the Burman center, the BSPP, and thus ultimately with the military. In public fora a such as the specialized UN agencies and commissions, Burma treated the minorities as a nonissue, downplaying their influence and diversity. Although the 1974 constitution specifically called for the retention of cultural rights by the minority groups, to attain national power one effectively had to be Burman, and the relatively few minority individuals who achieved positions of moderate influence played the game according to Burman rules. Even before the military, however, power was in Burman hands.

Since the elections of 1990, however, the military has been emphasizing minority issues. The institutional action in 1991 was the upgrading of the Sagaing Academy for the Development of National Groups to university status. This may be based on a Chinese model, such as the Yunnan minority institute in Kunming. It is designed to educate minority youth in Burman ways. There has been, in addition, a flurry of developmental activities, some sponsored by the UN Development Programme (UNDP), in some of the minority regions where the authorities have developed cease-fires with some of the groups previously in revolt. The cease-fires also serve to protect the lucrative trade routes to China. The essential issues are, however, neither more prestigious education for minorities (the academy—and all educational institutions—were BSPP training mechanisms for party inculcation), nor better infrastructure in the hills, the need for which cannot be denied. The minority issues center on the ethnic distribution of power.

The military has set forth its own tasks most clearly and defined the role of the population, and both focus essentially on avoiding ethnic dissolution. The three *tatmadaw* causes are: "nondisintegration of the Union, nondisintegration of national solidarity, and perpetuity of sovereignty. . . . Every citizen is to accept Our Three Main Causes of the *tatmadaw* as [his] duties as well and are [*sic*] to be always working for them." [34]

The minority groups on the border, now organized into the National Democratic Front, have long since given up separatist aspirations and for a number of years have sought some form of autonomous federal system. On December 18, 1990, a National Coalition Government of the Union of Burma (NCGUB) was formed, first in the border region with Thailand. It incorporates remnants of the NLD that fled to that area in 1990; later it moved to Washington, D.C. Formed as a result of a secret vote of some 250 elected members of the 495-person National Assembly (and thus a majority), the members regard themselves as representing the legitimate government, as they believe they represent the popular will. Their goal, in addition to providing a rallying point for national opposition to the present government, is reported to be to undercut the legitimacy of the SLORC/SPDC externally and within the population and the military. It has been formally supported by Norway, and the U.S. Congress requires that all UNDP programs be approved by the NCGUB and the NLD (see page 122n18). The SLORC indicated in an authoritative declaration that since the SLORC is not a political organization, "it has no reason at all to negotiate by political means with any armed insurgent organization." [35]

The military asserts it will have to approve the new constitution, which it claims will eventually be drafted and on which it and its cohorts are supposedly working. It preempted work on one by the NLD following its election victory. It must legally define the institutional sharing of central and regional power, but even more important within that context, it must deal with the issue in ethnic terms. That constitution, according to authorities, will also have to be popularly approved—by some sort of national assembly, constitutional convention including the minorities, and/or a national referendum, or by invoking the acclaim of the government-controlled mass organizations. The scenario is unclear and the timetable unspecified. The military has obviously used the minority issue as one means to delay the transfer of political power.

Yet the minority question is profound and the solutions exceedingly difficult since compromise is scorned by the state. Specialists may argue that ethnicity is not a static concept and that it can vary by time, location, and function. The SLORC/SPDC, and indeed all Burmese governments since independence, however, have regarded ethnicity in varying degrees of simplicity. They have underestimated the need to deal not only with the major minority groups (which are further subdivided into significant linguistic and cultural subgroups), but they have also avoided dealing with smaller groups that have singular cultural patterns and history but sometimes are not only smaller, but are less historically important or lack distinctive, contiguous geographical bases.[36]

The military designates all groups as "races," a term that accentuates at least international confusion in dealing with the admittedly complex issues of ethnicity. In fact, the *Working People's Daily* noted: "Nowadays, the term 'ethnic group' or 'minority' has no longer any serious meaning. It is found that the concept of 'national race' has come to have more and greater influence over the concept of an ethnic group, which is a component of a national race." [37] Thus the SLORC/SPDC conceptually stresses the people of the state as a whole, rather than its component groups.

In the attempt to slow the process of transfer of power, "race" now looms large in the compendium of state issues. The military, which had attempted to deny the importance of ethnicity for almost three decades, now brings forward the old colonial calculations of some 135 different ethnic groups (actually linguistic divisions) that have to be consulted in the formation of any new constitution. It notes that the "theory" of the big races "has been fading away from day to day." [38] It seems this is because the terms do not cover all ethnically designated insurgent groups, and it seems evident that the military is concerned about security in those smaller groups.

Ethnicity is one issue; regionalism is another, related, one. The failure of the BSPP to manage the state, according to one acute observer who was once high within the BSPP hierarchy, can be attributed to its increasing lack of responsiveness to local needs, some of which were in minority areas, while others were in purely Burman areas. This analysis is substantiated by the plethora of political parties that registered for May 1990 elections and contained ethnic or regional names. Thus although minority issues are exceedingly important, they reflect in more acute and virulent form problems of state responsiveness to local issues—the quintessential center versus periphery problem. The indigenous state has traditionally been centrist conceptually, although before 1962 it was administratively weak.

The unitary state, mandated in 1974 in spite of the commission of notables appointed by Ne Win who advocated some federal sharing of power, did not work. Conceptually it was anathema to some minorities and accentuated rebellions already in place or started new ones. It was also impossible to manage by a government that was as notoriously weak administratively as it was strong repressively and that equated military rank and party loyalty with administrative competence.

The SPDC is now attempting to come to grips with a central issue, if one may attempt to define its perception of the problem: how to retain centralized control or domination of the allocation of power in the military while appearing to share it with an acceptable civilian government and satisfying some internal and international needs for recognition of minority and regional interests, if it cannot directly satisfy the major minorities.

The military seems intent on retaining the unitary concept but in some new administrative configuration. In a significant article by a "senior military official" in the state-controlled press, the government is now maintaining that one cannot have 135 "races" provided autonomy on the basis of only eight separate (big races) groups (and their states or divisions).[39] "Unity within unity within unity" (these words broadcast in English) must be established. This might be done through the development of lower level autonomous units (i.e., lower than state or divisional levels), such as the townships (which have made up both states and divisions), "township zones," or districts.[40] The article notes:

> Through this [plan], disputes regarding the suitability of the notion of either the unitary or the federal system will come to an end. . . . It will be most appropriate if decentralization [in English] that assures freedom through autonomy for racial groups on the basis of racial concentration and distribution is coupled with centralization [in English] at the state level that ensures unity.[41]

The article continues: "The wishes of racial groups will be fulfilled if they are allowed to control the three branches of power [executive, legislative, and judicial] in the regions where they form the majority." National unity would be achieved through the centralized head of state (elected by the majority, which is Burman), a national assembly, and a supreme court.

The August 9, 1991, *Working People's Daily* is salient:
> The experiences gained [under the 1974 constitution] taught us that there were conditions which required one more level between the township-level and the State/Division-level. The State/Division level found that there were too many townships under it for it to manage them effectively and so there should be another level such as township zone or district placed between the State/Division level and the township level. However, this sort of arrangement will weaken the self-administrative theory as there will be many national races taking part in the State/Division level in practicing the self-administrative system by the national races. *Therefore, it will be more feasible and convenient if the central government controls the township zones/district administrative bodies to which the powers formerly exercised by the State/Division level administrative bodies have been transferred.* (Emphasis added.)

It is too early to assert that this model will be the one that the *tatmadaw* will eventually adopt, but publication with this attributed authorship is evidence of serious intent.

This legalistic approach to the issue of minority power does offer certain potential advantages for the smaller groups that have contiguous locations— for example, the Palaung (in the Shan State) who are located in relatively contiguous hill areas and who are distinctive linguistically (their language is part of the Mon–Khmer family, neither Sino-Tibetan nor Thai) as well as culturally. The attempts at the close of the century to resettle some 140,000–150,000 Wa in other areas of the Shan State closer to the Thai border, although explained as an effort to eliminate opium production by creating new agricultural and rural-based employment, may in fact be an effort by the Wa (with the consent of the Rangoon authorities) to expand their territorial reach so that by the time a new constitution is formed, the "autonomous" area of the Wa will be vastly expanded at the expense of the Shan.[42]

The real issue implied in this approach, however, is the effective breakup of whatever modest authority might have existed at the previous state level, devolving it down to a set of smaller administrative units, the townships, with the center holding power at the agglutinative group of townships (the districts or township zones). Although advantageous for certain smaller groups, it would effectively eliminate the exercise of power at the national level by any of the major minorities, such as the Shan, Kachin, Karen, Arakanese, Mon, or Chin. With the township zones/districts administered by the center, Rangoon and the military would effectively reach even further into the periphery. Thus while appearing to satisfy the need for regional autonomy, the *tatmadaw* may have devised a plan that will accomplish two of its objectives: first, continue to concentrate, or even strengthen, power in the hands of the center—those whom the *tatmadaw* deems worthy of support—and second, placate smaller minority groups with which truces exist (such as the Wa, Palaung, and Pa-O). This plan bears similarity to the South African example of establishing black native homelands and thus splitting black power.[43]

The plan is a move away from the constitution of 1947, which had a bicameral legislature—the upper house for the minorities while real power rested with the lower house. It is also seemingly different from the 1974 constitution, where power was starkly and bleakly centralized. If adopted, it would effectively continue the unitary Burman state by other means. For the military, it seems to be a feasible alternative to the unacceptable federal system most of the minorities want.

The leadership of the armed opposition and those in the provisional government along the border will probably oppose such a plan, for it would undercut their advocacy of a federal system that would provide significant autonomy to larger, more powerful administrative entities. Since all the states have significant small minorities (including Burman groups) within those territories, the effective administrative fracturing of the minority regions through elimination of the states and the reestablishment of the district or township zone would diminish minority influence at the center while increasing some minority rights at local levels. As the Burmese in the past have accurately accused the British of "divide and rule" ethnic policies, this plan would place the Burmans and the surrogates of the military in a similar commanding role by dividing while ruling.

When important changes were to take place on which the military felt public support was required (e.g., the 1974 constitution, the citizenship law), it has come up with a plan that is approved through controlled public discussions and meetings. It seems evident that whenever the preparation of a new constitution is completed, it will be presented to a meeting at which some of the myriad minority delegations will be present. This will likely be done with fanfare but with few or only marginal changes to what the military has predetermined is acceptable. Khin Nyunt has stated, "A firm constitution can only emerge with the full participation and *unanimous* agreement of all indigenous nationals, public service personnel, workers, and peasants" (emphasis added).[44] This underscores the pervasive interventionist role of the state. In 1991, then, the tactics of dealing with the minorities changed significantly, although the strategy and goals of the center seemed to remain constant.

The Power of Culture

The uses of cultural symbolism to reinforce regimes and provide legitimacy to governments are, of course, old and established. In Asia, the attempts are perhaps more obvious than in other areas, as clearer distinctions are perceived to exist between individual cultures and Western influences.

In Myanmar, the attempt to use culture as a legitimizing tool and an antiforeign weapon is particularly acute. It permeates the press on a continuous basis and seems a central focus of an authorized strategy of regime maintenance. Perhaps partly because of the lack of a clear popular mandate and as a means to counter extensive foreign criticism of the government, culture looms larger in Myanmar than in other states within the region.

The uses of culture to reinforce both nationalism and legitimacy, as well as the soundness and efficacy of present military policies, extend even to the origins of man. The *tatmadaw* is fostering research on paleolithic remains that would demonstrate that man originated in Myanmar. It has also claimed that archeological research on the stone age period has produced evidence demonstrating that different "races" (based on bone measurements) lived together peacefully because such bones were found intermingled without wounds. This is evidently to demonstrate that before recorded time, let along before the colonial period, the various ethnic groups were united—with obvious lessons for the present.

With the discrediting of the former state secular symbolic slogan, "the Burmese Way to Socialism" (and its ideological writings), Myanmar lacks a unifying theme. The use of Buddhism for this purpose, inherent in the U Nu period, was disruptive to some minorities, and at that time the military opposed its political use. The military has, however, reinvoked it on occasion, such as when Ne Win built a major pagoda, and in 1991, following an earlier crackdown in 1990 on monks in Mandalay. The public touting of the military itself, perhaps as an attempt to create such a unifying theme, seems to be internally questioned, for its incessant repetition may be indicative of a lack of responsiveness on the part of the people. Stress on indigenous culture may be seen to be the alternative answer.[45] As Bruce Matthews has written, "At the heart of the matter [of Buddhist cultural determinants of Burmese behavior] is the fact that the military regimes over the last three decades have appealed to certain key aspects of precolonial dynastic rule, to an older Burmese paradigm of authoritative government." [46]

To an outsider, Burmese (Burman) culture seems strong, even vibrant, and the repeatedly expressed fears that it will be subverted by foreign influences seem unwarranted and may indicate an internal concern over regime efficacy. By stressing culture in the SLORC manner, the state is denigrating, both implicitly and even more explicitly through the press, the role of all foreign cultures, especially those of the West, and of course attempting to counter the criticism of the regime by both Western governments and the press.

This theme is constant. For example, a cartoon says, "You must be careful to ensure that our Myanmapyi (the country of Myanmar), which has great cultural tradition, is not influenced by Western culture." [47] Another warns, "Then, uproot and get rid of all thoughts which hold high all that is foreign; and don't pine for the aunt over the shoulder of the mother." [48] Saw Maung said it most absolutely:

> The nation should be one in which only Myanmars reside and which Myanmars own. We will have to be vigilant against Myanmar Naing-Ngan [the Union of Myanmar], the home of Myanmar nationals, being influenced by anyone. And it is important that Myanmar Naing-Ngan does not become the home of mixed bloods influenced by alien cultures though it is called Myanmar Naing-Ngan.[49]

But the culture that is espoused, Myanmar-ism (to coin an inelegant phrase), is apparently that of the dominant Burman group. In the press it is generally defined more by what it is not, rather than what it is. It is not Western in any sense, and Western influences are to be eschewed. One actress was barred for five years "from acting in films, video films, plays and theatres; entertaining through the television, producing taped songs, appearing on covers of calendars, magazines and journals for having dressed up in alien and decadent attire contrary to Myanmar culture and customs when entertaining the public." [50]

Burman cultural practices dominate. For example, a government board was established to review all commercial music and tapes for foreign influences, ones that "contravene the rules for the composition of songs." It is supposed to act on the need to conform to "Myanmar culture," the definition of which is supposedly clear but is in fact inchoate.[51] We know who sets the rules, but what, indeed, are they?

As defined by the state, reflecting the Burman leadership of the military, that culture is no doubt Burman, however much the state may claim that its intent is to represent a broad spectrum of indigenous peoples. This creates major unresolved intellectual issues regarding any proposed constitution that will no doubt mention the protection of all indigenous cultures. An editorial in the official *Working People's Daily* warned against the danger of becoming un-Myanmar by losing the indigenous culture:

> Putting it bluntly, would anyone wish to see his son not as his own but someone else's? This is the raison d'être for the vigorous efforts being made for the preservation of our cultural identity and national personality. It is a natural reaction of anyone who cares for his own nation and his own people and is proud of his birthright![52]

Those who eat cheese or who wear pants or skirts (as contrasted with the traditional male/female sarong—the *longyi*) are considered un-Myanmar. There is a special fear and prejudice against Indians (especially Muslims), who are said to be destroying the Burmans by taking Burman wives and having a greater birthrate. There is a fear of the (Burman) race becoming extinct.[53]

The need for cultural preservation strikes a responsive chord among many observers who have seen the destruction of other indigenous societies. Yet the cry in Myanmar is strident, harsh, and so inclusive as to be, in effect, stultifying. It also indicates most blatantly the state's view of its role as comprehensive and intrusive and must bring into question the possibility, if these attitudes hold, of any organizational pluralism or real release of any aspect of the private sector from government domination.

For the immediate future, however, the problem is more acute. The infusion of foreign economic interests and individuals with the expansion of the private sector, the continuing need to understand foreign markets for Burmese primary products, the transfer of technology from outside to internal factories and institutions, and the training of Burmese abroad all create tensions between state needs and state ideology. When coupled with the impact of foreign ideas and news through the international media, internal duplication facilities, telecommunications that the government can no longer completely control (although it tries), and the planned influx of foreign tourists (for which the hotel structure of Yangon [Rangoon] has been transformed with foreign investment), the ability of the state to limit foreign exposure has ended even with its control over all media. Indeed, even as the state defines national interests in terms of imposing cultural limitations, it also recognizes the national need for foreign investment and better international markets.

Xenophobia, as noted, was evident under Ne Win and the Revolutionary Council, and it was formalized in the chauvinistic citizenship law of 1982, but the current authorities have carried it further to citizens who are seen to be too close to foreign ideas and concepts—who are "aesthetically un-Myanmar." The attitude of SLORC in summary is as follows:

> It is of great importance for weak multiracial countries like ours, that are situated between the super powers, to defend themselves from any foreign interference and influence. Therefore safeguards must be taken to exclude people who might have foreign influence, have less patriotic spirit, and lack any idea of

preserving national dignity, from any influential positions that can determine the destiny of the country.[54]

Culture is thus a salient element of the national purpose; if it was accurate to describe Burma in the 1960s as xenophobic, the SLORC accentuated that tendency. The legitimacy of the SLORC is related to that stress on Burman culture, but it is one that is at least in part in conflict with its own planned economic role.

Notes

1. Parts of this chapter appeared in James Morley, ed., *Driven by Growth,* 2d ed., and in a paper presented at Australia National University, August 1999 (see acknowledgments).

2. As calculated by the multilateral agencies and organizations for any of these countries, per capita GNP figures are questionable, and these were calculated before the Asian financial crisis of 1997, which lowered per capita incomes in Thailand and Korea. Even in Korea, which has the best statistics, estimates of the underground economy range from 20 to 40 percent of the entire economy. Thailand has an extensive smuggling record along all its frontiers with all its neighbors. Myanmar is the most problematic. The official rate of exchange (there are now also accommodation rates for various purposes) is 1/60 of the free market rate. Perhaps 70 percent of the economy is underground. Smuggling is a major source of income. Many types of investments, such as those from China, do not appear in official statistics because they do not pass through the National Board of Investment, and some estimates place the illegal narcotics trade as equal in value to the legal trade.

3. The Thai decision is more remarkable because at this time there were fears throughout Southeast Asia that the People's Republic of China would use the overseas Chinese community as a means to infiltrate and create revolutions in the societies in which they had settled. The similarity of the religion of the Thais and Chinese, although they are Buddhists of different persuasions, made integration easier than in Indonesia, with a predominantly Muslim population. Yet the Thai integration was more complete than in Burma, in which Buddhism predominated as well.

4. Manning Nash, *The Golden Road to Modernity: Village Life in Contemporary Burma* (Chicago: University of Chicago Press, 1965), p. 314.

5. See Robert Heine-Geldern, "Conceptions of State and Kingship in Southeast Asia," in *Southeast Asia: The Politics of National Integration*, ed. John T. McAlister (New York: Random House, 1973). Robert Taylor, in *The State in Burma* (Honolulu: University of Hawaii Press, 1987), has a more modern and comprehensive study of the issue. Michael Aung Thwin in his volume, *Pagan: The Origins of*

Modern Burma (Honolulu: University of Hawaii Press, 1985), has a number of cogent analyses of aspects of kingship during that critical period in Burmese history. See also Maung Maung Gyi, *Burmese Political Values: The Socio-Political Roots of Authoritarianism* (New York: Praeger, 1983). For a different approach, see Gustaaf Houtman, *Mental Culture in Burmese Crisis Politics: Aung San Suu Kyi and the National League for Democracy* (Tokyo: Tokyo University of Foreign Studies, Institute for the Study of Languages and Cultures of Asia and Africa, 1999), Monograph No. 33.

6. Lucian W. Pye, *Politics, Personality, and Nation Building: Burma's Search for Identity* (New Haven: Yale University Press, 1962), p. 146.

7. This is akin to the concept of the limited good in traditional agrarian societies, where if production went up or innovations were introduced by some element of a village economy, increasing its wealth, then the rest of that economy and population must necessarily suffer. See George M. Foster, "Peasant Society and the Image of the Limited Good," in *Peasant Society: A Reader*, ed. Jack M. Potter, May N. Diaz, and George M. Foster (Boston: Little Brown, 1967), pp. 300–23.

8. See Benedict Anderson, "The Idea of Power in Javanese Culture," in *Culture and Politics in Indonesia*, ed. Claire Holt (Ithaca: Cornell University Press, 1972).

9. Lucian W. Pye, *Asian Power and Politics: The Cultural Dimensions of Authority* (Cambridge, Mass.: Belknap Press, 1985), p. 99.

10. See Houtman for an extensive discussion of these contrasting forces. The following discussion is partly drawn from this work.

11. Pye, *Asian Power and Politics,* p. 147. See also his "Civility, Social Capital, and Civil Society: Three Powerful Concepts for Explaining Asia," *Journal of Interdisciplinary History,* 29, 3 (Winter 1999).

12. "Usually translated as 'goodwill,' in Burmese *cetana* means 'a union or accordance of mind with an object or purpose, inclination.' It presumes that for a government to work, all people must share the same deep intentions, and the same object or purpose. . . . The *cetana* of the generals thus demands a trusting response on the part of the Burmese that all will be well. There is no such thing as questioning the good intentions and there is no such thinking whether by being 'well-intentioned,' the regime might still do bad things for the country" (Houtman, pp. 162–63).

13. For a discussion, see Muthiah Alagappa, *Political Legitimacy in Southeast Asia* (Stanford: Stanford University Press, 1995). The theoretical discussion that follows is taken from that work.

14. Pye, 1985.

15. It was apparent that the struggle for independence was vital in the 1920s and 1930s. When it became clear that the Allies were going to win World War II, in the spring of 1945 the Burmese changed sides and joined with the Allies. The defeat of Churchill's government in England and the rise to power of the Labour Party effectively determined that India and Burma would become independent.

16. For a study of how the military views security as essentially internal, see Tin Maung

Maung Than, "Myanmar: Preoccupation with Regime Survival, National Unity, and Stability," in *Asian Security Practices: Material and Ideational Influences,* ed. Muthiah Alagappa (Stanford: Stanford University Press, 1998).

17. For a study of the uses of Buddhism for both internal legitimacy and foreign policy, see Juliane Schober, "Buddhist Just Rule and Burmese National Culture: State Patronage of the Chinese Tooth Relic in Myanmar," *History of Religions* 36, 3 (1997): 218–43.

18. For a study, see Robert Taylor's chapter in *The Politics of Elections in Southeast Asia,* ed. Robert Taylor (Washington, D.C.: Woodrow Wilson Center, 1996). He sidesteps the issue in his contribution. See also Taylor's chapter in *Burma: Prospects for a Democratic Future,* ed. Robert Rotberg (Washington, D.C.: Brookings Institution, 1998).

19. Mary Callahan questions whether democracy was an articulated goal even in the civilian period since it was not mentioned in the 1947 constitution; "Democracy in Burma: The Lessons of History" (National Bureau of Asian Research Analysis, 1998). See also Callahan's chapter, "On Time Warps and Warped Time: Lessons from Burma's 'Democratic Era,' " in Rotberg, ed., pp. 49–68.

20. Martin Smith, *Burma: Insurgency and the Politics of Ethnicity,* 2d ed. (London: Zed Books, 1999), p. 17. (Originally published 1991.)

21. The term was coined by Houtman.

22. See chapter 6, appendix C, for a list as of July 1998.

23. Houtman, op. cit.

24. For a discussion of the mechanisms (as contrasted with the political dynamics) of political parties, see Khin Maung Win and Alan Smith, "Burma," in *Political Party Systems and Democratic Development in East and Southeast Asia,* vol. 1, ed. Wolfgang Sachsenrodes and Ulrike E. Frings (Aldershot: Ashgate, 1998).

25. See David I. Steinberg, *Burma's Road toward Development: Growth and Ideology under Military Rule* (Boulder: Westview Press, 1981).

26. See chapter 1.

27. Burma "derecognized" North Korea. North Korea had violated the personal invitation of Ne Win to South Korean president Chun Doo Hwan. It was only in the summer of 2000, when North Korea joined the ASEAN regional forum, that Myanmar considered reestablishing relations.

28. The buildup was reported in *Jane's Defense Weekly,* June 15, 1991. On chemical weapons capability, see Elisa D. Harris, "Chemical Weapon Proliferation in the Developing World," *Rusi and Brassey's Defence Yearbook 1989* (London: Royal United Services for Defence Studies), based on congressional testimony by the U.S. Director of Naval Intelligence in 1988. Some claim that recruits are rushed into service so rapidly that they are poorly trained and motivated. There had been some discussion among the military to divide the *tatmadaw* into two armies—Irrawaddy east and Irrawaddy west commands—but this plan was dropped reportedly because of the fear of a split between the two.

29. *Working People's Daily,* August 14, 1991. This has a distinctly Confucian ring, but the origins probably lie within the Burmese tradition and concepts of Indian kingship and are prevalent throughout much of Southeast Asia.

30. SLORC Order 1/91 of April 30, 1991, reconfirms that all military and civil personnel must stay clear of party politics or labor organizations and cannot be members of or support any such activities, nor can their dependents. This was reiterated in an important speech by Khin Nyunt to public servants on October 4, 1991 (Foreign Broadcast Information Service [hereafter FBIS], October 7, 1991). In the 1950s U Nu also complained about the problem of divided loyalties in the ministries between the AFPFL and ministerial duties.

31. Cited in FBIS, October 7, 1991, from a speech by Khin Nyunt to public servants on October 4, 1991. Anecdotal reports indicate the purges were more widespread. They also included university teachers, who are considered public servants since education was nationalized.

32. For a discussion, see Robert H. Taylor, "Myanmar 1990: New Era or Old?" *Southeast Asian Affairs 1991* (Singapore: Institute for Southeast Asian Studies, 1991).

33. These ethnic groups are now called by the SLORC the "big races,"; see note 36 below.

34. *Working People's Daily,* February 22, 1991. The theme is constantly repeated in a wide variety of official media and other documents. See, for example, the editorial in the *Working People's Daily,* August 12, 1991.

35. SLORC Declaration 1/90 of July 27, 1990. All political parties were forced to sign this document. It also states that the SLORC will not accept an interim constitution. On the NCGUB, see "An Exile Government Fights to Be Heard," by Steve Hirsch, *National Journal,* September 23, 2000.

36. In fact, smaller groups have been omitted from the published population censuses. *The Burma 1983 Population Census* (Rangoon: Ministry of Home and Religious Affairs, Immigration and Manpower Department, June 1986) lists eight "races": Kachin, Kayah, Chin, Burmese (that is, Burman), Mon, Rakhine (Arakanese), Shan, and "other indigenous races," as well as "foreign races." "Other indigenous races" (the breakdown is unstated) amount to only 33,227 people (0.1 percent of the population), a blatant understatement. Presumably most have been lumped into individual state totals. Statistics on race or ethnicity must be regarded as questionable.

37. *Working People's Daily,* August 7, 1991.

38. Ibid.

39. Reported in FBIS, August 7, 1991, from *Loktha Pyeithu Nezin,* August 6, 1991. The official is also called a "high-ranking *tatmadaw* officer" in the *Working People's Daily,* August 7 and 9, 1991.

40. The district was a colonial innovation based on the Indian model that was retained after independence but eliminated by the military under the unitary state.

41. FBIS, August 7, 1991.

42. There has been speculation that the movement of some of the Wa has enabled, or even was planned, to encourage Chinese migration into those border regions.

43. There is, of course, no inherent or logical reason why such local autonomous units might not have national influence, but the fact of their formation by this government, in contrast to any other administrative system, points to their likely limited power.

44. Cited in FBIS, October 7, 1991, from a speech of October 4, 1991. In preparation for the 1974 constitution, a pervasive media campaign was launched to convince the public of its appropriateness. This was followed by a plebiscite controlled by the military. Even under these conditions, in some minority areas there were large numbers of votes against that constitution.

45. There also has been a major campaign in the press to accentuate the atrocities and injustices that all foreign groups have historically played on the Burmese peoples. This is designed to demonstrate that no foreigner can "love us" (the Burmese people).

46. Bruce Matthews, "The Present and Future of Tradition Bound Authoritarianism in Myanmar," *Pacific Affairs,* 1998.

47. *Working People's Daily,* June 30, 1990.

48. Ibid., May 10, 1991.

49. Ibid., February 22, 1991.

50. Ibid., June 12, 1991.

51. FBIS, June 19, 1991.

52. *Working People's Daily,* June 19, 1991.

53. Smith, paraphrasing the *Working People's Daily* of February 1989. When Khin Nyunt's son married a Singapore Airlines stewardess, Khin Nyunt placed a notice in the newspaper publicly disowning him. Regulations against officials having foreign relations—one of the factors the military has determined would not allow Aung San Suu Kyi to assume an important role in the new state— would theoretically also apply to Khin Nyunt.

54. FBIS, August 13, 1991, from *Loktha Pyeithu Nezin,* August 7, 1991. The dilemma for the government, and for foreign donors, is that the training of young Burmese abroad in modern skills needed for effective administration of the state automatically makes some of those trained suspect as being "un-Myanmar" as they acquire foreign-based skills, contacts, and possibly attitudes.

CHAPTER 3

The Military and the
Aftermath of the Coup

Military Perceptions and Roles

The *tatmadaw* occupies the pinnacle of power in the state.[1] It has forged an identity for itself based on its perceptions of its past, present, and future roles in the country; has created myths of its efficacy and place in the society; and has attempted to convince the populace that its vision is the correct, indeed the only, one. It is virtually obsessed with unity—of the state, of the military, of the concepts of governance, of ideas and the need for orthodoxy, and of the administration. As Foreign Minister Win Aung said, "Our program of democracy is secondary. Our fundamental program is national unity. Given the fact that we have so many diverse races living together, if we are not united, there will be no chance of survival. A new government can emerge, but unless we have solved our problems of national unity, it will not last long."[2]

The military is the most cohesive organization within the country; it occupies that position not only because of its taut command system, but also because since attaining power in 1962, it has consciously prevented the rise of any organization that it could not control or which was deemed a potential rival for any degree of autonomous power. Thus in the BSPP period, the party was founded by the military and dominated by both active duty and retired military, and all mass organizations were placed within its purview. In 1978, for example, of the 456 Pyithu Hluttaw members, 97 were active-duty officers and an additional 85 were retired military.[3] In the same way, but using different mechanisms, the SLORC/SPDC centralized control over all major organizations.

National Security Concepts

The military's natural preoccupation with national security explains many of its actions to ensure its commanding position within the state. As noted, the military seems to conceive of national security as internally focused. Yet most observers regard the usual and natural concerns of any military as protecting the integrity of the state from external violence. Thus the Burmese military's disposition to delve into all aspects of political, economic, and social control seems inappropriate. If, however, the most destructive enemies of the state are perceived to be internal (even if some have external relations), then this explains, but does not justify, the comprehensive efforts of the military to ensure the cohesive integrity of the state (as it sees it) through military domination.

The only national organization that for years was able to withstand pressures from the military's control was the Buddhist *sangha*. Composed of approximately 120,000 monks and perhaps 180,000 novices (and perhaps 20,000 nuns) in the late 1980s, it remained autonomous until the military, after repeated efforts, began to register and control the hierarchy in 1980. These regulations were supplemented in 1990 with decrees that ban any Buddhist *sangha* organization other than the nine approved by the military-controlled State Clergy Coordination Committee, which is indirectly elected by the monks.[4] Thus the only mass organization beyond the reach of the military has been brought into line. Now, with the exception of minority groups in active rebellion or those with which cease-fires have been negotiated—and in some of those cases (as with the Wa) considerable autonomy continues—the heartland of Myanmar is firmly in military hands. The NLD continues its tenuous and harassed existence in opposition, but with repeated forced and encouraged "resignations" from its provincial ranks and the closure of many of its local offices, it is a weak force even if some major segment of the society supports its goals.

The Burmese state in the precolonial period was at various times an aggressive kingdom and was often at war with its neighbors, and with considerable success.[5] Although none of Burma's neighbors offered any serious threat to the state, in two instances, however, neighboring countries expressed territorial aspirations at the expense of Burma. In recompense for Thailand's cooperation in World War II, Japan granted Thailand control of two of the amalgamated Shan States (Mongpan and Kengtung), which quickly passed back under British colonial governance at the end of World War II. Twentieth-century Chinese maps in both the Nationalist and the early communist periods showed parts of northern Burma under Chinese control.

Following independence, all the states surrounding Burma actively or tacitly supported groups in opposition to the central government. Thus the military was under constant threat from internal minority groups that often had significant foreign backing. Most prominent were the Thai, who in effect assisted in the creation of a series of small buffer zones along the Burmese littoral to protect the conservative government in Bangkok from the perceived socialist threat from Rangoon. So at local levels and with varying degrees of unofficial support (yet obvious official connivance), U Nu's rebellion in the 1970s was allowed to operate out of Bangkok, and various Shan, Karen, Mon, and Kayah groups in active revolt against the Rangoon government continued to exist, supplied through Thailand. Thailand has been the "sanctuary" for rebel groups. Even for a period after the SLORC came to power and the elections of 1990, the NCGUB, the external arm of the NLD, operated from Thailand until it was finally forced to leave in 1993 as Thai–Burmese relations warmed and the Thai obviously felt that the Burmese military would remain in command for some time.

In many cases, the operation of rebel forces was intimately tied to the production, transport, and trade in narcotics, especially opium, a trade that vastly expanded as the production of heroin became a major industry in the 1960s in the region. Some of the insurgents—with the notable exception of the Karen— were engaged in poppy production as a form of subsistence agriculture in the hills, and the vast profits to the leaders of some of these groups (in contrast to the poverty of the actual producers of the opium—the peasants), allowed them to buy weapons with which to continue their rebellions. In some cases, the ethnic–nationalist groups employed trade in narcotics (or taxing narcotics shipments as they crossed areas of their control) as a means to their ethnic-nationalist ends, but in other cases, such as with Khun Sa and the Mong Tai Army, ethnic nationalism was a cover for narcotics operations.

The weapons and narcotics trade could not have continued without the connivance and support of many Thai officials, most at the local levels but some, so reports indicated, among the higher levels of the Thai central administration. Although the Chinese and Bangladeshis were opposed to the narcotics trade, they in varying degrees supported the activities of rebel groups along their frontiers with Burma.[6]

The result was that the widespread nationalism among the Burman population was intensified by the justified suspicion of foreign intentions and the pervasive concept that significant elements among the minority groups wished for independence or, minimally, autonomy from the central Burman administration. Thus the focus of the military since Burmese independence has been the retention of the union of the country and the prevention of any minority attempts at seccession.

The minority antipathy toward the majority has been exacerbated by internal Burman imperialism toward many of the minorities. Some of the groups were denigrated because they were not Buddhist, and senior Burman military officers have sometimes indicated in off-the-record comments that they disdain the minorities. The fact that some significant percentages of certain minority groups, such as the Karen, Kachin, and Chin, are Christian is a cause for further concern because these groups are seen to have Western support owing to their religious identification. So, too, the Muslim Arakanese along the Bangladesh border are viewed as having divided loyalties and the support of Middle Eastern entities.

The Burman-oriented government has ceaselessly charged the British with following the policy of divide and rule (as noted). Indeed, the British did separate out the administration of what was called "Burma Proper," or the Burmese heartland, which was essentially Burman (but included Arakanese and Mon populations and some Karen in the Irrawaddy delta), from many of the hill frontier areas, of which some (e.g., the Shan and Kayah States) were allowed to keep their local administration under the hereditary *sawbwa* system. This was a pale imitation of the British control over the princely states of India. The military eliminated the administrative power of the *sawbwas* in 1959 under the Caretaker Government, but their social prestige continued.

As the military became entrenched in power following the coup of 1962, there seems to have been a conscious effort to limit the number of minorities in senior military positions. The Burma Army under the British had been composed of a number of ethnic regiments, and the British recruited from the "martial hill peoples" because the threat to colonial governance came from the Burman population. Only 13 percent of the British Burma Army in 1941 were Burmans (and 37 percent were Indian).[7] There is now no senior member of the Burmese military ruling elite who comes from a minority. This "Burmanization" has been one of the major social changes under the military.[8]

An exception should be made for Sino-Burmans. Ne Win and Aung Gyi, for example, came from Sino-Burman families, but they identified with the Burman population.[9] Under the military, one official, General David Abel, an Anglo-Burman, has held ministerial positions related to the economy, but he was never in or part of the inner circle of SLORC/SPDC; his role may have been dealing with foreigners, at which he was quite talented.[10]

Although the unity of the country is the central theme and the minorities a focus within it, the possible disintegration of the state as perceived by the military involves a far broader array of possible threats. The *tatmadaw* has stressed the threat to the integrity of the state from communist elements.[11] This threat has been intensively portrayed since the Caretaker Government in 1958–60. The collapse of the BCP in 1989 has not dimmed that fear. The military was greatly concerned over the possible exploitation by so-called communist elements of the unrest in 1988; it has repeatedly charged that the NLD had been infiltrated by communists and that if the NLD were to come to power, the communists would exert significant control over it. Some of these fears may be simply public relations efforts to provide the legitimacy that the military seeks to obtain and to seek the approval of governments such as that of the United States and Thailand, which it knows are anticommunist. There is probably some emotional basis to the concerns shared among the senior members of the army, as they fought against communist insurrectionists for two generations, and these attitudes may continue.

The Development of Dual Societies: Military and Civilian

As the military has solidified its power and expanded its reach, it has effectively created a separate, privileged society. If the minorities may be considered to be on the geographic, social, and power periphery of Myanmar, then the Burman population becomes the center. At that center is a core, which is the military; it is also Burman, but a select group. This core has been built up over time, so that its influence extends throughout the society. In effect, the military has created a state within a state within a state: the military, Burman society, and the periphery of minorities.

The military's reach is long and broad; it has become a self-contained administrative mechanism serving the needs of its expanding numbers and their dependents. As noted in chapter 2, it has significant economic enterprises and manages to control a large portion of the economy not only through its control over policy planning and the executive functions of the administration, but also directly through investments in local and international business and in joint ventures that make the military ubiquitous. There are military-controlled "private" banks (i.e., not state banks). The *tatmadaw* operates a major health care system for military families that is considered the best in the country. Its educational system for both dependents and staff operates when the public systems are deemed too explosive to be opened. To consider policy issues it has formed a think tank to which it invites private individuals for formal and informal discussions. Housing is provided for families, and military stores enable staff to buy all sorts of daily necessities at subsidized costs and below market rates (and which may be resold on the black market to supply needed extra income). The military has thus insulated itself from the external Burmese world as far as possible and is a protected institution. Further, by educating its children through military channels, the *tatmadaw* seems bent on continuing its control to the next generation.

As much as it is protected, it is protective—of the state, of itself, and of its leadership. This it has accomplished through a pervasive intelligence network—the Directorate of Defence Services Intelligence (DDSI, informally known as MI—military intelligence). Headed at the close of the century by Khin Nyunt, the DDSI is ubiquitous and is widely feared throughout the society. Because it collects information not only on the civilian population, but on the military itself, including the leadership, it accumulates data that can be used to keep the military in line. Ne Win used this group effectively, but when its heads became too powerful, they were dismissed and arrested or replaced, thus ensuring there would be no one who could threaten the position of "Number One." [12] There are, however, other military intelligence organizations, some reporting to General Maung Aye and some to individual regional commanders.

The military was created by Aung San, the father of Burmese independence. His legacy has been portrayed as critical to the country, and his assassination, along with others, in 1947 is still celebrated as a somber holiday; the room in the secretariat building (the ministerial headquarters of government) where this happened is still reserved as a shrine. Ironically, however, the "uses" of Aung San, the drawing upon his legacy and name, have now been drastically reversed. Ne Win, in the years of the BSPP, pointedly used his close association with Aung San in the independence struggle and in the "Thirty Comrades" to legitimate his position. The newspapers were filled with salient quotations from Aung San's speeches and writings, although drawn selectively to illustrate points that the Ne Win administration was anxious to make. Aung San's picture was on the currency. (It has since been replaced.) His photograph hung in government offices, in restaurants and buildings, and in a great many private homes. This picture, taken in a military overcoat with a military cap while he was negotiating independence with the British in London, gave him an otherworldly air—almost as if he were a *nat* (a Burmese spirit, often of a powerful person who died an unnatural and violent death). But after the SLORC came to power and Aung San's daughter, Suu Kyi, came into prominence, the relationship between the state and Aung San was deliberately downplayed. Photographs of Aung San disappeared from all buildings, and rarely is he quoted in the controlled press. It is Aung San Suu Kyi who constantly invokes her father, most prominently by using his name along with hers, and by speaking of how much she respects the military and its contributions to Burma—a military her father founded. Aung San's legacy is positive in many respects, but his political heritage is mixed (see chapter 10). Aung San in a sense has become a myth and has been exploited for political purposes and to provide political legitimacy.

As the military has expanded from its size at the 1988 coup of approximately 186,000 to one planned to approach the half-million mark in the near future, its control over the future of the state has expanded so that it has enveloped the society.[13] Many children of the high-ranking military are in the military academy or have chosen military careers. This tendency was already apparent under the BSPP but has likely increased, although precise data are lacking. The *tatmadaw* is creating a self-perpetuating elite. Further, the military controls all avenues of social mobility and can determine who has access to power. It seems most unlikely that it will voluntarily give up executive power.[14] Even though the military is feared and individual leaders may be disliked, the military as a career is still deemed desirable. Families outside the military try to get their children into the military, where the educational and health systems operate well. The military is perceived to be the only avenue to advancement to those within the country.

The change in name from SLORC to SPDC, when it occurred in November 1997, caused considerable speculation: did this mean a change in military policy, some openings to the NLD, or alleviation of human rights or other problems? Rumors abounded that the public relations organizations associated with the regime had warned it that the term SLORC did not help the regime's image. In fact, it sounded as if it were an evil organization out of a James Bond movie, bent on world domination. The name change to SPDC was, one must suppose, intended as signifying a shift from repression to development and a positive forward step. It also linguistically indicates a movement from the more temporary to the more permanent. That it took place soon after Ne Win made one of his trips to Singapore raised speculation, as such events usually do in Myanmar, that the impetus to the change came from Number One himself.

Whether that was true, there were elements in the shift other than the changing of the name. The composition of the elite group running the country was modified, giving rise—as always in a state that has been known for personalized politics and factionalism—to the suspicion that this represented the rise or fall of some of the top leadership. Aside from the retention of the four top leaders in the SLORC, all the regional military commanders were brought in to fill out the nineteen positions in the SPDC. They have become regional warlords because of their unambiguous authority within their command areas.[15] Since Maung Aye is commander of the army and all of these men report to him, there was speculation that this change may have strengthened his position, especially in relation to Khin Nyunt. Although there had been rumors of personal rivalries between these two men, few were predicting an overt split, at least in the near term. But in the future, when changes take place, the loyalties of the regional commanders will be critical to the regime. So, in effect, the ruling elite of the *tatmadaw* is held together because the members still recognize that they need each other.

If the military is under stress, even if it is more powerful than before, the NLD is under far more stress, and the strain is beginning to tell. It has been reported that there were strong differences of opinion within the NLD leadership over what the most appropriate strategy might be in dealing with the authorities and that those who wanted to negotiate with the SPDC were "traitors."[16] It seems evident that the NLD has made some decisions that may have been tactically maladroit, but the leadership feels the need for unanimity at almost any cost given the threats to its continued existence and the military's divide and rule strategy toward it. The central issue is dialogue with the SPDC, which the NLD wants as long as it can pick their negotiators (meaning Aung San Suu Kyi). Just as the military seems intent on trying to split Aung San Suu Kyi from her colleagues, she is fearful that this might come about. It is unfortunate that for personal reasons Kyi Maung, former spokesman for the NLD, has split with Aung San Suu Kyi and quietly retired. He was a stalwart and articulate member.

The vilification of Aung San Suu Kyi continues. In July 1999, an article appeared by Suu Naing Thu (lit. "Conqueror of Suu [Kyi]"):

> Like witches, ghosts, and ghouls hearing the recitation of *parittas* [religious incantations sometimes used for exorcism], the destructionists at home sweat and fear and become restless as they hear that Myanmar is getting on the same level with other Asian nations. They then approach their foreign voodoo masters for mantras that will enable them to continue to live their evil entities. What a pitiful life they lead.[17]

Defense Spending

Defense spending in Burma has traditionally lacked publicly consistent statistics, and in the past these have varied even in official Burmese publications for the same period.[18] Observers generally agree, however, that all the published statistics are understated. Moreover, figures on the size of the armed forces do not appear in government publications under public employees.

In the 1970s, official figures indicated that defense spending was between 25 and 40 percent of the national budget, varying by year and current expenditure or capital expenditure accounts. The U.S. Agency for International Development (AID) calculated that defense spending ranged between 3.63 and 6.32 percent of GNP from 1973 through 1977.[19] From fiscal year (FY) 1982/83 through FY 1986/87, current account expenditures officially were between

36.6 and 25.8 percent of the state budget and between 11.2 and 13.7 percent of the capital account.[20] Official Burmese figures after the coup indicated that defense spending (in a combined current and capital account) was 30.8 percent and 39.9 percent in FY 1991/92, or 3.4 percent of GDP.[21] Observers have believed that a more accurate figure would be in the neighborhood of 50 percent of the annual budget. The government admitted to allocating 31.6 percent of its 1997/98 budget to defense.

The state expanded the armed forces after the military coup of 1962, with more important increases under the SLORC. From a level of some 125,000, the armed forces increased to 186,000 by the mid-1980s, and to some 330,000–370,000 in the early 1990s. With this expansion went an increase in the capital intensity of the armed forces. Equipment was purchased from abroad, and China provided a major loan ($1.2 billion plus an additional $400 million) to upgrade and modernize a military that probably was one of the largest but most poorly equipped in the region. Burma's had been a labor-intensive military rather than a capital-intensive one, the latter the American model that influenced the Thai. It therefore had limited offensive capacity, but its officers were battle-hardened in rigorous campaigns.

The expansion of the military may have provided the seeds of its own eventual destruction and disunity. From a small fighting force it has become a massive bureaucratic entity in which rewards may be more in administrative compliance than military skills, and there may be jealousies and splits developing between the forces in the field and the military administration. Further, as the economy shrinks, the economic opportunities for the military elite may also diminish, causing competition for increasingly scarce advantages.

The economic impact of the military budget was significant. Expenditures on social services totaled only about one-third of the officially recognized defense costs and were not keeping pace with population increases and inflation, and funds expended on the military either undercut increased budgets for repair and renewal of aging infrastructure, or resulted in expansion of the money supply, thus fueling inflation. Also, the subsidized supplies and rations to military personnel were integral to the political and social position of the *tatmadaw* but outside of official figures. Military spending and control are also underestimated because local military units increasingly depend on local villages for logistic support, including food supplies and (in battle areas), forced porterage. These costs and extrusions from economically marginal peoples produce extensive hardships and are indicative of an even greater military involvement in the economy.

In addition to the official military budgets, and even beyond those funds not reported, the military's economic resources are considerable. Although the military-run DSI was nationalized after 1962 in the wave of socialistic fervor, as was the Burma Economic Development Corporation in 1961 (also military controlled), there are eight state-run corporations under the command of the military's Directorate of Procurement. (There are also the other military businesses such as the Myanmar Economic Holdings Corporation, Ltd., and the Myanmar Economic Corporation [see chapter 5].) As Selth noted:

> With this being the case, then it must be assumed that a high percentage of the profits of the joint venture deals embarked upon to date must eventually return in one form or another to the armed forces. The foreign exchange generated from these deals probably accounts for a large proportion of the arms and military equipment which has been imported from abroad since the SLORC was created. In addition, it is very difficult to establish any major business in Burma without the support of senior military officers, many of whom have their own interests in private companies throughout the country.[22]

How does the NLD view a military should it come to power? Unofficial reports indicate that a defense committee was established to explore the situation as a result of the NLD meeting in 1996. It determined the following:

> [As the 1996 NLD guideline established] the *tatmadaw* is an essential and necessary organization for the country. We have decided to endorse the NLD's position which says that the *tatmadaw* should be a dignified force that protects and fulfills the democratic practices. . . . The *tatmadaw* and the whole mechanism for defense will fall under the Executive. It will have to abide by the Constitution, and be a *tatmadaw* for the people and loved by the people. Only in specific and necessary times will the military stand as a separate pillar [from the executive, judicial, and legislative branches] owing to the importance of its task. . . . The national defense will be effectively equipped in the form of People's militias and military service will become compulsory for limited years for those of age.

It continued that the military should be armed from democratic countries and that military personnel should not generally hold civil service positions. It advocated a balanced ratio of women in defense and national security fields. It concluded that the strategy is "defense in depth," which will not succeed if the military stands alone outside and above the mainstream of government.[23]

The Role and Rule of Law

"Since 1988 the Burmese state has been delegalized." [24] Yet the SLORC regards itself as the defender of law. "Today's special characteristic is the rule of law: this rule of law is demanded by the present period," and the SLORC "has been compelled to resort to Martial Law in order to be able to curb violence and to usher in a new political system desired by the masses." [25] At the same time, the SLORC passed the Law Amending the Law Safeguarding the State from the Danger of Destructionist [*sic*] Elements, increasing the period of detention without trial from 180 days to five years.[26] Throughout its tenure, the SLORC has stressed law, fostered slogans in the press on law, attempted to portray itself as law-abiding, and minutely interpreted the laws that it has passed to serve its own purposes. Its very name, State Law and Order Restoration Council, itself created what might be called self-induced hypnosis in this regard. By fiat it sets the rules to serve its own ends and then enforces them; it then presents itself externally as concerned for abstract laws and rights. "The law" is, rather, a means to perpetuate its authority. Dr. Maung Maung, Burma's leading legal scholar, might have been an acceptable civilian (indeed, the one from whom the SLORC took power) to whom the military might have handed over power following its approval of a new constitution, a constitution that, according to Saw Maung, "is the foremost national task that must be undertaken." [27] Maung Maung has since died.

The ultimate expression of law lies in constitutions, which are sometimes designed to express reality, often aspirations, even to legitimate regimes, and also to act as a public relations offering toward either internal or external audiences. Burma has had two constitutions, the first formulated in 1947 before independence, and the last in 1974 that created the primacy of the BSPP and thus military rule. But between the coup of 1962 and 1974, the military ran the state by fiat, as the military has done since 1988.

The public announcement of the decision to create a new constitution through a National Convention came in 1993, following the disregard of the May 1990 elections and the replacement of Saw Maung with Than Shwe in April 1992. It seems likely that the military's own mass mobilization effort, the Union Solidarity and Development Association (USDA), was designed for the day when a new draft constitution would have to be approved by the people.

Having a pliant mass mobilized to service the military's policy goals would obviously prove invaluable under those circumstances.

The National Convention was composed originally of 702 delegates hand-picked by the military and theoretically representing various sectors of society; of that number, only 15 percent had been elected in the 1990 election. On November 30, 1995, the SLORC expelled the 86 NLD delegates who had boy-cotted the convention.[28] (Several years later the NLD wanted to return to the convention but was denied reentry by the state.)

The interminable drafting continues (with long periods of inaction) at this writing (Fall 2000), with the handpicked organizers meeting only occasionally and the controlled press continuing to avoid reporting on substance. Sessions have been suspended since 1996. Nevertheless, outlines of some of the key provisions have surfaced both officially and unofficially. The salient aspects of the document likely to emerge—and the military has repeatedly refused to designate a timetable for completion—will formulate a state in which the mili-tary will retain control over all critical aspects of the society. With a legislature that will be one-quarter active-duty military (the Indonesian model under Su-harto), the military will also be encouraged to engage in administrative work at all levels. The presidency will be filled by a complex process that effectively will ensure that the military will control the choice and that no person who does not have twenty years continuous residency and who (or whose spouse or dependents) is under foreign rights or obligations can assume that position. This effectively is an ad hominem exclusion of Aung San Suu Kyi. A multiparty sys-tem will be allowed—or so the military has promised—but such a system does not necessarily result in democratic governance. General Suharto, when he was in power, could dismiss Megawati Sukarnoputri (Sukarno's daughter) as the head of an opposition party. The Burmese military may look at Suharto's In-donesia nostalgically as providing a template for the continuity of military rule in spite of events since 1998. In any case, the leadership of the state will firmly be in military hands. It is believed that the military budget will not be subject to civilian review. Some in the military have discussed "disciplined democ-racy" as the goal. However linguistically modified, the reality is likely to be distant from any objective use of the term "democracy."

Some form of local autonomy will be included, but the debate that seems to be underway will limit the scope of such autonomy, including which areas and peoples will have it. It is unlikely to occur at larger geographic levels (where power may be aggregated) and to be limited to smaller regions. No doubt local autonomy will be partial recompense for some of the groups that have signed cease-fires with the state. But only local power will devolve to those levels, and it is likely that such groups will be fragmented, perhaps illustrating that "divide and rule" is not simply a prerogative of the imperialists.

Although the foreign press has been right to criticize the SLORC/SPDC for its arrest of foreigners who have come in to protest the regime and its excesses, the military has been exceedingly careful in how they have been treated if they were perceived to be no major threat to the regime. It has pronounced harsh sentences on those convicted (i.e., all accused), but most have been released and deported quickly and were not abused in prison, with important exceptions.[29] The authorities are obviously aware of the bad publicity that accrues to the regime and have tried to conduct damage control.

Law under the military is conceived of not as a protection of rights, but as a means of control. The SLORC in July 1991 formed the Law Scrutiny Central Board to examine all existing laws deemed not in the interests of the state. By 1996, it had repealed 151 laws. But old, even colonial, laws used for early control purposes were employed selectively to enforce the state's demands. They go back to the colonial period's 1908 Unlawful Associations Act (revised in 1957), the 1948 Official Secrets Act, and the 1956 Emergency Provisions Act against those spreading false information or violating morality, security, or stability.

One of the most notorious of the SLORC/SPDC practices has been commandeering forced labor for public or other works deemed important by the authorities. This has been called "slave labor" by the opposition activists and is a form of corvée. On May 14, 1999, the government passed Order 1/99, "Order Directing Not to Exercise Powers under Certain Provisions of the Towns Act 1907 and the Village Act 1907." Under these acts, villagers and town dwellers could be requisitioned for public service and labor. The order rescinds the acts except for emergencies such as flood and fire and "requisition for personal service in work or service which is of important direct interest for the community and general public and is of present or imminent necessity, and for which it has been impossible to obtain voluntary labor by offer of usual rates of wages and which will not lay too heavy a burden upon the present population." Thus the state can still requisition labor but more discretely. The rescinding of this act was probably prompted by International Labour Organization (ILO) criticism of the practice of forced labor.

Such SLORC/SPDC practices have been supplemented by a variety of other edicts and laws, among which are Order 1/90 of May 1990 against people who do not report others living "illegally" in their houses; Order 1/91 against public service officials or their dependents who become members of a political party or engage in politics or labor organizations; Order 5/96 of June 1996 against anyone even verbally criticizing the National Convention (on the writing of a new constitution) and preventing others from attempting to write such a document; and the July 1996 Television and Video Act and the September 20, 1996, Computer Science Development Law against unauthorized import, possession, or use of computers or network systems.[30] Burmese television reported that regulations for the internet and website uses prohibited any writing detrimental to the interests of the Union of Myanmar, directly or indirectly detrimental to the current policies and secret security affairs of the government, and writings related to politics.[31]

Political and Human Rights

The claim that Myanmar is unique is tautologically accurate when describing Burmese history and culture. Its preservation is a constant theme of the *tatmadaw* and no doubt strikes a responsive public chord among Burmans. The military is the self-appointed protector of this culture. The admonition, so consistently and loudly articulated, to preserve this cultural tradition in the light of what the authorities perceive as foreign political and cultural intimidation, is an appeal for political legitimacy.

Myanmar's uniqueness is, however, a misnomer when descriptive of the current difficulties facing the state—those generic problems that undercut the legitimacy the *tatmadaw* seeks: the definition of the role of the military, how far the tentative openings to the private sector should be allowed, the resolution of ethnic conflict, the efficacy of centralist government, the nature of the Union, and the personalized use of power. Myanmar shares all these conundrums with many states also confronting or appearing to confront problems of fundamental political and economic transformation. How much such transformations are intended in Myanmar is discussed below. The threads of protection of indigenous culture and foreign political and economic pressures are interwoven in the fabric of human rights.

There has been growing international concern with such broad issues as human rights, democracy, self-determination of peoples, and the role of the private sector. Events in the Soviet Union and its republics, in the former Yugoslavia and Eastern Europe, and elsewhere highlight the widespread political and economic liberalization that seems to be a general trend. Linking the two sequentially or in tandem is a separate and more difficult endeavor.[32]

The control exercised by the state is nowhere more evident than in its subjugation of publishing and the media. That the press and television are under state command is evident to any visitor, though the degree to which publishing is under military orders is less evident but no less real.[33] In August 1962, soon after the coup, the military promulgated the Printers' and Publishers' Registration Act, which established new requirements for such businesses and required all publications to be submitted to and screened by the Press Scrutiny Board (which still reviews publications and all book and magazine imports). New guidelines were established in 1975 to reject publications containing any of the following: anything detrimental to the Burma socialist program, to the ideology of the state, to the socialist economy, to national solidarity and unity, to security, or to the rule of law, peace, and public order; "incorrect ideas and opinions not in accordance with the times"; descriptions that are unsuitable; anything pornographic; nonconstructive criticisms of governmental departments; and any libel or slander of any individual. Before the September 1988 coup, in the heady days of the spring and summer, illegal but free publications appeared as the government lost control over society. But following the coup, things got worse:

> The PSB [Press Scrutiny Board], however, although a creation of the Burmese Way to Socialism, far from being disbanded, was strengthened; it tightened its supervision and continued to censor all publications in accordance with its previous guidelines, merely dropping the word "socialist." If anything, the PSB now appeared to writers in Burma to pursue ever more restrictive policies, becoming extremely sensitive to hidden meanings and democratic ideas in stories, poems, and articles.[34]

The international donor community has, at least rhetorically, become concerned over human rights, and not only toward Myanmar. The European Community ties foreign economic assistance to political as well as economic liberalization. Norway and Germany have in the past made representations to India on human rights issues. The United States has newly rearticulated this policy. Japan has done the same, and it monitors military expenditures as well. ASEAN members, such as the Philippines, have indicated concern, as has Thailand. The Myanmar authorities have, however, responded publicly most negatively to external public pressures from the West on this topic. Yet such pressures have had effects: the release of Aung San Suu Kyi from house arrest (perhaps under Japanese influence), the access to Arakanese refugees given to the UNHCR, and the interviewing of prisoners by the International Committee of the Red Cross (ICRC) all may be traced to such protestations.

Myanmar remains the most authoritarian and rigid of all Southeast Asian states in spite of its openings to the private sector. In contrast to Indonesia, which had been a militarized regime until 1998, Myanmar continues to be politically even more rigid and economically far less open than Indonesia had been in the Suharto period. Except for an ephemeral effervescence of liberalization in the summer of 1988 and what turned out to be the conclusive victory of the NLD in the 1990 elections (the results of which the military ignores completely), there was little hope for a solution to the myriad difficulties to which Myanmar is, by its own making, heir.

The *tatmadaw* has effectively crushed all internal articulate opposition to its political and economic power, arrested many opposition leaders, destroyed much of the political infrastructure of the NLD, and prevented the development of any autonomous institutions. At this publication, the military is in command, will likely remain in direct command in some form in the next few years, and into the foreseeable future will effectively control, and minimally have veto power over, any evolving government, political system, or economic regimen.

The opposition—in jail, harassed, in revolt along the borders, internally quiescent, or articulate abroad—has been rendered ineffective, at least at present, in influencing the SLORC/SPDC leadership. Secretary-1 and the foreign minister, among others, have maintained that there are no political prisoners in Myanmar. This may be literally true because dissidents have been arrested and detained under other legislation, but it is patently false because it is recognized that there are hundreds or even thousands who are incarcerated for what would generally be regarded as political views, associations, or dissidence; Human Rights Watch believes there are 1,300 such prisoners.[35] How long this repression will continue is unclear. There is always the possibility of singular regime ineptness leading to popular unrest (a theme often replayed in authoritarian societies) and public resistance. The Burmese emigré community, now totaling about one percent of the population, has been vocal in opposition to the regime. Whether the military can reform itself is an issue that will be explored below, but only one other authoritarian regime in the region has done so—Taiwan, and under special circumstances in its relationship with the People's Republic of China. The effective dissolution of a number of states— the Soviet Union, Ethiopia, Somalia, and Yugoslavia (the last an articulated model for post–Ne Win Burma in the early 1980s along the post–Tito paradigm)—raises issues connected with the "Union" that Myanmar was supposedly redesigning. The effects, if any, of these momentous changes on Myanmar are at present unclear. The military may regard these events as concrete evidence that it has continuously been right to stress the solidarity of the Myanmar state, and it may apply itself with more rigor and autocratic authority toward this end. China, instead of the USSR, may be the Burmese model.

Some of the minorities, on the other hand, may revive their earlier demands for independence, which they rescinded and replaced with those for autonomy or some form of federal union. Whether within or without the union, they will no doubt be encouraged by these events, even if disheartened by military campaigns against the border areas. How the general population will react is unclear. Communications technology now prevents Myanmar's authorities from completely insulating the society from these external events.[36]

International concern over law and human rights in Myanmar received added impetus in 1991. In late 1990, the UN Economic and Social Council's Commission on Human Rights sent Professor Sadako Ogata of Japan (she subsequently became the UN Commissioner for Refugees) to have "direct contacts with the Government of Myanmar." Her report was distributed on December 27, 1990, and subsequently discussed at the commission's 1991 spring meeting. Although confidential, the contents soon became well known. The report was a temperate but damning study. Ogata was neither allowed to see key dissidents, nor was she ever unaccompanied by government officials. Yangon later refused the commission's request to admit another observer and instead selected one. A second team visited Myanmar in October 1991 and attempted to see Aung San Suu Kyi, without success. Other special rapporteurs have visited Myanmar at various times since then, and their reports to the UN have been uniformly pessimistic.

At the UN General Assembly meeting in October 1991, U Ohn Gyaw, the Union of Myanmar foreign minister, defended his government's position on human rights:

> To the fullest extent permitted by our own national circumstances—not least among which is the continued existence of armed insurrection in remote parts of the country and the destructive activities of underground elements in urban and rural areas—we are doing our utmost to promote and protect fundamental human rights in conformity with the purposes and principles of the Charter and the provisions of the Universal Declaration of Human Rights. . . . However, a clear line must be drawn between the internationally binding character of the norms I have mentioned on the one hand, and the policy of implementing them by Member States in their own countries on the other. The modality of implementation is the primary responsibility of Member States, to be formulated by each according to its own best judgement, in keeping with its own local conditions.[37]

Since 1991, human rights issues have dominated the meager news from Myanmar. On November 29, 1991, the Third Committee of the United Nations unanimously passed a resolution urging the government of Myanmar "to allow all citizens freely to participate in the political process in accordance with the principles of the Universal Declaration of Human Rights." This was the rather innocuous product of a stronger draft that had expressed "concern also at the continued deprivation of liberty of a number of democratically elected political leaders," a phrase that was struck from the final text to ensure its acceptance. The approved resolution also reinforced the secretary general's appeals to the SLORC for the release of Aung San Suu Kyi. The Myanmar representative objected, claiming that some of the provisions "are based on unsubstantiated and politically motivated allegations, emanating mainly from unsavory anti-government and anti-people elements who are in league with armed terrorist groups."

As the Nobel Peace Prize was awarded in Oslo on December 10, 1991, and accepted by Aung San Suu Kyi's son Alexander on behalf of the Burmese people, the most significant demonstrations since 1988 broke out at the University of Rangoon, resulting in many arrests and the closure once again of all colleges and universities. They began to reopen three years later. Since that time, there has been an annual debate in the United Nations on Myanmar and attempted annual visits of special rapporteurs and others, with devastating results for that country in terms of public prestige. The practical effects within Myanmar, however, are minimal.

The debate over the UN Resolution on Myanmar (adopted November 24, 1997) is typical of the annual debates, all of which extensively catalogue the abuses of the regime, call for its adherence to many different UN resolutions, and urge reform and liberalization of political and human rights. The official Myanmar response of November 24, 1997 (as delivered by the permanent representative and alternate chairman of the Myanmar Delegation) claimed that the allegations of abuses were false and from "dubious sources," that the government does not condone human rights abuses, and that the resolution demonstrates a "clash of cultural values and traditions." [38]

The gap between theory and implementation looms large. In spite of this defense, the ample evidence since 1988 demonstrates that the SLORC continued its hard line on rights and had no intention of improving human rights or democracy or abiding by the results of the May 1990 election. Although the NLD was the clear victor in this election, the SLORC claimed that the NLD got only 32 percent of the votes and thus did not represent the people. The SLORC continued to maintain, however, that it would introduce a multiparty system.

In addition to the destruction of the legal system and the arbitrary arrests, detentions, torture, and surveillance carried out by the state, there is overwhelming evidence of mistreatment, forced porterage and labor, murder, rape, and military violence against various populations at local levels, far removed from any overt political rationale. Even if not expressly encouraged or condoned by the central authorities, the pervasive nature of the abuses, which are documented by the United Nations, the U.S. State Department, Asia Watch, Amnesty International, and other reporting, testifies to the problems that need no further explication here. Minimally the central authorities in these cases must take responsibility for not restraining their forces. The opposition internally and externally has emphasized this problem, sometimes with a lack of balance. (The term "slave labor" is graphic, but many cases correspond to corvée labor—a tax on the peasantry that, however unfair, should be stated as such.) In the past, the military have claimed that unpaid labor was voluntarily donated for public projects, such as road construction, and was a Burmese tradition. Labor has been gladly donated by the population for religious works, for it earns merit in the Buddhist karmic equation, but clearly the government's explanation was misleading in this context, and this was, in effect, corvée.[39] In mid-June 1999, the ILO passed a resolution that effectively prevented Burmese government authorities from attending ILO meetings and getting assistance from that organization because of the denial of labor rights. Since no member state of the ILO can be expelled, these were the strongest steps that could be taken.

The U.S. Congress in June 1990 passed the Customs and Trade Act of 1990. Under section 138, the president had to impose economic sanctions on Burma prior to October 1, 1990, if the Burmese government did not meet certain human rights conditions. After some legal maneuvering, on July 28, 1991, the executive branch indicated that Burma did not meet these conditions, and the United States did not renew a textile agreement between the two states that had expired on December 31, 1990. This prohibited some $9 million in Burmese exports into the United States (some 40 percent of all its exports to the United States) and affected some foreign-owned export-oriented firms (e.g., those of the South Koreans) operating in Myanmar as joint ventures. Such joint ventures were designed for export, not the local market, and to generate foreign exchange. The overall economic effect on Myanmar was minimal, but the message was evident: to discourage further foreign investment. To be effective economically, sanctions would have to cover third-party exports, such as teak or shrimp of Burmese origin from Thailand (with Thai value added), but this would conflict with various World Trade Organization (WTO) regulations. In 1997 the United States imposed sanctions on all new investment in Myanmar.

The United States (backed by Canada and Australia) also attempted to get ASEAN to protest the human rights situation in Myanmar at the ASEAN ministerial meeting in Kuala Lumpur in July 1991. In this it was, not surprisingly, unsuccessful, as most of the ASEAN states were blatantly exposed on their own human rights records, and those states do not criticize each other. ASEAN states preferred, they noted, to work through "constructive dialogue," meaning quiet, unpublicized efforts to encourage the Burmese to reform. ASEAN did agree, however, to send Philippine foreign minister Raul Manglapus to Yangon to talk to the SLORC leadership about these issues. Myanmar agreed to admit him only as the Philippine foreign minister, not as the ASEAN human rights messenger. It is apparent that some of the ASEAN governments, such as Thailand, although publicly silent at first, have expressed their growing concern about the situation in Myanmar. Thailand agreed to a formal visit by Saw Maung but only as chief of staff, not as head of state. It also initially refused to allow a trip by a Burmese delegation to present an award to Thai monks. In August 1999, Australia sent its human rights commissioner to Yangon to talk with authorities about the possibility of establishing an independent commission there. Although no one expected major advances in human rights, this was considered an interesting initiative that the government did not immediately turn down. It was criticized by the NLD.

The issue of human rights leverage—the effectiveness of public criticism in contrast to private discussion of reforms—is delicate at best, and not just in Myanmar. No nationalistic regime can afford to be seen as publicly subservient to foreign influence. This is especially true in Myanmar. At the same time, private discussions of the need for reform, even at high levels, are easily ignored. The governments under scrutiny are then seen to be autonomous and effective since international criticism is muted. The awarding of the Nobel Peace Prize to Aung San Suu Kyi was an important means to focus foreign interest and national attention on human rights in Myanmar through the actions and plight of a single individual. The controlled media in Myanmar for a considerable period did not announce that event, but through extensive radio broadcasts from abroad beamed into Burma the news was quickly spread.

Foreign governments may well wish to criticize the SLORC/SPDC for its excesses, its human rights policies, and the fact that it ignores its people's will. Some may also do so more because of the need to placate their own articulate and concerned populations than because they are committed to improving conditions in Myanmar. Such public criticism may be more important in worldwide fora than in Myanmar itself, where the regime has attempted to insulate the people from such influences, has employed nationalism as a response to any external denunciations, and may believe it can weather a period of foreign criticism. It must also be aware that states often have inconsistent policies toward different repressive regimes (e.g., the different U.S. approaches concerning China, North Korea, and Myanmar) and that such inconsistencies undercut the moral indignation of those who criticize.

It is unlikely in the case of Myanmar that either public or private foreign criticisms of human rights abuses or antidemocratic tendencies have had any direct effect on the government in terms of its overriding objective of maintaining control, although they evidently have affected its tactics and have led to modest changes, and although the Nobel Peace Prize may have affected the urban population. Thus, "leverage" is limited; that is, nevertheless, no rationale for not attempting to influence change, for such criticisms, if carefully couched, may affect other potential leaders over some indeterminate time. Economic isolation, in both the public and private sectors, is likely to be more effective over the longer term, even though more of the populace would suffer in the immediate future. (One cannot be sanguine at this possibil-ity if Cuba and North Korea are indicators.) But attempted economic isolation alone will not topple this government if Burmese history sets any precedent.

Myanmar can still limp along for a period economically at subsistence level, ignoring the needs of its populations—both Burman and minority—and falling further behind the economic advances of its neighbors. But regime attempts to isolate the country economically could not now succeed if tried, for its porous borders cannot be resealed. Myanmar needs the goods supplied by or through its neighbors, especially China, Thailand, and India. Burmese entrepreneurship has been most evident in the smuggling trade. Even more important, the state, even with controlled media, can no longer completely isolate its people from the outside as Ne Win could do in the early 1960s.

At the same time, it is evident that ASEAN has lacked strong concern about Myanmar human rights issues, in part because Thailand, Singapore, China, Japan, South Korea (before President Kim Dae Jung's government), and other states are not prepared to ignore regional economic opportunities. For their own perceived goals and to prevent other states from assuming a hegemonic economic position in Myanmar, each is pursuing its own (sometimes economic, sometimes strategic) roles. Thailand, China, and India are the principal actors.[40] Each has tried to fill the economic void that was Myanmar as that state moved from economic isolation into a more international economic mode. China, however, seems to hold the most pervasive economic power, with its aid, informal investment, emigration, and trade; the disintegration of the BCP along the border, together with the surrender of some of the insurgents, has strengthened China trade patterns. India, once regarded by Myanmar as its principal threat, muted its criticism after 1991 and developed trade and other ties. Thailand, under a more liberal foreign policy regime, advocated a policy of "enhanced interaction" when internal developments in any country had ramifications for other states.[41]

For change to occur, it is for both the leadership—civilian and military—and the people of Myanmar to determine what they are prepared to do, what type of regime they wish to see in their society, how power will be distributed, and the nature of their external relations. It seems unlikely that major changes in fundamental policies, or in attitudes toward how policies are formulated and their content, will come from within the SPDC. Although there has been much speculation on factions within SLORC/SPDC (and between "liberals" and "hardliners"), there is yet no evidence of serious splits. The military maintains that it is solid; yet if it continues in power for long, such splits would be likely, based on how power is perceived and on previous political history and the absence of a single strong leader in the post–Ne Win period. There is no present evidence that change is imminent.

Some observers have considered change as possibly instituted by the more recently recruited officer corps through the Burma Military Academy and the Officers' Candidate School. Positions in the academy, however, are reported to be 80 percent filled by children of the present or retired military and the rest with those who have influential friends among them. They are less likely to jeopardize their influential positions. The argument then continues that change within the military will come from second-tier officers and those who have better educational backgrounds from the technical services, such as communications and supply. Too little is now known to draw conclusions, but others argue that younger officers are more rigid and even more nationalistic than the older ones.[42]

The SPDC seems likely to continue in power for a considerable period, counting on the potential of natural gas revenues from the Yadana fields and the pipeline to Thailand, overseas remittances, and exports. Such gas revenues (initially estimated at $400 million annually but considerably less at this writing) might right the listing economic ship of state, but they are said to be mortgaged for some years. One SLORC member said, "We cannot say for how long we will be in charge of the state administration. It might be five years or ten." [43]

In a state such as Myanmar, in which culture and history pervade the inextricably intertwined fields of politics and economics, it is simplistic to attempt to separate sectors and disciplines for analysis. The dynamic and interplay between and among them is lost. Yet the need exists for some categorization the better to consider the nature of the challenges facing the country. The following chapters containing a set of cross-cutting issues is one such approach.

The SPDC is caught in its own web. With the international focus on Aung San Suu Kyi, it cannot eliminate her. It wants her to leave, but she has refused to do so (most recently in March 1999, in spite of the sickness and eventual death of her husband) without the effective overthrow of the present military system and the return to representative rights. Yet by retaining her the SPDC undermines the legitimacy that it tries so hard to achieve. If the military decided to force her into exile, what would this mean? She is a Burmese citizen, and the legal basis for such action would be questionable at best. Probably over time she would lose local support because of the *tatmadaw*'s ability to control the media, but she would probably gain more external publicity and certainly the regime would come in for more international censure. Thus in all likelihood she will remain because it is in her interests, as well as furthering her political ideals, but her constant presence is a cancer to the present interests of the SPDC.

Notes

1. The premier author on the Burmese military is Andrew Selth, whose publications on aspects of the *tatmadaw* should be required reading. They include the following book and working papers from the Strategic and Defence Studies Centre of the Australia National University, Canberra: *Transforming the Tatmadaw: The Burmese Armed Forces Since 1988* (1996); No. 113, "Transforming the *Tatmadaw*: The Burmese Armed Forces since 1988" (1996); No. 280, "Burma's Arms Procurement Programme"; No. 308, "Burma's Intelligence Apparatus" (1997); No. 309, "Burma's Defence Expenditures and Arms Industry" (1997); No. 313, "The Burma Navy" (1997); No. 315, "The Burma Air Force"; No. 334, "Burma and the Weapons of Mass Destruction" (1999); No. 338, "The Burma Armed Forces Next Century: Continuity or Change" (1999); No. 136, "Burma's Secret Military Partners [Germany, Pakistan, Israel, Singapore]" (2000); No. 351, "Burma's Order of Battle: An Interim Assessment," 2000; No. 352, "Landmines in Burma: The Military Dimension," 2000. For a study of the military in the period before 1962, see Mary Callahan, "The Origins of Military Rule in Burma" (unpublished Ph.D. dissertation, Cornell University, 1996). "The key to a contemporary understanding of the future of Myanmar's politics is an understanding of the army, just as it was in 1948, 1958, 1962 and 1988. If one is to understand the army, one has to comprehend the interests and attitudes of the current military regime. The army has been a dominating, if not dominant, institution since the regaining of independence in 1948" Robert H. Taylor, "Myanmar: Military Politics and the Prospects for Democratization," *Asian Affairs* 85, 1 (1998): 5.

2. *Time* magazine interview, November 15, 1999.

3. Robert H. Taylor, "Burma," in *Military-Civilian Relations in Southeast Asia,* ed. Zakaria Haji Ahmed and Harold Crouch (Singapore: Oxford University Press, 1985), p. 41.

4. Order 6/90. U.S. Department of State, "Annual Report on International Religious Freedom for 1999: Burma," September 9, 1999.

5. The Thai still remember the destruction of their capital at Ayuthia by the Burmese in 1767; Burmese-style temples still exist in northern Thailand; and it was Burmese invasions of Manipur and Bengal that brought on the First Anglo-Burmese War of 1824–26.

6. Chinese support to the BCP until the late 1970s enabled the party to avoid involvement in the trade, but when Chinese support ceased, the BCP became involved in the trade as well.

7. Taylor, "Burma."

8. "The government discourages Muslims from entering military service, and Christian or Muslim military officers who aspire to promotion beyond middle ranks are encouraged by their superiors to convert to Buddhism." During the 1990s, there was only one non-Buddhist at the ministerial level, and that person was the only non-Buddhist flag officer (U.S. Department of State, "Annual Report on International Religious Freedom for 1999: Burma," September 9, 1999).

9. Ne Win has denied this association.

10. "U.S. Report to the Congress for September 29, 1999–March 27, 2000, under Public Law 104-208," April 20, 2000.

11. For example, see Maung Aung Myoe, "The Counterinsurgency in Myanmar: The Government's Response to the Burma Communist Party" (thesis submitted for Ph.D., Australia National University, 1999, in process). The Indonesian authorities as late as 1998 also used the purported influence of the communists as a threat to the state. Whether there were cross-cultural influences is simply conjecture.

12. There was one attempted coup against Ne Win in 1976, but it was exposed and prevented. Tin Oo was arrested for knowing of the coup but not acting against it, even though he was never accused of being involved. Mary Callahan has written: "Three of the 23 DDSI intelligence detachments are responsible for surveillance of army, navy, and air force personnel. These detachments rely on informers from within the ranks, and dossiers are compiled on units and individuals in the military. The extent of DDSI infiltration into the ranks is unclear, but it is popularly perceived to be deep and widespread. This perception represents a formidable constraint on plots and conspiracies among aggrieved soldiers as well as senior officers" (Research Note: "Junta Dreams or Nightmares? Observations of Burma's Military since 1988," *Bulletin of Concerned Asian Scholars* 31, 3 [1999]: 56).

13. At the time of the 1962 coup, the military numbered about 125,000.

14. Military rule can, of course, be threatened, both internally from fissures that could develop among key leadership, and externally from opposition forces, such as the

NLD, which could come to power through some egregious errors committed by the military. But whatever scenario plays out over time, it is highly likely that the military will be insulated and protected from civilian management in any government and that its influence will be far more extensive than outside observers are likely to imagine.

15. For a discussion of their growing influence, and even their exalted presence in the military museum, see Callahan, "Junta," pp. 52–56. Some Burmese have privately commented that because the regional commanders are junior to the four senior generals on the SPDC, they will have little say in policy and will support the decisions of the four generals. The regional commanders are rotated far less frequently than under the BSPP, giving them greater power.

16. Roger Mitton, "How Things Look inside the NLD," *Asiaweek,* July 16, 1999.

17. "Whoever Jumps: It Won't Send up Dust," *Myanmar Alin,* July 12, 1999.

18. The comprehensive study of this elusive subject is Selth, "Burma's Defence Expenditures and Arms Industry."

19. For a discussion of military expenditures until 1980, see David I. Steinberg, *Burma's Road toward Development: Growth and Ideology under Military Rule* (Boulder: Westview Press, 1981).

20. Robert H. Taylor, "Burma: Defence Expenditure and Threat Perception," in, *Defence Spending in Southeast Asia,* ed. Chin Kin Wah (Singapore: Institute of Southeast Asian Studies, 1987), pp. 258–60.

21. Selth, quoting the U.S. Arms Control and Disarmament Agency, notes it was 4 percent of GNP in 1992 ("Burma's Defence Expenditures and Arms Industry," p. 17).

22. Ibid., p. 15.

23. NLD, Report of the Defense Committee of the CRPP, "Report on the Formation of a Modern *Tatmadaw* in the Democratic Era," no date (1999?), unofficial translation.

24. Andrew Huxley, "The Last Fifty Years of Burmese Law: E Maung and Maung Maung, *LawAsia* (University of Technology, Sydney, 1996), p. 9. E Maung was an advocate of the British legal tradition and Maung Maung wanted to make Burmese law indigenous. The latter was behind the destruction of the legal profession in 1972; the nationalization of law, lawyers, and justices; and the elimination of the separation of powers in Burma.

25. FBIS, May 13, 1991, quoting the *Working People's Daily,* May 1, 1991.

26. Reported in FBIS, August 13, 1991. Law 11/91 of August 9, 1991, legally allowed the SLORC to continue to detain Aung San Suu Kyi. In the *Working People's Daily,* the term used was "subversive elements."

27. FBIS, March 29, 1991, from Saw Maung's March 27 Armed Forces Day speech.

28. Janelle M. Diller, "The National Convention: An Impediment to the Restoration of Democracy," in *Burma: The Challenge of Change in a Divided Society,* ed. Peter Carey (London: Macmillan, 1997).

29. The military's concepts of public relations seem inconsistent. Although it released students, it held the resident honorary Danish consul, Mr. Nichols, who was personally close to Aung San Suu Kyi, on the charge of operating an illegal fax machine. He died in prison, and the military was accused of denying him appropriate medicine for his ailments. The government also miscalculated in denying the dying Michael Aris a visa, and its callousness was internationally condemned. The incarceration of a young, British activist, James Mawcsley, who appears to have been beaten in prison, has become a cause celebre for opponents of the military. He was released in October 2000.

30. Zunetta Liddell, "No Room to Move: Legal Constraints on Civil Society in Burma," in Burma Consortium Netherlands and Transnational Alliance, *Strengthening Civil Society in Burma: Possibilities and Dilemmas for International NGOs in Burma* (Chiangmai: Silkworm Press, 1999). The Computer Science Development Law mandates sentences of from seven to fifteen years for "carrying out acts which undermine state security, prevalence of law and order and community peace and tranquility, national unity, state economy or national culture" and includes the obtaining or sending and distributing of any such information. It may be one of the world's most stringent of such regulations.

31. January 20, 2000, as reported on the BBC.

32. For a discussion of this issue applied to Myanmar, see David I. Steinberg, "Democracy, Power and the Economy in Burma: The Donors' Dilemmas," *Asian Survey,* August 1991.

33. The following discussion is taken from Anna J. Allott, *Inked Over, Ripped Out: Burmese Storytellers and the Censors* (Chiangmai: Silkworm Press, 1993), pp.1–32. The author notes that ironically the location of the Press Scrutiny Board is in the building that housed the Kempetai, the Japanese secret police in World War II.

34. Ibid., p. 18.

35. Human Rights Watch, August 28, 1998, statement.

36. Although only 2 percent of the rural population has electricity, some 24 percent have radios, but how many are short wave is not known.

37. Statement at the forty-sixth session of the UN General Assembly, October 4, 1991. U Ohn Gyaw defended the record of the state related to Ogata's visit, environmental protection in Myanmar, and progress since the 1990 elections.

38. The texts may be found in a Washington publication, *Burma Debate,* vol. 4, November/December 1997, pp. 28–35.

39. Similar practices were attempted in Thailand in the 1960s but were often unsuccessful as the government's power to enforce regulations at the village level was limited (Charles Keyes, draft paper on language and violence in Asia and Thailand, 2000).

40. See David I. Steinberg, "Regional Rivalries in Burma: Economic Competition in Myanmar," *Asian Survey,* June 1990.

41. What effect the government of President Wahid in Indonesia will have is unclear. He visited Myanmar early in his administration and was said to have wanted to call on Aung San Suu Kyi, although this meeting did not take place.

42. Any organizational splits based on schooling were denied by Maung Aung Myoe, "Building the Tatmadaw: The Organizational Development of the Armed Forces of Myanmar, 1948–98" (Canberra: Australia National University, Strategic and Defence Studies Centre, 1998), Working Paper No. 327. This paper, basically an uncritical look at the military, does, however, contain much useful information on command structure and organization.

43. Lt. Gen. Aung Ye Kyaw, minister of construction and cooperatives, quoted in FBIS, September 12, 1991.

CHAPTER 4

Mass Mobilization, Civil Society, and Orthodoxy

E
ach regime in Burma/Myanmar has felt it incumbent to attempt to mobilize the population to support its perceived goals—the perpetuation
of its authority through expansion of its power base. In this, Burma has
not been unique, for this is a standard practice worldwide among both authoritarian and democratic regimes. Burmese governments, however, have done so
through different media, in some cases allowing the parallel growth of civil
society, and in others eliminating any element of pluralism. Political party and
nonparty mechanisms have both been employed at different times, and civil
society has been allowed to develop or been eliminated in other periods. The
implications of past practices for the future political process in that country are
likely to be important.

Mass Mobilization in Burma

Mass mobilization organizations have been major elements in the structure of
all Burmese regimes for political and economic reasons. From independence,
and the rule of the AFPFL, the formation of such controlled, ubiquitous groups
has been regarded as an important means of political control and power. Under
military rule, the leaders have mandated ideological orthodoxy as well.

In the AFPFL period (1948–58), mass groups were formed under the aegis of the AFPFL but were semi-autonomous. They were led by individuals who used the organizations both to achieve status within the AFPFL and to enhance their own party positions at the center. Prominent in that period were the All-Burma Peasants' Organization, led by Thakin Tin; the Trades Union Congress of Burma; and the Federation of Trades Organization (among others), all of which encouraged mass support for the policies of the party or group in power. Through the broad base supplied by the organization, the leaders could influence government to enhance their own positions in the central hierarchy and to advocate policies they favored toward their constituencies. They could attempt to deliver their constituents' votes. In a society in which power was highly personalized, a type of machine politics using these organizations was evident.

In the civilian period, which was characterized by high social mobility, one of the major avenues of such mobility, for both local and national status for even the relatively uneducated from any social class, was leadership of and through these mass organizations. They were important channels for the poor and the rural classes and helped give Burma an egalitarian society. (The other avenues were through free higher education, the military, and the *sangha*.)

A further important mass organization that predates independence but flowered thereafter has been the cooperative movement, a ubiquitous parastatal organization controlled by a cabinet-level appointment that had important, if localized, political implications. Although its direct political impact was limited because of its primary economic focus and because there were alternative means to achieve political ends, the cooperative movement, which reached most families, was an effort to instill political ideals as well as to provide goods to the populace. In periods of autarky, the cooperatives were especially important because they were a major legal source of consumer goods for much of the population; because prices were lower than in the bazaars, the resale of cooperative products was an important element of the black market. The importance of the cooperative movement lies not only in its economic effects, but also in its relationship to mass organizations as a whole (as the state has evidently viewed it). The leadership of the cooperatives has been coterminous with leadership of other, directly political, mass organizations in most of the military period, and with apparent design. The minister of cooperatives under the BSPP was also head of the Lanzin (BSPP) Youth League, and under the SLORC/SPDC, head of the USDA.

The uses of mass organizations have grown under military auspices. The military regimes, each in its own separate but related manner, have employed them to propagate the military's view of the issues in which it was most engrossed at any particular time. In each case, however, the organizations were primarily political in nature, used to further the military ideological line; they also served to preempt the formation of alternative, autonomous organizations that might question the military's view of reality.

Under the Caretaker Government the military began mass mobilization in a rather tentative manner. It set up a series of "National Solidarity Associations" to improve law and order and, of course, the capacity of the army to control the population. These proved to be ephemeral and withered away following the end of direct military rule in 1960. The experience gained during this period may have influenced later *tatmadaw* attempts to replicate this endeavor on a far grander scale.

Under the BSPP phase, the party structure itself became the primary venue for mass support and political indoctrination, although there were other related efforts as well. The slow buildup of the party from its founding in 1962 as a cadre organization to its expansion as a mass-based group probably reflected the military's perception of the need to have an effective, totally subservient means to mobilize the population for the leadership's perceived ends—a means more effective than functional groups because the military may have regarded the party as more easily controlled.

It is significant that the constitution that the military finally put into place in 1974, after ruling by decree since 1962, was promulgated and approved by referendum only after the BSPP became a mass organization, and thus could be used to support and legitimate the passage and acceptance of this constitution, which stipulated a unitary state composed of seven Burman divisions and seven minority states. It may have also been conceived as a means to provide mass support for candidates for the Pyithu Hluttaw, even though the system of elections legally involved only one party, the BSPP.[1] Opposition candidates were not tolerated. The BSPP also had various youth organizations associated with it, and stress was given to inculcating youth with the party's ideals, such as the "Burmese Way to Socialism." Before the formation of the BSPP as a mass organization, however, the Revolutionary Council (Ne Win's military cabinet) engaged in a series of mobilization efforts on which the BSPP eventually drew and which were coordinated at the apex of power. These were people's worker and peasant councils, called *asi-ayone,* or organizations. The workers' councils started in 1964 and had a membership of 1.5 million by 1970, while the peasants' councils, formed in 1967, had a membership of 7.6 million by 1980.

All of these organizations, both military and civilian, reflected the needs of those at the top of the hierarchy to convey down through an effective command structure the policies of a central government. Civilian mass movements varied significantly from those under military command. In the latter case, leadership and policies were predetermined by and controlled from the center, and no deviation from the policy framework was allowed, while civilian organizations responded to the interests of their superiors as well as those of the party. The military introduced ideological rigidity that the civilian governments avoided. Although civil society did exist under civilian rule, these state-sponsored mass organizations could not be considered as part of it, as they were too closely linked to the political process. None of the mass organizations sponsored by the military seems to have been viewed as a means to express to the top of the hierarchy the needs and opinions of those at the bottom. This myopic approach was a major cause of the failure of the BSPP regime.

Civil Society and Its Destruction

The term "civil society" has been prominent in the history of Western thought for about two hundred years. Its connotative vicissitudes, its origins and previous political uses (from Hegel and Marx and beyond) in a sense are a microcosm of both political and social science theory. For a time, reflection on civil society was out of style; it seemed to many to be an anachronistic concept replaced by more fashionable intellectual formulations. Today, however, the term has regained its significance. Here we are not concerned with its history, but rather with its contemporary use, as defined below, as one means to understand the dynamics of Burmese politics and society.

Although civil society developed in Europe, scholars worldwide have been restudying the concept of civil society and its past influence on and potential relevance to contemporary political and social cultures. They sometimes look for indigenous roots of civil society even though the concept was unknown, and sometimes they are successful, although the modern variants may be quite different from historical precedents.

A multitude of contemporary definitions abound; writers adapt the term to their particular predilections. What is important is not the search for one absolute definition applicable across all states—the "one size fits all" syndrome—but that we have a clear and distinct concept of what we mean and the analytical ends to which we employ the concept.

Civil society obviously means those institutions and groupings that are outside of government. There are nuances in different definitions, but the essential characteristic of what we call civil society lies in its autonomy from the state. It is also obvious that such independence is relative, and as no individual can be isolated, so no institution within a societal framework stands completely alone. The significance of the term today and its importance as an analytical tool to explore societies lie in the hypothesis that if civil society is strong and if citizens band together for the common good based on a sense of community or programmatic trust and efficacy, then this trust and efficacy somehow translate into overall trust in the political process of democracy or democratization and lead to the diffusion of the centralized power of the state.[2] Civil society is thus seen as an essential element of political pluralism.

In fact, many argue that civil society is a critical element of democracy. So democracy is not simply free and fair elections, which are a manifestation of part of the process but which in the popular eye are often equated with democracy, but rather democracy is composed of a variety of institutions, including a universal adult electorate, an elected legislature, an independent judiciary, a free press and media, and civil society—the ability of citizens to gather together in groups to express their common concerns. Parenthetically, then, the May 1990 elections in Burma were important when considering the issue of democracy in that country, but certainly not a reflection of more complex phenomena.

In civil society independent groups under an all-encompassing definition might include opposition political parties, the business sector or for-profit organizations, nonprofit groups, and even elements bent on the overthrow of the government through nonelective processes. It is thus no wonder that in many societies, such as China, the term civil society implies antigovernment activity, and its use is deemed inappropriate. This misconstrues the importance and place of civil society in much of the world and is not helpful to an analysis of Burmese issues.

In the case of Burma/Myanmar, civil society is best more narrowly defined. Here it is defined as composed of nonephemeral organizations of individuals banded together to pursue a common purpose or purposes through group activities and by peaceful means. These are generally nonprofit organizations, (nongovernmental organizations—NGOs) and may be local or national; advocacy or supportive; religious, cultural, social, professional, or educational; or even organizations that, while not for profit, support the business sector, such as chambers of commerce and trade associations. We are excluding from this definition in the case of Burma/ Myanmar businesses, political parties, and groups that are engaged in insurgent activities. However important these may be, they deserve consideration under other rubrics. They are included in more broad definitions and were especially important in the rise of pluralistic centers of power divorced from the thrones of Europe. The bourgeoisie played a particularly critical role there. Political parties in contemporary Myanmar, however, are excluded because those that are legal are severely circumscribed by the state and cannot operate independent of government power and considerable control or restrictions; the indigenous modern business sector (as contrasted with petty trading in the bazaars) is still nascent and developing within the government's formal and informal strictures; and all insurgent groups are excluded because civil society under this definition operates within the legal bounds of state laws and regulations and does not attempt to overthrow state authority.

The term "civil society" does not exist in Burmese and when used today (very rarely indeed) is left in English.[3] Although the term may not be used, the concept of individual organizations separate from the state did exist in the civilian period, even if conceptually they were not grouped together to form a cohesive intellectual construct.

The importance of civil society is that included groups have the capacity to act or advocate, autonomous of the state, for the common good, however that is defined and over however large a clientele—national, local, or specialized. They provide sources of pluralism in the society, thus diluting the possibility of a completely centralized autocratic or authoritarian state. They are not the only potential source of pluralism; this may come from the division of powers among elements of government, even within the executive branch itself and sometimes between that branch and the government's political party in power and, of course, from opposition political parties.

The organizations of civil society may span the spectrum of state relationships: they may advocate policies that support the government (if they are not its captive), call for stricter adherence to laws already enacted, call for new laws or activities, express interest in restructuring elements of policy, or simply do what its members regard as good, such as upholding traditional values or protecting the environment. For example, in Myanmar a village organization that was formed independent of the state to make offerings to the monks at a local temple would be part of civil society, but the hierarchy of the *sangha,* which is registered and under state control, would not be so considered. An organization may have to be registered by the government (in Burma, under the Companies Act, for example), but it could be part of civil society if it were autonomous in its actions and if its leadership were not subservient to, or chosen by, the state. It is conceivable that a private organization in part funded by the state might be within the bounds of civil society under this definition if it operated autonomous of the government.[4]

How autonomous must an organization be to qualify? It will depend on the culture and circumstances—how much space the state allows in intervening into the lives and activities of its citizenry, the extent of the privacy of the individual, and the autonomy of organizations.[5] In some societies—such as those evolving from the Confucian tradition, in which the state is idealistically presented as the benevolent father intervening for the good of the children, the people—that space tends to be quite narrow. In others, the gap is quite wide. In post-Confucian societies, not only does the state presume that intervention is appropriate and even necessary, but the citizenry also believes that some extensive degree of intervention is desirable or at least acceptable. This has important implications for human rights policies that are supposedly universally mandated. Concepts of privacy are culturally determined.

Civil society is often viewed as a threat by autocratic governments or those that do not wish to see their policies or programs undermined or even questioned. For this reason and to preclude the development and influence of such organizations even if they are allowed to be formed, the state will often sponsor mass organizations that are designed both to provide a popular or mass base for state policies and to preempt the formation of other groups that might oppose or threaten such policies.

There is little research on civil society in traditional Burma. Some might argue that such organizations existed or even were prevalent in the precolonial period. The whole structure of the traditional village headman, for example, might be construed as an element of civil society designed to ward off interference by the state in village affairs. As noted, it was transformed by the British from the highest level of local organization to the lowest level of central administration, thus changing its functions and roles.[6]

The quintessential examples of civil society, ubiquitous throughout Burmese history, have been religious organizations at the local level. Here people willingly and spontaneously gathered together to support Buddhist activities connected with seasonal ceremonies that formed an integral part of the social and religious scene. Since the British did not allow overtly political organizations, religion (a primordial loyalty closely associated with nationalism) became a natural focus for both religious good works and patriotic activities. The Young Men's Buddhist Association (modeled after and in competition with the YMCA) was one such group, with both social welfare and advocacy activities, and at the national level involved in the independence movement. Organizations of this type continue to the present, and they have been supplemented by others, especially beginning with the colonial era, to provide ethnic/religious solidarity among Christian, Muslim, and Hindu communities. Many of these organizations conducted social welfare activities often beyond the confines of their own immediate membership. The few studies published indicate that at the village level Burmese generally did not join together for civil society functions except for religious purposes, but such organizations were extensive.

Civil society did develop under civilian Burma. It seems to have been basically an urban phenomenon, except for the religious groups that continued in the villages but were also prevalent in the cities, many of which were socially extended, agglutinated villages. Professional and other organizations were formed and flourished in an era where considerable space did exist between the state and the society. That space was somewhat circumscribed because of three factors: the heritage of laws from the colonial period that were used to suppress political dissent and the independence movement, the insurgencies that prompted immediate concerns for state security, and a tradition in which state intervention was countenanced. There were, of course, close, interpenetrating links between the civil society groups and the government. This was to be expected because with a relatively small elite group and an extended family system, the relationships between the private and public spheres were often close. In politics as well, there were close familial ties between members of the insurgencies and the government at the highest levels.

Since independence the AFPFL dominated politics. The violent left wing went underground in revolt, the Karen were in rebellion, and the alternative to the AFPFL was the legitimate, far left-wing party, the NUF. Professional and nonpolitical organizations flourished, but since most employment of the educated population was directly or indirectly linked to government, these organizations, although independent, were in the mainstream of Burmese life. The AFPFL spawned a wide range of mass organizations designed to mobilize society for ends determined by the AFPFL and to keep it in power. The All-Burma Peasants' Organization and the All Burma Workers' Organization were just two of many groups with extensive membership that allowed the party to perpetuate itself in power, and to foster the individual roles of its leadership. The organizations under state control could not be considered as part of civil society. During the Caretaker Government, as in the AFPFL period, civil society did exist, and the military made no effort to enforce complete mobilization of the populace.

The election of U Nu and the triumph of his party introduced an ineffectual government that seemed as much mystical as it was developmental. Nu ordered 70,000 sand pagodas to be built to ward off disaster to the country, and the prominence of Buddhism as a state religion, which had been a campaign promise much opposed by the military, made some of the minorities restive. The military perceived that the threats to the unity of the state (based on compromise provisions of the 1947 constitution that unrealistically allowed the Shan and Kayah States to opt out of the Union of Burma after a ten-year hiatus and a plebiscite) were so extreme that they prompted the coup of March 2, 1962, which was to perpetuate military rule in that state. Some claim that the military was in any case bent on power, and this was the convenient excuse to assume control under the guise of the ever-popular slogan of the unity of the state—a slogan that reappeared with vigor under the SLORC.

The BSPP Period (1962–88)

Civil society died under the BSPP; perhaps, more accurately, it was murdered. All other political activity was prohibited as the military slowly built up the

BSPP from a coterie of Ne Win supporters to a mass mobilization system that had its first party congress in June–July 1971. The constitution of 1974 mandated a single-party socialist state along an East European model.

A year after achieving power, the military introduced a rigid socialist system that eliminated the private business sector. All private organizations, including private schools, came under state control; the only titularly private groups allowed to exist were those completely under military command. Burma instituted autarky, and outside contacts, via both ingress and egress, were eliminated as far as possible. No one legally left the country without authorization, visas for foreigners for a period were limited to twenty-four hours. For a period internal travel was greatly restricted, and foreign and domestic news subject to complete control or censorship. Foreign missionaries who left on leave were not allowed to return. Private foreign assistance organizations (the Ford Foundation, The Asia Foundation, British Council, etc.) were ordered to depart, and ties between internal groups and their foreign counterparts were truncated. Burma had turned from neutral to isolationist, and an official policy of virtual xenophobia was introduced.

The BSPP through its core organization and its various subsidiary youth groups dominated all social activity. The military succeeded for the first time since independence in registering and controlling the *sangha,* and legal retail economic activity was concentrated on the cooperative sector, which was also government controlled. Professional groups were either abolished or structured along lines mandated by the center and with leadership dominated by the state and very often composed of military officers, who also controlled central and local governments. The modest autonomy enjoyed by the constituent states was eliminated at first by fiat and then under the 1974 constitution, which established a unitary state.

The BSPP, controlled and in large part manned by the military, went to great lengths to mobilize public opinion and people in support of its activities. Although a feedback mechanism was established to provide the policymakers in the Pyithu Hluttaw with the views from the bottom, in fact it did not work. Fear of the hierarchy resulted in an inadvertent avoidance of unpleasantness. While civilians feared the military, the higher officers feared those in command, and even the cabinet feared the mercurial Ne Win and kept from him news it believed would anger him.

A few private organizations were allowed to continue—welfare and religiously oriented societies that kept far from politics or power. Those that had more than local potential were circumspect to a degree that vitiated the use of the term "civil society" in describing their activities. Advocacy groups were nonexistent except for those directly mobilized by the state or those underground or in revolt in the jungle. Dissent was publicly eliminated. Civil society had disappeared.

The SLORC

However tragic the failed revolution from below and however destructive and bloody the repression following the coup of September 18, 1988, the military regime that came to power was simply a cosmetic change from the military-mandated BSPP. Although the regularization of the border trade and the economic openings to both the indigenous and foreign private sectors and the decision to allow a multiparty political system are touted as accomplishments of the SLORC and so reported in the internal controlled press and the foreign popular media, this is not the case. All these changes, with important and in some cases positive implications for the future, had either been suggested by Ne Win at the close of his tenure as chairman of the BSPP, or had been proposed for implementation by the BSPP, but the chaos of the summer of 1988 and the coup of September intervened.

These changes were without question the most important liberalization of policies since the coup of 1962. As such, they were welcomed by many. However, they should not obscure the fact that actual power had not shifted and that it was evident from the very beginning of SLORC rule that it had no intention of reducing the ultimate control of the military over the society as a whole. What had happened was not even cosmetic surgery, but rather a thin new patina of powder over a constant power base.

The private sector was let loose where it did not threaten military rule but in fact supported the continuation of national power under military auspices through economic means. Events have shown, and history has indicated, that the military, and indeed any conceivable civilian government in the near future, will likely be highly dirigiste and not allow the market to control the economic future of the society; rather, the market mechanisms will be used within limits for perceived economic good that will redound to both the political and economic advantage of the state and its rulers.

The center's control over NGOs continued as before. It was subject to more external criticism not because it was effectively different from the repression of the BSPP era, but because the plight of Myanmar was emphasized in the international media, where there was for the first time a victim (Aung San Suu Kyi—attractive, poignant, and brave) with whom the world could identify. Moreover, times had changed for world opinion. The turmoil and killings of 1988 were not live on the world's television screens as were those of Tiananmen a year later, but world concern about the latter reinforced the former. The presence of a large overseas Burmese expatriate community where few had lived overseas in 1962 provided a convenient and dedicated base for protest. With the new communications technology it was effectively used in many countries to organize internationally as well.

The concepts of the nature of power and its organization remained constant between the BSPP and SLORC periods. Even if those wielding it were personally different, institutionally they were the same (the military). There was no let up in the attempt to prevent the rise of any pluralistic institutions in the society that could offer avenues of public debate or disagreement over state policies and the role of the military. Thus there has been no easing of state control and as yet no indication that an autonomous civil society will be allowed to exist. There are, however, mechanisms in place that could be perceived to allow more distance between state and society. The fact that the Yangon (Rangoon) Municipality Act could be interpreted to be a "liberal" measure because under it the municipality could accept foreign assistance without going through the central authorities—something that had not existed since Burma became independent—rather indicates that the military has planned a continuous hold on power at all levels and has confidence that it will endure, and thus local approval is tantamount to central approval and control.

But there have been changes in the way the state has responded to both mass mobilization and civil society. The focus of the BSPP had been on building mass mobilization organizations around the party mechanism. It became apparent in the May 1990 elections that there were dangers in pursuing mobilization directly through the party process. The BSPP did not work well, as the military came to realize and as we have indicated above.

To the same end of ensuring that there is a mass base for direct, vocal support for policies that the government (i.e., the military) wishes to pursue, the SLORC took a somewhat different route. Rather than mandating that the military and civilian personnel of the government join a party, which in the BSPP era was the only road to advancement, the SLORC moved to establish USDA.

The USDA

Since 1962, when the military destroyed civil society in Burma, there has been an obvious, systematic, and successful effort to control, coopt, or eliminate any organization that had a potential for societal influence beyond that at the most local level—village or ward Buddhist temples. The few private organizations that were allowed to exist in the BSPP era became essentially parastatal in nature. Although there is a far wider range of ostensibly private organizations under the SLORC/SPDC and private political parties are titularly allowed to exist, there are none that escape government surveillance and control. In a sense, the regime has attempted to recreate civil society in its own manner while suppressing alternative possibilities. Through the formation of the USDA, it has formulated a mass civil movement that it can control, that will do its bidding, that is ideologically orthodox, and that its leaders hope is building on the future by concentrating on the relatively young.

The USDA was founded on September 15, 1993, following the disastrous May 1990 elections, where the reincarnation of the BSPP, the NUP, won only ten seats in a series of elections swept by the NLD.[7] The founding of the USDA followed within two weeks of the SLORC decision to hold a carefully controlled and scripted National Convention to form a new constitution. This juxtaposition of events is not without significance. The change in leadership in April 1992 from Saw Maung to Than Shwe was possibly related to these new tactics. The buildup of a mass organization may have seemed necessary to the SLORC because it lacked an effective, nationwide means to spread the official word, even though the military held power through Law and Order Restoration Councils (LORCs) at all local levels of administration. Since the SLORC had promised that there would be a multiparty political system in place at some indefinite date in the future and since the military was involved in and tarred with the ignominious defeat of the political and economic programs of the BSPP, the SLORC may have considered that a mass organization should formally be kept out of the direct military process and divorced from formal politics. It may also have considered the need for some mass organization that could propagate the views of the military when the time came, as eventually it would, for the promulgation of the new constitution. The decision was therefore not to register this new group as a political party, but rather as a social organization under the Ministry of Home Affairs. Military and civil servants are not allowed to become members of political parties, but both may join the USDA because of its ostensibly nonpartisan nature.

The expansion of the USDA has been rapid. In late 1996, it had over 5 million members, according to Than Shwe, SLORC chairman and patron of the USDA. By 1999, it had over 11 million members. With membership beginning at age ten and with very extensive youth organizations attached to it (with precedents such as the Lanzin Youth League), the total population is potentially mobilized. This would mean that perhaps one-third of the adult population may now be members.[8] Together with the cooperative movement—and significantly the director general of the USDA is also minister of cooperatives, as was the head of the BSPP youth organizations in that period—there is virtually no family in state-controlled areas that has not been touched by the central government through one of these organizations.[9] The organization of the USDA parallels the administrative structure of the state. There is a hierarchy of offices; under the center there are 16 offices at the state and division level, 57 at the district, 318 at the township, and 14,356 at the ward or village levels. By June 1996, there were 111 USDA offices attached to the Ministry of Information's district and township offices. Perhaps only one-quarter of the villages have yet been directly involved by having some branch office of the USDA, but at each higher administrative level the structure seems complete.

At the third annual meeting of the USDA on September 12–15, 1996, the last day being the anniversary of its founding, the director general and minister of cooperatives, Colonel Than Aung, indicated that the membership was 4,635,777, of whom 1,456,000 were from Yangon. There were also at least 1.23 million trainee youths associated with the group who attended "Buddhist culture courses" at some 18,692 locations. The USDA also ran other courses, such as English proficiency, computer training, marine courses, and general aviation courses. At what level these courses operated is unknown, but education seems to play an important role in the youth activities of the organization, and this may be an attraction of membership. These courses are free and may provide both practical and ideological training. Some are open to nonmembers, who are encouraged to join the USDA on course completion. Since public schools were closed for extended periods, these courses have provided useful, if partial, services.

On the surface a review of the objectives, code of conduct, duties, and responsibilities of the USDA makes it appear to be a virtual counterpart to a type of scout movement, with one exception: explicit support to the military. The five objectives of the USDA are the nondisintegration of the Union, nondisintegration of national solidarity, perpetuation of sovereignty, promotion of national pride, and the emergence of a prosperous and peaceful nation. The eleven-article code of conduct stresses loyalty, good character, patriotism, and duty, while the fourteen duties and responsibilities are generally concerned with normal civic obligations.[10] There is evidently a supplementary community development focus to the USDA as well as the predominantly political one.

The USDA is ostensibly financed by a K. 5 membership fee for those over eighteen years old (less than $1 at the official rate of exchange), but in fact the support for services, such as office space, and probably personnel as well, has come from the government. When asked how the USDA planned to finance future activities, Director General Than Aung said that it intended to build buildings and rent them out.[11]

Since its formation, the USDA has expanded at the national and local levels into a variety of economic activities that serve to support the group nationwide. The funds raised from these activities cannot be accurately measured from the outside, but they evidently amount to a state-authorized subsidy and means to achieve economic independence, and the USDA's total access to funds amounts to billions of kyat. At the national level, it controls the Myan Gone Myint company, the gems market, part of Theingyi market, Myenigone market (which was later transferred to the military-controlled Myanmar Economic Holdings Corporation, Ltd.), and land in Hlaing township. In each division and state, the USDA has extensive businesses that range from bus and train transportation monopolies to fish ponds, plantations, taxes on local businesses and activities, import businesses, rice milling, and housing and real estate. The USDA "is undertaking commodity production services and enterprises as well as holding coordinations and signing contracts for joint venture services with foreign economic organizations."[12] Although some of these ventures are rather small, they are sufficient to support local USDA mobilization activities. The USDA involvement in the economy is now significant and is one further means for the military to control economic forces even if it civilianizes the government and continues to move toward a more market-oriented society. Support from the state is likely to continue to be significant.

The more overt activities of the USDA of interest to the state are the mass rallies, which, according to Than Shwe, a total of nearly 2 million people have "unanimously" attended. Schools and other institutions are said to be forced to provide massive attendance at these rallies, which are designed to focus on both support for the military and opposition to "destructive" elements. Some of these rallies are said to have mobilized 100,000 people and they have become potentially violent means to intimidate the population. Many of their activities are directed against the NLD and forces the SLORC has characterized as destabilizing:

> The patriotic youth, who are members of the USDA, are self-reliant; they have their own initiative. They have conviction and are full of confidence in themselves. Their strength, which is growing year by year, is used for the state; it is for our nationals. By using their strength, they will oppose anyone who will infringe and disturb the stability of the state. They will also isolate these elements in society. The youth mass will join hands with the public to totally remove these destructive elements if they try to disturb, damage, or destroy the state.[13]

Although many of the goals of the USDA are those to which most civic-minded individuals might subscribe in theory, in fact the USDA is clearly a means to extend and perpetuate the influence of the *tatmadaw*. It is likely to remain important as long as it is perceived to serve the interests of the administration and as long as the military provides sponsorship. From all reports it is neither a spontaneously generated organization nor one that can undertake autonomous activities. Its potential for destructive mobilization is evident if, as reports seem to indicate, the mobs associated with it were responsible for the attack on Aung San Suu Kyi's cavalcade in late 1996.

It is also evident that there is considerable ideological training given to the USDA leadership, and such training also includes military subjects. The USDA is viewed as a kind of civil guard supplementing military control mechanisms. As Than Shwe said to the USDA executive advanced management course:

> The trainees constitute not only the hard core force of the USDA, but also the *sole* national force which will always join hands with the *tatmadaw* to serve national and public interests. Hence, he said, they should be both morally and physically strong with sharp national defense qualities. Therefore, he said, the *trainees will be taught military parade, military tactics, and the use of weapons* (emphasis added).[14]

There are both positive and negative reasons for joining the USDA. There is said to be some coercion in schools and other organizations, such as factories. Membership is said to be very helpful for obtaining appointments, as was membership in the BSPP in the earlier period. It is also said that membership avoids continual harassment to join or to be involved in other activities. In a sense, membership is a kind of tax or corvée labor charge on someone's time and energies.

Even as the perceived need for a USDA-type mass mobilization organization may have evolved from both the Burmese tradition and the military's previous experience in two different administrations, the model may also be traced to Indonesia, where the "stability" (to use Khin Nyunt's phrase) of the military regime under Suharto was regarded in Rangoon as a pattern that might be emulated. As Rangoon was planning to copy Jakarta in placing active-duty military in the legislature, making the operations of the *tatmadaw* a state within a state, and giving the military a direct role in the economy, so too the Burmese may have explored the early Indonesian attempts to engage in mass mobilization. Indonesia tried this with GOLKAR, which was the military's effort to form mass support for it through an ostensibly nonpolitical organization in its *dwi fungsi* (dual functions—civil and military) roles. GOLKAR later became the military's political party. The USDA may also be so transformed.

The USDA is not the only mass organization founded by the SLORC. Functional groups have been formed under its command, such as a veterans' organization, and others may be expected. The USDA is important as the major national means available to SLORC for both civil improvement and support. The emphasis given to youth is an indication that the SLORC is building on what it may regard as a long-term approach to ensuring its continuing role into the next generation. Reality may intrude, however, and the USDA is likely to remain important only insofar as the military has an active role in governance. After all, the youth movement of the Lanzin Youth League was ephemeral as well.

The USDA may have several advantages to the SLORC and then to the SPDC. As noted, it is a convenient mobilization organization that can be used when a referendum or some equivalent is deemed necessary for the formal approval of a new constitution. It has some nationalistic elements of general appeal. It can be used against the NLD and Aung San Suu Kyi, as it seems already has been attempted. It may be considered by the SLORC as a potential counterpart to foreign NGOs that wish to operate in Myanmar to alleviate suffering. It is of the military, but not part of it, which may be an advantage if the military is internationally conveying the fiction that it is not in direct control. In a sense, it is a convenient community facade for the military that may (in the regime's eyes) also have peripheral social and developmental impact under the military's tutelage. But for the outside world to regard the USDA as autonomous and divorced from state authority would be a major error.

Another state-sponsored mass civic group, the Myanmar Maternal and Child Welfare Association, has about 340,000 permanent members and 1.1 million ordinary members.[15] It is headed by the wife of Khin Nyunt. Other mobilization groups include the Fire Brigade, which has 104,000 members, with a planned total of 300,000; it may have paramilitary training and functions. The Myanmar Red Cross Society, a reserve force for peace and stability in addition to its normal duties, has 250,000 members, including 160,000 "Red Cross Brigade" members.[16] But as the control of organizations is of extreme importance to the military, so is the control of ideas. Orthodoxy seems a requirement that may be related to the concepts of power discussed above. Not only does the military demand intellectual orthodoxy through its surveillance, censorship, and other means of control, but the opposition as well seems to demand its own brand. In May 1999, three hundred NLD members commemorated the anniversary of the May 1990 elections, and Aung San Suu Kyi called for party unity, opposing some party members urging unconditional dialogue with the military; she called those who disagreed with the formation of the parliamentary committee of the NLD "traitors." [17]

NGOs in Burma/Myanmar

NGOs are a phenomenon that has been prominent in Western political theory and practice for a couple of hundred years. Whatever their origins and however defined, they have become important in international affairs as well as in the internal development of pluralism. Those that operate internationally are normally inextricably involved with local counterpart organizations. To provide support, goods, and/or services in a foreign country, they have three alternatives: (1) operate directly with potential individual recipients; (2) operate through government as an intermediary; and (3) operate through local private organizations—that is, local NGOs (i.e., civil society). To conduct programs directly, such as running a medical clinic, may be effective for a relatively short period, but unless some local group takes over, the continuity of the program is lost. Operations through a restrictive government may undercut the integrity of the program and tend to ally the foreign NGO more closely with the state, thus adding legitimacy to its rule.[18] Working through and with local private groups is the most feasible approach, allowing the NGO to maintain its program principles while building continuity of the program and elements of civil society in the country, and thus pluralism.

Since in Burma/Myanmar the state is in control of, or has its imprimatur on, virtually every organization, it is difficult for many there to understand that organizations in foreign countries inherently may be autonomous of state interference and control. This misperception is as common as it is inaccurate. NGOs can support state policies, be opposed, or lobby to request the state to enforce its own rules more rigorously. Understanding these conditions is essential to formulating either a strategy for humanitarian assistance or the development of some of the elements for pluralism in a society.

Government Attitudes toward International NGO Activities

Burma has traditionally been attractive to foreign organizations. The warmth of its peoples, its diversity, long history, and interesting art and cultures have prompted strong attachments by many foreigners. Its neutrality during the Cold War encouraged increased interest, and the growth of poverty—more precisely the economic lag compared to other states in the region and the mismanagement of the economy first under the BSPP and then under the SLORC—all have prompted humanitarian concerns among many foreign governments and institutions.[19]

The SLORC/SPDC has greeted such interest with suspicion at the same time that it recognizes that its financial condition (including the massive expenditures on the military that consume some 40–50 percent of the state's budget—a budget that has been cut 47 percent in 1999/2000) prevents it from providing basic human needs to significant portions of the population, especially the minorities in peripheral areas where provision depends on the continuity of the cease-fires. The government clearly feels under siege, surrounded by larger, more populous and powerful states; decried by the industrialized nations; and vulnerable to foreign economic, political, and even cultural domination. These fears may no longer be justified, but that does not make them any the less real.[20] The leadership is generally highly insular and parochial, and the attitudes once prevalent have become imbedded in the military psyche and perpetuated and promulgated through the controlled press. Xenophobia is real even as personal relations with foreigners can be amiable and warm.

Foreign NGOs became interested in Burma after 1988, first in terms of gathering information about conditions there and then in increasing general awareness of the situation. In spite of good intentions and much good work, Zunetta Liddell notes, "there have been negative consequences, the most important of which is the dependence of these groups on their Western donors and the advent of donor-led agendas which meant many groups losing contact with the people inside Burma who should be their main supporters." [21]

In 1994, this writer visited Rangoon and discussed with some SLORC members the desirability of developing standardized regulations for the registration of foreign NGOs, memoranda of understanding, duty-free custom clearance procedures for educational and health supplies, stay permits, and other desiderata necessary for the effective operation of NGOs in the country.[22] There was even some interest in the SLORC about holding an international conference on this subject in Rangoon. In the end, however, the SLORC determined that it was not prepared to deal with the NGOs as a group but preferred to have their operations considered individually. Subsequent visits have indicated that the degree of control suggested by the authorities for a program operating in the poorer areas of the country varied widely. In extreme cases it would make it impossible to ensure the integrity of the program. In some cases, the military authorities wanted funds or supplies to be handled by the local military, which would be generally unacceptable to most international NGOs. In other cases, NGOs seem to be able to operate effectively.

In 1999 there were about seventeen international NGOs operating in the country, and some in sensitive areas, in contrast to more than fifty NGOs working in the border areas in Thailand and with refugees. Some have been provided with memoranda of understanding, which validate their operations, while others just as actively conduct programs without official authorization but with informal government approval. Some indicate that they have considerable local autonomy within the fields in which they work—all of these are, of course, avowedly apolitical. Some have found local organizations with which to work, or some local groups have been created to act as counterparts. Individual NGOs have said that the stringent regulations required at the center are sometimes lessened on the periphery; others report strong local military control. Regional commanders have virtual autonomy in such affairs, and the level of personal trust developed over time is important.

There are reports that some foreign NGOs operate in Myanmar on a non-resident basis by having visitors provide small grants to local groups doing humanitarian work. It seems evident, given the intelligence network of the state, that these activities do not go unnoticed but may be tolerated because they tend to supply the goods and services that the state itself cannot supply. It is also evident that a few indigenous organizations have developed in Myanmar that are incipient local NGOs. They may be formed of retired government officers (no active-duty personnel), and they may do poverty alleviation and environmental work, partly with foreign support. Obviously, such organizations are nonthreatening to the state, but insofar as they are autonomous and perform valuable activities, they are an important indication of the potential for slowly building civil society.

Overall, both domestic and foreign NGOs operate in a climate of suspicion that may be overcome, but only with time and sustained effort. If more NGOs come into Myanmar and seek counterpart organizations with which to cooperate, it is likely that the government will recommend parastatal organizations such as the USDA, the Myanmar Red Cross, the Myanmar Maternal and Child Welfare Association, or other groups that fall outside of our definition of an NGO and in fact are quasistate entities. Each foreign organization, depending on its program and charter, will have to determine whether this is an appropriate method of operation. At the same time, the NGOs can do valuable work. Their positive contribution to the image of the SLORC / SPDC will be considered below.

Opposition Attitudes toward International NGO Activities

The NLD has taken a very different position from the government on the operation of foreign NGOs in Myanmar. It views the activities of foreign NGOs in the country in terms of three negative factors. First and foremost, the presence of a foreign NGO in the country and the publicity that the state can engender about it through the controlled press serve to legitimate the government. Any activity—even through nongovernmental channels—any support for a government program, and even any presence tend to provide legitimation for a regime that the opposition (and much of the world) regards as illegitimate. Second, all local activities and the organizations with which most NGOs will work will benefit the military indirectly, through the USDA or other government-sponsored groups. If, for example, some international NGO were to dig wells for pure drinking water, who would get the contracts for such digging, and who would get the credit? The argument goes that it will be the state or state-sponsored groups.[23] Third, economic benefits come from investment, assistance, trade, or tourism. These the NLD wants to deny to the state, claiming that only the top echelon of the military would benefit and the rich would become richer while the poor would continue to suffer.

The NLD therefore has not wanted to see the operation of any foreign NGOs in the country. This position may now have been modified because it is untenable in terms of internal Burmese attitudes over time. The country is stagnating economically, and if either other governments or private organizations can help alleviate pockets of poverty and the opposition is perceived to be against this alleviation, then the NLD will be accused of having selfish and unpatriotic motives. This the military has already claimed. The continuation of the political stasis and the refusal of the NLD to approve or agree to NGO operations will eventually become politically indefensible. The NLD stance against poverty alleviation cannot long be maintained without its losing internal political support. The NLD has been especially critical of the Japanese, who have stretched the definition of "humanitarian assistance" to include repairs to the Rangoon airport and who continue to supply other forms of humanitarian assistance and debt relief. The NLD has now agreed to such assistance if it does not benefit the state but helps the Burmese people and if such assistance is cleared through the NLD. The difficulty is that since the organs of the state (direct and indirect) are ubiquitous, it is difficult to remain pristine in any such activities.

Civil Society, Pluralism, and the NGOs

The options open to a foreign organization or government in dealing with a pariah regime are several. One can deny relations, cut off dialogue and contact, and bring pressures to bear on the state through international sanctions and opprobrium over its policies. This is a policy that usually has an effect only over a long period and then is of questionable efficacy unless the state so singled out for judgment is geared into the international economic order and if its neighbors agree with that policy. This was the case of South Africa. This is not the case with Myanmar. No neighboring country agrees, and neither the leadership nor the economy is externally oriented.

A second option, often proposed by the international business community, is for openness and investment in the targeted society. This, it is claimed, puts pressure on the government to open up and supply additional information and transparency if it is to compete internationally, helps create a middle class that will push for liberal change, and ties states into the international economic order, which puts pressure on them to adhere to generalized concepts of the political good. If there is evidence for this, it is a very slow process, and past political events in Asia do not give one much hope for the success of this option in any reasonable time span.[24]

A third option is less considered because it is not only long range, but also less clear and distinct than the other two. This is to encourage local elements of civil society that can act as points for eventual political pluralism. Because this is a long-range process that usually begins with organizations that are either local in nature and apolitical or are national and support some aspect of the government's interests, their development is viewed as less of a threat. Fostering such groups is important, however, because insofar as they are local, they bring pressure on the state to devolve certain types of policies to local levels, and their influence, albeit limited to their parochial concerns, can still be a force for pluralism in the longer term.[25]

Insofar as foreign organizations are not prepared to use force to change situations—and in the case of Burma the use of force is not credible, in spite of the suspicions of some high in the *tatmadaw*—all options are longer range. Large-scale investment may bring greater immediate economic benefits to the people (or to a group at the apex of society, together with low-paying jobs at the bottom), but it results in far greater legitimacy for the regime and does not prompt it to consider change. Incremental change and gradual liberalization through the development of civil society through NGOs is more balanced, providing less legitimacy and yet alleviating the suffering of at least some in the society.

Notes

1. The expansion of the BSPP before the promulgation of the constitution of 1974 may parallel the development of the USDA beginning in 1992, prior to the formation and approval of a new constitution, which is still being drafted in November 2000. See below.

2. Francis Fukuyama, *Trust: The Social Virtues and the Creation of Prosperity* (New York: Free Press, 1995).

3. As Michael Aung Thwin has stated, "The word 'civil' has no equivalent in Burmese. The dichotomy [between state and civil] is a Western invention reflecting Western society. . . . The Burmese dictionary (English-Burmese only! not visa versa) defines civil from its Western roots— i.e., civitas, civilization, urbanization. It is completely modern and concocted. That's because the concept of society did not separate civil society from the state, military, or religious sectors but totally integrated [them]. Currently, I would guess that the term 'civilian' is not totally divorced from the state either (civil servants certainly aren't, since the old term *ahumdan*, or 'bearers of the royal burden,' is still used). If there is such a concept, it's entirely new, modern, and Western, and like the Chinese, antistate. The word doesn't exist unless you are talking to Westernized elites. 'Civil' law is 'social law' (*dhammathat*) as opposed to *rajathat*, which is king's law, so in law there's some distinction between civil and state so that civil law is applicable to nonpolitical things (like inheritance and marriage), but this isn't played out further" (personal communication).

4. Houtman notes that the term "civil society" does not appear to be used by the regime in its writings, although Aung San Suu Kyi has used it in some of her speeches: "The concept certainly does not have the currency as in the West, since it is not encouraged as a concept by the educational and intellectual exchanges within the country" (personal communication). One diplomat in Rangoon said that in his official translations between foreigners and Burmese, when the term "civil society" was used by the foreigner, he left it in English. In the past, terms from Pali were used to translate new concepts into Burmese, and if "civil society" as defined above is not an indigenous concept (although civil institutions did exist), it could be so incorporated into the language at some future date. Whether it would early become conceptually relevant in terms of diffusion of power is a separate issue.

5. The term "Gongo" (government NGO) is sometimes used to describe government-directed and often funded nonprofit organizations. They would not be considered as part of civil society under this definition.

6. See J.S. Furnivall, *Colonial Policies and Practice: A Comparative Study of Burma and Netherlands India* (Cambridge: Cambridge University Press, 1957).

7. The choice of the NUP name is simply a further indication of the military's concern over the unity of the state.

8. The Economist Intelligence Unit (*Myanmar [Burma] 3d Quarter Report,* 1999) estimates it as 40 percent of the adult population.

9. It is important to note that the economic significance of cooperatives has markedly declined as the availability of consumer goods has increased through cross-border trade and the openings to the indigenous and external private sectors.

10. *New Light of Myanmar,* September 12–15, 1996.

11. Personal communication.

12. *New Light of Myanmar,* September 12, 1996.

13. Cited in FBIS, May 16, 1996.

14. *New Light of Myanmar,* March 12, 1996.

15. Government Information Sheet No. B-1367(1), May 14, 2000.

16. Government Information Sheet No. A-0879 (1), May 6, 1999.

17. Economist Intelligence Unit, *Myanmar (Burma), 3d Quarter Report,* 1999, p. 12.

18. It is important to note that in recent U.S. legislation, Section 1106 of the Foreign Affairs Reform and Restructuring Act of November 1998 limits U.S. contributions to the UNDP unless programs "are focused on elimination of human suffering and addressing the needs of the poor," are undertaken through NGOs "deemed independent of the SLORC," no financial, military, or political assistance goes to the SLORC [SPDC], and must be "carried out only after consultation with the National League for Democracy and the leadership of the National Coalition Government of the Union of Burma [NCGUB]." The legislation does not recognize that the NLD and NCGUB do not officially or formally coordinate with each other (NLD personal communication, April 1999). This section raises important diplomatic questions that seem to have been unaddressed.

19. The most comprehensive study of NGOs is Zunetta Liddell, "Working Paper on International Policies towards Burma: Western Governments, Non-Governmental Organizations and Multilateral Institutions" (manuscript, 1999).

20. For a discussion of these strongly held views in relation to policy formation, see David I. Steinberg, "Burma/Myanmar and the Dilemmas of U.S. Foreign Policy," *Contemporary Southeast Asia,* August 1999.

21. Liddell, p. 21.

22. A previous study by an Australian NGO, the Australian Burma Council, had recommended the entry of foreign NGOs into Myanmar, but no action was taken ("Operational Strategies for Australian NGOs in Burma," October 1994).

23. NLD leadership, personal communication.

24. Consider that it took over a generation for the development of a middle class and changed attitudes that led to liberalization in South Korea, Taiwan, Thailand, and Indonesia.

25. For an analysis, see Catherin Dalpino, *Opening Windows: Letting Liberalization Lead* (Washington, D.C.: Brookings Institution, 2000). This volume questions the policy concentration on democracy rather than on incremental change through liberalization.

CHAPTER 5

Economic Changes:
Progress and Regression

The Economic Maelstrom

When we plan our economy, do not let us confuse issues by bringing in politics. I appreciate that economics and politics are intimately connected, but let us keep politics out for a moment. Let us not indulge in attacks on imperialism; let us not look for excuses.

—Aung San, 1947 [1]

I agree with our ASEAN friends that we are all in the same sinking boat, but the water level is rising faster in our part of the boat than in your part of the boat. We are not good swimmers. But we believe we have a lot of resilience and we think the "good resource base" we have in the country can be depended upon to serve as a lifeboat. This lifeboat is expected to see us through the present [economic] crisis.

—U Myint, 1998 [2]

All indigenous regimes in Burma have been dirigiste; the salient issues are to what degree and with what competence.[3] The monarchical state held monopolies on oil, teak, and exports; the civilian governments were restrained socialists; and the military has vacillated between rigid socialism in the 1960s, moderated socialism in the 1970s and 1980s, and controlled openings to the foreign private sector since 1988.

How much the past shapes Burma's present is of some controversy in politics: does a previous authoritarian pattern presage a nondemocratic future in the shorter or longer term, or does the civilian multiparty period provide a basis for a more pluralistic era? These questions are less of an issue in the sphere of economics because the past indicates a consistent pattern of state strength in economics, and these predilections are likely strongly to affect the future.

When the SLORC first came to power, it seems likely from the economic evidence that it did not anticipate remaining in direct control for the long term. Specifically, officials noted that they did not want to make long-range plans because a new (presumably civilianized but militarily controlled) government would soon come into power. After abandoning the planning of previous regimes, the SLORC began the practice of having one-year plans. This provided flexibility and had the political effect of indicating that the SLORC did not want to remain in power, but it prevented longer-range thinking.

Following the elections of May 1990, however, that approach seems to have been revised. Rigidity set in. After that time, the military came to realize that it could not trust the people to keep it in power without a longer-term commitment in mobilizing the masses and in preparing a constitution that would ensure its perpetual control. It was at this point that it began to make multiple-year plans.

The SLORC introduced a new Short-Term Four-Year Plan from 1992/93 through 1995/96, the principal objectives of which were longer-term growth and economic stability. It stipulated the following goals: the private sector was to be stressed, although its contribution to the GDP was expected to remain constant at 75 percent. Overall, the state planned to grow annually by 5.6 percent, but the primary sectors of agriculture and livestock/fisheries were to expand by 5.6 percent and 6.2 percent respectively. Government expenditures in FY 1993/94 were to fall by 19.6 percent in spite of the need for improved infrastructure. The state expected to improve the operations of existing manufacturing and processing facilities rather than expand them.

The Four-Year Plan was supplemented by annual plans. For FY 1993/94, the GDP was to rise by 5.8 percent, but agriculture was to climb by 8.4 percent, livestock and fisheries by 5.9 percent, mining by 5.6 percent, processing and manufacturing by 7.3 percent, and forestry by 6.8 percent.

In April 1996 (the beginning of the Burmese fiscal year), the government outlined a new short-term Five-Year Plan for 1996/97–2000/01.[4] It anticipated a growth rate on the average of 6 percent, with high priority given to trade: exports were to grow at 21.6 percent annually and imports at 13.7 percent. Internally, agriculture was the highest priority: it was expected to increase by 5.4 percent, livestock and fisheries by 5.8 percent, forestry by 2.8 percent, mining (especially oil, natural gas, and jade) by 1.8 percent, and processing and manufacturing by 7.4 percent, with special emphasis on value-added agro-based industries and the export of goods and services. At the last year of the plan, two-way trade was to total some $5.5 billion.[5] Per capita income was to rise from K.1,532 to K.1,873 (or 4.1 percent annually).

This penchant for planning, which has been evident throughout administrations since independence, is indicative of both the dirigiste approach to economics in Burma/Myanmar and the continuity expected of military-dominated regimes into the future. The SLORC, however, inherited both an economy and a predisposition to that sector that should be understood; thus some background is required.

The Precolonial Economy

The precolonial economy reflected the patterns of political ideology and practice under the Burmese kings. The capital, indeed the palace, was regarded as the symbolic center of the world, and the power of the monarch radiated out from that sacred site. The economic assets of the state, characterized as one that was low in population with abundant land, were considered the property of the king. He appointed officials who were recompensed for their labors by "eating" (collecting taxes from) the towns they governed and remitting a portion to the center. As noted, all exports were directly under the king, who also controlled the traditional oil wells of central Burma, the teak industry, and certain gem production.

The economic problems of the state were connected with low production because of low population. The result of the numerous wars between an expansionist Burma at various periods and its neighbors, as well as internal strife among Burmans, Shan, Mon, and Arakanese at differing times, was to move significant elements of defeated kingdoms to places under central control to increase production, construct temples, and supply greater forces for the military. Traditional irrigation systems in the dry zone of central Burma, many predating the Burman arrival in the region, were the means by which the Burman court and its military power could be maintained. The vast Irrawaddy delta, which became later the premier site for rice production, was largely forested and sparsely settled. Even before the advent of the British, Burma was exporting rice, and Western powers coveted its teak for use in shipbuilding. Traditional trade routes from China's Yunnan Province, which China effectively colonized only in the Ming period (1368–1644), were established and became important.

The Colonial Economy (1886–1948)

Burma had been a colonial economic success story. Underpopulated for its geographic size, Burma before World War II was the world's largest exporter of rice (3.123 million tons in 1940, a record since unequaled), as well as an exporter of oil and a variety of minerals (tin and tungsten among them), and it was known to possess the world's finest jade and rubies.

Before the opening of the Suez Canal in 1869 and the advent of steam navigation, which made European markets more accessible, Burma shipped some 400,000 tons of rice to India. The economic boom resulting from the conquest of lower Burma in the Second Anglo-Burmese War (1852) opened the Irrawaddy delta to investment and exploitation as the most important rice-growing region in the world. More capital was invested there than in any other agricultural area in any colony. Teak was a coveted commodity. Rubber also was prized, as was oil.[6]

The British regarded Burma as a potential avenue to the rich markets of southwest China. To help run the state and supply manpower for administration and jobs, which the Burmese either did not want or could not do at that time, Indians were imported in large numbers.[7] Chinese also came; some were from southeast China, others from Yunnan Province, pushed and pulled by both economic opportunity and local rebellions.

World War II devastated Burma. The British engaged in a scorched earth policy as they retreated into India, and the Japanese repeated the process as they were forced out four years later. The result was a country, although potentially rich in natural resources and with a vast agricultural base, that had little left in industry and infrastructure.

Socialism, in varying degrees of intensity, had been the guiding principle of Burmese economics since independence in 1948. This was an outgrowth of several factors. If the precolonial economy was traditionally state-directed, the laissez-faire colonial period resulted in alienation of much of the internal and export-led economy from the indigenous peoples and placed them in the hands of three foreign groups—the Europeans (especially the British); the Indians, imported by the British to help staff a variety of occupations and the lower rungs of the state bureaucracy; and the overseas Chinese. This was essentially a dual economy: a modern sector in foreign hands and a traditional, largely agricultural, sector under the control of an increasingly indentured Burman peasantry. The shift to a more market-oriented economy since 1988 has not been without difficulty because of this heritage. These factors, together with the moderate democratic socialist intellectual trends popular in England before World War II and the correlation of capitalism with imperialism, greed, and material concerns (and thus theoretically antithetical to Buddhism), made socialism, intimately associated with nationalism, the overwhelmingly prevailing policy orientation in the pre-independence period. Socialism was seen to be the means to place the economy back under Burman control and achieve social equity.

The Civilian Period (1948–62)

The natural endowments of the country should have made the newly independent but ethnically diverse and politically divisive state the economic envy of many of its neighbors. This advantage was lost through a series of civil wars, political upheavals, and economic policies that first stunted growth and then led to dramatic regression.

Moderate democratic socialism, introduced on independence in 1948, prevailed through the civilian period (1948–58, 1960–62), and this approach to economic planning was reflected in the Pyidawtha program of U Nu. The Caretaker Government (1958–60) stressed this as well. Foreign businesses and banking were allowed, although under greater control, and efforts were made to increase the Burman elements in the economy. The results were mixed, with many Burmans selling their import or export licenses to resident non-Burmans for quick, unproductive economic returns. The state, to further social equity and the appearance of modernity, established factories for a number of products from pharmaceuticals to steel without consideration of production costs or their comparative advantages. A large portion of the modern economy still remained in foreign, especially Indian, hands.

The Burmese Economy under the Military (1962–88)

The policies during the first year following the decisive military coup of March 2, 1962, also stressed this moderate socialist approach. The guiding, if eclectic, economic doctrine was "the Burmese Way to Socialism," which appeared shortly after the coup. It was followed the next year by the theoretical underpinnings for political and economic action, *The System of Correlation of Man and His Environment,* an even more abstruse philosophical potpourri. These documents were taught in required courses to civil servants, professors, and students at universities and colleges.

In 1963, the military proclaimed a major shift in economic policy and instituted a rigid form of socialism with nationalization of most private businesses, starting with major foreign companies such as the Burmah Oil Company and the Indo-Burma Petroleum Company.[8] Some 15,000 private businesses were expropriated by the state and some 200,000 residents from the Indian subcontinent forcibly expatriated without their economic assets. The military encouraged other nonindigenous peoples to emigrate. Officially induced nationalism, even xenophobia, was rampant. "The Burmese Way to Socialism" was to serve as the guide to an economy dominated by the center, and eventually by the BSPP, and thus by the military itself through the party, the bureaucracy, and all loci of power in a highly centralized, unitary state. Adhering to the Buddhist principle that all things are in flux in the material world, however, the document also regarded the ideology as finite and changeable.

By the late 1960s, even the military leadership realized that these economic policies were a failure. The policies were predicated on effective bureaucratic and planning capacities that were lacking. Indeed, whatever such capabilities had existed under the civilian governments had been dismantled by the military beginning in 1962, when officers without sectoral skills were placed throughout the bureaucracy in positions of leadership and the apolitical civil service purged

and subjected to political manipulation. Loyalty to the military was more important than competence. Trust was limited; the military distrusted most civilians.
The growth rate for the 1963/64–1967/68 period was –1.2 percent.

As mentioned in chapter 1, the first BSPP national convention in June–July
1971 discussed an official, devastating economic critique of regime performance. "The Long-Term and Short-Term Economic Policies of the BSPP"
advocated reforms within the socialist context but called for abandonment of
policies centered on industrial growth and the proletariat. It recommended instead concentrating on the development of Burma's natural endowment—agriculture, forestry, fisheries, and mining—and especially stressed oil production. A long-range Twenty-Year Plan was formulated, and implementation was
divided into five four-year plans. At the end of the planning period, 48 percent
of the economy was to be under state control, 26 percent under the cooperatives, and 26 percent in the private sector. Sectoral increases were to vary, and
per capita income was to double. The processing and manufacturing sector was
to increase from 11.5 percent to 22.1 percent of GDP. Burma was to stress state
agro-business growth.[9]

The BSPP paper commented that although diplomatic relations were good,
international economic relations were not. It sought foreign assistance in these
endeavors. This policy shift was approved by the party's Central Committee in
September 1972 and instituted slowly during the early 1970s. As noted, Burma
joined the ADB, the World Bank was invited back into Burma (from which it
had been excluded since 1963), and bilateral assistance was sought from a variety of world donors. Autarky was abandoned as a policy, but foreign private
investment was still shunned. (Although legally allowed in collaboration only
with the state, a German arms firm with ties to Ne Win was the only such
investment.) The private sector continued to be treated with great suspicion.

Some economic reforms, encouraged by the World Bank and the IMF, began slowly. The state raised agricultural procurement prices, instituted tax reforms, tried to rationalize the SEEs and create flexibility in management and
pricing, increased cost-of-living allowances to public employees (1976), and
raised interest rates (1975). These modest reformist policies were undercut by
local and national political conformity. Managers feared to use the authority
that had been titularly granted, reflecting a state of bureaucratic and social fear
that was endemic, and nationally the state moved in 1974 into a new constitutional mode, replacing the military's Revolutionary Council rule by decree. The

new state constitution of that year ratified the BSPP as the only legal political party and institutionalized both political and economic rigidity with the military in mufti in command.

These policies began to produce results, coupled as they were with the introduction and spread of the new high-yielding varieties of rice throughout the major 72 rice-growing townships of the state under strong government direction in what was called the "all-township" program. Foreign assistance also increased some twentyfold, from about $20–25 million annually (mainly from Japan) in the late 1960s to over $400 million toward the end of the 1970s. Paddy production expanded. Although acreage under production remained relatively constant, yields per acre increased by about 50 percent in an initial spurt of growth.

Growth rates rose to 6.4 percent during the Second Four-Year Plan (FY 1974/75–1977/78). They had been 2.7 percent during the First Four-Year Plan (1968/69–1973/74) period. Improvement was apparent. This improvement evidently vitiated the continuing need for structural economic change in the eyes of the military leadership, although it was apparent to outside observers that the goals of the Twenty-Year Plan were unattainable.

By the mid-1980s, however, the economy was again in crisis because of both internal and external factors. Foreign aid had produced massive foreign debt (see below), and the increase in the value of the Japanese yen, in which a substantial portion of that debt was valued (in 1994 it was 54.6 percent), exacerbated the problem, resulting in difficulty in servicing it. Rice production had reached a plateau because of limited irrigation, credit, and fertilizer, and the value of exports of primary products had dropped on the world market while the costs of manufactured imports had risen because of worldwide inflation in the wake of two oil crises. The current account was in deficit as the value of imports exceeded exports; imports had to be cut, so production of the fifty-six SEEs, already inefficient because they operated on political rather than economic principles, was reduced, creating a further drain on the state. The SEEs created a set of problems: they had in part been established for an ill-conceived import-substitution program, as well as for internal political image, ideological reasons, and external show. The SEE pricing policies reflected political considerations rather than costs, scarcities, or local considerations. They also employed a major portion (approximately 349,000 at one time) of the urban work force that could not be easily dismantled. Burma continued to function economically only because the country was largely composed of self-sufficient villages. The urban population relied increasingly on smuggling for consumer goods that the state could no longer produce and that competed with inferior local products.

In December 1987, the UN General Assembly voted to designate Burma an LDC, which would allow it to receive foreign assistance on more concessional loan terms and get debt relief. Although regarded by many Burmese as the ultimate public degradation of what had been generally considered a potentially prosperous nation, it was an appellation for which the Burmese government had assiduously lobbied. (It was perceived by the government to be such a sensitive issue that it was not announced until the end of March 1988.) Burma, however, was overly qualified to be in that category by its high literacy rate, which had been extolled since precolonial times.[10]

The growing crisis was exacerbated by the state's real leader, Ne Win. As detailed in chapter 1, on September 1, 1987, he inaugurated the most sweeping economic liberalization since 1962. Most of the agricultural economy, nine grains including rice, were allowed to be freely traded. Previously they had been subject to rigid pricing and controls and state purchase and regulation. Foreign observers hailed the move as perhaps the first sign of economic pragmatism in a regime previously characterized by ideological rigidity. They were wrong, however, as this turned out to be an astute political move without supporting policy changes. In fact, the reverse occurred.

On September 5, 1987, the state announced the demonetization without compensation of some 60 percent of the currency in circulation. Ostensibly designed to eliminate the black market, on which the government in fact depended, the change was widely rumored to be rooted in abstruse numerological calculations of Ne Win's astrological future. This third and most severe demonetization since military rule in 1962 (others took place in 1964 and 1985) had disastrous effects and destroyed the little remaining economic confidence in the military-led state. (It is significant that in 1993, in formulating the draft constitution, the SLORC felt it necessary publicly to guarantee no further demonetizations.) No one wanted to hold cash for fear of further demonetizations, and economic chaos resulted. Farmers held rice, their only major marketable asset, and urban dwellers bought any nonperishable commodities with whatever cash was available. There were four major results: increased inflation; a drop in the black market value of the Burmese currency; a precipitous rise in the price of rice in urban areas; and a dramatically increased demand for con-sumer (thus smuggled) goods, and with it the expansion of the border trade and Chinese influence, especially from Yunnan Province.

The need for consumer goods resulted in the growing economic role of China and the legalization of the overland China trade in November 1988 under the SLORC, even though it was announced by the BSPP in July of that year.[11] China could supply materials at cheaper prices and better quality than Burmese factories, where production had decreased through lack of raw materials, spare parts, fuel, and an uneven electricity supply, as well as through political ineffi-ciencies and the requirements of corruption. Observers estimated the informal China–Burma border trade at $1.5 billion at that time (formal trade in the early 1990s was reported to be much lower—see below). Chinese and Burmese needed no visas to cross frontiers, and Chinese capital and traders, as well as goods, began to dominate parts of upper and central Burma. The suppression of the student uprising in Beijing around Tiananmen Square in June 1989, reminiscent of Rangoon in 1988, solidified this China–Burma political and economic connection.

The economic and political malaise led to growing unemployment among the educated, postsecondary graduates; it was unrecognized in the statistics. About one percent of the total national population (but an educated one per-cent) since 1962 had fled the country (not counting the massive outpouring of refugees to Bangladesh in 1978 and 1991 and Karen and other minority refu-gees to Thailand)—most illegally before 1974 and thereafter with the tacit per-mission of a state that wished to rid itself of dissidents and to tax and obtain foreign exchange from those going abroad, ostensibly to work. Urban unem-ployment figures were generally quoted at about 9.4 percent in 1989 (down from 11.7 percent in 1985), but this did not accurately reflect reality because the figures represented only those applying for work at state-run unemploy-ment offices. The figures were probably substantially higher and underemploy-ment likely even more intense. Since there were few jobs in the private sector and the state could absorb no more staff (there were 552,000 in the national government, excluding the military, and 17,000 in local government, excluding the military and the SEEs) and politically the state could not fire many, some found sustenance in the black market trade.[12]

Inflation was severe, but civil service salaries remained frozen for about fifteen years. (The SLORC eventually raised them as a political expedient four times: in 1989, 1993, and 1998, and on April 1, 2000.)[13] Government shops and cooperatives stocked little at fixed, state-determined prices, so trading took place outside of approved circles at much higher rates. Civil servants were allocated access to staples at state stores, but many had to resell such goods on the black market to supplement their inadequate salaries. The legal exchange rate of the kyat to the U.S. dollar remained in the vicinity of K.6 to 1 (varying marginally and dependent on a basket of currencies; the kyat was pegged to 8.5=1 SDR [Special Drawing Rights] of the IMF), but the black market rate rose from three times the official rate in the 1970s to about sixty times in the late 1990s.

The SLORC thus took over an economy potentially rich but devastated by mismanagement, poor policies, political rigor, and the economic whims of its leaders, who eschewed foreign advice. The state did not trust, and did not want, outside economists learning of its inadequacies. Yet foreign advice was forthcoming from an unexpected source. In what seems to have been an unprecedented action by the Japanese at that time, in early 1988 the Burmese were privately informed that unless substantive (but unspecified) economic reforms were instituted, Japan would have to reconsider its economic relations, meaning its foreign aid program, with Burma. Since the Burmese economy was in shambles and Japan provided close to half of all bilateral and multilateral foreign aid to Burma—which was about $2.2 billion in the aggregate until 1988—and relations between the Japanese and Ne Win personally had been close, this alone was a significant incentive for change.

Patterns of Economic Change

The Economy under the SLORC/SPDC (1988–)

Economic conditions were dire when the SLORC took over in 1988. The Twenty-Year Plan had been a failure, and few targets had been achieved. Paddy production had leveled off. Oil, which had been the great economic hope for the BSPP, had indeed risen in production—from 3.81 million barrels in 1965 to 6.3 million barrels in 1971 to 9.55 million barrels in 1978. But plans had called for it to rise to 17 million barrels by 1981/82; in fact, it had fallen below

1971 levels—and even below the 1939 level of 6.56 million barrels—to 5.5 million barrels in 1989/90 and 4.28 million barrels in 1995/96. The output of most minerals had dropped, and capacity utilization of the industrial enterprises as a whole was 36.7 percent. External trade was in deficit by some $359 million in 1987/88—and the unofficial border trade probably increased that figure substantially—and remained so in 1999/2000.[14] In 1987/88, international net reserves (including obligations) were a minuscule $9.5 million, and foreign debt was over $4 billion. By 1998, external debt had risen to $5.883 billion. As noted, following the coup in 1988, most new foreign economic assistance stopped, although previously approved multilateral and Japanese projects continued. About 11.1 percent of the total labor force was employed by the state, and officially inflation was some 22 percent in FY 1987/88, although unofficial estimates indicate that it was much higher. The currency in circulation was K.8 billion in 1987 after demonetization but had risen to K.12.1 billion the following year. Per capita income hovered around $200. The GDP at factor cost (FY 1985/86 = base year) had declined by −1.1 percent in FY 1986/87, by −4.0 percent in FY 1987/88, and by −11.4 percent in FY 1988/89. There were few positive economic signs at that time.[15]

The SLORC was faced with a set of interlocking economic and political problems. Primary was the need for political legitimacy, but the economic needs that could contribute to that legitimacy were multifold: reforms; funds with which to implement them; incentives for savings (bank interest rates were below inflation levels); a skilled work force; an improved administration; better articulated institutions of management, finance, and planning; vastly renovated and expanded infrastructure; good planning and knowledge of international markets; and a set of rationally run state economic enterprises to replace those that were a growing economic drain on a poor regime.[16] Predictability, that essential element that provides the base on which economies flourish, both politically and in policy formulation and execution, was also lacking. Thus the state in 1988 was in economic and political extremis. The economy was out of control, inflation was high, economic and political discontent were merged and threatening the coup leaders, and private sector reforms were yet to be instituted. The border trade had mushroomed but was still uncontrolled, smuggling was rife, and the incessant insurgencies sapped the strength of the regime.

Eliminating socialism from the state's name and professing first an "open" and then a "market" economic system (this shift in itself may be significant) was quite different from allowing the private sector to work effectively. The past and present role of the state in the operational aspects of all activities within Myanmar, together with the present lack of intermediate autonomous institutions and countervailing social forces of any kind, must prompt skepticism about the intent of the state, and more specifically the military, to remain aloof from such a potential source of power. The military has in fact attempted both to coopt and to control the economy, first through the formation of a number of institutions (such as the Myanmar Holding Corporation, Ltd.)[17] through a network of military procurement factories run by the *tatmadaw* and through the Myanmar Economic Corporation (another military controlled entity), and second through regulations and hortatory statements that smack of coercion.[18]

When dirigiste characteristics are coupled with technocratic competence and a government that understands the nature of the economic processes or gives relatively free rein to economic experts, as in South Korea, the results may be highly effective, at least for a considerable period. When, however, dirigisme is coupled with misunderstanding or ignoring the nature of internal and external economic forces, a profound mistrust in the process of capital formation, and a weak bureaucracy in which loyalty to ideology is valued over competence, the results can be highly dangerous. Myanmar represents the latter case.

As we have discussed above, fundamental questions exist about the interest in, or capacity of, the military leadership. Those who seem to hold veto power over decisions are remarkably insular in their experience, limited in understanding and coping with economic change and Myanmar's entry into the world economy and, conversely, the world economy's entry into Myanmar. Although there are many competent technicians at the nonpolitical and nonpolicy levels, the sorry performance of the military may be interpreted in two ways: all economic decisions are determined on the basis of perceived political and power needs and thus are of secondary import, or the military itself has yet to comprehend some rather basic economic factors, such as the roles of money supply, exchange rates, and sound financial institutions. It shows even less comprehension of the private sector and the types of political-economic guarantees required to attract it on a continuing basis. The private sector requires predictability both at the political level and in economic policies, and even in levels of corruption. Myanmar offers little evidence that such guarantees exist or are likely to in the foreseeable future. Further, the state has virtually forced into exile a generation of trained people, for whom there have been no replacements.

The year 1988 was the economic nadir of Burma's foreign exchange holdings and international liquidity. But 1989 and 1990 were years of economic resurgence through the introduction of modest private sector openings and the sales of much of the state's natural resources (especially teak, which requires a fifty-year cycle of regrowth), with disastrous environmental consequences for short-term gain. During those years, the SLORC began major facelifting, superficial activities designed to brighten and modernize Yangon and other cities. It also moved significant numbers of the urban populations throughout the country to outlying satellite towns for reasons that are variously interpreted— from political harassment to better housing opportunities. Whatever may have been the motivation, it was coercively executed except in one area, where civil servants were offered plots of land at favorable rates and credit and thus were deemed good investments. Although accurate figures are lacking, the SLORC clearly has employed the temporarily effective expedient of printing more currency, which may seem falsely efficacious in the short term.[19] It will undoubtedly lead to longer-term and major political and economic difficulties. The SLORC had, however, learned one major lesson from 1987 and 1988: it has tried to keep the price of rice relatively low and the supply ample to the urban consumer. It is questionable whether this has succeeded, as the price has shot up, but the state has also dumped rice onto the market to mitigate the problem.

Inflation at one point was perhaps running at 60 percent. Khin Nyunt in a major speech listed the rise in prices of household necessities and noted that official figures might lag behind real price rises.[20] He accused businessmen of making too much profit at the expense of the consumer, harking back to an old Burmese prejudice that denied marketing as a productive force and its profits as a legitimate concern. This had been articulated by the military on many occasions since 1958, in part stemming from the historical fact that much of the trade and distribution aspects of the economy in colonial times were in foreign hands. Although U Nu could decry capitalism as breeding greed and thus being incompatible with Buddhism, evidence from other Buddhist societies would indicate that other, perhaps stronger, historical forces were prompting these attitudes. It is evident that the SLORC neither fully understood the economic forces that its own policies, both liberalizing and dirigiste, had set in motion, nor the requirement for reforms to be comprehensive—or it did not care.

As noted, foreign assistance virtually ceased.[21] The states that dispensed economic aid were, and remain, limited: China has been the major supporter, and South Korea has funded two projects. Thailand provided a loan for road construction in the Shan State. The UN agencies continued to operate. The country has declined to allow the IMF to advise on macroeconomic issues, although both the IMF and the World Bank have made economic analyses of the economy, the former under the normal surveillance associated with the annual Article IV consultations, and the latter most recently in 1999. Myanmar was in the early 1990s economically (barely) afloat through the encouragement of short-term extractive investment,[22] investment in labor-intensive export industries, receipt of funds from foreign firms on the signing of long-term oil exploration leases, the lack of some service of an extensive foreign debt of about $4.17 billion,[23] and the regularization of the border trade. The last activity, although providing considerable customs duties, has undercut the capacity of the SEEs to produce, further exacerbating the internal crisis. Civilians and military personnel have been exhorted to grow their own food as much as possible.

The common problem of states attempting to move from centrally planned economies to ones more open and market oriented relates to the stress placed on the polity. In the short run, inflation often increases, the poor suffer, and a small number become relatively wealthy. When this is coupled with the possibility that those who become wealthy will be those with access to capital—in the case of Myanmar essentially the Chinese, Indians, some of the higher-ranking military, and those engaged in the border trade—this could create major social tensions in the society. The very obviousness of the Chinese presence in central and northern Burma could become an issue if economic or social envy became apparent (see chapter 8).

If Eastern Europe is a guide, regimes that begin to cope successfully with the problem are those that have a broad and deep base of popular support and have the mass credibility to allow them to take actions that will negatively affect certain groups in the short term for long-term national benefits. Through a belief in its own public relations campaigns to convince the populace that the *tatmadaw* has such popular support, the military may think that it can carry out such change. There would be many, including this writer, who would doubt it.

It seems evident that the economic changes instituted by the SLORC indicate some progress, but they are half measures that will not succeed in solving either the social and economic problems facing the state or be sufficient to attract the amount of foreign investment anticipated. Vietnam, which opened its economy about the same time as Myanmar, has had about three times the volume of such approved investment.[24]

Openings to the private sector require fiscal prudence and rational exchange rate policies as well as the ability to attract indigenous savings. (Official bank interest rates in 1999 were 12 percent, but inflation was about four times that figure.) Myanmar must deal with the issue of SEEs, which have become increasingly obsolete and inefficient but which employ tens of thousands for whom other jobs are not now available. It has not done so. Further, past misuse of the economy for political purposes excites fears of more of the same. Rumors of another demonetization abounded in 1991 and had to be refuted by officials on several occasions. This is evidence of an intense level of economic mistrust of the state. At the same time, it is widely rumored that corruption has increased and has, in many instances, become egregious to the Burmese themselves. Khin Nyunt stated that 10,516 public servants had administrative actions taken against them for corruption.[25]

The SLORC has moved to acquire immediate gain from the exploitation of natural resources, while placing its hopes on the major returns over perhaps half a decade from both onshore and offshore oil exploration. Such measures carry economic and political dangers that any new SPDC-approved civilianized government may have to face. Oil revenues alone, as other states have demonstrated, do not necessarily produce sustained economic progress or development. The economic prospects for Myanmar are daunting.

The decline in the Burmese economy can be traced to several factors: the uncertainties caused by the still unresolved political and constitutional issues following the 1988 popular uprising, exacerbated by the government's studied inattention to the results of the May 1990 elections; the precipitous drop in foreign investment in the aftermath of the Asian financial crisis of 1997; the lack of fundamental economic restructuring; and the continuing international characterization of the regime as a pariah, which led to a U.S. imposition of sanctions. Poverty has increased, and the state seems bent on studied self-reliance in a period of world interdependence. The outlook remains bleak. This pessimistic assessment is justified in spite of some increases in the aggregate economic data since the coup (because the base data were very low) and the extensive efforts by the state to expand irrigation and double-cropping of paddy production, as well as to increase road and rail infrastructure.

The decline persists in spite of a potentially positive change in economic ideology; economic realities and complexities intrude on a more liberal approach to development. It is significant that none of the major parties that registered for the May 1990 elections invoked socialism as part of its party platform. Burma has largely remained an agricultural economy dominated by a single crop—paddy—and more recently by its exports of hardwoods, especially teak, and increasingly in the export of pulses.

Burma's experimentation with an enhanced private sector, increased trade, encouragement of foreign investment, and a greater willingness to engage the rest of the world had begun to provide greater potential for economic improvement but has declined. Structural economic changes, such as a devaluation of the currency, control of the money supply, adequate salaries for state officials, and privatization of the SEEs are still largely unfulfilled. The past, highly dirigiste heritage is also not easily overcome.

Here it would be useful to look at some of the sectors of the economy in more depth. Of primary importance has been and will continue to be agriculture and the rural sector, in which most of the population was employed and which generated most foreign exchange.

Agriculture and the Rural Sector

Burma was an agricultural economy in 1988 and remains so at the beginning of the millennium. In 1997/98, 62.7 percent of the total labor force was engaged in agriculture, which comprised about 58.8 percent of the GDP. The population was about three-quarters rural, and the agricultural sector was over 90 percent private (although it should be remembered that since independence the state has owned all land). The net value of the agricultural sector in FY 1986/87 (in FY 1985/86 constant prices) was K.22,343.3 million, but had dropped to K.18,706.7 million by 1991 and was K.25,697.6 million in 1996/97. In spite of the importance of agriculture to the economy, the state invested only 13.9 percent of the annual budget in that area in FY 1997/98.

Overall, the position of the peasant in Burma was better than in most centrally planned economies. Although the state nationalized all land on independence, it was never formed into communes, despite the rhetoric under the BSPP that this was a direction in which the government hoped to move. The farmer was not free, however. The state determined the crops to be grown (the variety of the crop in the case of paddy), the prices to be paid for these crops, and how and to whom they might be sold. Because the state was the ultimate arbiter of land and because of a lack of production capital, peasants made few improvements in the land that they tilled.

Burma was a state of smallholders. Land reforms in 1963, 1964, and 1965 were supposed to eliminate tenancy; the reforms seem to have alleviated the situation, but anecdotal evidence suggests that informal tenancy still existed. A significant number (said to be about 40 percent) of the rural population are said to be landless. In FY 1997/98, 61.4 percent of peasants tilled less than 5 acres (26.6 percent of cultivated area); an additional 25.1 percent held from 5 to 10 acres (32.3 percent of cultivated area), 10.9 percent from 10 to 20 acres (27.2 percent of cultivated area), and only 2.7 percent held 20 to 50 acres (11.0 percent of cultivated area).[26] Recent changes in government policy are designed to increase the commercialization of agriculture and develop large tracts of unused but arable land. If successful, they will benefit the state and the wealthy, but not the poor farmers. One of the attractions of Burma to the foreign donor community had been the perception of shared poverty, rather than the skewed incomes and large estates so apparent in the Philippines and Latin America.

In FY 1992/93, the state reported an increase in agricultural production of 12.8 percent over the previous year, when it had dropped by 3.9 percent. This compared to 5.2 percent in FY 1989/90 and 2.0 percent in FY 1990/91. The FY 1992/93 increase appeared to be misleadingly optimistic, both because of the low production of the preceding year and because paddy production rose only 4 percent over FY 1985/86, when the population had risen by about 13.5 percent over the same period.

The agricultural sector and the economy as a whole had been, and still were at the end of the century, dominated by a single crop—paddy. Paddy production and its availability in its edible form (rice), its distribution, costs, and level of consumption to a major degree determine the state's economic prosperity and political stability and the standard of living of the population. Paddy generally accounted for about 75 percent of agricultural output by volume. Paddy production is always subject to the vagaries of nature, and floods and drought constantly affect production in key regions. Even more important, however, are agricultural policies, including the availability and distribution of credit and fertilizers, government procurement and purchasing, land tenure, marketing, storage, and taxation. The high-yielding varieties of rice, to which the state had been committed for over two decades, required deft applications and controls on water and fertilizer to achieve maximum production. The 1970s saw a remarkable increase of 50 percent in paddy production because of the new seeds introduced through the International Rice Research Institute in the Philippines (in the 1990s, about 57 percent of paddy land was planted to these varieties), the enhanced availability of fertilizers from increased foreign assistance (use rose from about 50,000 tons in 1969 to over triple that amount a decade later), and a strong, government-directed mandatory system of production. The BSPP explicitly invoked regulations forcing peasants to conform to state production requirements, such as growing the new varieties, or lose their ability to till the land, which could be deeded to heirs only with the approval of the local BSPP committee.

Farmers, heavily taxed by the state through forced procurement at below-market prices, therefore were reluctant to engage in capital improvements to the land. A production plateau was thus reached. Paddy production doubled from independence in 1948 to about 10.5 million tons in FY 1979/80 and reached 13.6 million tons in FY 1987/88. A major intensified campaign to increase small-scale irrigation and encourage double-cropping of rice and other crops has resulted in increases in aggregate yields and sown hectarage but not in per hectare yields because of fertilizer shortages. In 1989/90 paddy production was 13.8 million tons and in 1998/99, 17.8 million tons, while per hectare yields remained relatively constant (2,916–3,079 kg/ha). These yields were among the lowest in Asia.

Water and fertilizer availability were limited. Only about 12.6 percent of the land was irrigated, and much of that was for insurance against a failed monsoon; only 14.8 percent of land was used for double-cropping in 1988/89. Irrigation, most prominent in the dry zone of central Burma, had existed since before the eleventh century, but the percentage of irrigated land was among the lowest in Asia. By 1997/98, the state had constructed a wide variety of smaller dams, raising irrigated areas to 17.5 percent. It had unrealized hopes of turning the dry zone into a "green area" by the year 2000, but progress was evident. Multiple cropping increased to 19.6 percent by 1997/98. Although there were large tracts of unused, potentially arable land equal to that under cultivation, most were in minority or other areas considered inhospitable to the Burman population; land under paddy production essentially remained constant.

Fertilizer availability reached a peak of 260,000 tons in 1987/88, declined to 137,000 tons in 1992/93, but by 1996/97 was 321,272 tons. Much of it was imported (only urea was produced in Burma), and sufficient imports were financially impossible as foreign assistance was lacking. In 1993, local production was 163,443 tons and imports 160,109 tons.

Restraints to production and availability remained. In 1993 the state procured some 11 percent of production of paddy at about one-sixth of market prices, although this practice was supposed to have been stopped in 1987. The result was that farmers attempted to grow more lucrative crops, understated their production to sell it surreptitiously, and smuggled rice to neighboring states where prices were higher. Some estimated that about 70,000 tons of rice were smuggled in FY 1993/94. Agricultural products counted for about one-third of all exports, and where once rice dominated that category, in 1992 it was only a quarter of the value of agricultural exports. In 1989/99, rice exports were about 5 percent of all exports. Rice exports were as follows;

Fiscal year	Metric tons	Million dollars
1989/90	168,500	40.18
1990/91	133,800	27.70
1991/92	183,100	40.00
1992/93	207,700	40.36
1993/94	270,100	43.20
1994/95	1,073,900	197.10
1995/96	354,000	78.0
1996/97	78,000	21.0
1997/98	28,000	6.0
1998/99	123,000	40.0 [27]

In 1998/99, the state procured about 2 million tons of paddy and distributed 0.7 million tons at subsidized rates to the military, civil service, and other selected groups.

Agricultural credit has been an important element in increasing production among an impoverished peasantry. In the colonial era, the state became concerned that the Indian subcaste of Chettyars from Madras had a virtual monopoly on rural credit and introduced cooperatives to counter increased Burman land alienation. During the Great Depression, much land was mortgaged and lost by the Burman population. On independence, state provision of agricultural credit was a political necessity. Such credit has mainly been used for paddy production and was essentially a seasonal or annual loan, not used for capital improvements. It had to be repaid in the following season or year. A small amount of development loans for longer term credit have been available (K.154 million in FY 1991/92).

In FY 1986/87, agricultural loans amounted to K.1,309 million (approximately $200 million at the official exchange rate), a sum that increased modestly to K.1,533 million in FY 1991/92. Under the military regimes, repayment levels have been very high because the state has had the capacity to enforce its will and because repayments are guaranteed by a system of village group responsibility. Under civilian governments, politicians manipulated credit and promised to forgive loans for votes. Estimates vary, but official credit has not been sufficient. In FY 1972/73 official credit was 11 percent of the costs of production and in 1969/70 about 17.1 percent of the formal credit market. By 1988/89, the last figure had dropped to 2.7 percent, and inflation and population increases had undercut its position. Informal markets for credit were illegal but prevalent, with interest rates of 3 percent per month with collateral and 5 percent without it.

Not only did the state enforce its will through credit allocations, but it also fielded 5,882 extension workers in FY 1992/93 to offer advice and ensure that farmers obeyed government directions. This number was expanded by over 10 percent from the previous year, although there remained questions about the level of training of these workers. Previously, when numbers were smaller, most were graduates of agricultural colleges; when demand overtook supply, they were recruited from high schools; thus they could help ensure compliance with government regulations but had less technical capacity to advise farmers.

By 1992 pulses and beans, which were in worldwide demand for animal feed, played a more important role than before. They accounted for 42 percent of agricultural exports. Their value in FY 1987/88 was $20.1 million but rose to an estimated $125.7 million in 1992/93 and $196.1 million in 1999. Pulse exports increased from 453,000 tons in 1989/90 to 1,678,000 tons ten years later. There were also increases in edible oil production. Wheat, maize, rubber, and sugarcane production remained relatively constant during the SLORC period. Rubber was 28 percent of the value of agricultural exports in 1991/92.

Agriculture remained in 1992 a captive of traditional technology in Burma in spite of some diversification of crops and improved seed. Only 4 percent of land was cultivated through mechanization, and draft animals were the essential means for plowing.

The government has engaged in a major land reclamation program on an extensive scale. The program began in 1998. Of a total possible 45 million acres, 23 million are now cultivated. Land is given on a thirty-year lease free of rent on condition that it be developed for agriculture in three years. The state provides technical assistance, and local banks are encouraged to provide loans. Fuel is provided at subsidized rates. Investors may export 50 percent of rice, are exempt from state rice procurement requirements, and have permission to import equipment. Although superficially this program seems helpful in increasing rice exports, "in purely economic terms the social costs of the project exceed its social value in that the combined social opportunity cost of the publicly supplied or subsidized inputs used by the project exceeds the value of the reclaimed land 'produced,' even if it assumed that the land would have had zero social value in the absence of the project." [28] The environmental effects are likely to be negative because of the wetlands.

Agriculture in the plains of the Irrawaddy, Chindwin, Sittang, lower Salween Rivers and in the Irrawaddy delta remained the backbone of the state. Yet in the hills, which generally lacked irrigation facilities, both wet and dry rice were grown in economies more attuned to subsistence levels. Infrastructure and transportation facilities were lacking, and cash crops had generally to be light in weight and relatively valuable for shipment. Thus tea in parts of the Shan State and poppies for opium (and eventually heroin) in the Shan and Kachin States were important for local economies.

Offshore fisheries were a significant although underutilized source of foreign exchange. Fish and fish product exports were valued at only $9.8 million in FY 1987/88 but had reached $23.1 million by 1991/92 and $51 million in 1998/99. Yet only half of the offshore allowable catch was taken, according to official estimates. These estimates must be treated with extreme caution, as Burma had very limited capacity to patrol its area and there were many reports of poaching in Burmese waters. [29]

Burma had 75–80 percent of the world's teak reserves in the 1980s because Thailand had earlier exhausted its resources. Teak was designated a "royal tree" in 1752, and in 1855 the British made it a state property. Disputes over it were a precipitating, if not fundamental, cause of the Third Anglo-Burmese War (1885–86). During the colonial period, Burma had what many regard as the finest forest service in the world, and it very carefully husbanded its resources. The cutting of teak and other hardwoods since 1989, however, has been a cause of considerable environmental concern.

Teak has remained a government monopoly, although foreign companies have participated in its extraction with the government since 1989. Published estimates that 57 percent of Burmese land was in forests must be regarded as suspect since the official figure remained unchanged since 1940. Estimates in the early 1990s placed the figure at about 39 percent, but even this may have been too high. Some 1993 figures indicate that 43 percent of land was in closed forests and 7.5 percent in "degraded forests," of which 2.2 percent annually became agricultural land. In the period 1960–88, Burma is said to have lost about 20 percent of its forest cover. Forests in which teak is significant cover about 15 million acres. Reserved forests were 40,137 square miles in 1996/97, up from 38,876 square miles in 1988/89.

Annual teak production in the 1936–40 period averaged 453,000 cubic tons, a figure that has yet to be equaled. It was 390,700 cubic tons in FY 1989/90, 439,800 cubic tons in 1990/91, and 362,300 cubic tons in 1991/92, but it declined to 230,000 cubic tons in 1998/99. In 1998/99 exports were valued at $136 million, compared to $94 million in 1988/89. Actual production was about half of estimated potential yields. Twenty-eight percent of production in 1992/93 was by foreign firms, mainly from Thailand (Thailand had twenty-six logging concessions along the frontier), and the drop in figures in 1991/92 may have been caused by the depletion and then closure of the Thai concessions in 1993. An average of about 50 percent of production was in logs for export. Burma abounds in a wide variety of other hardwoods that are also in increasing demand.

There have been questions raised throughout the period of military rule about whether government statistics accurately reflected the illegal export of timber, especially teak. Since Thailand had exhausted its reserves, and because a large portion of the border region between the two states was in insurgent hands and the transit of smuggled goods was taxed by them, many believed the illegal felling of such timber was widespread.[30]

Fears about illegal logging and the environmental consequences increased in 1989, when Thailand (which had banned all internal logging because of large losses of life from deforestation mud slides in the Burma border region the previous year) and Burma entered agreements for timber concessions along the border. Later China also participated in agreements with Myanmar for areas in the Shan State. There is said to be extensive deforestation along the Kachin and Shan States' borders with China. There is little question that at the time the SLORC initiated these concessions, the government was in dire need of foreign exchange, and the extraction that took place as a result of these agreements netted the state (with other concessions, especially from onshore oil exploration) considerable and immediate foreign exchange. A major decrease in forest cover was caused by both a growing population and the need for firewood for cooking since the government virtually stopped the production of kerosene. In 1990, some 10.3 million cubic meters of firewood were used for cooking, and the use was expanding by 1.1 percent annually. Rangoon alone used 900,000 tons of charcoal annually. In 1992, a new forest law was promulgated (with help from the Food and Agriculture Organization [FAO]), replacing the 1902 law under which forest land use had been controlled. It sets out conditions for forest conservation and land use and allows private sector involvement in forest management.

Foreign exchange earnings from exports dropped in the FY 1991/92 period as some concessions ended and as the easiest areas had been cleared. As Steinberg (1981) noted, "There are dangers that the Burmese may be overcutting their [teak] reserves, which require three to five decades to replace. The short-run advantages to the state are numerous, but the dangers are apparent." [31] In 2000, these comments remained valid.

Nonagricultural Production, Trade, and Investment

Mining

Much of the mining sector is a government monopoly. Burma produces tin, tungsten, lead, zinc, copper, antimony, silver, and gold, as well as nonmetallic minerals. Nonpetroleum mining in FY 1940/41 produced about 10 percent of Burmese exports, or about $16 million. Burma's mines were once exceptional; the Mawchi mine in the Kayah State was once the largest tungsten producer and the second largest tin producer in the world and was said to have reserves of 800,000 tons in 1982. The Shan State's Bawdwin mine was said to date from the eleventh century and in the pre–World War II era was one of the world's largest producers of lead, zinc, and silver. World War II devastated the field; with 1939 calculated as 100, the mining index in 1946 was 0.2 and had risen to only 12 by 1952. Before 1971, when policies began to emphasize mining, only some 6 percent of capital expenditures were allocated to mining; the figure rose to 15.3 percent in FY 1977/78. In 1998/99 allocations for minerals and nonmetallic minerals were only 0.1 percent of the capital budget.

The state investment in the mining sector (including energy—separated here because of the importance of oil, gas, and coal production) in FY 1992/93 was only 1.6 percent (1.3 in 1998/99). The sector is under exclusive government control, but joint ventures have been authorized. Although $500 million was approved for foreign investment in mining (exclusive of oil and gas) from 1989 through 1998, only a small percentage was actually invested during that period.

Mining has been a disappointment except for jade and gems; increases in jade production have perhaps resulted from the cease-fire in the Kachin State, where the mines are located. With 1985/86 as a base, the following table shows percentages of production for various minerals in three different periods.

	1988/89	1995/96	1996/97
Lead, zinc, silver	54.2	31.5	28.2
Tin, tungsten	43.7	50.4	34.4
Jade, gems	222.5	2,636.6	3,764.1
Industrial minerals	83.9	258.1	279.9

Most production has not equaled pre–World War II figures. This has likely been owing to the insecurity of government control over some of the mining regions for various periods; the lack of adequate transport, equipment, spare parts, and fuel; and because for much of the independence era the state refused to introduce new technology through cooperation with foreign firms.

Energy, Oil, and Natural Gas

In the pre-independence period, Burma was one of the few countries exporting both fuel and food, and traditional forms of oil production existed in the precolonial period. Before 1900, 32 million gallons of oil were produced annually. Since independence, the most important sources of energy in Burma were oil and natural gas, the latter only in production since the early 1970s. Coal production began in FY 1962/63. The hydroelectric potential is vast. Although the energy field was a source of great economic optimism in the 1970s, it became a frustration as production did not keep pace with expectations and needs.

Although Burma exported a small quantity of petroleum products in 1987/88, it had to import oil for a period, and the World Bank provided funds for fuel for its projects. A lack of fuel has slowed development activities throughout the country. Before the SLORC, all Burmese governments prohibited foreign participation in onshore oil exploration and production. With the fall of oil production, however, the SLORC in 1988 opened onshore exploration to foreign firms. Ten companies, including those from the United States, Britain, France, Holland, Japan, Australia, and Korea, initially received concessions, for which substantial initial payments were made to the state on execution of the contracts. The number of companies later rose to fourteen.

In the 1989–93 period, some $566.1 million had been invested in the oil and gas sector. The results have been disappointing to both the state and the firms. Finds were limited, costs of exploration high, and the state was said to be demanding. By 1997 only five firms remained. By 1994/95 crude oil production was only 4.2 million barrels, and by 1996/97 it had dropped further to 3.8 million barrels (or 37.0 percent of the base 1985/86 level).

Natural gas production is relatively recent in Burma. It started slowly with 4,575 million cubic feet in 1975 and rapidly increased. It reached some 40,000 million cubic feet in 1990, but dropped to 31,782 million cubic feet in FY 1991/92. This affected fertilizer (urea) production, which was a major product of the natural gas industry. (Urea production was 304,900 tons in FY 1986/87 but 133,000 tons in 1990/91.) The production costs of urea were K.4,072 per metric ton, while it was sold at K.2,160 per metric ton. Natural gas production rose to 58,575 million cubic feet in 1996/97. Under the SLORC, the Myanma Petroleum Enterprise capacity utilization was only at 28–33 percent.

Official gasoline prices remained unchanged from 1988 at K.3.52 per liter (somewhat less that $0.50)—among the lowest in the world—but gasoline was rationed, and a major black market existed for it. In 1993, the SLORC invited foreign bids for offshore exploration in eighteen concessions—thirteen in the Gulf of Martaban and five off the coast of Arakan. A major offshore natural gas find was announced by Total (France) in the Gulf of Martaban in the early 1990s, with estimated reserves of 3–8 trillion cubic feet. Called the Yadana project, it has developed into the major industrial project in the country and involves Total, Unocal (United States), the Petroleum Authority of Thailand, and the Burmese. Burmese investment will total $1.2 billion. Under this project, gas is transmitted first by undersea pipeline to the Tenasserim coast and thence overland to Thailand. This pipeline was the cause of much concern because of environmental issues, the forced resettlement of Karen and Mon in its path, and alleged human rights deprivations owing to forced labor in its construction. The gas is sold to Thailand, and Myanmar expects to gain annual revenues of some $400 million. The project came on line in 1998, but Burmese revenues are said to be mortgaged for several years. The problem is further complicated because Thailand is using less energy since the financial crisis than had been anticipated. A second field, called Yetagun, has been developed offshore and is to come online soon. Coal production hovered at about 35,000 long tons in the SLORC period.

Electricity generation in 1996/97 reached 3.945 billion kilowatt hours (bkh), of which 42 percent was from hydroelectric power and 55 percent from gas. Losses in generation, transmission, and distribution were about 38 percent of production, the highest in the region. In 1997/98 the government noted that 323 towns (probably township headquarters) were electrified, as were only 1,051 villages out of some 65,000. The Chinese have negotiated with the Burmese authorities to construct a hydroelectric plant in the Kachin State that would supply electricity to both Myitkyina and Bhamo. There have been plans for Chinese support for a major hydroelectric dam on the Salween, and more recently there have been negotiations with India for a dam along the Chindwin.

Industry (Manufacturing and Processing)

The Burmese industrial sector (known in Burmese statistics as manufacturing and processing) is a composite of state control over major industrial plants but a private sector preponderance in small establishments. Industry's share of the GDP was 9.2 percent in FY 1996/97. The state controls 28 percent of the GDP in manufacturing and processing. The sector employed 9.06 percent of the total

labor force of 18,359,000 in 1997/98. In common with many developing countries, it had major investments in food processing/beverages (209 of total state-
owned businesses) and in light industries such as textiles. In FY 1997/98, there
were 1,601 state-owned factories, 637 owned by the cooperatives, and 50,035
owned by the private sector (of which 28,818 were in food/beverages). Of all
industrial establishments employing under ten workers, 48,898 were private
firms and 811 were state owned. Of the few firms employing over 100 workers,
398 were state owned, while 101 were in private hands. Under the SLORC, the
sector lost some 174,000 workers.

The SEEs had been regarded as the backbone of the BSPP socialist system
and the 1965 Law for the Establishment of a Socialist Economic System. In
November 1988, the SLORC announced a number of reforms, including the
granting of more autonomy to the SEEs, limiting their capital expenditures,
and passing the Foreign Investment Law (see below), which allowed the SEEs
to enter joint ventures and technical agreements with foreign firms.

Under the SLORC, management became more centralized as the government tried to reform the financial system. In April 1989, all SEE debt was
canceled and converted into the State Account Fund. Progress and reform have
been slow, however, because of inflexible pricing policies; poor management;
lack of raw materials, fuel, and intermediate goods; aging and inadequate infrastructure; the necessity of buying local commodities at government procurement prices, which are below the market (thus leading to shortages of these
goods); and the import of many products competing with those domestically
produced. Thus capacity utilization of the SEEs was very low, ranging from
14–50 percent in 1991/92, depending on the industry.

The SEE deficits decreased from 7.1 percent of GDP in FY 1990/91 to
1.9 percent in 1991/92 and 1.5 percent in 1992/93, thus indicating some improvement. This partly occurred because of the change in accounting procedures and the practice of the SEEs to engage in countertrade to offset exchange
rate problems. In 1998/99 the deficit was 4.5 percent of GDP. The fundamental
problems connected with the SEEs are yet to be addressed. Ill-conceived enterprises continued, and the political impact of implementing needed reforms
and rationalization of employment were still prompting delays in dealing with
the issue. In January 1995, the state established the Privatization Commission,
which was to sell or lease off fifty-one small state enterprises. Only a few have
been sold because there is no realistic pricing policy.

The partial freeing of the economy and the salutary encouragement of the foreign and domestic private sectors have provided incentives to economic growth. By 2000 it was still too early to determine the degree to which the indigenous private sector was engaged in sustained production. The encouragement of the tourist industry proved a fillip for growth in associated construction (from overseas investment) and services, and a great deal of private sector activity was associated with both internal and external trade. The degree to which adequate internal capital will be made available to the private sector through the banking system (in contrast to funds for the cooperative movement and agricultural credit) may well help determine the nature and composition of the middle classes and the extent to which the market openings are regarded by the people as successful. To date, the SEEs have taken the bulk of available credit, leaving little for private sector activity and thus forcing greater reliance on foreign capital, which has not been forthcoming since the Asian financial crisis.

The Cooperatives

The cooperative movement in Burma goes back to the end of the nineteenth century. Fostered by the British to provide credit to help protect the Burman population, who was being exploited by usurers, the movement became an arm of the state after independence and since military rule has served the state as an integral element of economic and political control. Under the BSPP Twenty-Year Plan, the cooperatives were to control 26 percent of the economy at its close. Their contribution has been minimal and was only 2.1 percent of GDP in 1997/98. Yet from the state vantage point, cooperatives were critical for the distribution of state-controlled or produced commodities, including many consumer necessities. They had a modest role in the procurement of agricultural crops; in FY 1991/92, they purchased 8.2 percent of sesame production, 5.8 percent of pulses, 4.1 percent of paddy, and 3.7 percent of groundnuts. That year the government expended K.214 million on the cooperative movement.

In FY 1997/98, there were a total of 22,720 cooperatives in the country with 3.15 million members. There has been a decrease in cooperatives and membership since the SLORC, presumably because of greater imports and the liberalization of the grain trade. All the cooperatives were organized under a Ministry of Cooperatives, the minister of which during the BSPP period was head of the party youth league and a member of the BSPP Central Committee. As noted in chapter 4, the significance of the cooperatives under a more open economic system lies not in their economic function, but in the tie between them and the USDA, as the Minister for Cooperatives is head of both organizations, and both can be used for mass mobilization.

Trade

Burmese foreign trade remained seriously out of balance under the SLORC, as it had been under the BSPP government. In FY 1987/88, imports were $612 million and exports were $254 million (a deficit of $358 million). The following year the deficit dropped to $180 million, with exports rising to $351 million and imports dropping to $531 million. (Border trade was said to be in balance that year.) In FY 1989/90 the trade balance dropped to its lowest point in many years—$75 million—during which exports grew to $427 million while imports continued to decline to $502 million. The terms of trade index (1985/86 = 100) showed a rate of 65.7 in FY 1987/88, and by FY 1996/97 was only 48.8, which meant an increase in the deficit. In 1999, exports totaled $1.124 billion, but imports were $2.484 billion.

The shifts in the direction of trade between FY 1987/88 and 1991/92 reflected several factors: the rise of China's share in the Burmese economy; the continuing preponderance of Japan in imports (although the figures dropped with the absence of new Japanese economic assistance); and foreign investment. In FY 1987/88, exports to the industrialized countries (including Japan, with 5 percent) made up only 13.4 percent of total exports, while Asia received 60.4 percent. Exports to India were the largest (16.9 percent), followed by those to Singapore (11.4 percent). By FY 1996/97, the exports to Singapore were the largest, then to India, Thailand, Hong Kong, Japan, and China (but grossly undercounted). By 1993, 50.7 percent of total exports were handled by the private sector. In March of that year, there were 8,762 registered trading enterprises, including 4,596 exporters and importers, 933 business representatives, 1,986 Myanmar limited companies, 818 private enterprises, 166 branches of foreign companies, and 27 Myanmar joint ventures.

Some have claimed that the military intentionally distorts some trade statistics: "the government has sought to understate (by about 20 percent) the extent of private exports to offset the exclusion of military imports from the balance of payments account." [32]

Foreign Investment

During the long period in which socialist ideology was paramount, foreign investment was not allowed. In the early 1970s, however, the reforms theoretically encouraged foreign investment, but only with the state. Only one firm was allowed—Fritz Werner, a West German firm partly owned by the German government. It had close ties to Ne Win and the arms industry.

The November 1988 Foreign Investment Law allowed investments that promoted and expanded exports, exploited natural resources, brought in higher technology, supported production and services involving heavy capital expenditures, provided employment, saved energy, and assisted in regional development. Foreign investment under this law could involve 100 percent of foreign capital and joint ventures in which the foreign capital would be at least 35 percent. It had provisions for tax incentives, the prevention of nationalization during the life of any contract, and the repatriation of foreign currency at prevailing exchange rates.

By April 30, 1998, the statistics on permitted (in contrast to disbursed) foreign investment were as follows:[33]

Sector	Number	Value ($ billions)	Percent
Oil and gas	46	2.3	32.6
Manufacturing	113	1.4	20.3
Hotels and tourism	40	1.0	14.7
Real estate	18	0.9	14.1
Mining	43	0.5	7.1
Transport and communications	13	0.275	3.8
Livestock and fisheries	18	0.275	3.8
Industrial estates	3	0.193	2.7
Construction	1	0.017	0.2
Agriculture	3	0.014	0.2
Other services	5	0.013	0.19

In 1998/99, foreign direct investment approvals were only $29.5 million.

The U.S. Department of State estimates that only about 28 percent of approved investments have been realized, although official figures have not been released on this.[34]

By country, the figures were as follows:

Country	Number of investments	Value ($ millions)
Singapore	66	1,485.75
United Kingdom	32	1,352.28
Thailand	42	1,237.16
Malaysia	25	587.17
United States	26	582.07
France	3	470.37
Netherlands	5	237.84
Indonesia	8	236.37
Japan	19	218.87
Philippines	2	146.67
Hong Kong	20	121.32
Korea	20	99.33
Australia	14	82.08

Logging remained one of the most controversial of foreign investments. In March 1993, the state announced that twenty-six Thai logging concessions would be stopped by the end of 1993. The reasons given for ending these concessions were insufficient earnings, illegal felling, smuggling, border insecurity, and the need for conservation. International concern over the environmental consequences probably also played some role in the decision.

Burma has many attractions for foreign investors: a great need for facilities of all types, extensive and unexploited natural resources, low wages, controlled labor, and even officially approved means to avoid the unrealistic exchange rate. But problems remain: political uncertainties, inadequate infrastructure, high costs of doing business, and extensive corruption. Burma, like the communist states of Vietnam, China, and Laos, has attempted to keep its political system in tact while at the same time opening its economy. The tensions between the political and economic forces are intense. Burma in 1994 lagged behind these other liberalizing economies, making the tensions less explosive, but tensions in Burma also can be expected to grow in the years ahead.

The Financial Sector

The unrealistic exchange rate makes calculation of financial data for comparative purposes difficult. The nominal GDP rose from K.68.698 billion in FY

1987/88 to K.151.941 billion in FY 1990/91 and K.790.887 billion in 1996/97. In 1985/86 constant producer prices, the GDP was K.47.141 billion in 1988/89 and K.74.028 billion in 1997/98. Domestic savings fluctuated from 12.8 to 13.4 percent of GDP in those years, but distortions arise in using the official exchange rate to convert exports to kyat.

Three banking laws were enacted in July 1990. The Central Bank of Myanmar Law gave the Central Bank the authority to operate relatively independently and to set reserve requirements, discount and interest rates, and minimum cash margins. The Financial Institutions Law set the regulations for interest rates and reserves for commercial banks, finance companies, and credit cooperatives. Although the Central Bank was given more authority, as has happened in the past when economic authority has been delegated in Burma, it has been reluctant to exercise that authority.

The state owned five banks: in addition to the Central Bank of Myanmar, the Myanmar Economic Bank, the Myanmar Foreign Trade Bank, and the Myanmar Investment and Commercial Bank can deal in foreign exchange. The state also controls directly the Myanmar Agricultural and Rural Development Bank. (There was also the Myanmar Insurance Corporation, which had financial functions.) The Myanmar Economic Bank primarily deals with domestic currency. As of December 1992, it handled 82 percent of loans to cooperatives and 48 percent of loans to the private sector. Until March 1989, it had been responsible for the accounts of the SEEs; these subsequently were shifted into the State Account Fund. Because it has a large number of branches, it also handles foreign exchange accounts in the border regions.

The Myanmar Foreign Trade Bank handled most foreign exchange transactions for both the state and registered private traders. It was very profitable because it was the bank of deposit for non-interest-bearing foreign currency deposits (totaling some $88 million in April 1993). The Myanmar Investment and Commercial Bank became independent from the Myanmar Economic Bank in September 1990 to deal with foreign investors and joint ventures. It can deal in both foreign and domestic currencies. By April 1993, it had twenty-five correspondent banks. The Myanmar Agricultural and Rural Development Bank, founded in 1990, provided credit to the rural sector for seasonal loans, as well as for the purchase of equipment and machinery.

To encourage private savings, a Savings Bank Law was passed in June 1992. Interest rates were raised, and savings branches of the Myanmar Economic Bank and the Myanmar Investment and Commercial Bank accepted fixed-term deposits for three, six, and eight months. Foreign Exchange Certificates for foreigners have been issued since February 1993. They can be used as currency within the country, although dollars circulate widely. Savings rates, however, remained low because they were negative—less than the real rate of inflation.

The Central Bank of Myanmar began to grant licenses to private domestic and foreign banks beginning in February 1992. As of 1999, there were ten "private" banks, and thirteen private but "semi-governmental" banks, including the Myanmar Citizens Bank (jointly owned by government Joint Venture #3 and private citizens), the Yangon City Bank (owned by Rangoon city), the Myawaddy Bank (owned by the Myanmar Holdings Corporation), the Cooperative Bank (owned by the Ministry of Cooperatives), and the Yadanabon Bank (with ties to the military and the Ministry of Trade). Although the private sector banks are supposed to operate independent of government and provide loans solely in banking terms, the banks are under tight state control, and the state has significantly intervened in the allocation of credit. Lending and deposit rates in 1993 were controlled to six percentage points above and five points below the Central Bank prime rate, which was set in 1989 at 11 percent. Total domestic credit rose from K.31.554 billion in March 1988 to K.100.739 billion in March 1993. About 94 percent of the credit was allocated to the public sector in 1988, and 80 percent to it in 1993. The cooperatives in 1988 received credit of K.2.150 billion, the private sector only K.877 million that year. Virtually all of the nonstate sector credit by 1993 went to the cooperatives, but in December 1992, the private sector received K.11.018 billion. Of this amount, K.2.4 billion was provided to agriculture and K.8.5 billion to other private activities. A number of foreign banks had representative offices, but they were restricted in the types of activities allowed.

Inflation, the Cost of Living, and the Money Supply

Official estimates of inflation and the cost of living, as reflected in the Rangoon (Yangon) Consumer Price Index, have been a matter of considerable debate because the calculations have been based on official prices of items virtually unattainable by the people, were often inappropriately weighted (e.g., rice was less a percentage of expenditure than was actually the case), and did not reflect other parts of the state. A senior SLORC official publicly admitted in 1991 that inflation was higher than the official figures reflected.[35]

The official figures indicate that the Consumer Price Index rose from a base of 100 in 1986 to 233.7 in FY 1990/91, 301.8 in 1991/92, and 369.1 in 1992/93, and that it accelerated to 882.8 in 1996/97, 1,182.1 in 1997/98, and 1,762.2 in 1998/99. (On that scale, the index had risen ten times since FY 1970/71, but it had also doubled between 1963 and 1973.) Rice prices alone had risen 6.8 times from 1987 to 1992. The actual costs in Rangoon during that period were likely to have been much higher. Inflation under the SLORC officially averaged about 23 percent, but some observers indicated that it was more probably in the neighborhood of 50 percent and others that it was 100 percent.

The increases in the money supply also fueled inflation. From a low of K.8.1 billion after demonetization in 1987, the money supply rose rapidly. In 1990 it was K.27.1 billion and by 1992 K.57.2 billion, and in 1998 it was was K.282.791 billion. The printing of currency, carried out in Germany, was said to be under the control of the military, which then informed the Central Bank of the amounts produced. The actual totals may thus be different.

In spite of increases in civil servant pay, in March 1999 the highest monthly salary (ministerial level) was about K.2,500 (plus some rations). At just over $400 per month (at the official rate), the salary was inadequate for Rangoon living. Teachers averaged K.600 per month, or slightly under $100 at the official rate. The basic pay increased from K.450 to K.600 per month, and the minimum daily wage increased from K.15 to K.20 ($3.00 at the official rate). Supplementary incomes or black market activities were required to subsist. On April 1, 2000, the government increased civil service and military salaries by about five times, but the increase is still inadequate to cope with inflation. The increase itself will likely fuel more inflation as the state copes with the increased costs by increasing the money supply.

Growth in the GDP in FY 1992/93 was officially reported to be 10.9 percent, but estimates vary on its real growth; these range from 1.2 percent to about 8 percent that year (some knowledgeable observers estimated 4.6 percent) because of poor statistics and the low base on which it was calculated. The illusion of more rapid growth was created by later revising downward provisional figures of the previous year, thus creating contrasts that were later changed. The per capita income in 1998 was said to be K.1,670.

The Border Trade and Development

Border trade has been important since the military coup of 1962, but until 1988 it was surreptitious and concentrated along the Thai frontier. It intensified in the late 1980s because of the 1987 Burmese demonetization, which increased demand for consumer goods; Chinese internal economic liberalization, which increased capacity to supply such goods; and the clearance of border areas by the Burmese army and the collapse of the BCP, which improved access to the area. China began to replace Thailand as the principal conduit for consumer items, most of which were of Chinese manufacture. The Frontier Export Division of the Yunnan People's Export Corporation was a major factor in the trade.

By July 1988, the BSPP announced that the trade would be legalized and taxed. The SLORC formalized this plan in November 1988. Warehouses and hostels were built at critical junctures along the frontier, extensive barter and a realistic exchange rate were informally put into effect, and travel was allowed in both directions. Customs duties were levied, but anecdotal evidence indicated that the trade was far greater than officially recognized, and two-way trade was estimated at $1.5 billion. (Other sources in the early 1990s conservatively estimated the trade at $1 billion.) Burma was exporting all its primary products, including those proscribed for private trading (sixteen items including rice, teak, rubber, beans, pulses, oil, gems, and guns). China accounted for about 85 percent of border trade in FY 1988/89. Burmese statistics showed that the trade was in balance that year ($157.8 million in imports and the same in exports). By FY 1991/92, however, official statistics showed that exports from Burma were $100.3 million and imports $259.8 million, with Thailand controlling 39 percent of the trade.

The Myanmar Export Import Service controls the legalized trade by two methods: issuing licenses along the China border, with trade valued in dollars, and a "border" method, with trade locally permitted and valued in any currency. In October 1992, an "export first" system was introduced by the Burmese, under which exports must precede imports. In December 1993, the Burmese authorities indicated plans to increase the trading stations along both the Chinese and the Thai frontiers and to expand some stations to the Bangladesh border. In July 1993, China and Burma signed six agreements to increase trade and transport along the frontier.

After the SPDC took over in 1997, all border trade had to be financed by letters of credit in U.S. dollars. This created a strain on the trade because the facilities for issuing such letters were limited on the frontier, and many had to be issued from Rangoon. This regulation likely increased smuggling.

The border trade had important implications for Burmese manufacturing. Local Burmese manufactures could not compete in price or quality with Chinese goods, which flooded the market, and the porous border could not deter extra-legal imports. Thus the Burmese SEEs were deprived of a substantial, but unknown, percentage of the Burmese internal market and would have to concentrate on exports, probably under joint ventures, to be profitable. In effect, the state had sacrificed much of its manufacturing sector to assuage the urban population's demand for consumer goods that the state could not itself supply.

The SLORC announced a new Ministry for Progress of Border Areas and National Races and Development Affairs in September 1992 and promulgated the law for it in August 1993. This apparently was an aftermath of the cease-fires with a number of the minority groups and the demise of the BCP. The developments called for expansion of transport and communications facilities; improvement of health and education; and construction, trade, and the extraction of minerals. Work began in these regions in FY 1989/90, and through 1992/93 some K.1.120 billion was expended, of which K.499.91 million was from the ministry budget and K.620.51 allocated from other ministries. In 1993, the government reported the construction of 178 primary and 13 secondary schools, 31 hospitals, and 68 dispensaries. These figures were said to have risen by 1997 to 332 primary schools, 43 middle schools, 12 high schools, 40 hospitals, 78 dispensaries, and 74 rural health clinics. These minority regions, mostly in the Shan State, have been deprived of modern facilities and amenities, but critics argued that improved transport and communications would increase military capacity in the region. Extensive planned UNDP funding for projects in the region was blocked by the donor community.

In May 1993, the Chinese and Burmese met to discuss a regional "Golden Quadrangle Highway Network" to link more effectively China, Burma, Thailand, and Laos. Thailand was to lend Burma $12 million at 3 percent interest over ten years with a five-year grace period. Additional funds were to be sought from the ADB and World Bank when they began to lend to Burma once more. The ADB also has initiated discussions on establishing rail links between

Yunnan and the Shan State (a nineteenth-century British dream) and between Yunnan and the Kachin State.

Tourism

Burma has had a modest attraction for tourists since independence, although significant portions of the country have been off-limits because of security concerns. Since the military coup of 1962, tourist visas have been for as little as twenty-four hours (when the state discouraged foreign contacts), but in 1994, they had been liberalized to several weeks and tourism was encouraged. Official Burmese sources had disparaged foreign tourism as destructive of Burmese culture, pointing to the problems tourism has caused to such cities as Bangkok. The lure of foreign exchange, however, reversed that policy. The state created a Ministry of Tourism in 1992, and 1995 was designated "Visit Myanmar Year." It was later extended into 1996 and 1997 in the hope of reaching its annual goal of 500,000 tourists.

In 1987 Burma had the highest number of tourists in more than ten years— 41,904 (of whom 6,644 were Americans), and this brought in about $12 million in foreign exchange. Even this number was small compared to other countries in the region. Nepal had ten times that number in 1987, and Thailand had one hundred times more (4 million). Following the coup, however, tourism dropped even lower, to 5,044, and rose to only 8,061 in 1991 (1,095 U.S. tourists in 1992). In 1998/99 there were 287,394 tourists and 173,558 in the last half of 1999/2000.

State plans for tourism are, however, extensive. There have been major foreign investments in modernizing old hotels and building new ones, as hotel rooms have been very limited. By 1997 there were 8,300 hotel beds in Rangoon as a result of a building boom, although most of the hotels were running on minimum occupancy. There were 40 government-run hotels with 1,040 rooms; 69 private hotels, inns, and guest houses; and 97 tourist agencies. The Myanmar Holdings Corporation has entered agreements with JV Macau International to build a new hotel; the Strand Hotel has been rebuilt; the Inya Lake Hotel has been refurbished; and the Minatsu Construction Group of Japan has built a new Yangon International Hotel.[36]

Limited internal transportation will effectively constrain tourism. Air, land, and water transport are rudimentary and difficult. Tourist requirements to purchase some Burmese currency ($300) at the accommodation rate could cut travel. Chinese tourists have been allowed to cross the Chinese frontier, and plans were formulated to allow tourists to enter from Thailand and to fly directly to central Burma as well.[37]

The Environment and the Economy

Because of the favorable population-to-land ratio, the low level of industry, modest urbanization, and good forest management prior to the SLORC, environmental issues had received little attention until recently. There had been significant losses of wildlife (rhinoceros, elephants, tigers) because of the widespread availability of guns in the insurrections and the breakdown of state control in many areas over the years beginning with World War II.

Since the SLORC, however, international concern over environmental issues has become widespread. The need to garner foreign exchange led to the timber concessions to the Thai and the clear-cutting of large areas of teak forests along the Thai border. As noted, this resulted in pressures to restrict these concessions, and eventually they were closed. There also have been extensive shipments of logs to China. Many observers have questioned the rate of replanting of teak that the Burmese authorities have claimed in the past.

Salt water fisheries are also an issue. Although Burmese waters have been underfished because of the low level of technology available to the fishermen, by August 31, 1993, some $88 million in foreign investment had entered this field, and the level of technology (and thus the catch) had risen dramatically. The Burmese have little capacity to monitor internal or external compliance with regulations or agreements, and it is likely that the catches are far in excess of official figures and could lead to depletion of these resources.

Plans to construct dams on the Salween and Chindwin Rivers to provide hydroelectric power could result in major environmental damage, as well as displacement of local populations. Agricultural expansion through plantation is displacing ecologically fragile wetlands.

External Debt

There has been a major increase in Burmese external debt since the reassessment of foreign economic relations in 1971. In 1970, before major assistance was resumed, the total debt was only $106 million, when the GNP was $2.15 billion. The debt was completely incurred by the state. Of that amount, $72 million was from official creditors, of which $15 million was from multilateral donors (the World Bank) and $57 million from bilateral donors. Private creditors were owed $34 million, all of which was guaranteed by the state.

By 1980, however, the debt had risen to $1.39 billion, when the GNP was $5.756 billion. Of this debt, $279 million was to multilateral lenders and $829 to bilateral lenders. On the advent of the SLORC government in 1988 (GNP $11.765 billion), outstanding debt had risen to $4.22 billion, $983 million owed to multilateral agencies and $2.923 million to bilateral donors.

By 1998/99, the total debt was $5.883 billion, of which $2.973 billion was in bilateral loans and $1.064 billion in multilateral loans (including $720 million from the World Bank and $244 million from the ADB). The largest bilateral loans outstanding were from Japan ($2.239 billion) and Germany ($469 million). In 1992/93, Burma was $1.029 billion in arrears, and by 1996/97 the figure had grown to $1.454 billion.[38] In 1998, Myanmar went into arrears to the World Bank and the ADB for the first time. This was a deliberate decision of the SPDC.

Increases in exports since FY 1988/89 have lowered the debt service ratio from about 100 percent in 1987/88 to about 50 percent in FY 1992/93. Repayments proceeded according to schedule ($121 million) until 1989, but in 1990 repayments dropped to $45 million and to $29 and $26 million in 1991 and 1992 respectively. Burma had continued to meet all its multilateral debt obligations by 1994 but not its bilateral ones. It has attempted to negotiate debt relief; France has canceled F 500 million in debt, and Japan annually negotiated debt relief when Burma repaid Japanese loans, which were then returned to Burma as debt relief grants.

Relocation and Resettlement

Although the effects of relocation are not normally counted in terms of their economic toll, the magnitude of such efforts by the state must have important, immediate economic consequences. Estimates indicate that perhaps a million people have been internally relocated. Many of those are around major cities, Rangoon itself accounting for approximately one-third of a million. But each major urban area has seen forced resettlement of squatters and others to the peripheries of these centers. Whatever the longer-term effects may be, in the shorter term these have caused economic dislocations.

In the hill areas, the situation is worse. In the Kachin State alone, some 63,000 people were moved into camps, where they no longer can produce rice, and were cared for by the Kachin Baptist Convention. The military has forced similar relocations to control better the populations in the Shan State and in other regions. This has required internal imports of rice and other foods, and the government has seemed incapable or unwilling to meet these requirements effectively. No accounting is available of the implicit costs of these changes.

Corruption and the Economy

Incessant inflation, inadequate public salaries, poor state policies, and the need for the reallocation of material goods internally and externally have resulted in a pattern of corruption that is endemic and pervasive. Corruption is, of course, culturally defined, but when a society opens to world trade, corruption becomes an element of more than local concern and takes on international definitions. Smuggling, the illegal resale of goods from government stores, and payoffs (from procurement to legal fees) have, according to many citizens, become the means required to maintain even modest standards of living. The impact on the individual citizen is critical but outside the scope of this chapter, but the impact on the economy is profound. The unpredictability of the costs of doing business at all levels because of corruption amounts to a major disincentive for investment in any but the most exploitative or rent-seeking activities. Although the situation cannot be quantified, anecdotal evidence from foreign investors and residents alike indicates that the problem is severe and is likely to undercut the efficacy of government, its efficiency, and its political legitimacy.

In 1988, this author wrote the following:

> Burma by necessity has become a nation of illegal consumers and traders. Corruption is rife. Few get their legal weights or measures of scarce goods; a few pounds underweight on bags of rice or fertilizer, or a few ounces off a gallon of gasoline over time can support a family. Everyone must operate on the black market. One's ration of gasoline illegally sold can give one the same salary as a managing director of a government corporation. A trip abroad for a government official or a student, bringing back consumer goods and paying legal duties on them, can net the official traveler up to the equivalent of $15,000 (K.100,000) at the legal rate of exchange, or give a mid-level official his only chance for economic viability. . . . Everyone needs an extra source of income.[39]

The Future of the Burmese Economy: Problems and Prospects

The potential of the Burmese economy is extensive. Its natural resources are vast and as yet incompletely explored, let alone exploited. Its potential arable land is double that under cultivation. Its offshore mineral and fishery capacities are vastly underutilized. Its population is modest compared to its land area, and it is literate. The status of women is high, and few social forces integral to the society theoretically limit growth with equity.

The economic problems facing Burma are not primarily in natural resource endowments; they are in policies—both political and economic. For a generation and a half Burma had in effect cut itself off from new technologies, allowed its infrastructure to deteriorate, micromanaged an economy and a market it had few resources to administer, spent on the military rather than on investment, encouraged political correctness over competence, indirectly and then overtly encouraged many of its educated youth to leave, denied itself many of the resources of its border regions by refusing to negotiate settlements with its minorities in revolt, and disparaged foreigners and those Burmese who knew well the international markets and Burma's potential role in them.

As discussed above, the SLORC since 1988 has wrought some changes. The private sector has been encouraged within limits; the number of registered private businesses grew from 33,964 in 1990/91 to 51,738 in 1997/98, but state-owned enterprises dropped only to 1,600 from 1,765 over the same period.[40] Although not a market economy, Burma has become more sensitive to both internal and external market forces. Foreign investment has been advocated, and with it has come some new technologies. Indigenous investment has been fostered, but private businessmen and traders are regarded with profound suspicion by the military. Some administrative changes have been positive. Various subterfuges have been employed in foreign transactions to avoid wholesale devaluation of the kyat. Socialism as an ideology has been discarded, although the long arm of the dirigiste state is still ubiquitous and apparent.

Fundamental reforms in 2000 were still lacking. (See Appendix I for a November 1988 memorandum to the World Bank cataloguing the problems facing the economy. None of the issues raised there have been adequately addressed.) The money supply has remained uncontrolled. A formal, realistic, general exchange rate devaluation was avoided. Indigenous capital was still subject to political control. The SEEs were inefficient in both management and production. The private banking system was subject to extensive state direction. Although new financial institutions were formed, they had yet to prove their efficacy. The uncertain political future and problems with human rights, together with the lack of overall economic rationalization, limited the availability of foreign assistance, although low wages and a controlled labor force interested some foreign investors in labor-intensive industries.

New or recurring socioeconomic problems appeared. Because the state did not supply sufficient capital for private investment, those with access to such capital were from three groups: the indigenous and external Chinese community, the Indian community, and high-ranking military officials.[41] Thus the developing middle class, which will have a major role in the expanding Burmese economy, may become largely foreign. The Burman population may again see, as it did in the 1930s, the economy moving under foreign control, and this could result in a nationalistic, socialistic reaction.

The military will retain strong economic interests. In 1991, it formed the Myanmar Holdings Corporation. By 1994, the corporation already had joint ventures with foreign firms in manufacturing.[42] Through it, the military will be able to retain a substantial hold over the economy. For the next decade, military expenditures are expected to remain high, thus undercutting the funds available for both investment and social services. The future of the Burmese economy has continuously been held hostage to the political process, which continued to be dominated by the *tatmadaw.*

APPENDIX A—Selected Targets of the Five-Year Plan (1996/97–2000/2001)

	Base year 1995/96	1996/97	2000/01
Paddy (000 m/t)	19,568	20,865	23,369
Groundnut (000 m/t)	569	590	687
Cotton (000 m/t)	214	324	661
Sugar cane (000 m/t)	3,061	3,841	6,350
Teak (000 c/t)	256	220	250
Crude oil (million U.S. barrels)	6.87	10.95	12.78
Natural gas (million cubic ft.)	69,540	73,000	401,500

Table continues on next page.

APPENDIX A—(*continued*)

	Base year 1995/96	1996/97	2000/01
Tin concentrates (m/t)	492	505	1,787
Tungsten con. (m/t)	95	97	343
Gold (troy oz.)	22,496	24,480	24,580
Copper ore (000 m/t)	1,700	1,750	11,200
Jade (000 kg.)	335	400	600
Gems (000 carat)	5,155	5,500	7,500
Coal (000 long tons)	48.0	99.7	342.2
Cement (m/t)	523.5	527.0	637.8
Fertilizer (m/t)	300.0	300.0	825.0
Electricity (million kwh)	3,780	3,994	6,177

Source: An Outline of the Five Year Plan of the Union of Myanmar (1996/97–2000/2001) (Yangon: Ministry of National Planning and Economic Development, May 1996).

APPENDIX B—1999 World Bank Economic and Social Assessment Summary

Bradley Babson

Human Rights Watch Meeting, December 16, 1999 Washington, D.C.

Background

1. The draft report was prepared based on a mission last June that was conducted in a low key way in parallel with the IMF Article IV Consultation mission. The mission received a high degree of cooperation from the government and also the UN agencies and INGOs working in Yangon. The two senior members of the mission were invited to meet with Aung San Suu Kyi at a luncheon organized by the Australian Ambassador, and discussed their preliminary findings with her in a pleasant and substantive meeting.

2. The last Bank economic report on Myanmar was prepared in 1994/5, and we felt that it was important to update our knowledge of the situation and

especially the poverty and social conditions, in view of increased international attention to the situation in Myanmar and the impact of both economic policies and the Asian financial crisis on economic and social conditions.

3. Collaboration with the IMF has been an important part of this process. In previous years, Bank staff were invited to participate in the Fund's annual Article IV Consultation missions. These are conducted under the surveillance mandate that the Fund has with all its member countries. This year, we decided to send a separate mission in parallel with the Fund in order to undertake a broader economic and social assessment, with a particular focus on poverty. The Fund report incorporated information from the Bank's assessment and our report draws heavily on the macroeconomic and financial sector assessment provided by the Fund. The two reports provide the most comprehensive surveillance assessment ever conducted on Myanmar.

4. The draft report was given to the Myanmar authorities during the Annual Meetings here in Washington last September. We also sent a number of copies to the UNDP Resident Representative in Yangon and asked him in his capacity of UN Resident Coordinator to make copies available to local Embassies and to give one to Aung San Suu Kyi in anticipation of a proposed visit in October by the UN Special Envoy Alvaro De Soto with Bank participation. The report was discussed in general terms during that visit.

5. The government has not given us detailed comments on the report, but has requested that a Bank mission visit Yangon to obtain comments and discuss the report's findings and recommendations, with the intention of finalizing the report. We have asked the government for a clear indication in writing that the SPDC is prepared to address the core issues raised in the report and to provide their general comments, and this will affect the scheduling of any further mission. What we are looking for is some concrete indication that the SPDC is prepared to take the report's assessment seriously and to discuss the issues in a spirit of genuine policy dialogue. We are also insisting on an open process that includes the comments and concerns of civil society and the private sector. While the Bank is not permitted under our Articles of Agreement to take sides in the political debate, we do believe that all interested groups should have access to the report and have an opportunity to share their views and concerns. This is very similar to how we have conducted our role in Indonesia during the past year in a situation of significant political flux. As I mentioned before, the draft report has been provided to the NLD.

Major Findings and Recommendations

1. Let me now give you some more details of the report's findings and recommendations.

2. First, the basic conclusion of the report is that the kind of growth that Myanmar has been achieving has not been delivering improvements in employment, human development and poverty reduction that will be needed if Myanmar is to achieve its potential. Our bottom line assessment is that Myanmar needs both major reforms and external finance to obtain the kind of development that would best serve the country's long term interests. Progress on removing core inefficiencies will be needed before a broad structural reform process can get underway. Foreign investment and ODA will be needed, but these will only be forthcoming if Myanmar can satisfy the social justice concerns of the international community that are reflected in UN resolutions.

3. The core program that we recommend would seek to reform and/or dismantle (i) the fictitious official exchange rate and its rationing; (ii) the complex and inefficient mechanism for rice procurement, its domestic distribution and export; (iii) wide-ranging restrictions on private sector activity; (iv) budgetary priorities that squeeze expenditure on social services and infrastructure; and (v) inefficient state enterprises that claim a large share of public resources and government attention. Implementation of these reforms would set the economy on the path to broad-based growth and would create the room for implementing the large agenda of structural reform.

Poverty and Human Development

4. Although Myanmar's economy continues to register moderate income growth (GNP growth was 5 percent in 1998/99), the benefits of this growth are poorly distributed since most poverty and human development indicators are unsatisfactory. At $300 per capita, Myanmar is one of the poorest countries in the World. Life expectancy at birth is 60 compared with an average in East Asia of 68; infant mortality is 79 per thousand births, compared with the East Asia average of 34; child malnutrition rates are very high and represent the "silent emergency" in Myanmar. Wasting affects 30% of children under age 10, reflecting long term deprivation. Education is also a major concern. Official statistics indicate that a quarter of school age children never even enroll in

primary school, and that drop out rates are very high. Of those who begin the primary education program, only a third complete the full 5 years.

5. According to a government determined poverty line, about one quarter of the population of Myanmar lives below minimal subsistence levels. Poverty rates are approximately the same in urban and rural areas, but most of the poor (71 percent) live in rural areas. There is considerable regional variation in poverty rates. The highest rates of poverty are in the Chin State, Magway Division, and Kayah State, and the lowest rates are in the Tanintharyi Division and Shan State.

Structural Imbalances and Proposed Reform

6. Looking back over the past decade, the economy responded well to the liberalization of 1988. There was a significant expansion in investment, which reached US$800 million in 1996/97 compared to US$58 million in 1990/91. Exports tripled to US$1 billion a year between 1988/89 to 1997/98. GDP growth averaged over 7% per year up until 1997. In recent years, however, growth has run out of steam and has not benefited the poor, an acute currency shortage has emerged, and private capital flows have collapsed. The growth last year is estimated to have been 5%, fueled mainly by disbursements of foreign private investment on projects committed in the mid 1990's. Continued decline in growth is inevitable, unless Myanmar is able to attract new foreign investment, obtain aid flows that were cut off after 1988, or undertake reforms in public finance and banking to increase domestic resources for investment, which are extremely low by international standards. This has led to a situation where Myanmar is caught in a low-level equilibrium trap with serious macroeconomic imbalances.

Macroeconomic Imbalance

7. The official *exchange rate* is pegged to around 6 Kyats per US$1, while the June 1999 market exchange rate was 340 Kyats per US$1. Following the economic slowdown, tighter administrative controls have been put in place to ration foreign exchange. The foreign exchange controls generate substantial protection for state enterprises in their imports and create strong incentives for rent-seeking activities. Relative prices are distorted thus impeding

agricultural and private sector development, and rendering official statistics less credible.

8. Unification of the official and parallel market exchange rates would be equivalent to a significant *trade reform.* The present exchange rate system results in a large protection to the favored state enterprises, much larger than implied by the average tariff rate of 6 percent. In addition, the extensive trade barriers also need to be eliminated.

9. The *government budget* has remained unbalanced with substantial deficits during much of the 1990s. Fiscal deficits are financed automatically by credit from the Central Bank, a source of domestic inflation and instability in the economy. The ratio of taxes to GDP, at 3.5 percent, is very low by international standards. Although the government has sought to broaden the tax base by bringing more services into the commercial tax net (similar to a VAT), the system is riddled with exemptions given to both foreign as well as domestic investors. Tax revenues are also eroded by poor tax compliance (caused by corruption and a weak valuation system for imports) and inflation.

10. State enterprises are a drain on the budget but their true impact is clouded by the dual exchange rate system. *State enterprise reform and privatization must be pursued more vigorously. This must accompany a reform of the budget process* which, at present, continues in the tradition of central planning, with state enterprises driving the process rather than broader economy-wide revenue and expenditure projections.

11. A monetary policy that accommodates the flawed budgetary process contributes to the double-digit *inflation,* which peaked at 68 percent in mid-1998 and fluctuated widely during most of the decade.

12. A *public resource mobilization* effort needs to be geared up to protect public expenditures on basic services. The poor resource mobilization activity has adversely affected maintenance of essential infrastructure and the delivery of social services, impeding in turn broad based economic growth and human development. *The structural reforms recommended (including reform of the exchange rate, the budgetary process, state enterprises, tax policy and tax administration and others that follow) are urgently needed to strengthen resource mobilization to promote broad-based economic growth and human development.* Clearly a major issue is the balance between military expenditures and social and infrastructure expenditures. Published budget figures show that per capita spending on the military is 9 times that of health services and twice that of education services, and the trends have been worsening. It seems that mili-

tary expenditures have also been declining because of poor revenue performance, which means that a major area for policy dialogue and change is in the allocation of future incremental revenues.

Agriculture and the Environment

13. Rural poverty and agriculture are closely linked in Myanmar: for over half of poor rural households, agricultural production is the primary economic activity. And yet, agricultural growth has stagnated since the mid 1990s. The decline is even more dramatic in growth per capita. This lends support to the claim that recent overall GDP growth has not been sufficient nor has it benefited the poor. Also, it underscores the need for a second generation of structural reforms to rejuvenate agriculture.

1. Rice Procurement and Export. Rice is the most important crop in the Myanmar economy and removing distortions on procurement and export of rice would have wide repercussions.

- *First stage: Removal of exchange rate distortion:* As a first step, the state enterprise exporting rice, Myanmar Agricultural Produce Trading (MAPT), be turned into an autonomous corporation with independent management.
- *Second stage: Removal of price distortion:* The second stage of reform would aim at removing the distortions in price policy.
- *Third stage: Removal of MAPT monopoly* on exports; elimination of compulsory rice procurement; privatization of MAPT.

   1. Agricultural inputs and services: The reform program would not be possible without market based delivery of inputs to farmers. In particular, farmer access to credit needs to be improved.

   2. Land reclamation: The reform program outlined above would improve the use of existing cultivated land and move toward bridging the large yield gap between Myanmar farmers and their counterparts in the Association of Southeast Asian Nations (ASEAN). It would also redress rural poverty frontally by increasing agricultural incomes. The government has been following a different approach in recent years that emphasizes increasing agricultural output by bringing new lands under cultivation. We have some serious questions about the environmental and economic cost of these schemes and have suggested that there be a halt until further study and debate can take place.

3. Preserving forest: Annual de-forestation rates have doubled (to 1.4 percent) since the late 1980s. Population growth, inappropriate land use and poor forest tenure policies account for this. To check this alarming trend, priority should be given to developing a national land-use plan, clarifying land ownership and use rights, proper land titling, encouraging leases for establishing community-based forests in degraded forest areas and promotion of alternative fuels (including kerosene).

Private Sector Development

14. Myanmar's private sector is remarkably resilient and has survived the socialist era and the many hurdles and controls that continue to affect the costs of doing business. The need, of course, is to continue the consolidation of the private sector via a new generation of reforms.

- To allow the private sector greater room in the economy, the role of *state enterprises* will have to be scaled down. The inefficient state enterprises distort relative prices for the private sector, lay claim to the bulk of scarce credit and attract most of the government attention. Furthermore, their survival is possible only by curtailing private sector competition. Thus state enterprise reform must be a top priority.

- Following the establishment of a Privatization Commission in 1995, the Government has undertaken some steps toward *privatization.* In practice, however, progress has been slow. While it is difficult to make outright sales in the context of macro-economic uncertainty and lack of investor interest, authorities could do the ground work and clarify their intentions by developing and announcing a systematic Privatization Master Plan. This would focus on the institutional design for privatization, valuation of entities to be designed, and developing an appropriate regulatory framework for the privatized entities.

- A healthy *financial sector* is key to private sector development and economic strength. Myanmar is seriously under banked, the accounting and clearing systems need modernization, there is little competition to the large state-owned banks and the administered interest rates do not reflect scarcity of capital. Reform would require establishing a level playing field for state-owned and private banks (particularly in foreign exchange dealings and reserve requirements), a restructuring of state-owned banks and granting of bank licenses to joint ventures, and to foreign-owned banks to begin operations (initially for a limited range of activities).

- The legal framework for conducting private business is badly in need of modernization, particularly regarding the Foreign Investment Law, the Citizen's Investment Law, the Financial Institutions of Myanmar Law, accounting and auditing standards and the Insurance Business Law. The legal changes would aim at reducing regulatory burdens and restrictions on the private sector, simplifying transfer of ownership, facilitating repatriation of profits, improving access to foreign and domestic credit, and increasing the reliability of enterprise financial statements.
- Myanmar has taken some steps recently to improve its woefully inadequate infrastructure via pricing reforms in electricity and telecommunications. In the rural areas, isolation due to poor infrastructure is a severe problem. It prevents access to markets and delivery of social services. Improvement in rural infrastructure requires urgent attention.

Delivery of Social Services

15. *Health.* Some of the news on health outcomes is encouraging, but declining public confidence in publicly-provided services is of concern. A serious concern is that over the last 10 years, usage of public hospitals and dispensaries has fallen by 80 percent. This stems principally from low budgetary outlays (at about 0.2 percent public expenditure in Myanmar, is far below regional and developing country averages). This adversely affects availability of health care staff and medicines and the quality of equipment.

16. *Nutrition.* Data collected by both the Ministry of Health and UNICEF show high levels of moderate and severe malnutrition among preschool-age children. There is substantial scope for expanding supplementary feeding programs and maternal education programs. In designing an effective program, national and international experience suggests that the following should be borne in mind: i) food be supplied to needy children along with information to the care givers about good nutrition and feeding practices; ii) prevention of malnutrition is often more important than reversing severe malnutrition; iii) maintaining the already good breast-feeding practices is a priority; and (iv) supplementary feeding programs need to incorporate affordable and locally-available foods.

17. *Education.* As I mentioned earlier, low enrollment in primary education is a serious concern. It is impossible to provide good quality education services with the substantial erosion in education spending over the past decade. Current government spending in education as a share of national income is among the lowest in the world. Official data shows that real public spending per child has fallen from about 1200 Kyats per child (5-9 years) in 1990/91 to a dismal 100 Kyats in 1999/2000. Education financing is further confounded by the lack of affordability at the household level. The cost barrier is compounded by the poor quality of infrastructure and little adaptability of schooling (including schedules and curricula) to local conditions.

18. A number of long-standing, and well-known, basic issues need to be addressed to improve education outcomes in Myanmar: i) reversing the trend of declining public resource allocations for primary education; ii) exempting the poorest children from school fees and other substantial contributions while providing additional support to help cover such direct costs of schooling, as textbooks and uniforms; iii) developing flexible school hours to enable participation by children who need to contribute to family incomes; iv) increasing teacher salaries in real terms, and (v) reviewing transfer and departmental policies that encourage teachers to move out of rural areas.

Towards Better Economic Management

19. Implementing the reforms outlined above implies a different role for the government than the current one. At present the Government is all pervasive. This is a hugely demanding role that few societies have been able to sustain. It places a severe burden on scarce administrative resources; civil servants can be good regulators to protect the public interest but their training and education does not equip them to run factories. Furthermore, the dominant government presence in key sectors crowds out private individuals who could be generating economic growth and creating sustainable job opportunities.

Choice of Development Strategy

20. A macro-economic framework that is conducive to financial stability and one that sends correct signals regarding relative prices, including the price of foreign exchange;

21. Reduced government presence in direct production of goods and services;

22. Increased administrative capacity to monitor and regulate (in the public interest) private sector activity;

23. Use of appropriate fiscal tools (taxes and expenditures) to ensure that only those strategies are chosen that result in equitable income growth; and

24. Ensure adequate financing and institutional capacity to deliver social services that improve poverty and human development indicators and facilitate broad-based participation in growth.

Civil Service Reform

25. Myanmar has inherited a sound tradition of civil service that is badly in need of rehabilitation. The key to the transition outlined above would be the reform of the civil service to increase technical capacity and reward performance. Key elements of the reform would be in the areas of compensation and training:

- *Salary adjustment:* Salaries of public servants are low and have not been adjusted to keep up with inflation or with the private sector emoluments. A thorough review of the salary structure is needed to attract and retain the best talent in the civil service and to discourage corrupt practices.
- *Training:* Modern economic management requires continuous training. The lack of training assistance for the past 10 years has taken its toll on the middle level of the government, and this represents a significant drag on potential for improving policies and implementation of programs. The question of providing technocratic training assistance deserves to be revisited.

Working with Civil Society

26. NGOs already are playing an important if limited role in efforts to reduce poverty and promote human development in Myanmar. This can be strengthened by improving the working relationship of NGOs with the Government. Specifically, (i) the process for obtaining memoranda of understanding needs to be simplified and approval time reduced; and (ii) the framework for NGO operations should be clarified and standardized to facilitate day-to-day

operations and delineate longer term involvement in human development in Myanmar.

Conclusion

1. I have tried to give you a good understanding of the topics covered by our report and our views. Fundamentally, Myanmar is facing two major issues as the country grapples with its history and present day challenges. The first is the relationship of the State to the peoples of the country. And the second is the role of the State in the economy. Since it obtained independence after World War Two, Myanmar has been struggling to shape a national identity that can secure both stability and well being for the 48 million people representing over 100 ethnic groups. Social and economic policies followed by the military government since the early 1960s have given a high priority to maintaining stability at the expense of realizing Myanmar's potential for economic and social progress. The result has been an erosion of social capital and very low progress on building modern public institutions. Our basic assessment is that the policies that Myanmar has been following will not yield long term stability and development unless it adopts a more "pro-people" stance. It is for this reason that we believe that World Bank collaboration with the United Nations is a practical way to help Myanmar resolve long-standing political and human rights controversies, tackle poverty, and improve the social welfare of the diverse population. We hope that by working in a coordinated and not disjointed way we can use our respective mandates to promote social justice and poverty reduction to help Myanmar find the right path for the future of the country. I hope that our draft report can make a contribution to this objective.

Notes

1. Cited in Maung Maung, *Aung San of Burma* (The Hague: Martinus Nijhoff, 1962), p. 136.

2. U Myint at International Symposium on Interaction for Progress in Myanmar in ASEAN, Yangon, October 23–24, 1998. U Myint is senior economic affairs officer, ret., ESCAP, UN.

3. For a note on sources, see "Notes on Data," p. xxxiii.

4. Ministry of National Planning and Economic Development, *An Outline of the Five-Year Plan of the Union of Myanmar (1996/97–2000/2001)* (Yangon, May 1996).

5. Australia, Department of Foreign Affairs and Trade, *Burma (Myanmar)* (Canberra, May 1997), p. 24.

6. A British expedition was sent to the Kachin hills in the nineteenth century before the British annexation of that area to search for the *ficus elastica,* the rubber tree.

7. At the time of the 1931 census, Indians represented 7 percent of the total population of the country. See Teruko Saito and Lee Kin Kiong, *Statistics on the Burmese Economy: The 19th and 20th Centuries* (Singapore: Institute for Southeast Asian Studies, 1999), p. 15.

8. The shift took place with the waning influence of Aung Gyi and the rise of a strong leftist, Tin Pe.

9. David I. Steinberg, *Burma's Road toward Development: Growth and Ideology under Military Rule* (Boulder: Westview Press, 1981).

10. To qualify for LDC status, incomes were supposed to be below $200 per capita per annum, industrial production had to be below 10 percent of GDP, and literacy was supposed to be below 20 percent. Burma had won UNESCO awards for its literacy program, and official Burmese statistics claimed that Burma was over two-thirds literate (the United Nations calculated 78 percent) in 1986. By UN standards, Burma did not qualify for this dubious distinction. After receiving the UNESCO awards, Burmese statistics on literacy conveniently dropped from 78 percent in 1986 to 18 percent, but then mysteriously rose the following year to 82 percent in spite of school closures.

11. See chapter 8.

12. In 1987, when the government freed rice sales, it had 6,000 redundant employees who had collected rice, but the BSPP prevented their firing for political reasons (personal communication from a Burmese official). Given the number of those employed by the state directly in the civil service and casual labor, through the SEEs, and through the military, there are close to 1.5 million people employed. With an average family size of four individuals, some 6 million are directly dependent on the state, or over 12 percent of the population. It is difficult to calculate state employees of all sorts because figures vary widely. In one report, the government indicated there were 640,000 employees of the national government and 303,000 in the SEEs. Another figure indicates that total public sector employment was 1,410,000. Deducting these amounts, as well as a potential 17,000 in local government, leaves the military with 450,000. There can be no claim to the accuracy of these figures, but they represent a reasonable assessment of a complex problem.

13. The increase to the military and civil service on April 1, 2000, at the beginning of the fiscal year, was substantial—some five times previous levels—but several months later it had not been officially announced. Some officials told staff that this was to ensure their loyalty to the regime in the hard times expected ahead. How this would be paid for, aside from printing money, was unclear.

14. The trade balance has been in deficit since 1973/74.

15. David I. Steinberg, *The Future of Burma: Crisis and Choice in Myanmar* (Lanham: University Press of America and The Asia Society, 1990); Asian Agenda Report 14; IMF, 1993; Union of Myanmar, 1993.

16. IMF, 1993

17. The Myanmar Holdings Corporation had a potential capital of some 20 percent of official GNP in 1990. It had authorized capital of K. 10 billion, of which 40 percent is held by the Directorate of Procurement, Ministry of Defense, and 60 percent subscribed by service personnel, defense regiments, and veterans both individually and by unit. It had wholly owned ventures in banking, trade, tourism, gems, and real estate. It also had joint ventures with foreign firms in garment factories, consumer product factories, gems, wood products, and trade.

18. The Myanmar Economic Corporation has business interests in industrial planning, iron and steel factories, heavy industries, foodstuffs, trade, banking, tourism, gems, minerals, power, and transportation. It involves active-duty military, while the Myanmar Holding Corporation has both active-duty and retired military investors.

19. K.14,370.8 million was in circulation in 1986 (before demonetization), and in 1998/99, it reached K.282,791 million (*Review of the Financial, Economic and Social Conditions for 1991/92* [Yangon: Ministry of Planning and Finance, 1991], p. 220); World Bank, 1999. Rumors are that it was even higher. The black market rate for kyat exploded from about K.70 to $1 to K.90 and had reached as high as K.360 in late 1999. The official rate is about K.6.3.

20. FBIS, May 22, 1991, from a May 21 radio address.

21. Japan, the primary donor, has provided some debt relief and has continued previously approved projects but has started no new ones. See chapter 9 and David I. Steinberg, "Japanese Economic Assistance to Burma: Aid in the Tarenagashi Manner?" in *Managing Japan's Foreign Aid: Power and Policy in a New Era,* ed. Bruce Koppel and Robert Orr (Boulder: Westview Press, 1993), and also in *Crossroads* (Northern Illinois University) 5, 2 (1990).

22. For example, teak production increased from 291,000 cubic tons in 1988/89 to 440,000 cubic tons in 1990/91, the peak since that date.

23. This is the last official published figure from December 1989. The state has not published data since that time (the IMF and the World Bank have, however). Myanmar is servicing its multilateral debt and some of its Japanese debt but is in arrears on that and on German debt. The French in 1991 forgave much of Myanmar's debt.

24. Vietnam has experienced a drop in foreign investment of some 60 percent since the Asian financial crisis of 1997, but in Myanmar it has been even more precipitous. Both had massive investments from ASEAN countries. There have been growing problems with the Vietnamese administration, but they are far less severe than those in Myanmar, at least in part because the legitimacy of the Vietnamese government is not in question.

25. FBIS, October 7, 1991, from a speech of October 4, 1991. This figure may be cumulative for 1988–91.

26. In 1975, 86 percent of farmers had less land than they needed to rise above the poverty level (Steinberg, *Burma's Road toward Development,* p. 79).

27. IMF 1993; Union of Myanmar 1993; World Bank 1999, U.S. Embassy reports. See Myat Thein and Maung Maung Soe, "Economic Reforms and Agricultural Development in Myanmar." ASEAN Economic Bulletin, Singapore. April 1998.

28. Peter G. Warr, "The Failure of Myanmar's Agricultural Policies," in *Southeast Asian Affairs 2000* (Singapore: Institute of Southeast Asian Studies, 2000), pp. 219–33.

29. Thailand had overfished its waters and needed new areas to exploit. This led to a number of fishing contracts with Myanmar in the early 1990s., When Myanmar suspended its fishing contracts, allegedly Thai companies were losing more than $3 million per day—four times the recorded average daily crossborder trade of both nations.

30. The data are further complicated by factors such as the Thai illegally cutting inside their own borders, then shipping the logs into Myanmar, and then claiming they were imported. A scandal was uncovered in 1998, but it obviously had been going on some time and under earlier Thai governments. It might be recalled that General Chavalit's family had logging interests in Thailand that could not legally be exploited because of the Thai ban on internal logging, and thus the Burmese connection was especially useful. Chavalit was commander of the Thai army in 1988 and remains an influential politician.

31. Steinberg, *Burma's Road toward Development.*

32. Australia, Department of Foreign Affairs and Trade, p. 25.

33. The figures as taken from the U.S. Embassy, *Burma Country Commercial Guide,* 1999, p. 87.

34. "Investment Climate Statement: Burma," Rangoon cable 001939, unclassified, July 23, 1999.

35. Inflation in the past decade has never fallen below 16 percent, but it is based on a 1986 consumption basket and reflects only official prices, with the implication that such data are badly underestimated. IMF Staff Country Report 99/134, rev. 1999.

36. The tourist business has greatly expanded judging from the statistics:

	1992/93	1997/98
Tour guide businesses	87	2,763
Hotels and lodge houses	46	548
Tourist transport	71	1,620
Tourist enterprises	69	622

Source: Industrial Development and Reforms in Myanmar: ASEAN and Japanese Perspectives, a report of a symposium by the Sasakawa Southeast Asia Cooperation Fund (Bangkok: White Lotus, 1999), p. 27. (Cited hereafter as Sasakawa Report.)

37. In 2000 NGO human rights groups protested the publication of a new guide to Myanmar by the Lonely Planet group on charges that it would encourage tourism.

The NLD had opposed tourism as it economically supported the regime and enhanced its legitimacy.

38. Sasakawa Report, p. 30.

39. "Neither Silver nor Gold: The Fortieth Anniversary of the Burmese Economy," in *Independent Burma at Forty Years: An Assessment,* ed. Josef Silverstein (Ithaca: Cornell University, Southeast Asia Program, 1989). The exact configuration of corruption may have evolved, but the basic forces remain quite constant.

40. Sasakawa Report, p. 24.

41. Minoru Kiryu, "The Role of Small and Medium-Sized Enterprises in the Industrial Development of Myanmar," lists five sources of private capital: (1) overseas Chinese; (2) local investment from commercial funds; (3) Burmese working abroad and returnees; (4) former bureaucrats; and (5) armed forces investment in the economy. He notes that remittances from overseas workers were only K.520 million in 1991 but were K.2,470 million in 1996. There were 20,000 Burmese workers in Japan, of whom 60 percent were illegal, and they remitted Y 8 billion in 1996 alone. (In Sasakawa Report, pp. 13–15.) The World Bank calculates that "net private transfers" (essentially remittances) rose from $76.5 million in 1990/91 to $514.6 million in 1998/99 (World Bank, 1999). The Tun Foundation Bank Report estimates remittance transfers at $800 million to $1 billion. In the spring of 2000, the government abruptly announced that all Burmese working overseas had to remit 50 percent of their incomes to Burma, where families would receive the equivalent in foreign exchange certificates. The uproar was immediate, and the plan was quickly dropped. Overseas Burmese are still taxed 10 percent of their income.

42. The Sasakawa Report lists six, but there are believed to be more: Myanmar Segye International—clothing (Korea); Myanmar Noveau—rubies, sapphires (Thailand); Rothmans of Pall Mall, Myanmar—cigarettes (Singapore); Myanmar Daewoo—clothing (Korea); Myanmar Brewery—beer (Singapore); Myanmar Daewoo International—garments, drinks (Korea). Together these firms employ over 5,000 people.

CHAPTER 6

Multiethnicity and the
Burmese State

*Now when we build our new Burma, shall we build it as a Union or as a
Unitary State? In my opinion, it will not be feasible to set up a Unitary
State. We must set up a Union with properly regulated provisions to safe-
guard the rights of the National minorities. But we must take care that
"United we stand" and not "United we fall."*

—Aung San, 1947[1]

*We want to establish peace in our country. It is not a time to confront
each other because we need national conciliation. We have reached
cease-fire agreements and the next step is political dialogue. We must
establish trust. After bloodbaths lasting nearly half a century, we must
establish trust with the view that one day reconciliation will come about.*

—Nai Shwe Kyin, Head, New Mon State Party, 1996[2]

*We [minorities] must first survive as a people, then we can talk about
democracy.*

—Karen leader, 1998[3]

Aung San's 1947 comment, wisely sensitive to the threats to the incipient Burmese state, was in part reflected in the constitution of 1947,
ignored to the peril of the military in the constitution of 1974, and
likely to be dismissed to a significant degree under SPDC rule. The issue is the

most problematic one facing any Burmese regime, and far more significant than issues of economic policy or even representative government. It is the single most enduring question facing any Burmese government, and yet it is treated with less attention and sensitivity than it deserves.

The diverse ethnicity that was, and is, Southeast Asia was completely ig-nored in the Western political scramble for access and power in the modern era. The European introduction of rigidly demarcated boundaries, to which power and sovereignty horizontally radiated and which was based on political and sometimes geographic circumstances, failed to consider the ethnicity or other forms of self-identification among the peoples of the region. The result was the formation of states but not of nations with a shared vision of their solidarity. There is no country in Southeast Asia that is essentially homogene-ous in ethnicity or language. The creation of such nations, the search for unity and cohesion and a sense of power justly shared, has been the task, never easily fulfilled, of the newly independent countries of the region.[4] Nowhere is this better illustrated than in Burma: "Each government of the Union of Burma has attempted to create this sense of nationhood—a sharing of national values and will amongst all of its diverse people. Yet, each effort has to a major degree been unsuccessful. Although a 'Union of Burma' as a state was titularly cre-ated, a union of people as a nation was not."[5]

The issues of minority and majority, ethnicity, race, and related questions have been made more complex by intentional inattention, obfuscation, ethnic nationalism, a lack of realism, military arrogance, and questionable termi-nology. As noted in chapter 2, the SLORC/SPDC has insisted on using the term "race" for the diverse groups within the country. Ironically, they count the number of such "races" as 135, which is a figure from the colonial era and was based on a survey of linguistic diversity, including a variety of dia-lects, and certainly not race in any internationally acceptable use of that term.[6] Even concepts of ethnicity have undergone revisions. The static identifica-tion of peoples has been subject to intellectual criticism, and even the con-cepts of "majority" and "minority" in ethnic or linguistic terms have been revisited.[7]

The traditional Burmese kingdom was expansionist when central authority was strong, and the Burmese invasions of Bengal and Manipur in the early nineteenth century were the precipitating causes of the gradual British dissec-tion of the kingdom. The amalgamation of various ethnic groups of greater or lesser political sophistication within what became the Burmese Empire was neither prompted by ethnic considerations nor by ethnic enmity, but by the control of peoples in that land-rich but people-sparse area. Ethnic conquest did exist, but the focus was not primarily on ethnicity.

The gradual British occupation of what became Burma stopped a pattern of ethnic movement that had been pronounced in earlier times. The Kachin southward migration was truncated by the British conquest of Upper Burma, and previously Shan kingdoms had been established as far away as the Chindwin valley. The Irrawaddy delta, which had been sparsely populated, mainly by Karen, became inundated with Burmans as the area was cleared for extensive rice cultivation. Today, the Burman leadership is sponsoring the expansion of Wa-occupied territory southward in the Shan State.

The Burmese have continuously accused the British of pitting one ethnic group against another—the "divide and rule" policy. To a degree this was true, but the British did not need to divide to rule; they had sufficient power. It was rather convenience that prompted them to separate "the hills" from the Burman-dominated river valleys. The periphery, a horseshoe arc of hills and mountains on the west, north, and east where many of the minority peoples resided, was governed separately from Burma Proper, or Ministerial Burma, the homeland of the Burman ethnic group (but including the Arakanese and Mon).

As the British recruited military forces in Burma, they did so from what was called the "martial races" (the hill peoples), as they had done in India, and some regiments were formed based on ethnicity—e.g., the Kachin Rifles. Approximately 87 percent of the Burma Army in the colonial period was composed of non-Burmans. Since it was the Burmans who were occasionally in revolt and who offered the major political problem as nationalism and anti-colonialism developed, the use of minority forces was a means to ensure loyalty among the troops because they would support the British and be presumed to be less reluctant to fire, if necessary, on Burmans.[8]

In addition, with British rule came the expansion of Christian missions. But the Burmans, devout Buddhists as were the Shan, were essentially impervious to missionary activity, while many of the non-Buddhist minorities were converted.[9] The tie between some of the minorities and the colonial power, especially the Karen and the British, was quite strong, and the Karen insurrections, first for an independent Karen state, which some British had unofficially advocated, and later for autonomy, became the major insurgencies after independence and continued in truncated form at the close of the century.

It was only the force of will of Aung San that was able to bring the minorities together at the Panglong Conference in the Shan State in February 1947, from which the Union of Burma was finally forged. Significantly, the Karen, who went into revolt in 1949, attended the meeting only as observers. But it was a tenuous union, for (as noted) under the constitution of 1947 the Shan State and the Kayah State were theoretically able to secede from the union after a ten-year trial period and a referendum. This was an impractical alternative that few, except some of the minorities themselves, believed could ever be implemented.

The union that was formed gave modest autonomy to the ethnic states, which had their own administrations but which were closely geared to the Burman central system. To rise in the union, one might be from a minority group, but one played by Burman rules, spoke Burmese, and went to a university where courses were taught in Burmese. Minority languages were not, and still are not, formally taught in the public education system, and they are seemingly actively discouraged. The welter of rebellions that broke out soon after independence was markedly left-wing political, not ethnic, except for the strongest—that of the Karens. At its height soon after 1949, the Karen insurrection occupied many of the major cities in the country for short periods and reached even to the suburbs of Rangoon. That continuing rebellion may be the longest in the twentieth century.

The history of the minority peoples and their tenuous relations with the Burman state are found elsewhere.[10] From independence, Burma has been a fragile state caught in conflicting tides. Bordering the huge states of China and India and with significant minorities of Chinese and Indians within the country, as well as indigenous minorities (some of whom looked with envy at developments among their linguistic cousins across international boundaries), Burma has had to deal gingerly with both states. Burma was caught in the Cold War struggle and sought to maintain its neutrality. Internally it was beset with two communist insurrections, the revolt of some of its paramilitary forces (the People's Volunteer Organization), the intrusion of Chinese Nationalist (Kuomintang) troops on its territory, and the insurrection of Muslims on the East Pakistan (later Bangladesh) frontier. The major powers (and some of the minor ones) were perceived to be in collusion with some of these divisive elements. Burma for a number of years appeared to be a besieged state. It is this siege mentality that still pervades military thinking today and is a cardinal element in the *tatmadaw*'s continued emphasis on the need for unity—for the country, for the military, and in administration and ideas and ideology.

With the coup of March 2, 1962, which heralded the military's determination that no minority peoples could hope for secession or for significant autonomy, a series of ethnic uprisings began or were accentuated, and they supplemented the two communist rebellions and the continuing Karen revolt. These uprisings probably reflected a number of changed circumstances and fears: more stringent central government control through the military; the concept of the Burman military as an occupying army in minority regions; the rise of ethnic nationalism much as Burman nationalism had grown; stricter center control over illicit trade, including narcotics, on which much of the periphery depended; and perhaps general frustration as well, for the "union" that had been created was titularly a type of federalism, but in actuality was highly centralized.

Foreigners may have consciously or unconsciously fostered these revolts by sympathizing with some of them because of concern for the underdog or Christian minorities, thus giving the minorities false hopes that they would somehow be rescued with foreign support. This specter of potential foreign intervention (specifically by the United States), however unrealistic, is one that still haunts some of the SLORC/SPDC leadership. Some unrest, especially among the Kachin, started before the coup, when U Nu announced as a political platform for the 1960 elections that he wanted to make Buddhism the state religion. It always had a special role in Burma, but the state was essentially secular in administration even as it was Buddhist in feeling.

As military control increased, the rebellions mushroomed, often driven by factional issues within some of these groups. By the 1980s, there was no major ethnic group that did not have some element of its population in revolt.[11] It must be stressed, however, that in no case was the impetus to revolt unanimous among any group; there were many instances in which those in revolt were in a distinct minority, sometimes a few hundred, and had little military power. In other cases, however, the rebels gained control of significant amounts of territory and were well armed.[12] At the start of the SLORC period, perhaps

60 percent of the land area of the country as a whole was insecure to the government at varying periods, while this represented perhaps only 10 percent of the population.

These rebellions represented an enormous financial drain on the state. Aside from the Vietnamese communists, the Burma Army was probably the most battle-hardened force in Southeast Asia, and although it remained relatively small, it was a major expense on a government whose ken was limited. No insurgency, separately or in unison, could threaten the existence of the center after the initial success of insurgents in the first few years of the republic, but they did exert pressure on the treasury, denied to the government the development of the extensive and potentially valuable resources located in those areas, allowed the minorities to engage in extensive smuggling (thus denying revenue to the center), undercut the legitimacy of the state, and kept much of the minority population in poverty.

Although it had been evident since 1962 that secession from the Union was never to be allowed as long as the military had a significant say in governmental affairs—and since independence it held veto power over critical decisions—the problem was devising a system of control that was the least repugnant in minority eyes. In 1968, Ne Win established the Internal Unitary Advisory Body, composed of civilians, many of whom had been jailed after the coup. The group was to consider what kind of administrative system for governance of the whole state, including minority areas, should be promulgated in the new constitution that the military was in the process of considering, and make recommendations to the authorities in six months. The majority finally decided on a federal system, but it was divided on whether the state should be a single-party or multiparty system. In the subsequent constitution of 1974, the military opted for a unitary state under a single-party mass mobilization system, where all power was held by the party—which meant the military—and at the center—which meant the Burmans. To create the fiction of a "union," the seven minority states (Shan, Karen, Kayah, Kachin, Mon, Arakan, and Chin) and seven divisions were proclaimed. Minority members might run for election to the Pyithu Hluttaw as government-sponsored, single-party candidates in the BSPP, but power was in Burman hands and the BSPP was to do the military's bidding. If, instead, some form of federalism had been followed, in all probability much of the subsequent bloodshed would have been avoided.

Unity was a commanding theme in military thinking in Burma, and the need for such unity at almost any cost, or perhaps the great fear of disunity, on which precipice all institutions including the state and the military tottered, dominated military policies in a variety of fields and has affected administrative structures, human rights, and ideological orientation as well.

Force held the Union together, not a sense of national unity or ethnic equity.[13] The attempts to instill a national ideology that would be cohesive proved impossible. As Burmese nationalism rose, so did ethnic nationalism. Yet as the military continued its control over minority regimes, the army acted more as an occupying force than as a locally supportive group. When U Nu thought of Buddhism as a unifying force, the minorities considered it divisive.[14] When the military inserted socialism as the nonsectarian means to unite the people, it operated as if loyalty and enthusiasm for implementation of orders were more important than competence. Now it has moved beyond all those supposedly unifying themes to concentrate on the military itself as both the unifying principle and force of the country.

With the advent of the SLORC, there were changes. Led by military intelligence under Khin Nyunt, the military sought to arrange a series of cease-fires with as many of the insurgent forces that would adhere to simple principles: if the rebels stopped fighting the army, then the minorities might engage in their traditional agricultural pursuits and the military would support increased educational facilities (in Burmese) and opportunities, improved health services, and better transportation and infrastructure in those regions. Many of the minority groups had been fighting for so long whole generations grew up that had never known peace. The cease-fires had precedents in previous practices but were double-edged. In the 1960s, the military had tried to stem the ethnic rebellions in some areas by essentially incorporating the rebel forces into a kind of local militia called the Ka Kye Ye (KKY).[15] The same criteria applied that were used later: no fighting with the Burmese military (and in some instances fighting against other rebels), and the rebels could retain their arms and engage in their traditional agricultural pursuits, which in some cases involved cultivation of the opium poppy. In the 1990s, however, the military had expanded and had modernized its equipment; although it could not wipe out the rebel forces in the vastness of the mountains and jungles, it could inflict more damage than heretofore. As each successive cease-fire was signed, this freed some troops for further counterinsurgency activities. The sole function of the Ministry for Progress of Border Areas and National Races and Development Affairs is to improve conditions along the periphery. Its work, in conjunction with line ministries such as health and education, was said to cover 64 townships with an area of 74,905 square miles and affected a population of 5.2 million. Total expenditures on the border areas since 1989 were K.8,542.0 million (about $24 million at current curb market rates), of which K.4,191.9 came from this ministry and the remainder from the others.[16]

As the government expands the road network, which is essential to moving these areas out of subsistence livelihoods and into regional (if not national) markets, it increases its grip by providing easy access. Previously, the government had little or virtually no control over some of the areas of the periphery and thus could plausibly deny responsibility for narcotics or other illegal activities. With improved access, however, the state will necessarily have to assume greater responsibility for the activities within those regions. Unless the military acts with greater discretion toward the minorities and educates its own leadership to this necessity, greater contact with the Burman majority may result in increased, rather than lessened, tensions along the border areas.

The center is represented in the periphery by a regional military commander who has the real power in the area (and who is now on the SPDC). Insofar as he may be sensitive to local issues, the relationship will be less confrontational. Before 1988, regional commanders were rotated, but this practice has diminished. There seems to have been no central and/or effective attempt to control local excesses, including gross human rights violations. There are charges, for example, that in the Chin State the local commanders have engaged in an anti-Christian campaign that exacerbates local tensions and is in contrast with the relative liberalism of worship in central Myanmar.[17]

More structural and more immediate is the question of arms. As noted, in accordance with the cease-fires, the former rebels have been able to retain their arms, even though they are not supposed to use them. In some areas, such as the Wa region on the China border, the former rebels are so strong that Burmese troops are disarmed on entering, although this is not the normal pattern in other regions. The real problems, yet to be faced, are twofold. According to present plans, when a new constitution is finally promulgated, the minorities will be required to surrender their arms. This, according to SPDC authorities, is the only way to ensure a fair election.[18] Yet it is highly unlikely that a sufficient level of trust will then exist that the minorities will be willing to do so in any manner other than as a symbolic token. Thus the potential for further trouble is likely to remain. The second issue is the government's promise to change for the better the quality of life on the periphery. In 1997/98, only about $2 million (at market rates of exchange) were allocated for such projects, a great many of which were in the transport sector and thus of little immediate benefit to the local population. If the state cannot deliver on its promises, if economic conditions continue to deteriorate, if foreign NGOs are not trusted to help provide support in those regions, and if significant foreign economic assistance is still absent (and all of the above are likely in the short term), then minority frustration could grow and impatience increase, threatening the cease-fires.

The issues will relate to what kind of a state will be proposed under the new constitution. As long ago as August 1991, in an article in the controlled press under a pseudonym, some high-ranking military official wrote that local autonomy would be provided to some of the minorities. It has become apparent that the local autonomy that will be included in the new constitution will be of a marginal nature and related to small, local groups at township or district levels. The Burmese authorities now claim that the seven large minority states, dating in part from the original constitution of 1947 and then augmented under the 1974 constitution, will no longer exist as units of governance since each of them has a variety of minority groups, many of which have been excluded from any role in government. The proposal is that smaller units of self-government be formed, and it is expected that these will essentially be located where cease-fires have been signed.

What may evolve is a system of self-government in which, for public relations, some autonomy will be granted over local issues, but in which any semblance of national power among minority groups will be avoided. The *tatmadaw* will be able to point to this system as indicating the prevalence of political and human rights in those areas, and some foreigners may be convinced that this represents a liberalizing trend. This would be inaccurate. This move may temporarily satisfy some of the smaller groups that have never had any local authority since independence, but it will not placate the major minorities and will not defuse the potential ethnic time bomb ticking away.

The government may not be fully aware that it is on the horns of a dilemma. If the national economy continues to decline or remains in a slump, then the state will not be able to deliver the improvements promised to these peoples. If, on the other hand, the central economy does well, then the minorities (as in the past) may claim that they are not receiving their just share of economic growth. In either case, the military will be hard pressed to maintain the balance necessary to prevent further violence along the frontiers. In the past, the military has often acted with brutality in these regions, although this may not have been a national policy. It is likely that because of the relative autonomy of the command structure in dealing with local problems, together with a social milieu that encourages the demeaning of minorities, there will be incidents that trigger bloodshed.

The future relations between the Burmans and many of the ethnic minorities are based on perceptions that inhibit the development of the trust necessary to ameliorate the current confrontations, even though some of the perceptions may not be accurate, apply only historically, or may be only partially true. For the cease-fires are no more than that—temporary halts in killing that could resume under a number of possible provocations.

The Burman perceptions indicate a degree of internal insecurity combined with disdain for many of the groups (as opposed to individuals within those groups). They include the following:

- The legitimate unifiers of Burma have been the Burmans. These unifiers have always been Buddhist.
- The validity of Burman hegemony was reaffirmed by Burman leadership in the anticolonial struggle.
- The Burmans are the only major ethnic group whose total population resides within the territorial bounds of the state, and thus they have a legitimate claim to power.
- The name of Burma or Myanmar is an indication of this legitimacy, and the "Myanmaification" of the state by the military reflects this.
- Minorities, foreign nationalities, and foreign powers have traditionally and in more modern times threatened the political power of the Burman unifiers.
- Foreign minorities usurped the economic power of the Burman population in the colonial period. In traditional Burma, power was always centralized in theory, even if in fact it was fragmented.
- Western Christian powers are inherently prejudiced in favor of the Christian minorities and identify with them, and vice versa.

- The military has tried to deal fairly with the minority groups and with *cetana* has provided social and other services out of a very restricted national budget.
- Some of the minority groups cannot be trusted, and some are "primitive."
- The minorities would secede from the Union if possible.

The minorities have a different set of perceptions about the Burman majority.

- The Burmans are prejudiced against the minorities and consider some of them to be less civilized.
- The state apparatus and the military have increasingly and unfairly been dominated by the Burmans.
- The coercive power of the state is in the hands of the Burman leadership.
- The traditional autonomy of the minorities has been eliminated, even though the traditional leadership of some of the minorities was retained during colonial rule.
- The autonomy promised the minorities under the first constitution has never been fulfilled.
- Although minority areas are rich in natural resources, the profits from their exploitation have not been adequately shared with the minorities, and the minorities have been denied adequate economic development.
- Both the Burman monarchy and the British recognized the independence of the Kayah State in 1875.
- Minority religions (Christianity, Islam) have been placed in jeopardy by the state.
- The Burman military has acted arrogantly toward the minorities and inflicted atrocities on them. It has acted as if it were foreign occupying troops.
- The provision of possible secession by the Shan and Kayah States in the 1947 constitution has been eliminated.
- The minorities have been denied the right of education in their native languages.[19]

Ethnic issues are most problematic along the Thai frontier. There, waves of migration and movement caused by the rebellions and the actions of the Burmese military, together with economic hardships, have created a wasteland of misery. About one-third of all Karen in the Karen State have been displaced from their homes.[20] There are about 120,000 Karen in refugee camps along the border in Thailand. (The figure includes some Kayah and Mon.) In addition, because of the creation of what are essentially free-fire zones in parts of the Shan State, where there have been antigovernment activities resulting in the forced resettlement of thousands, there are in northern Thailand thousands of Shan who remain unclassified as refugees and who eke out meager incomes in menial jobs and are exploited by unscrupulous businessmen. These are in addition to the approximately 700,000 illegal Burmese workers in Thailand who seek modest incomes in a variety of legal and illegal activities and who have become the conduit for the spread of disease in the region. Thailand has tried to avoid the problem of refugees; with the economic crisis in Thailand, it has tried to send back across the border thousands of these illegal workers. Burmese authorities are reluctant to accept them and have arrested some.

In the longer run, there are plans being formulated for major economic changes should human rights and international relations permit. One, the Golden Quadrangle (noted in chapter 5), envisages a major transportation network in the border areas of Myanmar, China, Laos, and Thailand and the creation of road and rail links that would change the traditional patterns of commerce and control in the region. Such a development, a long way from fruition because of both political and economic considerations, would link the minorities with each other and the outside world. Whether or how much the minorities would directly benefit from these grandiose plans is a major question, but even the beginnings of such an effort would signal that the violence had dropped; at least that would be progress. However, any such plans would be seen further to legitimate the Myanmar military government and thus would likely be opposed by the NLD.

In the immediate term, the situation continues to be poor. Unless major concessions are made by the military and by the minorities and a sense of trust is established, the tensions that are now in check beneath the relatively placid surface of cease-fires will again explode to the detriment of all the peoples of the state and perhaps of neighboring states as well. Herein lies the danger.

APPENDIX A—Linguistic Groups of Burma/Myanmar

Sinitic

Chinese
Panthay
Haw

Tibeto-Burman

Lutzu
Nakhi (Moso)
Kachin (Chingpaw), including Atsi, Lashi, Maru, etc.
Achang
Hpon
Kadu
Lahu
Rawang
Akha
Nung
Burmese
Naga (divided into many subgroups)
Karen (including Pwo, Sgaw, Bre, Karenni, Padaung, Pa-O)

Malayo-Polynesian: Malay

Selon

Miao-Yao

Yao
Miao (Hmong)

Mon-Khmer

Mon
Palaung
Wa

Tai

Shan
Hkamti Shan

APPENDIX B—Ethnically Related Rebel Groups in Burma, 1983–84

Abi Group (Lahu)
Arakan Liberation Party (Rakhine Liberation Army)
Arakan National Liberation Party (Rakhine Muslim Liberation Party, Mujahids)
Kachin National Union (successor to the Karen National Defense Organization)
Karen Liberation Army
Karenni National Progressive Party
Karenni State Nationalities Liberation Front
Kayah New Land Revolutionary Council
Lahu National Unity Party
National Democratic Front (umbrella organization)
Muslim Liberation Front
National Socialist Council of Nagaland
New Mon State Party
Palaung Patriotic Army
Palaung State Liberation Organization
Pa-O National Organization
Rohingya Patriotic Front
Shan State Army
Shan State Nationalities Liberation Group
Shan State Volunteer Organization
Shan United Army
Shan United Revolutionary Army
Wa National Army
(unnamed) Chin group

Other Rebel Organizations

Burma Communist Party
Arakanese Communist Party (Rakhine Communist Party)
Yang Hwe-Kang group (Chinese Irregular Forces)

APPENDIX C—Ethnic Cease-Fires as of July 1998

Main Cease-Fire Organizations Date

Myanmar National Democratic Alliance Party 1989
United Wa State Party (or Myanmar National Solidarity Party) 1989
National Democratic Alliance Party 1989
Shan State Army/Shan State Progress Party 1989
New Democratic Army 1989
Kachin Defence Army (KIO 4th Brigade) 1991
Pao National Organization 1991
Palaung State Liberation Party 1991
Kayan National Guard 1992
Kachin Independence Organization 1994
Karenni State Nationalities Liberation Front 1994
Kayan New Land Party 1994
Shan State Nationalities Liberation Organization 1994
New Mon State Party 1995

Other Cease-Fire Forces Date

Democratic Karen Buddhist Army 1995
Mongko Region Defence Army 1995
Shan State National Army 1995
Mong Tai Army 1996
Karenni National Defence Army 1996
Karen Peace Force (ex-KNU, 16th Battalion) 1997
Communist Party of Burma (Arakan Province) 1997
Mergui Mon Army 1997
Source: Smith, *Burma.*

APPENDIX D—Forces in Revolt (July 1998)

Arakan Liberation Party
Chin National Front
Karen National Union (1995–96 talks broke down)
Karen National Progressive Party (1995 cease-fire broke down)
Lahu National Organization
Mergui-Tavoy United Front (ex-BCP)
National Socialist Council of Nagaland
  East
  Main Faction
National Unity Party (Front) of Arakan
Rohingya National Alliance
  Arakan Rohingya Islamic Front
  Rohingya Solidarity Organization
Shan United Revolutionary Army (reformed 1996)
Wa National Organization (1997 talks broke down)
Source: Smith, *Burma.*

Notes

1. Aung San, 1947 before the formation of the republic.
2. Quoted in Martin Smith, "Ethnic Conflict and the Challenge of Civil Society in Burma," in *Strengthening Civil Society in Burma: Possibilities and Dilemmas for International NGOs* (Chiangmai: Silkworm Press, 1999), p. 37.
3. Personal communication.
4. For a good summary of the ethnic issues together with NLD recommendations on the formation of a new liberal constitution, see Josef Silverstein, "Fifty Years of Failure in Burma," in *Government, Policies and Ethnic Relations in Asia and the Pacific,* ed. Michael E. Brown and Sumit Ganguly (Cambridge, Mass.: MIT Press, 1997), pp. 167–96.
5. David I. Steinberg, "Constitutional and Political Bases of Minority Insurrections in Burma," in *Armed Separatism in Southeast Asia,* ed. Lim Joo-Jock and Vani S. (Singapore: Institute of Southeast Asian Studies, 1984).
6. Appendix A contains a linguistic breakdown of the peoples of Burma. This appeared in Steinberg, *Burma's Road toward Development: Growth and Ideology under Military Rule* (Boulder: Westview Press, 1981), but was an older, U.S. government source.

7. For a discussion in the Burmese context, see Lim and Vani S., eds.

8. Although this is not verified, it has been suggested that the Burmese military used Chin forces to fire on demonstrating Burmese at various times since 1962. If so, they ironically followed the British pattern.

9. In some areas, such as parts of the Kachin State, the missionaries essentially divided up the territory, with different Christian sects allowed exclusive missionary activity in various valleys.

10. For the most comprehensive study, see Martin Smith, *Burma: Insurgency and the Politics of Ethnicity* (London: Zed Books, rev. 1999; originally published 1991). For an earlier study, see Josef Silverstein, *Burmese Politics: The Dilemma of National Unity* (New Brunswick: Rutgers University Press, 1980).

11. A list of ethnic-related rebel groups of the 1983–84 period is in Appendix B of this chapter. Appendix C lists groups that have been parties to cease-fires, while Appendix D lists those still in revolt.

12. In 1999, a senior military official said that Khun Sa's forces in the Mong Tai Army were better equipped than those of the Burmese military.

13. Indonesia, an even more ethnically and geographically diverse state, attempted to impose a national ideology on the society, *pancasila* (five principles), to which all groups had to adhere. It does not seem to have been effective. On the other hand, Thailand, far less diverse ethnically and religiously, has successfully employed the monarchy and Buddhism as cohesive forces.

14. In this case the military had been correct; it recognized that the promulgation of Buddhism would be detrimental to the unity of the state, and was against it. Now it seems in favor of it and supports proselytizing.

15. Incorporating warlord armies into central government troops or militia had been a pattern followed in China in the republican period (after 1911).

16. Union of Myanmar, *Review of the Financial, Economic and Social Conditions for 1997/98* (Yangon: Ministry of National Planning and Economic Development, 1998), pp. 218–20.

17. See U.S. Department of State Report on Religious Freedom (Washington, D.C., 1999). Promotions within the military to relatively senior levels seem to require at least titular adherence to Buddhism, and such conversions are sought. Personal communication from former military officer. The government claims there are 5,122 Buddhist monestaries, 5,200 Christian churches, 3,215 mosques, and 1,010 Hindu temples in the country.

18. Personal communication, March 1999.

19. Adapted from Steinberg, "Constitutional and Political Bases of Minority Insurrections in Burma."

20. Smith, "Ethnic Conflict and the Challenge of Civil Society in Burma," p. 35.

CHAPTER 7

The Politics of Social Issues

T he late nineteenth century guidebooks prepared for the British trav-
eler to Burma would often remark that the visitor, once stepping off
the gangplank in Rangoon from India, would breathe a sigh of relief.
There was none of the poverty and degradation associated with Calcutta, with
its overwhelming numbers of the poor and abject misery creating an oppres-
sive atmosphere. Burma was a pleasant, if backwater, component of the British
empire.

This perception was in general accurate. Here was a country rich in natural resources with a relatively sparse population compared to its arable land
and one that had not in memory been subjected to the famines that seemed to
plague India or China. There was, at least among the Burman population, none
of the grinding social discrimination associated with the Hindu caste system.
Although there was not equality of income, the great disparities of wealth
seemed to have escaped Burma—shared but not desperate poverty seemed to
be the norm. The Burmans were considered, condescendingly it is true, as
charming and perhaps naive, and although that characterization was in many
ways inaccurate (as are all such stereotypes), it was far more benign than those
associated with the subcontinent.

This impression of Burma was reinforced by its traditional and colonial
achievements. Burmese (Burman) women had much higher status than the
women of either India or China, and this was refreshing to foreigners. They
never performed suttee, as did widows in India, nor were they subject to foot-
binding, as were women in China. They controlled much of the retail trade,

inherited equally with their male siblings, and kept control over their dowries on marriage and divorce, thus making separation an economically unattractive pursuit for males. Burma was said to have the highest literacy rates between Suez and Japan; this was probably true because to be a good Buddhist, each Burman child would by custom be educated in a monastic village school, where he, and to a degree she, would be taught to read and write the Buddhist scriptures. In the early nineteenth century, Trant (1826) speculated that female literacy in Burma might have been higher than in England.

In the decade following the independence of many countries in Asia, there was a major "brain drain" of talented people, either educated or seeking education, who decided to reside in the West, especially in the United States. The lack of opportunities commensurate with their educational attainments and the relative affluence of the West were attractions. Although such individuals contributed greatly to progress in the countries to which they went, many in the West spoke out against their decisions to deprive their original state of the talents that were needed for national development. Some states, such as South Korea under the military after 1961, tried to cajole or encourage their learned citizens to return, but with limited success.

Before 1962, however, Burma was distinct, if not unique, in that there was no brain drain and those trained abroad returned to their homeland to contribute to national growth. Standards of living were, by Western measurements, low, and even the highest officials and professors were paid a pittance. Yet the style of living was attractive and the social milieu comfortable, so many Burmese turned down lucrative positions in the West to return.

This changed radically after 1962. The political repression, the violence associated with the perpetuation of military rule, the ubiquitous intelligence surveillance, the requirement for intellectual orthodoxy and subservience to the military, the lack of appropriate employment opportunities, and the rigidity of the "Burmese Way to Socialism" all prompted an outflow of educated peoples. The repression of Muslims in the Arakan caused refugees to flee to East Pakistan (later Bangladesh), and revolts prompted Karen and other minorities to cross over the Thai border. As few were legally allowed to leave, many fled under great hardships, walking across mountainous frontiers and through malarious areas. Later, after the student demonstrations of 1974 and then in the 1980s and 1990s, when the state recognized that it might be more desirable to let potential dissidents leave than create trouble at home and that the state could gain considerable foreign exchange by encouraging work abroad (taxing those who went), the government allowed many to depart. In addition, the massacres associated with the coup of 1988 and then the chance for employment of peoples who had no livelihood, many of whom had been forcibly removed from their villages in the hills in the Shan, Kayah, Karen, or Mon States near the Thai border, prompted some three-quarters of a million quietly to move over time to Thailand, which at that time was experiencing a major economic boom that required masses of low-cost labor to perform the manual jobs that the Thai increasingly found distasteful. The permeable frontiers that character-ize Burma and its neighbors, together with ethnic relations that create cross-boundary ethnic and linguistic kin, have led to movements of people and goods back and forth, creating statistical problems of unrecorded economic data, rela-tive ease of narcotics trafficking, and the transmission of disease, particularly HIV/AIDS, throughout the region.

With these changes have come an exchange of information. No longer was Burma isolated, but people began to learn of opportunities in other countries and sought relief there from their plights at home. They began to compare the lack of progress in Burma with clear changes among their neighbors. This was not all envy, for many Burmese felt that the Thai economic advances had been sustained by the destruction of Thai culture, at least in Bangkok, and this many Burmese did not want to happen to Rangoon.

The decline in the quality of life in Burma from 1962, however—at least in comparison with its neighbors if not in absolute terms—was a travesty of which many Burmese have been deeply chagrined and ashamed. Many Bur-mese officials have recognized this disgrace. That is why the military concealed from the public for four months (until March 1988) that Burma had been rec-ognized by the United Nations as "least developed." Even with the financial crisis of 1997 that affected so much of Southeast Asia and Korea, but from the worst effects of which Myanmar was insulated by its relative isolation from the world economy, the decline in the Thai standard of living is but a minor irrita-tion compared to the continuous stagnation, even decline, in the quality of Bur-mese life, both for the majority of Burmans and the minority peoples.

Five social aspects affecting the quality of life need explication because unless changed, they will negatively influence the future development of the state, as well as its international acceptability, under whatever government comes to power. These are issues of poverty, education, health, the status of women, and narcotics. They are intimately related because poverty is the single largest cause of school dropouts, and it obviously affects the health and nutritional standards of a significant segment of the population. The production of narcotics is complex; it affects the economic and social well-being of the population and is related to security concerns, and although it is a health problem in itself, it has also led to the spread of HIV/AIDS.

As discussed above, the large military expenditures on defense and the related military establishment restrict the ability of the state to deal effectively with any of these issues. Furthermore, insofar as the elite of the military are insulated from the problems of health and education because the *tatmadaw* runs its own vastly superior systems for its staff and families, they are less inclined to feel that improvement in public systems is a priority concern of the state. As a matter of international prestige, the authorities have been reluctant to admit to social problems, claiming that the "traditional cultural values" of Myanmar (read Burman values, which are as based on sentimental and selective memories as are those in the West) inhibit the spread of AIDS, prostitution, or drug addiction.

Poverty

Poverty is culturally defined beyond the basic nutritional standards to sustain life and reproduction. It was not for a period considered a derogatory term in Burma.[1] In the 1930s, a major political party was even named the Sinyetha, or Poor Man's Party. It had popular appeal.

Although shared poverty may have been the plight of many, Burma was considered a rich country before World War II. It was a rarity—a country that exported both fuel and food. It was self-sufficient economically, and although the image of a peaceful Buddhist society was inaccurate—especially after the effects of the Great Depression hit Burma in the early 1930s, when poverty spread and crime rose—it was by comparison a prosperous region.[2] But this image and reality were destroyed in the scorched-earth policies of both the British and the Japanese in their respective retreats from Burma in World War II. Independence brought little relief, for Burma was plagued once again by war, this time by the insurgents, who at the apex of their power reached the suburbs of Rangoon, so that the appellation of the "Rangoon government" was as literal as it was figurative. It was not until the late 1970s that the per capita income of the Burmese reached prewar levels, and even then it was low.[3] Although the population was deprived, grinding poverty and famine were not known. Certain of the hill areas were traditional subsistence economies that depended on slash and burn agriculture and periodic migration for sustenance and were thus poorer than other regions. Although figures are lacking on income distribution during these periods, the unverifiable but likely hypothesis is that income distribution, as might have been measured by the Gini coefficient had such studies been attempted, would have made Burma one of the countries with more equitable income distribution in Asia.

The increases in production as a result of the introduction of the high-yielding varieties of rice were an important component of that equity and change, and land reform earlier had leveled farm income. Since some 80 percent of the population was rural, these had a major impact on statistics. There was, in addition, a general paucity of industrial wealth; what little existed was in the public sector (and often was not profitable). Entrepreneurship, even in the presocialist economy of the 1950s, was not common among the Burman population. This was partly due to the unavailability of appropriate credit (which was more accessible to the Chinese and Indian minorities through their own castes, clans, and linguistic networks) and the uncertainties of economic policies, which made longer-term investments more risky and thus less desirable. Capitalism was culturally remote. It was more profitable to build a pagoda, where the social rewards were high (the donor could then be addressed as a *payataga,* or "pagoda builder," a great compliment) and the karmic rewards were certain, while investment in productive industries was insecure and government policies opaque, bureaucratic harassment extensive, and corruption prevalent.[4]

The quality of life was markedly affected by the system of taxation on the bulk of the population—the rural sector. The state lacked the administrative capacity effectively to collect income and other complex taxes from the rural population. Taxes were on production, especially rice. The state, for much of the time since independence, maintained a (theoretical) monopoly on the export of rice (much was smuggled to neighboring countries, especially Bangladesh), and (as noted) the state's revenues in large part depended on the price differential between the low price it paid producers and the export price. Under the military, until 1987, farmers were forced to sell their surplus rice (beyond fixed amounts calculated per capita for family consumption, seed, and monastic donations) to the state at set, low rates, thus encouraging smuggling and surreptitious sales and discouraging increased production. Even after the reforms that freed sales, the implicit tax on farmers between the percentage of the crop that had to be sold to the state and the market price was substantial—some 36 percent.

The agricultural policies of the state and the unavailability of off-farm employment for most of the rural population have resulted in poverty levels affecting at least 22 percent of the total population, and 70 percent of that poverty is located in rural areas. The IMF believes that 30–40 percent of the population lives below the poverty line.[5] Farm size is too small for more than subsistence living for much of the population, and the productivity of the available land is low in comparison with many states in the region. As discussed in chapter 5, this is due to lack of fertilizer and related to inadequate credit at reasonable interest rates (usurious credit is available but is illegal and can cost up to 6 percent per month), the paucity of effective and reliable irrigation for double cropping, and the mechanized means of soil preparation and harvesting. In 1975, 25 percent of the rural population was landless, and some 86 percent of farmers held less land than they needed to rise above the poverty level. Some statistics show that 40 percent of the rural population in the 1990s was landless.

In the socialist era, goods were rarely available for sale in the market towns, so even the material incentives for increased production were lacking. This has changed with the opening of the legal private economy and the extension of smuggling. Farmers are certainly better off than they were during the socialist era since a large percentage of their rice crop could be freely marketed after September 1, 1987, but much more might be done in terms of policy reform to improve their lot.

Although poverty is widespread, it is not evenly distributed. The Magwe district of central Burma (in the dry zone) and the Chin and Kayah States are said to have the most pervasive poverty. The problem has been exacerbated by the extensive relocations, most of them forced, throughout both urban and rural areas.

A singular pattern of forced resettlement has been consistent under military rule. During the Caretaker Government and following the coup of 1988, the military moved hundreds of thousands of people to new satellite towns, in the early period providing few if any services, and in the later one varying support by particular places. The older towns created by the military in 1958 (North and South Okkalapa and Thaketa) are still among the poorest neighborhoods in Rangoon, although the planting of trees has softened the appearance of poverty.[6]

The number of people moved to the new satellite towns around Rangoon beginning in 1988 is unclear. Statistics vary from 331,000 to 447,323.[7] Among the new towns, Hlaingdaya (across the Hlaing River from Insein) is the poorest and physically resembles those new towns of 1958. Dagon Myothit, however, is one of the premier towns, and civil servants and military have been offered land on favorable terms, and many view such sites as investments, although they prefer to live closer to the city. Forced relocation has also occurred in many other urban areas in central Myanmar, including Mandalay and the ancient capital of Pagan. Mya Maung estimates that perhaps 1–2 million have been so moved, although the latter figure seems high. The motivations behind these moves are unclear, but several have been assumed, including the breakup of political opposition sites, reduction of fire and health hazards in slum areas, and the use of land for other lucrative purposes. Although the state since independence has held the ultimate ownership of all land under all constitutions, the manner in which the military has carried out the relocations, in both 1958 and 1988, has often been brutal and seen as arbitrary. In creating a new university in a new Rangoon suburb, one official indicated that part of the motivation was to keep students out of downtown Rangoon and thus minimize potential disturbances.[8]

Mya Maung estimates that 1–2 million people from central Burma and 3–4 million from minority areas have been relocated, although these figures seem high.[9] Such relocation has been a product of military operations, denial of population to rebel organizations, and retribution against what the regime regards as terrorist acts. As noted, free-fire zones have been created, forcing peasants to move to other areas and pushing them across the border to Thailand. Minority farmers have been forced into settlements where they are under stringent military control, similar to British policy in fighting the communists in Malaya and the "strategic hamlet" program of the South Vietnamese.[10]

Poverty and deprivation are in part due to the increasing need of the urban population to spend more on food. The staples, such as rice and cooking oil, had been a relatively small percentage of family expenditures two decades ago, but inflation has meant that a larger percentage of family income must be spent to provide the necessary components of living. One estimate indicated that 70 percent of income was spent on food. Another noted that the average monthly wage of a doctor in 1996 (K.1,500) was not enough to pay for the monthly cost of rice consumption.[11] Inflation, caused by massive increases in the money supply (see chapter 5), has eroded family surpluses. Government statistics on inflation are considered to be inadequate and undercount the real increases in prices both because calculations represent official prices while people are forced to buy at unofficial rates because of the unavailability of produce at official outlets, and because the basket of prices on which calculations are figured are improperly weighted.

As discussed in chapter 5, the salaries of civil servants as recently as 2000 have not kept pace with inflation. For example, the monthly salary in 1999 for a director general of a ministry was K.2,500 (plus some rationed staples and food), and for a junior clerical officer, K.800–900. Thus civil servants have had to sell on the open market some of the government-provided materials that are dispensed through state stores to which they have privileged access; have more than one family income;[12] or engage in some illegal or inappropriate means to make ends meet. For example, the sale of small amounts of gasoline, rationed to car owners at highly subsidized rates (some ten times less than their market value), may be resold.[13] In an effort to reduce subsidies, and thus government deficits, the electricity rates were increased tenfold in the spring of 1999, which will increase urban hardships. At the same time, the opening to the private sector and the encouragement of foreign investment and tourism has meant an increase in income for some, even though the total program must be considered a failure in national terms. For a period, employment improved so that the minimum urban wage (K.20 daily at that time) was not sufficient to attract workers, who often received double that amount. The spurt in construction is now over, as buildings remain empty or incomplete.

The increased data on poverty and its effects on health, however incomplete, are welcome because without them policy changes are unlikely and the most appropriate approaches to ameliorating the problem will not evolve. Yet the data are likely to be inadequate, and there is every probability that in peripheral areas poverty levels are likely to be higher than those reflected in the presently available data.

Available data indicate that 22.9 percent of households live below the poverty line that foreign observers have calculated. (The government has no official level, and thus there is no official poverty, although it has set a standard of 2,400 calories per day.) An additional 33.9 percent of households have expenditures that are less than 10 percent above minimum subsistence; thus over half the population should be considered poor, and this may be an underestimation. There is an obvious and growing disparity between the top and bottom of the economic ladder: the lowest decile represents 3.2 percent of consumption, while the top decile represents 26.6 percent. Food costs some 16 percent more in urban areas. It is significant that (in contrast to other Asian societies) the overall percentage of the population that is poor in Myanmar (23.9 percent) is slightly higher than the percentage of rural poor (22.4 percent), although the absolute numbers are greater in rural areas because the bulk of the population is rural.

The quality of life in rural areas is still more bleak. Only 2 percent of the rural population has access to piped water, compared to 17 percent in urban areas; 38 percent of the former have sanitary facilities, compared to 82 percent of the latter; and 10 percent of the rural population has electricity, while 68 percent of urban people do.

The link between poverty and education is direct and twofold. Not only are children forced to drop out of school because they are needed for farm labor (since hired labor is too expensive) or because informal school fees (uniforms, books, supplies, etc.) are too high, but also the decline of public education has meant that a whole separate industry of "tuition schools" has been established.[14] These are private endeavors and are designed to accomplish two ends: provide students with the education that the public schools have failed to do, and provide teachers with supplemental incomes without which they could not live. A very substantial portion of disposable incomes for urban families with young children is consumed by educational expenses.

The Destruction of the Educational System

Education has been a priority of all governments since independence, but their commitment to it has varied over time. Three policy pronouncements from the socialist period illustrate their views. As early as 1963, the Revolutionary Council wrote the following:

> The Revolutionary Council believes that the existing educational system un-equated with livelihood will have to be transformed. An educational system equated with livelihood and based on socialistic moral values will be brought about. Science will be given precedence in education.[15]

> Our education target is to bring basic education within the reach of all. As regards higher education, only those who have promise and enough potentialities and industriousness to benefit from it will be especially encouraged.[16]

Further, the constitution of 1974 explained that every citizen had a right to an education and that primary education (kindergarten through fourth grade) was compulsory.[17]

Primary education did expand under the socialist system and as the government regained control of some of the areas previously under insurgent influence. In 1965, some 58 percent of primary school-age children were in school, and by 1977 it was said to be 87 percent. Since the coup of 1988 and the fall in incomes, the school attendance figures have dropped, and now a significant percentage of children do not finish primary school; in 1998/99 only 25 percent of students completed primary school, although about 70 percent entered kindergarten.

The government claims that in 1997/98 there were 35,877 primary schools, 167,134 teachers for those schools, and 5,145,396 pupils (provisional figures). The comparable middle school figures were 2,099 schools, 56,955 teachers, and 1,545,601 pupils; for high schools the figures were 923 schools, 17,089 teachers, and 385,112 students. During that year, there were 53 universities and colleges (including separate technical institutes), 7,625 professors, and 374,112 students, of whom 195,130 were in "distance education" (see below).[18] It is noteworthy that the number of students officially listed in colleges or universities in 1995/96 was 647,038. Presumably the massive drop the subsequent year reflects the closure of schools because of student demonstrations in December 1996.[19]

The good reputation of Burma as a literate society eroded, although it had been reinforced by the quality of Burmese education following independence—Burmese medical degrees were recognized in England while those from India were not without an examination. The Burmese level of English was first very high, and many of the elite attended private, mission-run middle and high schools. A conscious effort was made to make higher education available to the population.

The level of mobility in Burma was pronounced because in Burman areas (in contrast to some of the hill areas) the old royal families essentially disappeared in the wake of the colonial era, and the precolonial elites did not return to significant power as they did in so many postcolonial Asian societies. As noted, the avenues of mobility were open not only through education, but also through the *sangha* (and no social stigma was attached to entering or leaving at will), through the mass political organizations that were formed under the aegis of the AFPFL, and through the military itself. Significantly, this mobility was not limited to Burmans, but was more widely open to minorities who could speak Burmese and respect the Burman culture. Local cultures and languages were relegated to the family; all state instruction in minority areas was in Burmese (except some subjects at university level, where English was necessary because of the paucity of textbooks in Burmese). Some Shan in the Shan State would surreptitiously show primary textbooks they had illegally received from the Shan Autonomous Region in Yunnan Province (Sip Song Banna) that were written in Shan (the Thai–Shan languages are widely spread in that region) and point them out with considerable envy.[20]

In its efforts to isolate the state, the military in the BSPP era destroyed the efficacy of the educational system and cut it off from international contacts. All mission schools were nationalized. English was eliminated as a medium of instruction in 1966 and reintroduced only much later into the curriculum.[21] Political indoctrination substituted for content in many courses, and both students and faculty were forced to attend political education courses. Orthodoxy was mandatory. In 1991, questionnaires were distributed to teachers and students asking for their opinions on a variety of topics, including the opposition and the United States. They were a form of loyalty oath. As a result, some 7,000 teachers were dismissed, as well as several hundred university professors, when their responses indicated insufficient orthodoxy.[22] There is a certain Orwellian atmosphere to the educational system; references to the role of Aung San as the father of independence have been eliminated from the primary and secondary curriculum.

The students at university, and even in high school, were fervently nationalistic but at the same time critical of the restrictions imposed by the military and the brutality with which it treated the population. When students at the University of Rangoon protested against the coup of 1962, the student union building, which had a long history in the nationalist struggles of the 1930s, was blown up by the military and many students were killed (unofficial figures estimate as many as 400). The universities were then closed for a long period. When students demonstrated against the demeaning burial of U Thant in 1974 (when deaths again were extensive), the universities were again closed. To prevent the concentration of students in Rangoon and Mandalay, the urban seats of most student protests, the military closed the universities again on several occasions. Universities and even high schools have remained closed for years, following the demonstrations and coup of 1988, after demonstrations in 1996, and at other times. Since 1962, colleges and universities have been closed about 20 percent of the time. Under the SLORC/SPDC, most universities and colleges have been closed for over eight years in the 1988–99 period, but they reopened in June 2000. Thus there is a backlog of students waiting to graduate from high school and enter college. There were said to be 400,000 students awaiting college entry in 1999, but there are less than one-quarter that number of places in the colleges and universities.[23]

In 1974 the military began a program to develop sixteen regional colleges, which opened in 1977 and were the equivalent of community colleges; each state or division had its own institution. The concept was twofold: keep a large number of students out of the urban areas of Rangoon and Mandalay, and provide vocational training so that students could on graduation get local jobs. Neither goal was achieved. The training was not provided by practitioners of the trades or skills, so the education was not truly geared to the job market, and students still accumulated in the major urban settings. Over time these colleges were turned into universities and "distance education" was added. Although "distance education" gave those who worked an opportunity to learn without actually being resident at university, it also served the political purpose of keeping the students off campus.

Although government figures for expenditures on education show marked increases over the years, those increases have not kept pace with inflation and with population expansion, so the state is in fact investing less per student than it did three decades ago. From 1989 to 1994, the percentage of the national budget for the social services sector (including education and health) declined from 32 to 23 percent, while military expenditures in the same period were about 46 percent. Real public spending per child on education for 5–9 year olds decreased from K.1,200 in 1990/91 to K.1,000 in 1999/00.

Corruption has crept in and become flagrant in education, as teachers must be engaged in outside employment to meet monthly expenses. As noted above, many teach in tuition schools. Illegal "entrance fees" for the prestigious high schools in Rangoon are said to involve bribes of up to K.100,000 and lesser amounts for other institutions. Examination questions are said to be available for a price.

Educational standards for the population as a whole seem to have deteriorated. Over 70 percent of both poor and nonpoor populations have not gone beyond the fourth grade, and only an additional 14.7 percent have received a Burmese middle school education (grades 5–8; grades 9–10 are high school, as the curriculum is only ten grades). Employment is scarce for those who complete the bottom as well as the top of the educational curriculum. This was also true in the BSPP period; students were not motivated to study even when colleges and universities were open because there were no jobs. Enrollments for women are increasing, while male enrollments are declining, presumably because of a lack of employment.

Health

The health status of the Burmese has always been fragile. The tropical climate and the inability of the government to deliver effective goods and services have meant that endemic diseases were problems for all administrations. Burma produced good medical staff, but cultural factors often prevented their effective use. Burman doctors often refused to serve in peripheral and isolated areas, so the civilian government hired Indian doctors. In the pre–World War II period, about half the doctors were Indian. Burman women were culturally not supposed to have physical contact with nonfamily males, so they did not become nurses. This was left to the Karen and other minorities who had no such restrictions. As a result, many Burman women became gynecologists and pediatricians, so that they could practice effectively within cultural norms.

In the socialist era, the health objectives of the state were appropriate: help the poor and working people, give priority to preventive measures, and narrow the gap between the availability of services in urban and rural areas (among others).[24] In part, this theoretical approach might have been because at that time the Ministry of Health was staffed at higher levels with professional medical people, in contrast with the bureaucrats in most other ministries. However, it was weak in terms of its relative power within the cabinet, which controlled budgets. Although the theoretical approach to health expenditures was admirable, in fact more funds were devoted to curative than preventive medicine. In 1997/98, 44 percent of government spending was in curative (hospital) care, and 26 percent was on public health. At that time, the priority medical concerns were malaria, tuberculosis, anemia, tetanus, prenatal morbidity and mortality, hypovitaminosis, leprosy, and cholera.[25] The endemic medical problems today are still malaria and tuberculosis. The malaria rate in 1985 was said to be 5 percent. In 1995 it was 22 percent.

Infant mortality is officially listed at 46 per 1,000 live births in some data but at 71 per 1,000 in 1997. Even the latter figure is probably low. It was said to be 252.8 in 1951, 129.9 in 1961, and 53.8 in 1975, although the last figure realistically might have been double, since the collection of data at that time was incomplete and sporadic.

It is likely that two major changes have taken place in the health field in the past decade. The first is an increase in malnutrition, especially among children under five years old, and the second is the spread of HIV/AIDS. Malnutrition is high, although caloric consumption is generally at acceptable levels. About 5 percent of infants under six months were moderately malnourished, but the figure climbs to about 35 percent at age one. The rates have been declining. In spite of these promising developments, improvements are not comparable with those in other countries that were economically expanding, indicating that all classes are not benefiting equally. Because economic growth has slowed, the rates may increase.

Each society seems prone to perpetuate the myths of what in the United States are called "family values" and what in Burma are said to be the traditional systems of morality, which are far more strict than contemporary practices. For this reason, the government has been reluctant to admit that there is an HIV/AIDS problem in Burma, and it has denied that a "sex trade" exists, in spite of observations, even in Rangoon, to the contrary. Such an admission would also undercut attempts to woo tourists to that relatively un-spoiled land.

Yet HIV/AIDS is exploding at remarkable rates. Part of the spread is through increased intravenous drug use, which has mushroomed. Among these narcotics users, the rate of infection in some small surveys carried out in the north runs about 90 percent. Rates of HIV infection in 1993 were over 85 percent of tested intravenous drug users in Mandalay and 94–95 percent in Myitkyina and Bhamo. In six villages surveyed along the Kachin–China bor-der, HIV rates were 40 percent. Moreover, because of poverty, the relocation of families from their traditional homes, and the demand for cheap prostitutes in Thailand, an increasing number of women have been infected in Thailand and then return to their home areas and spread the disease. The rapacious ac-tivities of the Burmese Army also spread the illness.

Although the government will not admit to the severity of the problem and surveys on the disease are limited, the little information that is available is startling and disquieting. In one case, a company testing Burmese males for overseas work found an infection rate of about 9 percent,[26] and there are indi-cations that the military rate may be as high as 15 percent.[27] Some estimates maintain that there are a minimum of 440,000 HIV cases in Myanmar (some say 500,000), making it the second worst area of AIDS epidemic in Asia. Reports indicate that the adult infection rate may be 1.8 percent (others say 2.4 percent; the United Nations estimates 2 percent of adults), with cumulative cases by mid-1997 of about one million and 86,000 deaths.[28] In September 1998, 0.7 percent of Rangoon and 0.97 percent of Mandalay blood donors tested positive. UNICEF claims that there are some 15,000 orphans in Myan-mar as a result of AIDS. The government, however, admits to only 23,669 HIV cases, and 3,195 AIDS cases from 1988 to June 1999.[29] Thailand, where the disease has reached endemic proportions, now spends some $200 million an-nually to stop the spread. Burma spends some $2 million (less than 50 cents per capita). Without a concerted effort that involves a recognition of the prob-lem, technical assistance from abroad, and major increases in educational, pre-ventive, and treatment expenditures by the state, we may expect the problem to expand and reach devastating proportions.

Government statistics indicate that the spending on health has seriously decreased. Although the state spent only 0.83 percent of GDP on health in 1992, that figure had dropped to 0.45 percent in 1995, 0.3 percent in 1997/98, and 0.18 percent in 1998/99.

The Status of Women

The status of women in Burma/Myanmar is the subject of some dispute and a great many broad-brushed remarks that do not do justice to one of the traditional virtues of Burman society. In the past decade, as poverty in the hill areas has become more intense and widespread and as the army has engaged in forced resettlement and in virtual free-fire zones, there has been a flow of people from Myanmar into Thailand. Many of these have been women, especially from the minority areas of the Shan, Kayah, and Karen States. Many have been economically forced or sold into prostitution in northern Thailand, where they make up a significant (but unknown) percentage of the brothel inhabitants. There are said to be some 40,000 Burmese (mostly minority) women in these brothels.[30] There have been a large number of credible stories of rape of minority women by the Burmese military. These stories have captured international attention, with many drawing erroneous conclusions about the past and present status of Burmese women. Whatever degradation these women suffer, it is not representative of the past or the present situation among Burman women as a whole. In 1889, one author wrote:

> If you were to ask a Burman "What is the position of women in Burma?" he would reply he did not know what you meant. Women have no position, no fixed relation towards men beyond that fixed by the fact that women are women and men are men. They differ a great deal in many ways, so the Burman would say; men are better in some things, women are better in others; if they have a position, their relative superiority determines it. How else should it be determined?[31]

The deleterious effects of poverty in Myanmar on the status of women, especially some of the minority women, should not detract from the traditional high status enjoyed by Burman women. (The traditional status of minority women has varied by ethnic group.) This has been noted by foreign observers for the past century and a half. Today, in spite of military control by an army that is predominantly male, this status has not eroded. It is significant that in 1959, when the military Caretaker Government passed a draft law, it treated women equally with men. The constitutions of Burma have specifically mentioned the equality of the sexes.

Although the Census for British Burma in 1872 may have exaggerated somewhat when it stated that female education was a fact in Burma before Oxford was founded, 24.28 percent of the pupils in lay (nonmonastic) schools were female in 1870. Some comments by Western observers, past and present, make the case, which has implications for the future.

> They [the Burman women in 1882] have the further inducement that they enjoy a much freer and happier position than in any other Eastern country, and in some respects are better off even than women in England. All the money and possessions which a girl brings with her on marriage are kept carefully separate for the benefit of her children or heirs, and she carries her property away with her if she is divorced, besides any she may have added to it in the interim by her own trading or by inheritance. Thus the married Burmese [Burman] woman is much more independent than any European even in the most advanced states.[32]

> The Burmese [Burman] women [in 1896] are such an important and unique feature of Burma that I feel they demand, ay, and deserve, a chapter to themselves. In no country, I think I may say—except in America—have women such a prominent position as in Burma. Utterly unlike their miserable Mohomedan and Hindoo sisters, they enjoy absolute liberty—a liberty of which, if rumor proves true, they make ample use! Women's rights are not in Burma an illusive dream. A thing to be shrieked and struggled after, they are an accomplished fact.[33]

And finally, from the foremost anthropologist on Burma, Melford Spiro:

> Burmese women are not only among the freest in Asia, but until the relatively recent emancipation of women in the West, they enjoyed much greater freedom and equality with men than did Western women. Today . . . they control not only the family economy but most retail trade as well—village hawkers-—and the proprietors of the stalls and shops in town and city bazaars are predominantly women. Women are well represented, too, in large business enterprises. Moreover, except for engineering, women are liberally represented in the professions. In the villages, women participate in the productive phases of the agricultural economy, and they receive the same wages as men for the same work (even though, according to men and women alike, men accomplish more because of their greater strength). . . . Finally, women enjoy social equality with men. Such customs as the veil, purdah, child betrothal, foot binding, widow immolation— these, and all other disabilities suffered by the women of India, on one side of Burma, and China, on the other, have always been absent from Burma.[34]

The traditional high status of women has been obscured by military rule, although there are women in the *tatmadaw,* but not in high command positions. Many of the higher civilians in government, however, are women. It is of some significance that when some high military officers have been arrested for corruption, it has often been the wife of the officer that has stood accused of the illegal business connections because of female control of many businesses.

The abuses suffered by women as a result of military occupation, dislocation, and migration should not obscure very favorable patterns of gender relations historically and in the heartland of Burman culture. The contemporary controlled literature does not stress this historical role of women, for to do so would be seen as strengthening the position of Aung San Suu Kyi and legitimizing her potential role, which the military by all means has attempted to deny. Significantly, it has generally not done so on the basis of her sex, but on her foreign connections and supporters. Historically, there have been some very influential queens in Burma, and to deny that a women could lead the country would fly in the face of sociological and historical precedent and could well backfire.

Narcotics and the Economy

Until 1959, opium sales were legal in the Shan State, and the *sawbwas* derived a modest revenue from taxes on it. After the Caretaker Government in 1959 declared opium illegal, trade in it began to expand. The demand increased as refineries were set up in the Golden Triangle region (the border area of Burma, Thailand, and Laos) to process the opium into morphine base and then into heroin.[35] Estimated production increased from a few hundred tons to about 2,500 tons in 1997–98. Until the cutoff in foreign assistance in 1988, the United States supplied funds and equipment for antinarcotics activities, including helicopters and materials for aerial spraying. The SLORC and previous military governments had made major public campaigns against drug use and had continuously publicized their eradication of poppy fields.

Much controversy surrounded narcotics production in Burma and its export through Thailand, China, and other neighboring countries. As noted in chapter 3, there was evidence that some insurgent groups, the KMT troops, or local "warlords" used narcotics sales or transit taxes to finance their rebellions, private armies, and localized power bases. Most famous was Khun Sa, who controlled a significant segment of the Thai–Shan border region with some 10,000 troops. Some critics argued that the military at a local level, or perhaps even at the national level, was fostering the trade for its own profit. Others claimed that demonetization and a lack of faith in local currency encouraged production, and others believed that aerial spraying forced diversification and thus increased production rather than diminished it.

Whatever the causes, the lucrative nature of the trade and the tenuous control of the central government, together with low wages, limited the potential for eradication of both production and trade. The subsistence agricultural economy of the hill areas in a period of increasing population and limited transportation encouraged the production of cash crops of high value, labor intensity, and low weight, of which opium was a prime example. While the contribution of opium/heroin was critical in financing many of the rebellions, it is unclear how important it was to the Burmese economy as a whole. Mya Maung calculates that in 1995, the value of Burmese heroin in New York was $3.6 billion, or 54 percent of the legal GDP at the prevalent black market rate at that time.[36] The 1989 comparative pricing of No. 4 heroin (the purest variety) has been calculated as follows:

Production site	Cost ($/kg.)
Burma—production site	3,670–5,082
Rangoon	4,500–6,500
Bangkok	6,300–7,450
Hong Kong	12,000–13,200
United States	104,000–220,000[37]

Ronald D. Renard notes that statistics on opiate use in Burma are notoriously unreliable because the state does not control much of its territory; the criminalization of use means that few register because once done, it cannot be reversed; there are different forms of drug use; and the government is embarrassed by frank discussion of it. He continues:

> Burma can be commended for its attempts to create a distinctive Burmese culture following its considerable suffering in the hands of Western adventurers in Burma. The distrust Burmese leadership feels toward the West is understandable. Measures to counteract it indicate an effort to instill new values in Burmese society. However, Burma's acceptance of the idea that narcotics is a problem constitutes a Western influence in the country that is not widely recognized as such. The Burmese will never reduce opiate use by following outmoded, unsuccessful Western models. And while it is impossible to return to precolonial practices, the country's leadership can try to re-create the balanced approach it once employed.[38]

The elimination of poppy production is a complex activity involving environmental, economic, social, and political considerations. Although repression, including crop spraying and burning, has been attempted, these methods have not proven successful in this region. This is an area of subsistence agriculture, and the elimination of poppies will depend on offering substantial economic alternatives to the producers. (The traffickers in any case will want the trade to continue because no other product offers such great returns.) Crop substitution has been attempted in Burma and Thailand, but with limited success until alternative employment and economic infrastructures, such as adequate roads and marketing facilities, have accompanied such efforts. It took about four decades to control opium production in northern Thailand, and it was accomplished only after massive economic changes were made and political control was strengthened. According to the (Chinese) Xinhwa News Agency, there were 86,537 drug addicts in Myanmar in 1999, as reported by the official Central Committee for Drug Abuse Control. Of this number, 50 percent were opium addicts, 37 percent heroin addicts, and 7 percent marijuana addicts. The figures are likely to be much higher, however.

In an effort to explore innovative modes of assistance, the Japanese have been experimenting with crop substitution in Myanmar, encouraging farmers to grow buckwheat to be used in the production of Japanese soba noodles. Buckwheat cultivation has expanded from 200 acres in 1997 to 2,150 in 1999. Yet buckwheat is relatively cheap, and transportation costs from the remote areas of production are high. Japanese subsidies are likely to be unsustainable, and other, more valuable crops suited to the hill areas of the tropics have to be found.[39]

The United States charges that Burma is a "narco-state," directly benefiting from the narcotics trade, harboring drug criminals, and countenancing money laundering from the trade. It has asked for the extradition of Khun Sa, who lives in a Yangon suburb in comfort. That Burma is the site of one of the most intensive narcotics production areas in the world is obvious and accepted. In the past, the state could disclaim responsibility because the periphery was beyond its control, while recognizing that the reputation it was developing would hurt the state. This has changed in part because of the extensive expansion of state control over opium production areas, and the military has made promises of a staged elimination of opium production as its control solidifies and the cease-fires become institutionalized, which in itself is a question. But as state control over the periphery expands, the military cannot evade more responsibility for control of the trade.

There is no solid evidence that the state directly receives income from the illegal trade. Circumstantial evidence is present, however, and many official observers question where the foreign exchange has come from to arm the military and engage in other activities. Mya Maung has commented, "As in the case of many South American and authoritarian regimes around the world, the ability of the Burmese military junta to stay in power is directly linked to its ability to derive hard currency from drug trade and money laundering in order to fortify its military might." [40] Although this may be disputed because the evidence is circumstantial, there is no question that local commanders in critical areas receive benefits, either directly from the heroin factories or from a transit tax on opium or heroin, for otherwise the trade would stop. The United States has commented:

> In 1999, poppy cultivation and opium production continued their three-year decline, falling 31 percent and 38 percent respectively. Although the government has conducted eradication and crop-substitution programs, the decline in opium poppy cultivation was largely attributed to recurring drought. . . . While there is no evidence that the government is involved on an institutional level in the drug trade, there are continuing reports that corrupt army personnel may be aiding traffickers. [41]

There is also no question, as military leaders freely admit, that there are advantages to giving Khun Sa and others asylum: their drug-related rebellions have ceased, government military casualties that were too high to be sustained have stopped, and the funds from their activities, now "laundered," contribute to the economic development of the state through investment in businesses. This, they argue, is an effective means to stem the drug trade. [42]

Internationally the trade is too lucrative, minority relations within Burma/ Myanmar too complex and fragile, and central control too tenuous and likely to remain so for quite some time to expect that this production and trade will soon end. It is likely that any foreseeable Burmese government will likely have to make accommodations on narcotics production and trade to ensure titular central control over some of the minority regions. There are some in the U.S. government who call for a direct renewal of the antinarcotics program in addition to the activities carried out by the UN Drug Control Program. The quiet debate continues.

There has been an alarming explosion in the production, sale, and use of amphetamines and methamphetamines. This has directly affected Thailand, which has become increasingly concerned about use and addiction. Reports estimate that the import of some 600 million "ecstasy" tablets, as methamphetamines are called, is a serious social problem. Although there are ecological, social, and economic reasons for poppy cultivation and opium production in the Golden Triangle region, there are different factors in the production of amphetamines. These are chemically produced and thus are not dependent on appropriate growing conditions. Their production is determined by the availability of markets, chemicals, and (most important) a safe haven for factories. Thus the issue is no longer the poor minority peasant, but rather sophisticated drug entrepreneurs who understand that they are beyond the reach of any law or enforcement authority. This effectively changes the equation in the Golden Triangle into one far more politically charged than previously had been the case. The chemical production of amphetamines, however, will not necessarily conflict with the continued production of opium in the region, for there still is a worldwide market for the latter.

Notes

1. The term "deserving poor" is not one that is prevalent in the West today, although it once was popular.
2. Although the murder rate remained relatively constant, dacoity rose from 551 cases in 1930 to 4,656 the following year, and other types of robbery increased from 1,806 to 3,073 cases in the same period. This was caused by the Saya San Rebellion, which was in part prompted by the decline in living standards and in part by the rise in Burman nationalism. See Teruko Saito and Lee Kin Kiong, *Statistics on the Burmese Economy: The 19th and 20th Centuries* (Singapore: Institute for Southeast Asian Studies, 1999), p. 246. The British and Western historians have treated the Saya San Rebellion as an obscurantist backlash, but Burmese historians and younger Western scholars have given it new importance. The military has put Saya San's picture on the currency.
3. See David I. Steinberg, *Burma's Road toward Development: Growth and Ideology under Military Rule* (Boulder: Westview Press, 1981).
4. Western notions of people as simply "economic animals" often did not apply. When asked who bought a Burmese-made rice cooker for five times the cost of the Chinese one next to it in the bazaar in Mandalay, a shopkeeper replied that people bought the Burmese one to feed the monks, thereby gaining more merit for having spent more.
5. IMF Staff Report, May 22, 1998.
6. Some of the worst antimilitary rioting took place in those areas in 1988, and there may be a causal relationship.
7. Mya Maung, *The Burma Road to Capitalism: Economic Growth versus Democracy* (Westport: Praeger, 1998), pp. 41–44. For a study of the capital, see Than Than Nwe, "Yangon: The Emergence of a New Spatial Order in Myanmar's Capital City." *Sojourn*, Vol. 13, no. 1, 1998, pp. 86–113.

8. Personal communication.

9. Mya Maung, p. 41. There is speculation that some forced movement of peoples in the Shan State is to make way for the reservoir of a major dam across the Salween, planned to be built with Chinese assistance.

10. The author saw such settlements moved close to roads under the Caretaker Government in the Tenasserim area.

11. Mya Maung, p. 249.

12. In one national survey covering urban and rural areas, the bulk of the families had more than one wage earner.

13. There was speculation that the proliferation of political parties registered for the May 1990 election was not only because of perceived political liberalization and ethnic nationalism, but also because such parties had priority access to telephones and extra gasoline rations. The provision of a gasoline ration is said to have been eliminated in late 1999.

14. UNICEF reported that 26 percent of parents said they could not afford to send their children to primary school. Quoted in John Brandon, "The State's Role in Education: An Overview," in *Burma: Prospects for a Democratic Future,* ed. Robert Rotberg (Washington, D.C.: Brookings Institution, 1998), pp. 233–46. Athough government expenditures on education were 0.9 percent of GDP in 1997/98, they had fallen to 0.64 percent in 1998/99. By then, they were about half of the percentage for 1995/96. See Myat Thein and Khin Maung Nyo, "Social Sector Development in Myanmar. The Role of the State." ASEAN Economic Bulletin, Singapore. December 1999.

15. *The Burmese Way to Socialism* (1962).

16. *System of Correlation of Man and His Environment* (1963).

17. Total education consists of ten years of schooling plus kindergarten.

18. Union of Myanmar, *Review of the Financial, Economic and Social Conditions for 1997/98* (Yangon: Ministry of National Planning and Economic Development, 1998), pp. 188–89. The University of Distance Learning was introduced in 1992, largely to prevent the concentration of students in areas where they might demonstrate.

19. Even if we use the 1995/96 enrollment figures for tertiary education, these were one-half of Korean enrollments at the same level, although the national population statistics are about equal.

20. Personal communications, 1960–61 period.

21. The BSPP in 1980 reintroduced English into the curriculum, it was plausibly said, because Ne Win's daughter failed a London examination to study medicine because her English proficiency was weak.

22. Brandon, p. 240.

23. Some specialized schools and institutes reopened in 1999.

24. Burma, Ministry of Health, "An Analysis of Country Health Programming Experience in Burma" (1977).

25. In 1973 the Defense Intelligence Survey of the U.S. Medical Intelligence and Information Agency noted that the leprosy rate for Burma was 8.6 percent when a 2 percent rate would normally be considered high.

26. Personal communication, 1999.

27. Other informal estimates place it at about 8 percent. This is not unique to the region. Infection rates in India, China, and Thailand are hightest on the Myanmar border, indicating that it has become the nexus of the disease in the region. See "AIDS in Burma: A Growing Disaster," David I. Steinberg, *International Herald Tribune,* September 30, 2000. In 1999, Cambodia's minister of health publicly admitted that one out of every seven soldiers and police was infected by HIV/AIDS. Entry into the army is rejected on what are commonly called the "a, b, c grounds": if one has AIDS, if one has hepatitis B, and if one is Christian. Personal communication.

28. Population Services International, Myanmar, a commercial firm, compared seropositive rates of infection with the virus as follows (in percent):

	1992	1998
Commercial sex workers	4.20	29.4
New military recruits	0.56	2.17
Pregnant women	1.90	2.3
Intravenous drug users	62.3	59.3

29. Khin Nyunt, January 20, 2000; *AsiaWeek,* January 21, 2000.

30. "Working Paper on the Humanitarian Crisis, Aid, and Governance in Burma" (Johns Hopkins University, School of Advanced International Studies, May 24, 1999).

31. H. Fielding Hall, *The Soul of a People* (London, 1889), p. 185.

32. Shwe Yoe, *The Burman, His Life and Notions,* 3d ed. (London: Macmillan, 1882), p. 53. This still remains the best single volume that is descriptive of Burman society. Shwe Yoe is the pseudonym of Sir J. George Scott.

33. G.T. Gascoigne, *Among Pagodas and Fair Ladies* (London, 1896).

34. Melford Spiro, *Kinship and Marriage in Burma: A Cultural and Psychodynamic Analysis* (Berkeley: University of California Press, 1977), pp. 257–58. A traditional Burmese saying is that women are four times smarter than men, six times more diligent, and eight times more sensual.

35. Opium is processed into heroin at a rate of approximately 10 to 1; thus 100 lbs. opium = 10 lbs. heroin.

36. Mya Maung, p. 196.

37. Ronald D. Renard, *The Burmese Connection: Illegal Drugs and the Making of the Golden Triangle* (Boulder: Lynne Rienner, 1996), p. 103. It is said that 70 percent of the heroin in the United States comes from the Golden Triangle, and of this amount 98 percent is from Myanmar. The 70 percent figure may reflect interceptions rather than availability.

38. Ibid., pp. 96, 112.

39. The *Bangkok Post* (December 14, 1999, reported on Burmanet News the same day) said that Japanese importers are offering $300 per ton, f.o.b., yet they pay Chinese producers $280 per ton. In 1962, Burmese authorities asked The Asia Foundation to import the crocus bulbs for experimentation in producing saffron, which is labor intensive, very high value, and light weight. Bulbs were ordered but at just that point The Asia Foundation, along with other foreign organizations, was asked to leave Burma, and no follow up was possible. (Personal communication.)

40. Mya Maung, p. 197.

41. U.S. Report to Congress, April 20, 2000; Six-Month Report, September 29, 1999– March 27, 2000. Under PL 104-208, the State Department also noted that the hectarage of harvestable cultivation dropped from 160,000 in 1991 to 130,300 in 1998. Potential yields also fell from 2,350 metric tons to 1,750 metric tons in the same period (U.S. Department of State, Bureau of International Narcotics and Law Enforcement Affairs, March 1999).

42. Personal interview, 1998.

CHAPTER 8

Foreign Affairs:
Myanmar as Regional Nexus

The China Factor

For some years, previous to the date of the expedition (1868), of which the progress is narrated in these pages, the attention of British merchants at home and in India has been directed to the prospect of the overland trade with western China . . . and a direct interchange of our manufactures for the products of the rich provinces of Yunnan and Szechuan might well seem to be advantages which would richly repay almost any efforts to accomplish this purpose.

—Anderson, 1876[1]

In January, 1875, the British mission reached the City of Bhamo, the point of departure for the great overland trade route between India and China. The importance both politically and commercially of the reopening of this route had long been acknowledged by the Indian Government.

—Augustus Ramond Margary, 1876[2]

The traditional patterns of China–Burma trade have been turned on their head. From the middle of the nineteenth century and the Sino-British Opium War of 1842 , for a century China was the destination. Opening the great, unexploited markets of southwest China and Yunnan was of importance to the British and part of their rationale for encompassing Burma in the

British Empire. It was the potential northern flow of trade that appeared to be most enticing. Toward the end of that century, competing with the French, who from Vietnam were attempting to build a railroad to Kunming, was an important secondary motivation. The northern focus continued until the mid-twentieth century. Burma was the southern link, via the Burma and Ledo roads to China, to supplying that beleaguered country with supplies and war materiel during World War II.

Today, geography has been reversed. Bhamo, a sleepy little town on the eastern bank of the Irrawaddy River where only two decades ago horse-drawn "taxis" predominated and once considered as the northernmost pivotal point of economic advance into China by the British, is now viewed as a southern point of influence to the Chinese, for from Bhamo the navigable Irrawaddy River gives inexpensive access south to Mandalay and then to the Bay of Bengal. The easy road access from China to Myitkyina in the Kachin State and the old Burma Road from World War II from China to Lashio in the Shan State provide passages to the rail heads in those two towns and thence to Mandalay and Rangoon. The China factor has become the single most important influence on foreign policy in the region, of which Myanmar has become the nexus.[3]

Chinese relations with the pre-Burman areas now known as Burma were well known, as this was one of the ancient trading routes west during the Chinese Han Dynasty. Relations with the emerging Burmese state historically have not been as close as contemporary public relations specialists of both governments would have us believe—they have not always been *pauk hpaw* (siblings). Kublai Khan destroyed the first Burmese kingdom of Pagan in 1298, and various regional and local Chinese armies have subsequently clashed with the Burmese along the frontier. One Burmese king became known as "He Who Fled from the Chinese." In other periods the Burmese repelled Chinese armies.

But times have changed. Since independence, Burma was most careful with its China relationships. It was the first to recognize the People's Republic of China (PRC) and in the civilian period exchanged numerous leadership delegations and received some foreign assistance. Burma was most concerned in 1950, when Kuomintang forces fled into Burma, because the Burmese felt the PRC might pursue them. Under the Caretaker Government, the military signed a border agreement with the Chinese, and the BSPP regime withdrew from the Non-Aligned Movement in 1979, when it became too close to the Soviet

Union, thus upsetting China, who accused the Soviets of hegemonism. Burma has been able neither to police nor to control its long China border.[4]

The emergence of Myanmar from the chrysalis of Burma in 1988, however, heralded a major shift in regional power relationships and concerns. This shift was not caused by the redistribution of internal power in Burma, which remained in the hands of the military as it had been since 1962, but rather in external interest in Myanmar in the light of important and significant internal Burmese and Chinese policy changes related to trade and investment. Belated openings to the private sector generated regional rivalries in the pursuit of profits. Coincidental with the openings to the private sector in Burma came internal Chinese liberalization, which encouraged the development of private sector trading and development. The Burmese military expansion and modernization raised questions. The exodus of refugees from ethnic fighting and even greater movement of Burmese migrants for work in neighboring states, especially Thailand, sometimes in unseemly occupations, raised security and health concerns as HIV/AIDS spread. As long as Burma remained essentially economically supine and inert, no neighbor was concerned, and the state was ignored even as a modest border smuggling trade prospered and the surreptitious narcotics trade continued.[5] But with potential markets and minerals newly open to foreign investment and as internal policies affected external relations, Burma moved from the penumbra, creating regional rivalries reminiscent of an earlier age.

If China looms largest in its influence on Burma's foreign policy, Japan has played the critical role in domestic policy changes that in turn affected foreign policy. The impetus for such changes, as noted in chapter 5, came in 1988, when Japan warned the Burmese that significant reforms would have to be made in their economic policies. But economic changes were also generated internally. The demonetization announced by Ne Win in 1987, the third and most devastating, destroyed faith in an already markedly overvalued currency. The unrecognized but obviously highly profitable China trade expanded, although much of it went unreported. The Burmese citizenry needed to hold durable and consumer goods, which created a spurt in demand for imports. Burma on all its borders survived by smuggling—consumer goods in, and raw materials out. One estimate indicated, for example, that some 20 percent of the Arakan rice crop was smuggled to Bangladesh. But it was China that has proven to be most important.

Myanmar has become a critical nexus in the China–India connection.[6] As Mohan Malik has written,

> Seeing India as a potential challenger in South and Southeast Asia, China has sought to contain it through strategic alignment with Pakistan and Burma. China's evolving naval doctrine envisages a coordination of efforts with its allies such as Iran, Iraq, Pakistan, and Burma to ensure dominance and control over trade routes and energy resources in the event of a regional or global crisis. This strategy leaves China free to act without the constraint of either a regional balancer or a regional counterweight on mainland and maritime Asia.[7]

From an Indian perspective, the situation is reversed:

> It is commonly averred that Indian security concerns over the fifty years since Independence have focused on two visible neighbors—Pakistan and China, in that order of priority. However, using the term strategic in a more rigorous sense, this article argues that India's primary strategic security concern is China, and if so, Myanmar occupies the next slot. In other words, if China takes the number one position in terms of strategic priorities/challenges to the Indian state, then Myanmar is 1A, while Pakistan follows in the next position. . . . One can even argue that Myanmar can affect the interests of the USA in the region, so that this country emerges as the single most significant swing factor in shaping the strategic balance of southern Asia.[8]

The China commercial connection has become vital to Myanmar in the dozen years since it exploded.[9] China has become a major supplier of Myanmar's consumer products. Although the China trade was regularized and taxed in October 1988, official figures mask its importance and may represent as little as 20 percent of its real value. Whatever the actual figures, the Yunnan People's Export Corporation in 1988 indicated that some 2,000 separate kinds of goods were exported to Burma.[10]

The Sino-Burmese relationship has extended to intelligence activities as well as arms supplies and trade. Desmond Ball catalogues the factors that have made this true: "China is Burma's only major intelligence partner." Although Singapore has supplied equipment, "virtually all other elements of Burma's intelligence modernization have been provided by China."[11] Chinese support seems aimed at improving its access and intelligence in the Bay of Bengal.

China needed the south. At a meeting of southwestern Chinese province officials and academicians in Chengtu in the mid-1990s, participants noted that it was impossible for those provinces to compete internationally with the eastern provinces, where foreign investment was extensive and shipping costs low.[12] Therefore, the natural markets for goods from the southwest were in Burma, Thailand, Vietnam, Cambodia, and Laos.[13] During the earlier period of SLORC, assignment to the Chinese frontier area was considered so potentially lucrative that bribes were given for such postings.[14]

China as a foreign policy issue cannot be separated from the indigenous aspects of Chinese relations in Burma, which have shifted as have the international components of the relationship. The Chinese population of Burma, a figure subject to controversy, was estimated at 350,000–400,000, 1.3 percent of the population, before World War II. The overall Chinese population was estimated at 233,470 in the 1983 census, although this figure is no doubt smaller than the numbers who may consider themselves to be at least part Chinese.[15] The problem of determining the number of Chinese was complicated when Chinese Nationalist forces fled from the communists in 1949–50 and occupied a part of the Shan State, hoping later to reenter China. They were assisted by the United States through the CIA, the Thai military, and Nationalist authorities in Taiwan and were countered by PRC forces that conducted operations in the Shan State.[16] Although many were evacuated, some remained in Burma and others went to northern Thailand. In both areas they are said to be heavily engaged in the drug trade. The Sino-Burmese community has been important; it has relatively easily assimilated into the Burmese society—partly because many of the Chinese are also Buddhists—although their presence is in no way as profound as in Thailand. Many prominent figures, such as Ne Win, Aung Gyi, San Yu, and Tin Pe, are said to be Sino-Burmese. Unless Chinese (among other nonindigenous nationals) can prove the Burmese residence of their ancestors before 1824, they cannot become full citizens under the Citizenship Law of 1982 and thus cannot hold certain official positions or even attend universities.

The Chinese, at 1.5 percent of the labor force, were concentrated; they were 9.7 percent of the mining industry and 6.9 percent of trade. Current figures for the Chinese in the labor force are lacking.

Of special significance is the increased importance and visibility of the Chinese. There has been an influx of Chinese from southwest China who do not need visas for border crossing but manage to stay in the country and permeate many urban areas. Much of the economy has moved into Chinese hands, with potentially dire consequences for social unrest. Mandalay, the seat of Burman culture, is said to have 200,000 recently arrived Yunnanese Chinese out of a population of one million: "Chinese entrepreneurs dominate Mandalay's central business district, raising concerns among local Burmese about their role and the extent of Chinese immigration, much of it illegal." [17] Less visible, but no less important, may be the influx of rural Chinese who are absorbed into the countryside. Because of flooding in Yunnan and opportunities in Myanmar, many Chinese are "changing the whole demographic balance in Northern Burma," and their estimated numbers range from several hundred thousand to over one million in the past several years (an informal but official Chinese estimate).

In the past, foreigners have sometimes been the scapegoats for internal economic or social failures. In 1967 antiregime sentiment was channeled into anti-Chinese rioting, ostensibly because of local Chinese students involved in the cultural revolution, but the more likely underlying cause was the obvious and dominant role of the Chinese in retail trade during an extremely difficult economic period.[18] There are dangers that a Burmese government could redirect resentment onto the Chinese community, as it did in 1967 and as has happened in Indonesia. As one former Chinese ambassador was quoted as saying, "We [Chinese] are walking on eggshells [in Myanmar]." Because of the massacres in Indonesia, the PRC has become more vigilant in calling for the protection of overseas Chinese. These internal factors are additional to regional concerns related to Chinese influence in the Bay of Bengal, Burmese reliance on Chinese military supplies and equipment,[19] and the financing of Burmese infrastructure designed to improve Yunnan trade with Burma.[20]

China has been supporting the building of a complex network of bridges and roads designed in part to increase Chinese trade with Burma. It also has supported trans-Irrawaddy bridges (some say with a view toward access to the Indian border), and Chinese improvement of airfields in Mandalay, Meiktila, and Pegu potentially give China avenues toward the Bay of Bengal.[21] China is also supposedly assisting in developing port facilities along the Burmese littoral, at Hainggyi and Ramree Islands in the Arakan and in Tenasserim, and there have been rumors of a Chinese tracking station in the bay on Great Coco Island, close to the Indian-controlled Andaman Islands and the Indian naval base there.[22] Construction was supposed to have started in 1991 or 1992 and was detected by U.S. satellite in late 1992.

> Given the location and extensive capabilities of the Great Coco Island SIGINT station, it undoubtedly has several functions, including: helping the Burmese "to protect their long coastline and police their exclusive economic zone,"

collecting intelligence on regional military activities, especially naval and air movements in the eastern part of the Bay of Bengal, monitoring activities at the Indian naval base and tri-service garrison at Port Blair in the Andaman Islands, intercepting telemetry associated with Indian ballistic missile test launches over the Bay of Bengal.[23]

From a stagnant backwater, Myanmar has been transformed into a source of regional concern and understated, but nonetheless significant, rivalry.

Chinese economic and military assistance was significant, but more important was the increased official and unofficial role of the Chinese in trade and their physical presence in the state. As noted, to facilitate the border trade, Chinese and Burmese were authorized to cross the borders without visas. Although there were said to be many Burmese working in Yunnan Province, the increase of Chinese in northern and central Burma was apparent. Chinese were said to be buying real estate as far south as Mandalay (using Burmese identity cards).[24] The Burmese have allowed the Chinese to establish businesses in both Myitkyina and Bhamo. Chinese products flooded northern Burma, extending even to Rangoon. Godowns and hotels were established along the frontier to further trade, and Chinese were seen operating openly in central Burma as well as along the frontier. Chinese goods, materials, shops, and hotels dominated Mandalay, turning northern Burma into baja [lower]-Yunnan.

Even official trade figures, which, as noted, are suspect and grossly understated, show a marked change. In 1988 Burmese exports to China were $1.81 million and imports from China $7.7 million. By 1989, they were $24.6 million and $53.43 million respectively, and by 1995 they had grown to $202 million and $480 million respectively (estimated).[25] Statistics on overland trade are notoriously questionable, both because of smuggling and because legal imports are undervalued for customs purposes and inspectors are appropriately rewarded, but China in 1988/89 was said to control 27 percent of official Burmese imports, while Thailand held 4 percent; in 1994/95, China made up 12 percent, while Thailand's share had increased to 10 percent.[26]

China has been important to Burma, and reporting on the incessant delegations between the two countries (including regional delegations from Yunnan Province) has been standard fare in the state-controlled *New Light of Myanmar (Working People's Daily)* in Rangoon.[27]

The new and changed economic pattern, which became more important as all foreign donors except the Chinese cut off foreign assistance, altered the pattern of power in the Bay of Bengal littoral. As noted, China became the main supplier of arms (including sophisticated equipment) to the military. It is said the purchases were paid for by mortgaging Burma's future oil revenues.[28] The supply of Chinese armaments has included fighter aircraft, patrol boats, artillery, multiple rocket launchers, tanks, armored personnel carriers, and other equipment. China started training Burmese military personnel in 1989. Chinese investment did not go through the National Foreign Investment Board and thus was omitted from national data. Such investment may be the largest infusion of capital from any state. Official figures placed cumulative Chinese investment through 1996 at $16 million, a ludicrous understatement.

Thailand became concerned. It had evidently come to view itself as the economic hegemon of mainland Southeast Asia and was interested in control over the region's economy, but it believed it was losing out to China. The prime example of this was when Prime Minister Chatichai presented an aide memoire to President George Bush at the Japanese Emperor's funeral in February 1989, in which he called for U.S. collaboration with the Thai in expanding diplomatic and trade relations with Indochina and, significantly, also with Burma. The United States, at least publicly, ignored this invitation, which received little publicity in the American press, although it was prominently featured in Thai newspapers.

Authoritative sources within Thailand indicated that the Thai government was concerned with Chinese economic control over Myanmar and the resulting spread of Chinese influence, as well as the close alliance between the Chinese and Burmese military and the loss of Thai markets. That individual Thai (and Thai military-controlled) firms developed important teak and other concessions with the Burmese military was thus considered useful in checking Chinese influence.

India could not be immune to any developments in Burma. Relations between India and Burma have traditionally been poor, even when the two countries were under joint British colonial rule. (Burma was governed first from Calcutta and then from Delhi until 1937.) Although history may not be precedent, the First Anglo-Burmese War (1824–26) was fought because of Burmese expansion into Bengal and Manipur. The British encouraged Indian migration into Burma to provide labor for various industries, as well as to help staff the administration in its early stages. The British also used troops from India to subdue the Burmese. Indians came to control a large share of the economy and were essential lenders of capital to the impoverished Burmese peasantry. Rangoon was considered essentially an Indian city. Economic and cultural disputes prompted anti-Indian (Muslim) riots in major Burmese cities in the 1930s. The result has been a strong, continuing Burmese prejudice against the Indians for a century, a prejudice that has been economic, political, international, religious, and racial.

According to the census of 1983, a document that must be treated with some caution, Burma was 0.5 percent Hindu and 3.9 percent Muslim.[29] The report states that there were 428,428 Indians, 42,140 Pakistanis, 567,985 Bangladeshis, and 73,511 Nepalis in the country. Although the subcontinent groups have lost their stranglehold over the economy, they are influential in some aspects of trade. There is little question today that Myanmar regards India as a potential enemy, even if relations are formally appropriate.[30]

Even before the coup of September 1988, India in August had backed the development of a democratic alternative to the Burmese military (although eschewing the "parallel government" that U Nu had declared).[31] From that time, India became the most vociferous critic of the SLORC and the military regime in Rangoon.

This criticism was persistent and was expressed through All India Radio (AIR—India's equivalent of the BBC or Voice of America [VOA]), which employed U Nu's daughter in the Burmese service. There is little question that although the SLORC complained about all three international networks, it was particularly incensed with the AIR. Its criticisms were expressed through the controlled press, and a major series of articles on earlier Burmese history was published expounding on foreign, but especially Indian, degradations of Burma, its culture, and its peoples. They were clearly intended to foster antipathy toward India and its resident population in Myanmar. In late 1990, when some members of the NLD escaped to the rebel region along the Thai border, the Indian authorities provided modest support to their activities. Also in 1990, when Burmese dissidents hijacked a Thai Airways plane and had it flown to India, Indian officials released the hijackers on bail, much to the anger of the SLORC.[32]

Changes in the Chinese-Burmese relationship happened to coincide with the internal liberalization of the Chinese economy, which allowed China to respond to the new Myanmar situation with speed and relative efficiency. It employed an effective economic intelligence system to pinpoint local production, shortages, and preferences and recommend various products for import.

For example, an exceedingly popular checkered male *longyi* of a particularly virulent shade of blue was originally smuggled in from Madras but was later replaced by Chinese goods of the same design. Moreover, Chinese goods were cheaper and of better quality than locally produced goods.

Internal Indian events also fostered Indian interest in Burma. The government of Rajiv Gandhi was exerting its regional power. It had moved militarily into Sri Lanka and the Maldives. It was engaged in a dispute with Nepal: because Kathmandu had bought Chinese weapons, India had closed the frontier, thus causing extreme economic hardship to landlocked Nepal, the imports to which had to traverse India if they were to come by land. The Indian navy was expanding its operations in the Indian Ocean—more specifically in the Andaman Sea and the Bay of Bengal.

Burma was important to India. It was not directly confrontational, as was the Chinese presence in Tibet. Although the frontier held none of the traumatic possibilities of the Pakistan–Kashmir region, the echoes of the Sino-Indian War of 1962 remained, and the eastern portion of the disputed Sino-Indian border had never been formally resolved. Northeastern Burma flanked both the Chinese and Indian interests, and the area was inhabited by smaller ethnic groups that straddled that triangular region. India had encouraged the migration of tribal peoples from China and Burma onto the Indian frontier to act as a buffer to Chinese expansion in a sparsely populated area.[33]

Throughout the Indo-Burmese border, there were other concerns as well. The revolt of the Naga rebels in India was supported by the Naga peoples on the Burma side of the frontier, and rebels moved across the remote frontier, which was ethnically heterogeneous throughout. If Nagaland was a problem to India, Mizoram was an issue as well. In Burma, the Chin peoples call themselves "Zo" and are closely related to the Mizo of India, who were also a splinter group.[34] India provided covert support to ethnic rebels within Burma, including the Kachin Independence Army, one of the most formidable of the rebel groups, which in turn helped train Kuki and Chin forces that could be used against Naga rebels fighting the Indian government. Indians also assisted Chin rebels, and in turn the SLORC supported Naga and Manipuri dissidents against the Indian government.[35] India also provided funds to the opposition NCGUB.

The Indo-Chinese competition in Myanmar has brought in Pakistan. Evidently, if India has backed the Burmese opposition, Pakistan (with its additional links to China) has supported the SLORC. There have been exchanges of military missions, and there were persistent reports of Pakistani shipments of arms to the *tatmadaw,* but whether under loans or grants is unknown. Clearly Pakistan viewed an India engaged on its eastern border as in its longer-range security interests.

It is, of course, simplistic to consider either India or China as monolithic internally or temporally. Policies in both countries may change in focus or emphasis. The Indian case is illustrative. Following the death of Rajiv Gandhi, the new government seemed to tone down its anti-SLORC line, and new policies were begun in 1992–93, but over time the stridency gradually decreased. On the other hand, China for years supported the activities of the BCP along the China frontier and trained many cadre, claiming that party-to-party relations were distinct from state-to-state relations.

The new economic policies of the Indian government, which encourages both the foreign and domestic private sectors, may influence economic and political relations with Myanmar. India may find itself more competitive in a broader spectrum of goods in the Burma market than heretofore. Although the China border is both long and serviced by the Burma Road from the border to the railhead at Lashio in the Shan State, the Indian market is available by sea and also quite inexpensively through Tamu and down the Yu River into the Chindwin and Irrawaddy to Mandalay and then to Rangoon. That route has been increasingly popular for the smuggling of chemicals for the production and export of heroin from Myanmar through India to broader, more lucrative markets. Thus India may become more involved with Myanmar economically, and Myanmar may want to regularize and tax the commercial trade as it has done with China. There have been negotiated trade and other agreements with India, and relations have significantly improved.

China's national interests clearly involve Myanmar. "Seeing India as a potential challenger in South and Southeast Asia, China has sought to contain it through strategic alignment with Pakistan and Burma. China's evolving naval strategy envisages a coordination of efforts with its allies such as Iran, Iraq, Pakistan, and Burma to ensure dominance and control over trade routes and energy resources in the event of a regional or global crisis." [36] Some Burmese have evidently become concerned over the extent of Chinese influence. The SPDC reportedly turned down a Chinese proposal to establish a container port at Bhamo and improve the port facilities at Kyaukpyu in the Arakan.

Yunnan Province clearly benefits from the Myanmar trade, although it is impossible to determine to what degree either the legal or illegal trade contributes to the Yunnan economy. Yunnan may be the conduit through which trade flows, but the products themselves come from all over China. Thus Kwangchou beer and cigarettes have been cheaper in Mandalay than Mandalay beer and Burmese cigarettes, and both have been more easily accessible. Should any future central Chinese government desire to restrict this trade, for political or other reasons, it would probably be difficult.

The issue of drugs cannot be ignored in this complex equation. As discussed in chapter 7, there have been reports of the movement of drugs from Burma into China, with increasing addiction and spread of AIDS.[37] Some argue that the increase in drug traffic was a result not only of the increasing markets and marketing possibilities, but also because of aerial spraying and/or because of the demonetization of the Burmese currency, forcing hill dwellers to hold opium as lowland farmers held rice instead of cash.

Myanmar's close alignment with China serves the immediate needs of the SLORC for guns, funds, and friends, but it may not be in the longer-term interest of the Burmese state. The alignment has exacerbated rivalries that may in the future be dangerous, even if China has neither territorial nor revolutionary ambitions. It seems now evident that the Burmese are slowing down the close association because the military may fear Chinese economic domination, southern migration, and the potential of internal Burmese backlash first against the Chinese and then against the military who brought about a condition of virtual Chinese hegemony.

To what degree can China help modify Burmese policies? China is Myanmar's most important neighbor. If in the Orwellian sense all states with diplomatic relations with Burma are equal, China is more equal than others. Informal Chinese approval may have been given, for example, before Burma solicited economic assistance from the United States in the late 1970s. There are rumors that China has been suggesting to the SLORC that it modify its repressive policies, but these are not confirmed.

Chinese interests in Myanmar are clear, as are Indian interests in preventing too strong a Chinese role. "Closer Sino-Burmese ties are now seen as 'of great significance to the national security of China.' "[38] Burmese interests in China have been more complex. Fear of Chinese expansion has been an obvious concern. Chinese maps in the 1950s and earlier had included northern Burma in Chinese territory. It is said that Ne Win's pronatalist policy on families was based on fears of Chinese population expansion into an underpopulated Burma. The famous "Burma Surgeon" of World War II fame, Gordon Seagrave, who operated the best hospital along the Chinese frontier, argued that Chinese migration into Burma had traditionally been stopped only by a particularly virulent strain of malaria to which the Chinese seemed vulnerable. Strong Chinese relations also preclude the United Nations from taking any adverse action against Myanmar, such as sanctions, since China has veto power in the Security Council. Perhaps the supply of new arms from China placates some of the more junior members of the Burmese military, who might have become restive under present leadership.

Other, more vital problems in the Sino-American relationship (WTO issues, trade, Taiwan, human rights in China, etc.) probably preclude serious discussion of Burma. Secretary of State James Baker in a 1991 China visit had Myanmar on his agenda to discuss with the Chinese leadership. It was obviously low on the list and may not have been discussed or stressed.

Sino-Indian relations in the formal sense have improved. Li Peng, the Chinese prime minister, visited India in December 1991, and Indian prime minister Rao reciprocated in 1992. India seemed to support Chinese sovereignty over Tibet, and competition on the periphery, such as in Burma, seemed to play no role in the discussions. Burma will not replace those areas of foreign policy that are considered directly threatening to the Indian national interests, but along the periphery Burma will likely loom larger. The presence of the Chinese, even in a solely commercial aspect, on the Bay of Bengal, long considered an Indian preserve, would exacerbate Sino-Indian problems and focus even more attention on Myanmar. It is likely that the Thai would also view such a development with some concern. Although the Cold War fears of Chinese political or ideological expansion are over, regional rivalries still play important roles in national policies.

Japan is naturally concerned over the growing power of China since these two nations are the only potential hegemons in the East Asia region. Myanmar figures in both the Chinese and Japanese equations. Unofficially, former Japanese defense officials have indicated that the strengthening of the China–Myanmar connection—for example, if China is able to import oil to southwest China via Myanmar, thus avoiding the Malacca Straits and the South China Sea—would not be in Japan's long-term interests.[39] Yet according to J. Mohan

Malik, China's strategy for the twenty-first century involves securing oil access to the Middle East by sea, much as it will attempt to control central Asian pipelines into China via Xingiang. As India views China as a potential adversary, so China views India as a state that could control the supply of significant oil shipments to China.[40] In addition to Japan's sentimental attachment and commercial interests in Myanmar, which are considerable, the possibility of weaning Myanmar away from China may be an additional and strong impetus for the resumption of major Japanese foreign assistance to Myanmar.

The military implications for Chinese influence in Myanmar have been stated as follows: access through Myanmar allows China to outflank both India and ASEAN; access also enhances China's signal intelligence (SIGINT) in monitoring India (especially from the Coco Islands) and ASEAN; a pliant Myanmar gives China access to the Indian Ocean, making China a two-ocean country; even a benign relationship will alter the existing maritime/naval balance of the world; and Myanmar becomes a "rimland" state, giving China a natural advantage.[41]

The alternatives to Chinese economic and strategic domination of Myanmar may also have been a factor in ASEAN's successful efforts to make Myanmar a member.

How do the Burmese react to Sino-Indian rivalry, Thai concerns about the Chinese presence, and U.S. policies in Asia? Although surface relations between Myanmar and India and Thailand are cordial, there have been historic deep-seated problems with both countries. India is considered a potential enemy of Myanmar, and Thailand and Burma have been centuries-old rivals, Burma having destroyed the Thai capital of Ayuthia (still the name for Thailand in Burmese) in 1767 and controlled much of what is northern Thailand for long periods. The Burmese remain deeply suspicious of the United States. That suspicion prompts the military to consider U.S. support (moral and financial) to the opposition and related groups along the Thai border as an effort to strengthen the forces containing China to prevent it from assuming a hegemonic role in the region. The Burmese officially have written:

> [As China becomes a major power, there is a strong lobby in the U.S. for containing China.] One approach to the problem is to influence China's immediate neighbors to take a more pro-Western stance. Therefore, from a Western point of view, Myanmar could be deemed to be the weak link in the regional China containment policy, as primarily advocated by the U.S. Their attempt in creating Myanmar as a Client State is quite obvious in their blatant interference in Myan-

mar's internal affairs and the actions against her. But if their actions become successful, Myanmar will be once again turned into a nation of warring ethnic groups and proxy war.[42]

Thus, rather than seeing U.S. policy as devoted to humanitarian and social goals, including human rights and good governance, the military sees the United States as using Myanmar as part of a scheme antagonistic to China and thus dangerous to Myanmar. To the authorities in Rangoon, this creates even greater problems than concerns over human rights.

The ASEAN Issue

The decision in May 1997 to allow the entry of Myanmar into ASEAN, which took place in July of that year after considerable international debate and lobbying by both proponents and opponents, was the culmination of over half a decade of Burmese interest in that organization after two decades of studious avoidance. This was a major foreign policy change by the SLORC, which had moved away from the essentially isolationist precepts of the BSPP regime. Before the elections of May 1990, there had been informal soundings by Burmese officials on whether there would be U.S. opposition to Myanmar's joining this club.[43] At that time, and before the SLORC seemed almost perpetually frozen in its authoritarian mold, there were those who would have welcomed such membership because Burma had been so secluded for about thirty years from most international dialogue that exposure to outside views and more transparency in international relations would have been conceived as progress, even for a regime that had come to power in a bloody coup.

As repression in Myanmar continued, however, this view in the West dramatically shifted. This was especially evident after the SLORC studiously ignored the results of the elections of 1990 and with the house arrest of Aung San Suu Kyi (which had taken place earlier). As it became evident that the SLORC had no intention of allowing a nonmilitary government to be formed and as human rights and democracy became more central to the foreign policy of a variety of states, especially the United States, U.S. attitudes toward Myanmar's joining ASEAN became vigorously negative.

This was not true, however, among the ASEAN members. ASEAN operated through an informal system of consensus, not confrontation, and noninterference in the internal affairs of the member states. The Treaty of Amity and Cooperation and the ASEAN Concord, signed by the members in Bali in 1976, stressed these factors. The member states saw opportunities for trade and investment that could be better pursued within the ASEAN context. Led by Thailand, they developed the rather ambiguous slogan of "constructive engagement," which theoretically was to transform Myanmar into a more open society through increasing trade, investment, and economic relations, but which in practice seemed more devoted to pursuing short-term profit-making than to fostering long-term political reform. Most member states themselves could not be accused of devout adherence to an international (or Western) standard of democracy, and military rule in Myanmar may have seemed to some of those governments a better alternative than the chaos or communist control that the SLORC continued to stress would have taken place had it not come to power. There was, in addition, a growing concern among some ASEAN member states that the overwhelming influence of China in Myanmar needed tempering and that this might be accomplished through increased ASEAN relations, reliance, and trade.

The apparent Chinese influence within Myanmar was said to be of some concern to elements of the Burmese military, although never publicly articulated. The general official atmosphere of xenophobia, mostly directed toward the West but prevalent in government pronouncements as a whole, probably contributed to the regime's desire to moderate its Chinese dependency. Joining ASEAN was probably conceived as both adding international prestige and legitimacy and a form of protection against economic domination by China. It may also have been viewed by some as a means to ensure the Burmese border and to prevent potential Chinese encroachment.

Myanmar in 1995 was invited to attend the fifth ASEAN summit, which was held in Bangkok, and at that time signed the Southeast Asian Nuclear Weapons Free Zone Treaty. That same year, Myanmar became an observer at ASEAN and some months later joined the ASEAN Regional Forum (ARF). It was an offshoot devoted to dialogue on regional security matters. It had been apparent for about two years that Myanmar would not be excluded from formal ASEAN membership, but two issues were evident: when or whether some outrageous new act of oppression would prompt entry denial or lengthy delay.

The push for Myanmar admission to ASEAN was led by Malaysia, which hosted the thirtieth anniversary meeting in Kuala Lumpur in July 1997 and wanted the symmetry of all ten of the Southeast Asian nations in the organization. ASEAN was seen as a stabilizing force, and thus complete Southeast Asian membership was considered desirable. Myanmar's entry was cleverly orchestrated jointly to include Laos and Cambodia, so that any problems connected with Burmese inclusion would be mitigated by group action and perhaps, if necessary, diplomatically postponed based on diffused difficulties if pressures became too great. The coup by Hun Sen in Cambodia just prior to its projected entry caused considerable consternation among the ASEAN states and resulted in Cambodia's temporary exclusion from the club. Even that took pressure off Myanmar. The American secretary of state, Madeleine Albright, vigorously protested Burmese entry, although other ASEAN dialogue partners, such as Japan and South Korea, remained silent. Some have argued that because the United States so vehemently opposed Burmese entry into ASEAN, the ASEAN states pushed for admittance so that they could not be perceived as submitting to U.S. control. This raises two dilemmas for U.S. policy: the degree to which adherence to a moral foreign policy position toward a state in which the United States has few strategic or economic interests (Myanmar) will take precedence over close relations with a region (ASEAN) where such interests are exceedingly important, and the discrepancies between the U.S. positions on human rights in China and Myanmar.

There seems little question that in the near term, entry into ASEAN strengthens Myanmar internationally but prompts little in the way of significant political or economic changes in the Burmese system. Yet some believe that the SLORC allowed, without overt interference, the NLD to hold its convention September 27–28, 1998, to celebrate the anniversary of its founding because of the country's recent entry into ASEAN, thus placating any misgivings among some of its members. Others argue that each fall the SLORC modestly eases its repression (but not its control) because of the annual UN General Assembly debate that has occurred since 1990. This gesture never significantly altered the power equation in Myanmar, which is still heavily weighted toward the SLORC/SPDC.

Over the longer term, however, entry into ASEAN, with its opaque consensual style, will prompt Myanmar to conform to ASEAN standards of international trade and other economic desiderata. (An ASEAN free trade zone is planned, and Myanmar has ten years from 1997 to conform to ASEAN tariff standards.) Myanmar must adhere to the ASEAN framework agreements on services, industrial cooperation, intellectual property rights, investment protection protocols, and transparency on trade laws and regulations. These are all positive forces that may push more rational international economic relations, but politically the pressures are likely to remain relatively light, given the policy of noninterference (somewhat compromised by the Cambodian coup, with Malaysia calling for a new policy of "constructive intervention" and the Thai wanting "enhanced engagement") and the internal political anomalies in the majority of ASEAN states. It is unlikely that Burmese entry into ASEAN will mitigate Chinese influence, as some contend, through diversification of investment or support; whether it will diffuse the potential for an anti-Chinese backlash is highly questionable, should there be a popular feeling that the Chinese control the economy or if there is a severe internal economic downturn. Since much of the investment entering Myanmar is from Singapore and Thailand (with their strong ethnic Chinese business communities) and perhaps indirectly from Taiwan (with which ironically Myanmar has no diplomatic relations but growing economic ties) via Chinese intermediaries in Southeast Asia, the overt Chinese presence is likely to remain. The people have had a penchant for xenophobia whipped up by the governments of Myanmar/Burma in the past. To the Burmese, fine national distinctions are likely to be secondary to ethnic origins in times of crisis.

Contacts at very senior levels with ASEAN states may have produced some change. In a highly unusual circumstance, Ne Win visited Indonesia in September 1997 to meet with Suharto, in return, it is said, for Suharto's previous visit to Myanmar. This set off speculation that consultations were taking place on issues of internal importance for potential change in Myanmar, for, as noted in chapter 4, Indonesia has been the unarticulated model for the SLORC/SPDC. Although the trip was officially said to be personal, few believed such a rare occurrence was without political import.[44] The change in name from SLORC to SPDC may have arisen as a result of those discussions. In early October, Khin Nyunt visited Singapore, whose government has been supportive of the Burmese regime, and called Singapore a staunch ally of Myanmar. Singapore's trade with Myanmar had doubled from 1991 to $856.21 million in 1996, and Singapore became Myanmar's largest official investor ($1.3 billion) since Chinese investment is not included. It is widely believed that Singapore is a major supplier of military and telecommunications equipment to Myanmar as well.

The United States and the Issue of Sanctions

The position of the United States toward Myanmar has remained rigid, perhaps because U.S. national interests in regard to Myanmar have been marginal. There has been no question of the recognition of the SLORC (and now the SPDC) regime. (It was only the Japanese who had to re-recognize Burma after the 1988 coup; other states simply regarded the new military government as a continuation of the old through different personnel.) However, the United States has refused to appoint an ambassador to Rangoon after the stalemate following the 1990 elections (the embassy remained open with a chargé who now has the stature, if not the title, of ambassador) and has continued (with the NLD) to call the state by its old designation, Burma, thus making nomenclature a political statement. Long past is the period in which Rangoon was a critical listening post for the United States in the Sino-Soviet split, and as opium production and the drug trade expanded, U.S. interests shifted to that issue. As democracy and human rights became more prominent in U.S. policy and as elements of the bureaucracy were formed to pursue those concerns, these issues assumed major proportions in official U.S. thinking.

The United States has called for respect for human rights, suppression of the drug trade, and the recognition by the SLORC of the results of the May 1990 election, overwhelmingly won by the NLD, and thus the formation of a new government that would be led by Aung San Suu Kyi. The proposed constitution is, however, specifically designed to prevent her from assuming any political office, as well as keeping the military in fundamental control of all organs of state power.

Thus the United States has found itself in direct confrontation with the SLORC/SPDC with little prospect of ameliorating the impasse while both governments remain in place and continue in their stated positions. The United States charged that the SLORC had done little to eliminate the heroin trade. The contention, as some charge, that the SLORC/SPDC has directly profited from the drug trade (as opposed to corrupt local military commanders and their subordinates) is disputed, as no direct evidence has appeared (see chapter 7).

Previously, the United States had enforced an arms embargo on Myanmar and had refused to renew a textile agreement, but these actions caused little outcry, as those affected were very few. As internal political pressures within the United States were expanded by human rights activists and some NGOs, as the policy bureaucracy was in place to respond to these concerns, and as "vital" U.S. interests were not threatened (as they were in China, with the enormity of U.S. trade and investment there and the potential for more), the United States has the luxury of adhering to its proclaimed foreign policy morality. So pressures for a stronger policy toward Myanmar have emerged.

There were divergent domestic reactions to the situation in Myanmar. Business groups, and even some members of the administration, were opposed to sanctions against the regime. They were interested in the rich potential that Myanmar offered both in terms of eventual markets and more immediately in its extensive raw material base and its cheap, controlled, and literate labor force.[45] They were also concerned lest other foreign investors, who seemed to have strong interests in Myanmar, staked claims that would prevail and make later market entry difficult. Some were opposed to sanctions on new investments because they felt they would have little effect since trade with Myanmar was an infinitesimal percentage of U.S. trade and a small proportion of Myanmar's potential trade. Many believed that once imposed, sanctions would be difficult to undo because that would require some concrete and persuasive positive change in the Burmese administration that was unlikely to be either forthcoming or convincing.

In March 1997, however, the Congress passed the sanctions bill on new investment (old investments remained untouched). Even some Congressmen who feared the restrictions on trade and were concerned about the inconsistencies in U.S. foreign policy (such as U.S. reactions to China and Myanmar on trade questions) said that politically they could not oppose sanctions because they would be seen as supporting the SLORC regime, which had become a worldwide pariah.

This was a testament to the strength of the anti-SLORC lobby in the United States (and to the new media technology that allowed virtually instant and inexpensive communications among parties interested in a particular issue), which had become effective in mobilizing public opinion against the Burmese regime at both the national and local levels. More than fifteen local bodies, including the state of Massachusetts, have passed legislation prohibiting companies that invest or trade in Myanmar from contracting with such local governments.[46] The Federal District Court, however, determined in 1998 that the Massachusetts law was unconstitutional because the state was preempting the federal government's right to make foreign policy. This decision was appealed in 1999, and in 2000 the Supreme Court overthrew the Massachusetts law.[47] There has been some significant business exodus from Myanmar as a result of the economic pressure, but perhaps more important is the opprobrium attached to sourcing production there or engaging in trade.

The Congress has also passed legislation that prohibits SLORC/SPDC members, families, or senior employees from obtaining visas for travel in the United States. There are the obvious exceptions for diplomats accredited to the United States or activities involving the United Nations, but in a highly mobilized state such as Myanmar, where every schoolteacher or professor is considered a government employee, how or whether this will be enforced is still unclear. In 1999 and 2000, the State Department turned down informal requests from private groups to allow the Burmese foreign minister to visit Washington and participate in academic fora.

Relations between U.S. Secretary of State Madeleine Albright and Aung San Suu Kyi are said to be personally close, and there have been informal consultations with the latter on multilateral foreign assistance, such as with the UNDP. There has been a successful movement among some members of the Congress to formalize such consultations, although to do so would be tantamount to recognizing the NLD as a virtual government-in-exile, an action that would be of questionable legality and destructive of any future possibility of dialogue with the SPDC or its possible and eventual military-in-mufti successors.

Although Canada and the European Union have followed the U.S. lead on sanctions on new investment and travel restrictions, other states have refused to do so. Japan, potentially once again the largest donor to Myanmar, has indicated that it would be prepared to resume assistance beyond the modest humanitarian support currently provided if there were indications of change in the regime's political rigidity and a movement toward dialogue with the opposition and/or economic reforms.

In spite of the strong Japanese–U.S. relationship, there are important differences in the approaches of the two countries toward relations with Myanmar, despite similar objectives and a "common agenda." [48] Japan's foreign aid program has provisions for concern about human rights, excessive military spending, development and production of weapons of mass destruction, and movements toward a market economy. Known as the Kaifu Doctrine (after the prime minister at that time), the doctrine was initiated in April 1991, but it has often been ignored when national policy interests dictated otherwise. Elichi Hoshino contrasts two approaches to dealing with Myanmar: the "asphyxiation" and "oxygen" strategies, the former applied by the United States and calling for essential isolation of the regime unless changes are forthcoming, and the latter calling for engagement and action. Both alternatives have intermediary positions (partial asphyxiation and partial engagement). The argument proceeds that the Japanese are more interested in group rights, stability, and social stability as prerequisites for economic growth, while the United States is concerned with individual rights, participation, and democracy as preconditions. "Disengagement [from Myanmar] is asphyxiation. The United States has good reason to follow this policy in terms of its ideological interests and domestic political concerns. Japan, absent its fear of losing its global partnership with the United States, has much less reason." [49] Hoshino argues for several factors in approaching the sanctions issue in Myanmar: synchronized policies so the Japan–U.S. alliance is not affected; respect for ideological interests; avoiding pushing Myanmar into a corner; positive sanctions (as opposed to negative ones); and the recognition that "economic development and 'civilian pain' are no less important than political gain." [50]

Japanese business is anxious to expand in Myanmar, and in 1997 Keidanren opened an office in Yangon. South Korea, which wanted to ensure that Japan's potential role in Myanmar would not exclude it, runs a modest foreign assistance program, including both loans and grants and a volunteer program (along the lines of the Peace Corps), and it has a significant level of investment there (some $100 million in a variety of projects including some with the military). It has no compunctions regarding human rights, and it congratulated Myanmar on its entry into ASEAN. However, with the election of President Kim Dae Jung, who has long held strong views favoring democracy in Burma and admires Aung San Suu Kyi, Korea backed the United States in the United Nations in introducing a resolution against the regime in Rangoon in 1999.

There are subtle differences in policy toward Myanmar between the United States and the European Union. The former has called for honoring the elections of 1990, as well as the usual catalogue of political rights and freedoms; the latter has articulated these rights as well but has stipulated that there be new elections instead of honoring those of 1990. Myanmar was prohibited from attending the 1998 Asia European Meeting (ASEM) in London but did go to Portugal in 2000. The European Union proposal may be more realistic in that the SPDC might be more prepared to follow that course in the future while maintaining its intelligence apparatus and building up mass support through organizations such as the USDA and through attempting to improve economic conditions and internal security.

Migration and Refugees

The essentially forced isolation of Burma under the BSPP was partly reversed under the SLORC/SPDC. From 1974 and the riots connected with the dispute over what to do about the burial of U Thant, Burma's most illustrious citizen, the military began to let a selected number of Burmese leave the country. Its motivations may have included the desirability of letting a number of dissidents leave; also, those who legally left had to claim to have a job and had to pay taxes and other fees, so the state was able to garner significant foreign exchange through this process. Although the regime lets people out, it still attempts to retain a monopoly on information and news coming into the country.

After 1988, however, the pattern changed. There was an outflow of those who had been against the 1988 coup and who felt, with reasonable assurance, they would have been persecuted for their political views had they remained. And then there was an outflow of both refugees and workers. Those who left without permission were stripped of their citizenship rights.

Refugees leaving Burma were nothing new. In 1977–78, over 200,000 Muslims fled the Arakan and crossed over into Bangladesh to escape Burmese Army harassment and intimidation—and perhaps worse. Many returned after UN intervention, but a similar occurrence again took place under the SLORC in 1991–92, when 250,000 refugees again fled to Bangladesh; of these all but 21,000 returned by the end of the 1990s. Muslims in the Arakan strongly feel the prejudice of the Burmese military, and Burma's antipathy toward its Muslim minority has been continuously pronounced.[51]

As noted, the porous nature of the Burmese borders means that the movement of peoples and material in both directions creates regional issues of importance for both Myanmar and its neighbors. The Burmese view these issues as the internal affairs of their government alone, but this view cannot be

sustained in light of the regional consequences of internal political and economic decisions. This then complicates the issues connected with both internal
reforms and foreign policies.

In October 1999, five Burmese student dissidents calling themselves the
Vigorous Burmese Student Warriors seized the Myanmar Embassy in Bangkok
to make known their objection to the Rangoon regime. After a tense period, the
Thai negotiated a peaceful settlement in which, with Thai Deputy Foreign Minister M.R. Sukhumbhand Paribatra as a guarantor of their safety, the dissidents
were flown to a Burma border area and released. The Thai interior minister
remarked that the dissidents were not terrorists but rather democracy activists.
The Burmese were incensed by the Thai reaction and closed the border with
Thailand, thus cutting off trade that was especially critical to Thai fishermen.
It took a visit by the Thai foreign minister, Surin Pitsuwan, to provide an opportunity for both sides to appear winners. The border was opened once again
in late November, just prior to the ASEAN meeting, which included the leaders
of China, Japan, and South Korea and at which Myanmar did not want to appear obstreperous.

In January 2000, a few insurgents from a splinter Karen fundamentalist
Christian insurrectionist group called God's Army, with which the student dissidents had taken refuge, hijacked a bus and seized the Thai hospital at Rat-
chanaburi, where they held some 500–700 patients and staff hostage. Thai
troops attacked the rather incompetent rebels, killing them and freeing the hos-
tages. It was claimed that there were a few hundred in God's Army. It was led
by two twelve-year-old twins said to have divine powers. These troops were
subjected to both Burmese and Thai shelling, causing them to attack the Thai
to try to put an end to their fire and to treat their wounded. The Burmese, who
had been greatly upset by the lenient Thai treatment of the student dissidents,
complimented the Thai on the solution to the dilemma. The quick Thai reaction was probably an effort by the Thai to encourage better relations with the
Burmese.

These latest incidents are not without precedent. For example, in 1990, Burmese students hijacked a plane from Bangkok to India. It is evident that the
audience for these events is not internal to Myanmar, where information is
controlled, nor is it the SLORC/SPDC. Rather such incidents are staged for the
outside world to keep the issues in which the dissidents believe so strongly in

the public limelight. The Thai, for their part, would like all this quietly to disappear and all refugees and other illegal workers to return to their home states. They want to avoid the political problems, but they also want to avoid international opprobrium by not forcing them to return, although there are Thai who have advocated just that. It seems likely that from time to time other incidents will occur, perhaps not as dramatic as the embassy seizure, but ones nevertheless that will seek to focus world attention on the plight of those abroad, who are political refugees in fact if not in name and who cannot return to their own state under the present circumstances. Although arrangements have been made to allow dissidents to leave for some "third country" (possibly the United States), such departures would marginalize the dissidents' political influence along the border areas.

The SLORC/SPDC period has vastly increased the importance of Myanmar to the region and beyond. The country has assumed economic and strategic relevance that had previously been lacking. The fora in which it can participate have increased, thus giving it greater external voice and also subjecting it to more extensive criticism. Even its internal problems, which have led to illegal (and legal) migration flows into and from the country, affect regional stability. The transnational spread of epidemic diseases, with social and economic consequences of great moment, can no longer be considered solely internal affairs. Narcotics production of traditional (opium, heroin) and nontraditional (amphetamines, methamphetamines) drugs has created serious international concerns. Even the testing of international policies toward democracy and good governance is in part focused on Myanmar. Thus the backwater that was Burma has evolved into the maelstrom that is Myanmar.

Notes

1. Anderson, *Mandalay to Momein* (London, 1876). Quoted in David I. Steinberg, "Burma: A Political Economy in Crisis," Report to the World Bank, August 1, 1988 (unpublished).
2. *The Journey of Augustus Ramond Margary from Shanghae to Bhamo and Back to Manwyne* (London, 1876); quoted in ibid.
3. For a discussion of the pivotal role of Myanmar, see J. Mohan Malik, "Myanmar's Role in Regional Security: Pawn or Pivot," *Contemporary Southeast Asia* 19, 1 (June 1997): 52–73.

4. In the civilian period, border markers were surreptitiously moved south by the Chinese, only to be moved back by the Burmese. The game was said to have continued for some time.

5. Since the bulk of Burmese narcotics production in the form of heroin went to the West, it was there, and especially in the United States, that concern about Burma existed. If the United States had any national interest in Burma after U.S. relations with China improved, it was in antinarcotics activities, and this was reflected in the antinarcotics aid program.

6. See David I. Steinberg, "Myanmar as Nexus: Sino-Indian Rivalries on the Frontier," *Studies in Conflict and Terrorism,* Spring 1993.

7. Mohan Malik, "China's Asia Policy: Implications for Japan and India," Monash University, Australia, Internet Virtual Forum, June 29, 1999. See also "China's Ambitions in Myanmar. India Steps Up Countermoves." International Institute for Strategic Studies, Vol. 6, no. 6, July 2000.

8. C. Uday Bhaskar, "Myanmar: Advancing India's Interests through Engagements," in *Securing India's Future in the New Millennium,* ed. Bramah Challeny (New Delhi: Orient Longmans, 1999), pp. 415–16, 419.

9. See Chi-Shad Liang, "Burma's Relations with the People's Republic of China: From Delicate Friendship to Genuine Cooperation," in *Burma: The Challenge of Change in a Divided Society,* ed. Peter Carey (London: Macmillan, 1997), pp. 71–96.

10. Interview, June 1988.

11. Desmond Ball, *Burma's Military Secrets: Signals Intelligence (SIGINT) from the Second World War to Civil War and Cyber Warfare* (Bangkok: White Lotus Press, 1998), p. 219. Ball covers the Chinese extensively, pp. 219–30, and the Chinese Nationalists, pp. 195–210.

12. Chengtu is the Chinese military command center that is responsible for Myanmar affairs.

13. Personal communication, 1996.

14. Personal interviews, 1988–94.

15. According to the 1931 census, the Chinese in Burma were calculated at 194,000, or 1.3 percent of the population. Teruko Saito and Lee Kin Kiong, *Statistics on the Burmese Economy: The 19th and 20th Centuries* (Singapore: Institute for Southeast Asian Studies, 1999), p. 15.

16. See Ball, pp. 195–209.

17. *The New ASEANs: Vietnam, Burma, Cambodia and Laos* (Canberra: Australian Department of Foreign Affairs and Trade, 1997), p. 135. Figures on foreign investment are also quite misleading because Chinese investment does not pass through the Board of Investment and thus is grossly understated. *Jane's Intelligence Review* notes sources that believe that the Mandalay population of 1.2 million is 30–40 percent ethnic Chinese (Anthony Davis, "Burma Casts Wary Eye on China," June 1, 1999, as quoted in *Burmanet News,* no. 1290 [June 10, 1999]). The esti-

mates conclude that Chinese have entered Mandalay at the rate of about 30,000 annually.

18. At least 50 people died in the riots, and along the border 113 Burmese were reported killed and 250 wounded. These official figures may be too low. A Chinese military attaché noted that Burma was in China's geopolitical interests and that the Chinese would support SLORC in the face of a coup or even in a popular uprising (although he admitted that would be more difficult). Personal interview, 1996. This should not be taken as a definitive statement of Chinese policy, which would likely be far more pragmatic if faced with such contingencies.

19. The *tatmadaw* has become dependent on China for much of its armament. The usual figures are $1.2–$1.6 billion in military assistance, but Ball (p. 219) speculates that the figure may be as high as $3 billion.

20. One view is that China will have to import oil, probably from the Middle East, and a secure sea route to southwest China through Burma would enable China to avoid the Straits of Malacca and the South China Sea and thus increase Chinese security. A former Japanese official said this was not in Japan's national interests (personal communication, 1999).

21. In the spring of 1998, the Indian defense minister remarked that the real potential enemy of India was not Pakistan but China. Northern Burma outflanks the northeast Sino-Indian frontier, which has not been formally demarcated and on which border fighting took place in the Sino-Indian War of 1962. One former Burmese military officer remarked that the potential use of Burmese airfields by the Chinese would make an Indian aircraft carrier in the Bay of Bengal virtually irrelevant.

22. Observers may be forgiven for speculating on whether Chinese from a Burmese post tracked the Indian test firing in the Bay of Bengal in April 1999 of the Agni 2 missile, which has the range to cover all of China.

23. Ball, pp. 221–22.

24. Chinese are said to buy the registration papers of deceased Burmese and alter them so that they would be deemed eligible to buy land. Costs are about $10.00. See Masahi Nishihara, "Myanmar's Relations with the Big Powers." Research Institute for Peace and Security, Tokyo. *Myanmar and Cambodia in a New ASEAN,* March 2000.

25. Liang, p. 83.

26. Mya Maung, *The Burma Road to Capitalism: Economic Growth versus Democracy* (Westport: Praeger, 1998), pp. 183–222.

27. When the author complained to a senior military officer about the sorry state of the Burmese press, the official replied, perhaps only half jokingly, that it was the fault of the United States; since the United States cut off contact and assistance, all the press staff have been trained in China, and what did I expect from such training anyway? (June 1997.)

28. A $1.2 billion purchase was supplemented by an additional $400 million purchase in 1994.

29. *Burma 1983 Population Census* (Rangoon: Ministry of Home and Religious Affairs, June 1986).

30. A senior Burmese official acquiesced to this characterization. Personal interview.

31. *New York Times,* September 13, 1988.

32. See Andrew Selth, "Burma and the Strategic Competition between China and India," in *Burma: Myanmar in the Twenty-first Century. Dynamics of Continuity and Change,* John Brandon, ed. (Bangkok: Chulalongkorn University, 1997), pp. 146–68.

33. Personal interviews, Putao, 1961.

34. For a study, see Vumson, *Zo History* (Mizoram, India: Aizawl, n.d).

35. Selth, "Burma and the Strategic Competition between China and India," pp. 151–52.

36. Malik, "China's Asia Policy." For a general discussion of the issues, see Donald M. Seekins, "Burma–China Relations: Playing with Fire," *Asian Survey* 37, 6 (June 1997).

37. See the recent reporting by Bertil Lintner in a variety of the issues of the *Far Eastern Economic Review.*

38. Malik, "China's Asia Policy," p. 115.

39. Personal communication.

40. Malik "China's Asia Policy," p. 116.

41. Bhaskar, p. 432.

42. Lt. Col. Hla Min in *Political Situation of Myanmar and Its Role in the Region* (Yangon: Office of Strategic Studies, Ministry of Defense, 1998), p. 21. Hla Min is the spokesman for the SPDC.

43. Personal communication from a Burmese official.

44. How much Ne Win's visits to Singapore influenced policies is also a matter of some speculation.

45. The ILO has protested the Burmese control of labor, as has Amnesty International and Human Rights Watch.

46. For a study of the issue, see David Schmahmann and James Finch, "The Unconstitutionality of State and Local Enactments in the United States Restricting Business Ties with Burma (Myanmar)," *Vanderbilt Journal of Transnational Law* 30, 2 (March 1997): 175–207.

47. The Myanmar case is prominently included in an article by Brannon P. Denning and Jack K. McCall, "States' Rights and Foreign Policy," *Foreign Affairs,* January–February 2000, pp. 9–14. The article notes that the U.S. Court of Appeals for the First Circuit upheld the Federal District Court decision on the Massachusetts law, but that decision applied only to areas within the courts' jurisdiction. The authors are against sanctions and attribute the success of lobbying for sanctions to

both globalization and the growing influence of the NGO community—especially those concerned with human rights.

48. These are effectively discussed in Eiichi Hoshino (University of the Ryukyus), "Economic Sanctions against Myanmar and the Japan-U.S. Alliance" (unpublished, no date). For a study of the Burma issue in Japan, see Donald M. Seekins, "Japan's 'Burma Lovers' and the Military Regime" (Tokyo: Japan Policy Research Institute, September 1999); Working Paper No. 60.

49. Hoshino, p. 23.

50. Ibid., p. 25.

51. The outflow of refugees from Burma into Bengal/Bangladesh occurred in 1784, 1811 and thereafter, 1977–78, and 1991–92. "Burmese Refugees in Bangladesh: Still No Durable Solution," *Human Rights Watch* 12, 3(c) (Washington, D.C., May 2000).

CHAPTER 9

Foreign Assistance:
Tensions and Needs

*I tell you that no country can ever be really free as long as she depends
on the charity of foreigners for her revenues. We must achieve our freedom by ourselves with our own money.*

—Aung San, 1947[1]

Since independence, there has been tension between Burma's need for
foreign assistance to help accomplish the economic goals the state has
set for itself and its dependence on external influences. This strain is
further intensified by the nationalistic sentiment inherent in all regimes since
1948 that calls for autonomy, neutrality, and self-reliance. This has meant that
such assistance has had to be couched in language and attributes that were not
perceived to undercut the sovereignty of any regime. Military authorities have
continuously maintained that any assistance could not have strings attached,
but in fact strings were always involved; the issue was what kinds of strings.
Traditionally, even while becoming indebted to foreign organizations, Burma
maintained a fictive neutrality. When the Soviet Union gave assistance in the
1950s, Burma repaid the assistance with rice. When the U.S. foreign assistance
program was expelled from Burma for covert support to Chinese Nationalist
troops in the Shan State in the early 1950s, the Burmese government picked
up the costs for the American technical assistance program from its own
funds.

Yet Burma was dependent on foreign assistance, which at various junctures was essential to the economic survival of the state. Aung San had said before independence that Burma should not become dependent on foreign support, and yet it was foreign support of all kinds that was needed: military, economic, training, and technical. But assistance had to be carefully couched. For example, the U.S. foreign assistance program requires that the United States receive an official request for aid. Yet the Burmese would not make such a request. So a compromise was made under which the United States would write a letter inquiring whether the Burmese might be interested in such a program, and they would write back indicating that they might be interested, and this exchange of correspondence was deemed sufficient to satisfy the requirements of both sides. Moreover, it has been the continuous policy of both civilian and military governments that when Burmese were sent abroad for training under any auspices, including all foreign assistance programs, the individuals to be trained were chosen by some state organ, not foreign groups.[2]

The vicissitudes of foreign assistance to Burma in a sense mirror the events in that country. After independence, Burma took aid from everyone in a balanced, neutral style as if it were its due. Following the coup of 1962 and in the socialist period that followed, most aid programs halted except those from the Japanese and the United Nations. But with the recognition of the failure of the economy in the late 1960s and at the inaugural mass meeting of the BSPP in July 1971, the need for foreign economic assistance was obliquely recognized as regularizing foreign economic relations. In 1988, following the coup, most foreign assistance programs again stopped, although the Chinese expanded their support. Under UN regulations, any member may have UNDP assistance, as well as that of other UN agencies (UNICEF, WHO, etc.). Some Burmese expatriates demanded that such programs be halted because they were seen to help prop up the military and give that government added legitimacy, but they continued, although not without controversy.[3] Historically, however, of all the programs, the singularly most important was that of the Japanese. It could play such a role in the future.

The Japanese Assistance Program

Japan had a special relationship with Burma before World War II, when the Japanese set up an intelligence-gathering organization to counter the

British. The famous "Thirty Comrades," including Aung San and Ne Win, were trained by the Japanese to oppose colonial rule. After the Japanese victory in Burma, a quasi-independent state was set up by the Japanese. The Burmese became disillusioned with it, and in the spring of 1945 they turned against the Japanese and sided with their colonial masters, thus making it politically easier for the British to grant them independence, which would have come in any case in the wake of India's freedom. In spite of this, many Burmese look back upon the Japanese with affection.

The Japanese retained a sentimental attachment to Burma after the war, partly because of the trauma and a certain amount of guilt over that era, partly perhaps because of the attraction of Burmese Buddhism, and partly because at certain levels there was real affection between the Burmese and the Japanese.[4] This was reflected in the poignant Japanese novel (and then movie) *Harp of Burma,* which is still popular.[5]

The initial Japanese motives for beginning a foreign assistance program to Burma in 1956 were probably multiple.[6] They included remorse for the suffering and destruction caused by the war, the reestablishment of the Japanese position in the region, the access to Burmese raw materials, the possibilities for Japanese investment in a new and potentially sizable market, and the resurrection of Japanese exports and industry. Important as well became Japan's self-perceived obligation to provide foreign assistance to less-developed nations because it was a member of the industrialized world, and Japan wanted to meet its social responsibilities and gain the respect of other such nations.

The Japanese program started as reparations for war damage and then moved to what was called "semi-reparations" and then to loans and grants, loans predominating in the later period. There have been six distinct periods or decisions that affected Japanese assistance: (1) the decision to provide war reparations in 1954 as a result of the peace treaty with Burma on November 5, 1954; (2) movement from reparations to economic cooperation in the 1960s; (3) the decision to increase aid tenfold in the 1970s; (4) the decision in March 1988 to issue the Burmese a warning about their economy; (5) the cutoff of aid following the September 1988 coup; and (6) the decision to restart old projects in February 1989. (Details are provided in appendices A and B.)

The reparations were grants for the supply of Japanese goods and services; for much of the early period of Japanese assistance, support was tied to Japanese industry and technical assistance. Total assistance was to be $200 million over a ten-year period, with an annual grant of $5 million for technical assistance.[7] This, together with similar support to other Asian nations, provided a spur to Japanese industrial expansion, which had already been assisted by American offshore procurement in Japan during and after the Korean War. Through September 30, 1960, Japanese assistance was 37.8 percent of all foreign assistance delivered to Burma.

The Japanese economic program in retrospect was deemed by many senior Japanese as a failure in Burmese terms—that is, it really did not assist the development process to a great degree. In political and international relations terms, however, it was a great success because it solidified Japan's place in Burma. The economic assessment, however, is overly pessimistic. The best foreign assistance project in Burma was probably the Japanese hydroelectric project at Lawpida in the Kayah State. On the other hand, the early construction of four industrial factories (at an initial cost of $29.2 million) to produce consumer goods under Japanese license was a massive failure; they never were profitable, relied on Japanese components, and thus were a continuing drain on foreign exchange reserves and increased debt.

Japan and Burma renegotiated a new reparations agreement in 1963 and arranged that $200 million additional assistance start in 1965 over a twelve-year period; of this amount, $140 million was to be in grants and $60 million in concessional loans. Disbursements continued through 1975. Since most of the assistance was in yen and much was in the form of loans, the revaluation of the yen upwards by over threefold resulted in the increase in Burmese debt.

The reappraisal of the economic malaise by the BSPP in 1971 led to an explosion of foreign assistance because the reappraisal was viewed as the most important liberalization move in a decade. Japanese support increased from $30 million to $178 million annually at the close of the 1970s. It peaked at $244 million in 1986, representing 6.3 percent of all Japanese assistance worldwide. During the 1980s, assistance to Burma ranked either third or fourth largest of Japan's assistance to any country. From the beginning of the program through 1990, Japan has provided $876.3 million in grants and $1,380.0 million in loans.

The salient characteristic of Japanese assistance was that it did not interfere in the internal affairs of any state and thus officially did not press for economic reforms or change. The World Bank, the United States, and the ADB all provided policy advice, even when it was not requested. Further, until 1986, Japan did not design a development or aid strategy for any country; the first time it did so was for the Philippines in that year (prompted by the end of the Marcos era). This again was in contrast to other major donors. Thus what happened in Burma was an important precedent for Japan.

On two occasions, however, it was Japan that was the decisive influence in Burma. In the mid-1960s, at the height of the socialist fury in Burma, when the economy was so bad that even Ne Win admitted that the country could not feed itself, Japanese assistance probably sustained the regime. Neither Burma nor Japan would probably care to verify that statement, but it seems reasonably evident that this assistance was critical. The second occasion was the unprecedented (in Japanese terms) warning to the Burmese in March 1988 that if they did not reform their economy Japan would have to cut its foreign assistance. It was this warning, although not couched in terms of specific suggestions for reform, that led Ne Win in the last days of the BSPP to advocate the abandonment of socialism and the opening to the private sector. Although the impact did not begin until after the coup of that year, the change can be attributed to the Japanese. In spite of a lack of fundamental reforms and suspicions by the government about both the indigenous and foreign private sectors, this was the most important liberalization move since 1962.

With the coup of 1988 and in accordance with Japanese law, the new government had to be re-recognized, and thus the foreign assistance program was halted. The re-recognition of Burma took place in February 1989 and was just before (and prompted by) the Japanese emperor's funeral.[8] A month earlier, thirteen major Japanese firms petitioned the Japanese Embassy in Rangoon to restart the aid program, as they were losing money without it. But under intense pressure from the United States, Japan has refrained from restarting its foreign assistance program beyond humanitarian aid, although in Japan there is great pressure from ministries (other than the Ministry of Foreign Affairs) and the business community to do so. Japan regards the U.S. relationship as more important than improvement in Burmese affairs but seems to be moving toward more assistance if there are modest economic or political changes and even if they may be cosmetic in terms of distribution of power.

Japan did not start new projects, but it did restart old, unfinished projects, supply debt relief, and provide humanitarian assistance. From 1993 through 1997, Japan provided thirteen grants for debt relief, plus humanitarian assistance for grassroots projects. In that same period, Japan provided $432.3 million in grants, $44.45 million in technical cooperation, and $75.36 million in loans (excluding repayments), making the total of Japanese assistance to Burma from the beginning of the reparations program $2.613 billion, of which $1.665 billion was in loans.[9] In 1998, it restarted with funds of over $20 million the reconstruction of the Rangoon airport on "humanitarian" grounds because without such assistance, the Japanese argued, the airport was too dangerous and many people might be killed. This was a blatant stretch of the definition of "humanitarian" to begin to accomplish what the Japanese hoped to achieve— the resurrection of their preeminent economic position in Myanmar. The NLD has been urging Japan not to strengthen the military regime by restarting its assistance, and it has been critical of the Japanese position.

The Japanese evidently are waiting for a slight thaw in the political stalemate in Myanmar to reward the regime with significant economic "cooperation" (the word "assistance" is eschewed). The importance to Japan is said not to relate to the degree of democratization, but to the vector of positive change. Honoring the past elections or holding new ones are not necessary desiderata. The issue for Japan will be to determine whether the thaw is simply cosmetic and does not change the internal balance of power in the country. Japan has internal guidelines on democratic governance and military expenditures for assessing whether a foreign assistance program should be pursued, but it is likely that the opportunity to regain its position in Myanmar will outweigh any of the theoretical criteria if there is surface movement toward political dialogue and away from stasis. In a real sense, then, Japanese policy is in opposition to that of the United States. In March and June 1999, this writer recommended to the Japanese government that yen lending not begin and that a program of strictly humanitarian assistance be conducted through Japanese NGOs in order to have positive effects on the Burmese people, strengthen the Japanese NGOs, possibly develop Burmese NGOs and thus civil society, train specialists on Burma who will be important to Japan in the future, and ease confrontation with the United States, as humanitarian aid through NGOs was likely to be the most acceptable approach to assistance.

The *Japan Times* reported that Japan might resume official assistance to Myanmar as part of an aid package to the countries involved in the Mekong River development planning;[10] these include Thailand, Vietnam, Laos, and Cambodia. This would provide a regional rationale and political cover for

Japanese assistance. It is also evident that Chinese commercial interests may be forthcoming for Mekong development, and some of such support would go to projects in Myanmar.

Japanese assistance was not only bilateral, but it was also multilateral. In addition to its support through the World Bank, Japan founded the ADB and played a dominant role in that institution.

It is significant that at the ASEAN ministerial meeting in Manila at the end of November 1999, Prime Minister Obuchi met with Than Shwe, the first meeting of the heads of state of those countries since 1984. Further Japanese assistance may be forthcoming if the Burmese make an appropriate gesture, such as dialogue with Aung San Suu Kyi or major economic reforms, but the initial reporting seemed to indicate that neither side was prepared to make changes, which raises questions as to why such an important meeting was arranged.

Burma informally asked Japan for $1.45 billion in assistance under the Miyazawa Plan, which was a Japanese promise of assistance to the countries affected by the Asian financial crisis of 1997. However, Burma was not eligible as it had not met the criteria for such assistance, which included World Bank–IMF mandated reforms.[11]

The U.S. Economic Aid Program

The U.S. economic aid program was probably more consequential for the very fact of its existence than for its results. Although it supported a variety of projects—including port reconstruction, a major teak mill, and a new campus for the University of Rangoon, as well as other infrastructure—it was through technical, engineering, and economic advisory services that it probably had the greatest, if ephemeral, impact.

The beginnings of the aid program in the early 1950s were predicated on security considerations (as was the whole aid program in East Asia)—to help stabilize the government against two communist insurgencies and the perpetual threat of a newly communist China, whose expansionist intentions at that time seemed ominous. As noted, it was terminated in 1953 by the Burmese because of covert U.S. support to the fleeing Kuomintang (Nationalist troops), who entered the Shan State (as Ming troops had done fleeing the new Ch'ing Dynasty in 1644). Burma, which was the first country to recognize the PRC, has been neutral with extreme sensitivity toward the PRC and the balance of world power. The program was restarted in 1956, and even after the coup of 1962, the program continued for a period. It was at this time that negotiations took place for U.S. support for a new road from Rangoon to Mandalay, the main avenue of land transport for about 400 miles, to replace a two-lane overly used and badly constructed thoroughfare. Disagreement over the most appropriate route stopped the project at Burmese request in 1964, after $1.5 million had been spent on survey work. At that point the Burmese said it would be built using convict labor—prohibited under U.S. legislation if it involved U.S. support. This, together with the intensity of the socialist dogma prevalent in Rangoon, effectively ended the U.S. effort for over a dozen years. Until that time, the United States had provided a total of $121.79 million. (For details, see appendices C and D.)

In 1978, the Burmese unofficially approached the United States to determine whether it might restart its aid program. Although evidence is lacking, the end of the Vietnam War may have provided the political possibility for such a change, thus easing the delicacy of Burma's neutrality and the sensitivity of the long, indefensible border with China. There were rumors that the Burmese might have consulted with the Chinese on this, and the Chinese indicated they were in favor of, or at least did not oppose, such assistance. A U.S. team was sent to Rangoon to meet with various officials and recommended a program focused on "basic human needs" and technical training.[12] Because the basic agreement between Burma and the United States on the operation of resident foreign assistance had never been abrogated but simply set in abeyance, the restart of the program did not need formal government approval or the renegotiation of an agreement. The first project that was informally suggested by the Burmese was the rebuilding of the Rangoon airport; it was turned down immediately in Rangoon by the U.S. team as not meeting USAID guidelines for basic human needs projects. Early assistance focused on both training and rural health delivery systems. The program closed again following the coup of 1988, and the USAID mission was dismantled.

The usefulness of the U.S. program was certainly never in its magnitude; it was small compared not only to the Japanese, but also to the West German and other efforts (see appendix E). It was significant because as the largest donor worldwide at that time (now outdistanced by the Japanese), the United States gave a moral leadership to bilateral loans and grants (especially grants, as the

Japanese provided most assistance after reparations and before 1988 in loans) and was influential in the World Bank and the ADB. It is significant that during the 1970s and 1980s, human rights was not deemed a significant issue in the question of whether the United States would provide assistance, although it was titularly pursued in the case of other countries, such as the Philippines.[13] This was true even though the Carter administration (1977–81) was a strong advocate of human rights; the BSPP regime was just as repressive as the SLORC, perhaps more so in that it was a single-party mass-mobilization society with not even a titular opposition and with a ubiquitous military intelligence system operative.

Since the election stalemate of 1990, the United States officially has been concerned about the plight of political refugees. It has assisted projects for those displaced outside the country and has supported organizations designed to foster democracy. The U.S. Congress has been allocating funds for work among the displaced peoples who have fled Myanmar and has authorized humanitarian assistance within that country subject to extensive conditions. USAID has developed a strategy for such assistance that is based on a number of questionable assumptions, including the following:

- "The SPDC regime is financially, economically, and politically unsustainable. A transition in government will occur, but not necessarily soon."
- NGOs have the capacity to develop meaningful programs within and along the Burmese littoral.
- International donors may be treated as a united front opposed to the regime (aside from China, of course). This assumption is clearly inaccurate with Japan poised to restart major assistance.
- The United States has no geopolitical interests in Burma.
- The United States could conduct an effective counter-narcotics program with a more receptive government installed in Rangoon.
- A civilian government installed as a result of the 1990 elections would be democratic.
- The Burmese outside Burma (if their capacities develop) would have a role in reshaping the country internally should the administration change.
- The experience of holding elections, workshops, and the like outside Burma would be transferable inside Burma.

Significantly the objectives of the program leave out alleviation of poverty, except as a humanitarian response to war or natural disasters. In addition to refugees and economic migrants, the strategy omits consideration of the one percent of the population (an educated one percent) who have migrated around the world for political and economic reasons, who transmit funds back into the economy, and some of whom might return under other political or economic circumstances. Two stated objectives of the program use the term "pressure," which is unlikely to be productive, and no mention is made of building civil society. This strategy is likely to have marginal impact on those inside or outside Myanmar.[14]

Multilateral and Other Donors

Burma has been sporadically involved with multilateral organizations virtually since independence. In addition to the United Nations and related agencies, it has had programs with the World Bank and associated institutions and with the ADB. They have loomed large in the past and may, under other circumstances, play an important role in the future.

The World Bank

Burma became a member of the World Bank in 1952, the International Finance Corporation (IFC) in 1956, and the International Development Agency (IDA) in 1962. During the 1956–61 period, three transportation loans were made totaling $33.3 million (of which $0.2 million was canceled). From 1962 until 1972, during the socialist period and before Burma reconsidered its external economic relations, no lending took place. In 1973, the World Bank again became active, and 30 IDA credits were provided totaling $804 million, of which $752.8 million resulted in projects and the remainder were canceled. The largest component of the loans was for agriculture (26 percent), followed by energy and power (24.2 percent), transportation (17.3 percent), forestry (16.2 percent), telecommunications (7.1 percent), and the remainder in mining and manufacturing. (For details, see appendix F.) In the 1980s, the bank provided policy advice on taxes, revenue, macroeconomic policy, exchange rate reformation, and private sector development. Some of the sector-specific recommendations were followed, but major structural changes did not take place.

Since July 1987, there has been no new lending, and the last project closed on December 31, 1993. Since September 1998, Myanmar has been on a nonaccrual status with the bank and was overdue on interest payments of $25 million at the end of June 1999. The bank conducted economic studies in 1991, 1995, and June 1999. The last Consultative Group meeting of donors on Burma was held in Tokyo on January 14, 1986, under World Bank chairmanship.

In 1999, a still confidential bank draft report on Myanmar was leaked to the press in Thailand. The report, which was critical of the government's policies on poverty, education, health, the private sector, and agriculture, linked the issues of economic performance to political liberalization and the development of social capital. At this writing (September 2000), the SPDC is considering the report and has invited bank officials back in for consultations but has made no response on specific areas for change. The United States still effectively blocks bank activities in Myanmar until there are political changes. (For a summary, see appendix I, chapter 5.)

The Asian Development Bank

Burma joined the ADB in 1973 (following its reconsideration of foreign economic assistance), and the bank started operations at that time. To date the bank has provided thirty-two loans totaling $530.9 million for twenty-eight projects. Fifteen of the loans were for agriculture and agroindustry (59.5 percent), 11.9 percent for health, 8.0 percent for transport and communications, 7.8 percent for industry and development banks, 6.8 percent for water supply, and 6.0 percent for energy.

Since 1988, no new lending has taken place, and as of July 19, 1999, the total overdue payments to the bank were $28.7 million. Although no direct assistance has taken place since the SLORC came to power, Myanmar does participate in the program of Economic Cooperation in the Greater Mekong Subregion, and the ADB has been developing plans for a new transportation network in the Golden Triangle. The project is referred to as the Golden Quadrangle and would involve Myanmar, China, Laos, and Thailand.

The International Monetary Fund

The IMF has conducted annual reviews of the Burmese economy under Article IV of its agreement and has made a number of economic studies, basically focusing on macroeconomic issues. It does not provide financial assistance in project form, and its major support goes to states that need assistance in structural adjustment—that is, major restructuring of economic policies and institutions. To date, Myanmar has not been prepared to engage in such reforms.

United Nations Programs

UN programs cover a broad spectrum of activities in Myanmar. Thirteen UN agencies and organizations operate in that country. They range from the UNDP to WHO, UNICEF, the UNHCR, the UN International Drug Control Programme (UNDCP), Food and Agriculture Organization (FAO), the World Food Programme (WFP), and many other groups. Central to the UN program are fourteen Thematic Working Groups, which concentrate on such problems as primary health care, reproductive health, poverty alleviation, women/gender issues, and the environment.

Most programs focus on basic human needs broadly defined. Important has been the campaign for immunization against polio, which has reached 98 percent of children under five (in 1996). The UNHCR has been working with refugees in Rakhine State (Arakan). HIV/AIDS has been the focus of projects, and primary education and rural potable water supplies have received concentrated attention by various UN organizations. Central to the UN activities has been stress on community development and fostering civil society through working with local, national, and international NGOs.[15]

The Future Role of Donors in Myanmar

What might the role of foreign economic assistance in Burma be in the twenty-first century should conditions permit the resumption of major support? What might these conditions be? What are the lessons of the previous aid efforts? The potential donor role[s] are influenced by factors both external and internal to Burma. One factor—a major international trend in which Myanmar may be considered—is almost universal agreement among major bilateral donors of the Development Assistance Committee (DAC) in Paris (including the European Union, Japan, and the United States) that human rights and political issues, as well as limitations on military expenditures, should and will play a role in the allocation of foreign aid (although adherence to these criteria seems sporadic and selective). Priority is also given to the development of a vibrant private sector, sound banking policies, and the minimizing of state-owned enterprises. The World Bank and the ADB are now considering such requirements, although these were not within their original charters. In addition, the World Bank is paying significantly more attention to issues of poverty and governance, including corruption. IDA 12 (World Bank assistance policies) gives priority to countries that demonstrate good performance in economic policy and management. The World Bank considers core reforms more important than mobilizing official development assistance (ODA), although significant amounts of assistance and foreign investment will both be necessary for Myanmar to progress. In any case, the bilateral donors have a pervasive influence in those multilateral institutions and could effectively block loans to any country in violation of these principles. China and South Korea previous to the Kim Dae Jung administration were the two exceptions to those states expressing concern about Burmese human rights. Conversely, it is also apparent that if the record of U.S. bilateral assistance is examined for the period when human rights were said to be a major policy concern (i.e., the Carter administration), then it is clear that there was considerable slackness in the execution of that policy, both because political/security considerations were paramount and because assistance was designated to go to the poor. Yet as those in foreign assistance know, money is fungible, and foreign aid for one project might free local government funds for some less "desirable" endeavor. Although the human rights effort may have created an admittedly important impression of concern, reality lagged far behind rhetoric. But because no major donor (except China) believes it has strategic interests in Burma, the human rights considerations are likely to carry considerable weight unless there are important changes within Burma. As Chinese economic influence grows, greater concern on the parts of Thailand and India may be expected, both to limit China's potential role there and to feed from the same trough.

As noted, Japan is under pressure from Japanese business interests to lend to Burma once again, but as Japan is a member of the OECD, the diplomatic influence of other donors may sway it. Yet a senior Japanese official stressed in 1994 that the Kaifu Doctrine would not affect a $1 billion lending program to Indonesia, a state that had at that time questionable political and human rights records.[16] Japan is the critical bilateral donor, and its policies toward Burma will be most important. Its principles may be shaky where its political or economic interests are seen as transcendent. For Japan's own articulated policies to be effective in Burma it may take the coordinated influence of other donor states.

There are several lessons to be learned from previous foreign aid efforts in Burma. First, foreign and economic policy advice is officially anathema to the military, at least if publicly voiced. Initiatives for change must be seen to be coming from inside the regime; if they are suggested from abroad, they must be quietly pursued. Second, the military will continue its strong interventions in the economy and society as a whole; dirigisme will out. Third, too much assistance (as in the 1970s and 1980s) will effectively reduce Burmese interest in substantive economic reforms. Fourth, coordinated economic planning involving intersectoral considerations (as opposed to individual projects) has been beyond the capacity of the state both because of the lack of trained staff and because such planning normally involves complex political decisions.[17] This is likely to remain so. These factors should provide a backdrop to and cautions about thinking on foreign assistance.

The new century may provide, *mirabile dictu,* clear and distinct alternatives, although at this writing this seems remote. On one end of a theoretical spectrum, political stasis could continue indefinitely, with the *tatmadaw* ruling by decree. At the other extreme, power could be turned over to elected representatives, the SPDC dissolved, and the military returned to the barracks, not to intervene in politics again. The former alternative seems far more likely than the latter, although both are improbable.

If the SPDC continues its present policies and stasis is maintained, major donor assistance (aside from China) is unlikely on new activities. The government, together with Japanese business firms, will likely put pressure on Japan to restart new programs. China and perhaps South Korea (in the post–Kim Dae Jung era if Japan appears to be active there) would remain donors of some significance. Other foreign assistance would probably be denied, even through the multilateral donors. A liberal and civilian regime would no doubt attract relatively large-scale assistance. There are dangers in this latter, if remote, eventuality as well.

More likely are less Cartesian situations, mixed politically and economically. It is likely, as the SLORC/SPDC maintains, that a multiparty political system will evolve. The timing of that system, if it does come, however, is unclear, and it will probably develop slowly rather than quickly. A multiparty system also does not necessarily mean a democratic system, nor one not subject to military veto. It also may not mean one in which many basic human rights are honored. Any ethnic autonomy granted may not mean ethnic power.

If one looks further into the future, when political changes will most likely take place in Myanmar, then the donors will have to assess whether those changes are conducive to the broad political goals that they have set for themselves (assuming those goals still exist—there has been a plethora of fadism in foreign aid) and provide a framework into which economic reforms may fit. This will be a judgment individual donors will have to make, although they may be influenced through stances taken by the OECD or other international fora. The present outlook seems decidedly mixed.

But if, as previously discussed, political reforms are required before economic reforms are both meaningful and sustainable, then where do donors begin? The following plan for donor assistance is based on four premises:

1. There is a primary focus on political issues in Myanmar, and economic reform is held hostage to these considerations. Parallel approaches for the two are needed.
2. The SLORC/SPDC and perhaps many Burmans (both in the military and among the civilian elite) believe their own propaganda for over two generations that both foreign powers and indigenous minorities wish to see the breakup of the state. There is considerable historical evidence that this desire was once true.
3. The minorities have abandoned their earlier positions for independence and now are prepared to settle for some sort of appropriate autonomy within Burma.
4. The SPDC underrates the degree of foreign antipathy to the regime and its policies.

Because Myanmar military authorities view policy suggestions as interference in the state's internal affairs, foreign public exhortations for change, the protection of human rights, and the redistribution of power might create an internal backlash. That does not mean that external pressures for change are not necessary, but necessity and effectiveness do not necessarily go in tandem. It may well be, and indeed seems likely to this writer, that the SLORC/SPDC generally believes its own pronouncements concerning the potential breakup of the state because of ethnic rebellions, since its three "causes" center on unity of the state and its sovereignty. Yugoslavia and the Soviet Union may be regarded by the SLORC as object lessons to be eschewed, and thus it may harden its position concerning how much or little autonomy it can get away with allowing the minorities—and which minorities.

To solve this deadlock, some action seems necessary, although the question should be asked: what is different now from the previous three or four decades that could prompt change? There are, in fact, many changes, both positive and negative. The military is far more powerful today, but the 1990 election has diminished the legitimacy of the government. The Nobel Peace Prize to Aung San Suu Kyi further diminishes the regime, at least internationally. The NCGUB provides a focus for the opposition. And there is a cumulative burden of decades of incessant warfare increasingly difficult to bear by all parties.

The first priority to begin a process of government-opposition discussions might be to eliminate or limit the flotsam of misperceptions, leaving the most difficult of political issues—the redistribution of power, especially in regard to the minorities—for later. The objective would be to set the stage for later negotiations by clarifying the scene and eliminating some articulated concerns, assuming, of course, that they are beliefs rather than propaganda ploys.

The UN's Economic and Social Commission for Asia and the Pacific (ESCAP) might bring together the five neighbors of Burma: India, Bangladesh, China, Laos, and Thailand, all of which are members of ESCAP and all of which have previously negotiated border agreements. ASEAN or the ARF could do this as well for general moral support now that Myanmar is a member. The ARF might be persuaded to issue a statement guaranteeing the territorial integrity of Myanmar at the approved borders. This, of course, would be the re-ratification of the status quo and thus be considered as nothing new. Yet reiteration of the borders might indeed be viewed as a new step and might sufficiently reassure the military that Burma as a nation would not be destroyed. The minorities might then be prompted to indicate that they have no intention of leaving an appropriately structured "union," leaving to later what the detail of that union might mean.

This step would not commit any group to anything it might not later approve, but it could be the prelude for internal negotiations—in effect, in contemporary usage, a "confidence-building measure." A constitution might later be devised, negotiated internally without outside influence, to better satisfy the needs of the minorities for autonomy within some sort of union and the needs of the Burmans (and especially the military) to ensure the solidarity of the state as a whole.

Although full of pitfalls and abounding with questions, this approach might provide a more favorable means for all parties to begin a process of reconciliation. Under this proposal, no one has negotiated, foreign powers have not interfered, and face is universally saved. There are a few other foreign options, as I will discuss. I am not sanguine about their possibilities, but they would be first steps. If, in addition, donors were to indicate privately that successful completion of various stages leading to eventual solution could prompt selected and phased economic assistance, this might be an incentive.

The events of the past may make this scenario more difficult. The military may truly believe that it will eliminate the rebels through force alone. It may be extremely troubled by the collapse of Yugoslavia and the Soviet Union and (more recently) Indonesia's problems of national unity. It may not wish to negotiate. The rebels may be encouraged by the same events and heartened by the Nobel Peace Prize.

If one seeks an economic assistance policy for foreign states toward Myanmar, then it might be appropriate to begin anew, based on some plan along the lines suggested above.[18] If there is substantial progress toward a plan that might lead to a constitution acceptable to the general population and compromises are reached with the minorities, broader foreign assistance then might be considered. Such assistance should be conditional on economic and political reforms; it should be modest, phased, and carefully monitored by residential representatives of the multilateral donors, not through fleeting and hurried missions from headquarters. This should be the case under any regime.

In the meantime, however, there is an intermediate issue that has appeared and has been highly controversial. That is whether donors should provide planning (such as sector studies) for future indeterminate lending or training for Burmese. The arguments run along the following lines: The negative effects are that pressures on the SPDC to reform are diminished, that the military would receive added legitimacy in being offered such assistance even if it had no short-term economic effect, and that foreign donors would have difficulty in assuring that the most appropriate people were trained, or that data for studies were accurate. On the positive side, there would be less of a hiatus between planning and execution of development projects, and thus economic recovery would be speeded if and when conditions again become ripe for foreign assistance. The World Bank study of August 1999 focusing on poverty, education, health, agriculture, and the private sector is an example of what is needed. But some controversy arose over the negative conditions reported and whether the very fact of preparing such a report legitimates the regime or increases pressures for action. Such studies also require a greater degree of access to data and an openness to share such materials. These have been lacking in the past.

There is an important dichotomy between the reality of authoritarian regimes and some foreign assistance (and internal NLD) policies. The NLD argues that no training should go to members of the regime, and the United States would agree. But the evidence from other authoritarian states is that if the elite and their children are sent for training, because they are trusted, they could have a far greater impact for change than can those who are politically neutral or neutered. The trade-offs between these two opposing views should be considered. The debate is legitimate. In its extreme form, it is disputed by those who determine that no discussions on any issue should take place with the SPDC because such activities are used to enhance regime legitimacy. Many would say that discussions instead should be held with the NCGUB.

The prudent course for foreign donors, however, is to attempt to provide the external preconditions for internal resolution of Burmese problems, as outlined above, and at the same time to continue the dialogue with the SPDC or other authorities in Rangoon, as well as with the opposition, recognizing that there are trade-offs in this approach. This dialogue should include discussion of economic reform measures. The timing of the two efforts might be dovetailed; studies and training might be offered as the process of constitutional negotiations is accepted or started. The immediate gains from such discussions may seem less than the legitimacy a clever government could pull from them, but over the longer term such dialogue could assist positive change.

One cannot be sanguine about the results of any such approach. Burma is likely to have major unresolved problems that defy foreign intervention and complicate internal resolution. Foreign assistance has not been, and will not be, a panacea for Burma's political or economic ills. Mao Tse-Tung once said that politics were in command. They seem to be in Burma, where the relentless attrition of the economic well-being of the populace continues; all seem caught in the net of internal power politics. If foreign assistance is forthcoming without at least a partial resolution of the economic and political issues that are inextricably bound, the results will be less than efficacious. Over the past decades, the roles of foreign powers have not been as constructive as they might have been. Now the world has changed, the Cold War is over, and tensions are more regional than global. The powers, through appropriate organizations such as the United Nations and its agencies, could begin anew the process of reconciliation by making positive gestures. There is a need to move ahead, even if the process is slow, tedious, and halting, and there will no doubt be blind alleys in the maze of Myanmar.

APPENDIX A—Japanese Aid Projects

Japanese Reparations Projects ($ millions)

1.	Beluchaung hydroelectric		28.8
2.	Four industrial projects		29.2
	Agricultural machinery plant	[4.4]	
	Small vehicle plant	[9.2]	
	Electric goods plant	[8.6]	
	Bus/truck plant	[7.0]	
3.	Railway rehabilitation		20.2
4.	Automobiles		17.2
5.	Rangoon port rehabilitation		17.2
6.	Technical cooperation		7.5
7.	Other		76.0
		Total	200.0

Source: Japanese Embassy.

APPENDIX B—Japanese Economic Assistance to Burma: Loans, Grants, Reparations *(Current $ millions)*

Year	Grants	Loans	Total
1950–57	45.7	—	45.7
1958	26.0	—	26.0
1959	18.7	—	18.7
1960	21.4	—	21.4
1961	13.6	—	13.6
1962	24.4	—	24.4
1963	27.0	—	27.0
1964	16.6	—	16.6

APPENDIX B—(continued)

Year	Grants	Loans	Total
1965	11.6	—	11.6
1966	10.2	—	10.2
1967	6.4	—	6.4
1968	10.2	—	10.2
1969	—	30.0	30.0
1970	11.9	—	11.9
1971	16.7	7.1	26.7
1972	18.1	11.6	29.6
1973	14.8	41.9	56.3
1974	12.1	34.2	46.4
1975	17.1	7.1	21.6
1976	17.7	21.5	27.3
1977	8.0	12.2	20.6
1978	10.6	96.7	107.3
1979	30.0	153.3	178.1
1980	37.2	122.3	152.5
1981	33.2	100.1	125.4
1982	21.3	76.5	97.8
1983	48.4	65.1	113.4
1984	47.1	47.1	95.4
1985	49.4	104.9	154.1
1986	68.9	175.2	244.1
1987	67.3	104.7	172.0
1988	91.3[a]	168.3	259.6
1989	0.1[b]	—	0.1
1990	33.0[c]	—	33.0
Total	886.0	1,380.0	2,266.0

Sources: Burmese and Japanese data.

Note: Totals do not add up because of rounding and discrepancies. All figures are in current dollars. Some figures are in question because some sources do not discriminate between commitments and disbursements. Figures do not include repayments. Grants include reparations, semi-reparations, cultural grants, debt relief, and food production programs. Loans include project assistance and commodity loans. Grant assistance between FY 1975 and 1986 included Y 329 million for culture and cash grants for debt relief of Y 3,003.

[a] May not include $450,000 in emergency food aid and $29 million in debt relief.

[b] Emergency fire victims relief, $150,000.

[c] Untied debt relief of Y 3.5 billion, announced July 24, 1990, by Kyodo News Agency. FBIS, July 30, 1990. Note that this took place following the elections of May 1990 and may have been predicated on the "liberalization" apparent at that time.

Reparations grant commitment, 1954	$200.0 million
Semi-reparations grant commitment, 1963	$131.4 million

APPENDIX C—U.S. Assistance Program Fiscal Obligations as of August 15, 1967

	U.S. Contributions		
	Dollars	**Public Law 480 Kyats**	**$ Equiva-lent** [a]
1957 ECONOMIC DEVELOPMENT LOAN	$750,390	K. 3,816,000	$801,680
Rangoon general hospital			
Rangoon water supply	1,104,000[+]	4,703,210[++]	988,069
Rangoon sewage system	515,000	634,000	133,193
Expansion of teak production, ph. II	3,480,000	12,600,000	2,647,059
*Inland waterways fleet improvement	4,564,794	–	–
*Land and water resources development	3,400,000	–	–
Expansion of teak production, ph. I	1,444,222	–	–
*Reconstruction of Kabo Dam	1,586,521	–	–
*Timber extraction	661,669	–	–
*Rice handling and processing mech.	152,213	–	–
*Telecommunications	153,016	–	–
*Rice mill, spare parts	54,759	–	–
*Land restoration	5,353,200	32,318,000	6,789,496
*Union of Burma Applied Research Inst.	857,998	5,650,000	1,186,975
*Civil aviation, airport development	406,031	–	–
*Village water supply and sanitation	569,661	8,527,000	1,791,387
	25,053,474	68,248,210	14,337,859
POLICE EQUIPMENT LOAN			
*Police assistance	8,724,011	–	–
GRANT ASSISTANCE			
Rangoon University liberal arts col.	2,245,413	28,157,136	5,915,364
*Rangoon–Mandalay highway[b]	1,533,021	535,500	112,500
*Namsang area development	730,918	–	–
	4,509,352	28,692,636	6,027,864
GRANT/LOAN ASSISTANCE			
Hospital and school construction	–	82,358,171	17,295,233
GRAND TOTAL			
Loans plus grants	38,286,837	179,299,017	37,660,956

* Completed projects.

+ Includes $76,838 from special trust fund.

++ Includes K837,210 from special counterpart acct.

[a] K4.76 = $1.00.

[b] This project was terminated at the request of the Burma government in May 1964. The funding referenced here is that required to complete payments for previously completed surveys and designs.

APPENDIX D—Summary of Actual and Committed U.S. Assistance to Burma, 1950–66[a] *($ thousands)*

Economic development grant, 1950		19,700
Rice for technicians, 1956		1,100
Economic development loan, 1957		25,000
Indian rupee exchange, 1958 (rupees)		5,000
Police equipment loans, 1958 and 1959		8,800
Rangoon–Mandalay highway[b]		1,533
Preliminary surveys and studies	Direct dollars	(1,102)
Engineering design	Direct dollars	(409)
U.S. Corps of Engineers terminal activities	Direct dollars	(22)
Rangoon University liberal arts college		2,250
Public Law 480 loan, 1957 (kyats)[c]		17,300
Public Law 480 grant, 1959 (kyats)		6,600
Public Law 480 loan, 1960 (kyats)		800
Public Law 480 loan, 1961 (kyats)		8,450
Public Law 480 grant, 1962 (kyats)		1,900
Public Law 480 loan, 1962 (kyats)		5,331
Public law 480 grant/loan, 1966		17,295
Namsang area development		731
Total		121,790

Source: USAID.
[a] As of January 31, 1967.
[b] This project was terminated at the request of the Burma government in May 1964. The funding referenced here is that required to complete payments for previously completed surveys and designs.
[c] Public Law 480 loans and grants are authorized under the following agreements:

PL 480 agreement signed February 2, 1956	$22,700,000
PL 480 agreement signed May 27, 1958	18,000,000
PL 480 agreement signed November 9, 1962	9,520,000

APPENDIX E—Official Development Assistance to Myanmar, 1989–97 (Development Assistance Committee Countries and Multilaterals)[a] *($ millions, net totals)*

	1989	1990	1991	1992	1993	1994	1995	1996	1997
Australia	4.2	2.2	0.6	0.5	0.2	0.4	1.9	1.5	1.7
France	0.9	9.7	8.0	3.3	3.4	2.0	4.3	2.1	1.9
Germany	4.6	2.4	4.0	3.2	1.6	1.4	1.3	1.5	1.4
Japan	71.4	61.3	84.5	72.1	68.6	133.8	114.2	35.2	14.8
UK	1.2	0.2	0.1	0.1	0.3	0.6	0.4	0.4	0.5

Table continues on next page.

APPENDIX E—(*continued*)

	1989	1990	1991	1992	1993	1994	1995	1996	1997
United States	2.0	1.0	—	—	—	—	—	—	
ADB	25.3	6.2	2.4	−0.3	−3.4	−10.1	−10.3	−10.5	−11.7
IBRD (IDA)	52.0	54.0	38.0	9.7	0.3	−1.7	−9.5	−10.8	−7.0
UNDP	7.4	13.3	17.9	12.6	8.6	10.9	14.3	5.8	14.0
UNTA[b]	3.1	1.7	3.3	2.1	4.3	2.4	7.9	2.8	4.2
UNICEF	6.6	7.9	6.4	6.6	7.5	6.5	6.9	8.0	8.4
Other Multilaterals	1.8	3.1	2.7	1.4	2.0	0.7	1.5	5.1	1.6
Arab agencies	−3.4	−2.9	0.2	0.2	4.7	1.8	—	—	—
TOTAL	176.3	164.0	179.4	115.1	101.5	161.6	151.3	56.2	45.2
Japan loans	37.7	28.0	42.8	35.5	26.9	26.5	16.0	6.1	—[c]

Sources: Geographical Distribution of Financial Flows to AID Recipients: Disbursements, Commitments, Country Indicators (Paris: Development Assistance Committee [DAC], OECD, 1994, 1999).

Note: Totals include other DAC countries and other multilateral agencies. Net figures include repayments. All figures are grants except as noted.
[a] Does not include China or other non-DAC countries.
[b] UN Technical Assistance.
[c] Included in above totals.

APPENDIX F—The World Bank, Myanmar: Loans/Credits Summary (*$*)

	IBRD	IDA	TOTAL
Original principal	33,350,000	803,950,000	837,300,000
Cancellations	226,057	92,649,970	92,876,027
Disbursed	33,123,943	752,813,342	785,937,285
Undisbursed	0	0	0
Repaid	30,378,965	64,291,153	94,670,118
Due	0	737,487,415	737,487,415
Exchange adjustment	0	0	0
Borrower's obligation	0	737,487,415	737,487,415
Sold third party	2,744,978	0	2,744,978
Repaid third party	2,744,978	0	2,744,978
Due third party	0	0	0

APPENDIX F—(*continued*)

		Project		Amounts in $ millions			
Financier	ID	Description	Ccy	Principal	Undisb	Disbur	Approval date
IBRD	P003336	RAILWAY	USD	5.4	0.0	5.3	04 May 1956
IBRD	P003335	RANGOON PORT	USD	14.0	0.0	13.9	04 May 1956
IBRD	P003337	RAILWAY II	USD	14.0	0.0	13.8	13 Jan 1961
IDA	P003338	INLAND WATER TRANSPORT	USD	16.3	0.0	16.3	26 Jun 1973
IDA	P003339	RAILWAY III	USD	16.7	0.0	16.0	26 Jun 1973
IDA	P003340	IRRIGATION I	USD	17.0	0.0	16.8	13 Jun 1974
IDA	P003341	FORESTRY	USD	24.0	0.0	23.5	11 Jul 1974
IDA	P003342	TELECOMMU- NICATIONS	USD	21.0	0.0	21.0	27 May 1975
IDA	P003344	LIVESTOCK I	USD	7.5	0.0	7.3	23 Dec 1975
IDA	P003343	LOWER BURMA PADDY	USD	30.0	0.0	28.1	15 Jun 1976
IDA	P003346	PORTS II	USD	10.0	0.0	10.0	21 Dec 1976
IDA	P003345	INDUSTRY MINING	USD	16.0	0.0	15.8	08 Mar 1977
IDA	P003347	SEED DEVELOPMENT	USD	5.5	0.0	5.4	01 Nov 1977
IDA	P003348	LOWER BURMA PADDY	USD	34.5	0.0	33.8	06 Jul 1978
IDA	P003349	RUBBER REHABILITATION	USD	4.5	0.0	4.1	06 Feb 1979
IDA	P003351	FORESTRY II	USD	35.0	0.0	24.9	09 Aug 1979
IDA	P003352	TELECOMMUNICA- TIONS I	USD	35.0	0.0	35.0	27 Nov 1979
IDA	P003350	IRRIG II NYAUNGGYAT	USD	90.0	0.0	87.0	29 May 1980
IDA	P003353	GRAIN STORAGE	XDR[a]	23.0	0.0	17.2	06 Jan 1981
IDA	P003354	WOOD INDUSTRIES	XDR	32.0	0.0	26.3	17 Mar 1981
IDA	P003355	POWER I	XDR	80.0	0.0	82.0	13 May 1982
IDA	P003356	CONSTRUCTION IND. I	XDR	20.0	0.0	19.8	25 May 1982
IDA	P003358	TANK IRRIG.	XDR	19.0	0.0	17.7	21 Dec 1982
IDA	P003360	PORTS III	XDR	50.0	0.0	60.6	24 May 1983

[a] Special Drawing Rights. IMF credits based on a basket of currencies. Slightly more than a U.S. dollar.

Notes

1. Aung San, "Appeal to Pay Land Revenue, Rent, and Agricultural Loans," in *The Political Legacy of Aung San*, ed. Josef Silverstein (Ithaca: Cornell University, Southeast Asia Program Series No. 11, 1993), p. 61.

2. This meant that requests for training were sent to the appropriate Burmese authorities, such as the Ministry of Foreign Affairs, without specific names of Burmese but with generic qualifications of those who were suited to the program. This was then forwarded to the appropriate ministry that chose the trainee. There were informal means around this regulation, but the fact that it existed under all governments is important.

3. Programs that had been designed to assist the development of transportation in the minority areas had to be scrapped after criticisms that this would give the military greater access. The UNDP program was rewritten to exclude direct government assistance, and there were informal consultations with the NLD, as well as formal approvals by the government.

4. In 1999, two very senior retired Burmese officers spontaneously remarked how attached they still were to the Japanese, who helped train them, because the Japanese showed a continuous interest in them, as contrasted with the British and the Americans.

5. It portrays a Japanese soldier who stays behind in Burma after the war to help bury the dead.

6. The assistance amounted to $1 per capita annually. For a discussion of Japanese aid, see David I. Steinberg, "Japanese Economic Assistance to Burma: Aid in the Tarenagashi Manner?" in *Managing Japan's Foreign Aid: Power and Policy in a New Era*, ed. Bruce Koppel and Robert Orr (Boulder: Westview Press, 1993); also in *Crossroads* 5, 2 (1990). See also Donald M. Seekins, "The North Wind and the Sun: Japan's Response to the Political Crisis in Burma, 1988–1998," *Journal of Burma Studies* 4 (1999): 1–34.

7. Japan also supplied $200 million to Indonesia and $400 million to the Philippines.

8. A senior Japanese official remarked that if Burma had not been recognized, protocol would have demanded that the Burmese delegation be seated next to the formally unrecognized Palestine Liberation Organization at the funeral, which would have been a major insult. Personal communication.

9. *OECF [Overseas Economic Cooperation Fund] Yearbook 1998* (Tokyo, 1999), p. 232.

10. June 28, 2000.

11. *Burmanet*, no. 1461 (February 12–13, 2000).

12. *Report on the Resumption of Bilateral Assistance to Burma*, May 17–27, 1978 (Washington, D.C.: Agency for International Development, Department of State). The authors were David I. Steinberg (team leader), Richard Newburg, and Albert Boucher. Much of the history of the aid program reported here is taken from that report and its appendices.

13. U.S. assistance continued for basic human needs projects in the Philippines, but the United States abstained on some major infrastructure loans from multilateral organizations. The period when U.S. aid was being reconsidered for Burma (i.e., 1978) was at the height of the Carter administration's concern for human rights.

14. A number of organizations receive funds from the U.S. Department of State (specifically authorized by Congress) to engage in Burmese-related activities. The National Endowment for Democracy in its 1999 annual report lists grants totaling over $1.6 million to a broad variety of organizations, including those ethnically related and those in publishing, research, and labor affairs. It also supports aspects of the Democratic Voice of Burma (Norway based), some work of the NCGUB, and the Burma Fund.

15. "United Nations in Myanmar" (Yangon, United Nations, October 1997).

16. Personal communication.

17. Personal communication with a vice minister in the BSPP period.

18. Multilateral donors are bound to continue projects already started or approved if internal aspects of such projects allow. The UNDP is a right of all member states. Bilateral donors have different approaches, ranging, as noted, from that of the United States, which stopped all projects already approved, to that of Japan, which continued approved projects but did not start new ones.

CHAPTER 10

Conclusion:
Burma/Myanmar—
Its Future and the
Dilemmas of Foreign Policy

Nebo, nyasa!
(For today, [we can only think about] our evening meal!)[1]

There are eight essential tensions facing Myanmar that have been caused or exacerbated by military rule. Unless these tensions are lessened through explicit administrative and institutional avenues and solutions fostered by the national leadership, the future of that complex of societies known as Burma/Myanmar will be compromised. These are the tensions:

- Between authorized and encouraged Burman nationalism and growing ethnic nationalism;
- Between bureaucratic centralism and pluralism;
- Between military and civilian sectors of society;
- Between globalization and nationalism;
- Between the need for ideological orthodoxy and pluralistic views of state-society relations;
- Between officially fostered Buddhism and other religions;
- Between the vested interests of those profiting from the narcotics trade and societal goals;

- Among regional powers that variously view the state as potentially supporting or subverting the national interests.

The authorities to date have articulated a different set of tensions, referring to them as "threats" to the state. From their vantagepoint, these are:

- Challenges from regional powers;
- Globalization (cultural and economic);
- Communications and media influence (negative to state goals and procedures);
- Competition and trade disputes within ASEAN and the outside world;
- Migration from Bangladesh, India, etc. (significantly China is not specifically included);
- Rapid expansion of the urban population;
- Problems of transnational crime, drug trafficking, ethnicity, poverty, HIV/AIDS, and environmental degradation.[2]

It is evident that the analyses of the problems facing the Burmese state are quite different, thus leading to misperceptions among contending organizations and among nations as well.

Subsumed in all of these categories are issues connected with democracy, governance, and human rights. These are stressed by the NLD, most potential donors, and the international media but are often ignored in the popular press in reports on the problems of Myanmar. Concentration on democracy, which, as we have seen, is often equated only with elections, may lead an observer to ignore some of the more fundamental issues on which democratic governance is normally based.

It is important to distinguish the intellectual legacy of Aung San from his daughter's views; his heritage is quite different from her public position. It lies not in democracy, but in the struggle for independence and the trust he generated with the minorities. The aura of Aung San, as we have noted, has been used by Ne Win to legitimate his early rule and later by Aung San Suu Kyi for the purposes of her party. There seems little question that Aung San is beloved, but his was not a democratic heritage. Aung San advocated a single-party state system, and he said, "One nation, one state, one party, one leader. There shall be no parliamentary opposition, no nonsense of individualism."[3]

Times have certainly changed, and Aung San Suu Kyi has written eloquently on democracy. The question is not whether to invoke Aung San for his now outdated views, but rather whether the civilian era has provided a base of experience that will make the introduction of democracy in a generally accepted sense workable, however much the NLD leadership may espouse it. There are many, both in the opposition and in academia, who say that that base is there from the civilian period, for the society was pluralistic; others would disagree. Mary Callahan has captured the issue:

> To date, U.S. policy has held the military junta solely responsible for bottling up a transition to a more responsive, representative form of governance. The weakness of this position is that the junta is only part of the problem, albeit a big part. The real problem undermining U.S. and Burmese opposition party attempts to promote a transition to democracy in Burma lies in the decades-old political and socioeconomic structures that not only block meaningful political reform, but also undermine the authoritarian regime's capacity to achieve its own goals. . . . Beyond the obvious anti-democratic measures taken by the military junta, three significant political and socioeconomic conditions stand in the way of establishing democratic governance in Burma: (1) an inadequate political base for federalism in this multi-ethnic society; (2) a century-old crisis of state capacity rooted in the fragmented nature of society; and (3) an institutional intolerance for dissent that is found in authoritarian as well as democratic organizations.[4]

Closely related to democracy is the issue of human rights, democracy being the political aspect of such rights. Regimes in Asia have rejected the imposition of Western values, claiming that "Asian values" are distinct and involve collective rights (but the extent of that "collectivity" is often selectively drawn). The most articulate advocate of that position has been Lee Kwan Yew of Singapore, but the Myanmar military has also used this approach and has charged the United States with using its influence to force states into ideological submission. Secretary-1 has stated the official Burmese position unequivocally:

> At present, we keep hearing two overworked cliches. Those are the terms human rights and democracy. The Western nations are using these two cliches at every turn in order to indoctrinate the people of developing nations to suit their ulterior motives, in what could be termed a form of psycho-colonialism. Thus developing nations such as ours must perforce exercise human rights and democracy within the bounds suitable for us. There are vast differences between the countries of the East and those of the West—differences in our culture, customs, traditions, and historical development. And there is no way to force them into the same mold. Progressive changes and reforms consistent with the conditions and nature of our country and our people will be gradually carried out

as time and circumstances permit. The type of permissiveness and uninhibited rights found in the West are certainly not for us at this point in time.[5]

Related to the issues of democracy and human rights and whether these should be the immediate priorities, as the NLD claims, or whether they (however they are interpreted) are supplementary issues to be faced after the unity of the state is assured and military guidance enshrined, as the *tatmadaw* believes, is the political confrontation that is the focus of internal and international attention. But should democracy be somehow introduced in the country, this will not automatically solve the minority issue, which is the most intractable problem facing the state.

The struggle between the *tatmadaw* and the NLD has continued. The past few years have been a gestation period of intensified confrontations between the Burmese military authorities, the SPDC, and Aung San Suu Kyi and the NLD. What may be born from this heightened, painful labor is problematic. What we have witnessed in the past years is but a continuation of the struggle since the March 1988 student demonstrations, albeit in somewhat different contexts, not presently blatantly brutal but no less potentially bloody and critical.

If the foreign observer is frustrated by the political stasis and the paucity of balanced and nuanced information in and about Burma/Myanmar, consider for a moment what all those involved must feel in relation to the current situation.[6] The SPDC must also be frustrated in spite of joining ASEAN in July 1997 and gaining the very modest additional legitimacy that derived from membership (a legitimacy that the regime evidently sought and that the United States sought to deny). One of the military's primary objectives in seeking membership in ASEAN was likely the expected inflow of foreign investment from member states. This has been denied, not because the ASEAN states would not take advantage of the opportunities in Burma if they could—however uncomfortable some of their governments might feel with the reputation of the SPDC—but because of the unfortunate timing of the Asian financial crisis that began in July 1997 in Thailand and then spread and has undercut the capacity of businesses in ASEAN states to invest.[7] Foreign investment at the turn of the twenty-first century virtually dried up because of both the financial crisis and continuing U.S. sanctions against the regime.[8] Myanmar, probably unexpectedly to its delegation, was the obvious target of a liberalized Thai Foreign Ministry resolution through ASEAN to explore the internal affairs of member states, a heretofore inappropriate ASEAN consideration.

The SPDC must also be frustrated by the reluctance of the multilateral financial institutions, such as the World Bank and the ADB, to provide badly needed assistance; they have been prompted to withhold support in large part by the United States, whose sanctions on new investments are probably more of a moral than an economic force. The 1999 World Bank study of poverty, health, education, agriculture, and the private sector was still being studied by the Burmese authorities at publication. Although no foreign assistance from multilateral organizations is expected until some form of political liberalization coupled with economic policy reforms either is agreed upon or takes place, the study provides a guide for possible future action. The United States was opposed to such a study at the time it occurred, believing it would prompt a return to economic assistance.

The policy influence of the United States extends beyond its own borders and affects countries that indeed would want to resume economic assistance to Burma if they could do so without antagonizing the industrialized international community and its allies. Japan is the prime example of a state torn between a foreign ministry concerned about international relations and the American alliance, on the one hand, and, on the other, certain elements of the Diet and ministries devoted to trade and investment, which reflect a domestic business constituency intent on exploiting a potentially lucrative market, a source of raw materials, and the contracts that would necessarily flow from renewed and massive economic assistance. The public pronouncements emanating from the November 1999 Manila meeting between Prime Minister Obuchi and Than Shwe indicated little progress. The Japanese called for some political movement, and Than Shwe did not indicate any change. Following that visit, former prime minister Hashimoto, as a representative of Prime Minister Obuchi, visited Rangoon on a quiet, supposedly "unofficial" visit. Such meetings are highly significant and would not have been publicized without some hope for progress, however. The public statements may be for external consumption and mutual "face," while more substantial accommodations may evolve later, supposedly separate from these events but actually based on them. Some form of Japanese assistance to Myanmar is likely under some auspices, and some cosmetic conciliation by the SPDC is possible, with perhaps some modest internal economic policy changes, but real internal liberalization that would move the military from the center of political or economic power is highly unlikely.

The *tatmadaw* is evidently frustrated by the NLD and its intransigence, together with the stubborn courage of Aung San Suu Kyi; the continuing publicized confrontations with the NLD, heightening international concerns; and the deterioration of the economy, inflation, and the international opprobrium attached to the regime, although its hold over the society has increased as the ethnic cease-fires have been maintained, and military operations on the borders have subsided. Ironically, as military control has expanded, economic efficacy has deteriorated.

The NLD must also be frustrated. It has seen its once extensive and powerful, if harassed, political infrastructure destroyed by the military, its provincial chapters closed or truncated, and its local leadership arrested or forced to resign.[9] The campaign against the NLD, and personally against Aung San Suu Kyi, as reflected in the controlled and authorized press, is vehement and unrelenting. As Than Shwe said on the seventy-ninth anniversary of Union Day (December 2, 1999), "Neo-colonialists and their subservient negativistic internal axe-handles wearing the cloaks of human rights and democracy are violating all kinds of laws, moving to incite anarchy and interfering in the internal affairs of the nation and are even perpetrating terrorist acts transgressing the sovereignty of the state." [10] The regime has severely cut into the party as a political institution and destroyed its regional base but not affected its core. The army has also clearly attempted to split the NLD from Aung San Suu Kyi, as some of the leadership may be more interested in compromise than is Aung San Suu Kyi, without major effect to date but with some signs of disaffection. In May 1998, twenty-five elected NLD members criticized Aung San Suu Kyi concerning the formation of the Committee Representing People's Parliament (CRPP) and were charged with being disloyal to her. Prolongation of the stasis undercuts the legitimacy of both the government and the opposition but in the long run may hurt the NLD, and more specifically Aung San Suu Kyi, as economic conditions continue to deteriorate and she is more blamed, however unfairly, for intransigence than is the military regime. The military's goal is clearly the elimination of the NLD or at least the elimination of Aung San Suu Kyi as an effective political force and rallying focus for foreign and domestic critics.

To prevent its marginalization both internally and externally, the NLD has engaged in an extensive series of confrontations with the government.[11] These include:

- Aung San Suu Kyi's forcibly truncated—and internationally well-publicized—attempted visits to local party chapters, which were prevented by the army, leaving her stranded in the countryside or at the Rangoon train station;

- Demands to rejoin (after NLD representatives walked out of it) the National Convention and to open it to real debate;
- Insisting that the elected (mostly NLD) representatives of the May 1990 election be seated by August 21, 1998;
- Distribution of NLD flyers by eighteen foreign students and other young people;
- Attempting to hold a party convention (resulting in the arrest and/or detention of hundreds of party followers or officials);
- Formation of the CRPP, a committee of ten empowered by the NLD to act as a parliament.[12] Since the NLD won the May 1990 elections, it believes it is the legitimate government. One of its first official acts was to declare that it had the authority to void all laws and regulations imposed by the SLORC/SPDC over the past decade and then to declare all laws of the military illegal; in January 1999 it sued the military, specifically military intelligence, for attempted destruction of the party. The Burmese court, which surprisingly heard the case, not so surprisingly dismissed it in October of that year.
- Struggling to obtain a Burmese visa in 1999 for Michael Aris (Aung San Suu Kyi's husband), who was terminally ill from cancer in the United Kingdom. The SPDC refused him a visa before he died, and Aung San Suu Kyi was unwilling to trust the SPDC, in spite of its promises, that it would allow her back into Myanmar should she have left to join him. Clearly, the SPDC lost considerable international credibility in not allowing his visit.[13]

The NLD has walked a very fine line. While deprecating the SLORC/ SPDC-induced laws and regulations and even declaring many of them illegal, it has adhered to a great many and specifically avoided actions that the regime could declare to be blatantly illegal. Had the NLD broken the arbitrarily imposed laws, it would have given the authorities an excuse to declare it an illegal entity and shut it down. This is probably what the SPDC would wish to do, but without a clear violation of regulations, such as the NLD's advocating or resorting to violence, it has been willing to tolerate its presence since the military would be subject to even more intense international criticism if it were to close it down. This may also be why the NLD and NCGUB claim to have no direct contact.

Expatriate dissident groups tried to evoke mass demonstrations against the regime on September 9, 1999 (9-9-99), reminiscent of August 8, 1988.[14] Some disturbances were reported, but they did not threaten the regime, although the government took precautions, even delaying the visit of the UN assistant secretary general.

In October 1999, when the Vigorous Burmese Student Warriors stormed the Myanmar Embassy in Bangkok, the NLD specifically did not claim that it had sponsored the act, but Aung San Suu Kyi indicated the NLD would not disown all those who fought for freedom. These events have generated considerable international publicity and sympathy for the NLD; their consequences internally are far less evident.

The NLD has endorsed sanctions, which have increasingly been questioned outside Myanmar; counseled against investment as benefiting only the regime; deplored tourism and advised tourists to stay away; criticized foreign humanitarian assistance (especially the Japanese) as legitimating and benefiting the government and not the people; and discouraged international NGOs from working inside the country.[15] The NLD strongly criticized an August 1999 Australian initiative in which the Australian commissioner for human rights visited Yangon and met with both the authorities and the opposition to discuss the possibility of setting up an independent Burmese human rights commission, modeled on one in preliberalization Indonesia. The NLD regards any increase in military visibility or financial gain as legitimating and prolonging military rule.

The minorities may feel that their cease-fires, although effective in stopping the killing, have not resulted in the delivery of the goods and services anticipated: the lives of the citizenry have not improved. Poverty is said to be especially pronounced in the Chin and Kayah States, although circumstantial evidence and reports from occasional observers indicate that it is likely to be pervasive and deep elsewhere as well. The Karen, fighting for two generations in what has sadly become a hopeless cause, are fragmented and are militarily ineffective. Their leader, Bo Mya, after decades of command, finally resigned in February 2000, although he retains the chair of the Democratic Alliance for Burma (DAB). Forced resettlement in minority areas, most dramatically in the Shan State, has caused dire economic and social conditions. The minority cries for some form of federalism have gone unheeded (except by the NLD), and there is growing concern among some of them that their primary objective must be to ensure the survival of the ethnic groups, with democracy a secondary concern. The general Burman population may also be frustrated by the continuing economic decline, growing inflation, increasing poverty and malnutrition, blatant corruption that undercuts regime capacity and acceptance, and general political climate that continues to be as repressive as at any time in Burmese history, perhaps even more so because the state has greater capacity for monitoring and control of its population.[16]

Dilemmas and Current Conditions

The friends of the diverse peoples of Myanmar face multiple dilemmas. First and primary, how can the lives of the population be improved? Basic needs are at best only marginally met. Education has eroded.[17] The health services are lacking, and agriculture is still undeveloped. (At the same time there is a parallel path: the health, education, and living standards for the military are far superior.) Then, how can personal and political rights be expanded to give individuals greater access to information and the ability to move around and associate and develop a sense of political efficacy? How also can power be shared among ethnic groups in some manner that is seen by all those involved as appropriate and nonthreatening? Which of these comes first, if any, and how?

The military has opted for economic and security advances, which suit its political agenda of control. The opposition has cried for democracy first; economic and ethnic issues could, it argues, be resolved relatively easily after democratic governance is instituted. Some of the minorities want their rights before other questions are resolved. Foreign observers are frustrated, many believing that political and economic reforms go in tandem. There are no easy answers to any of these questions; clear and distinct Cartesian answers are not realistically possible.

Internally, the evidence is overwhelming that the military is determined to maintain solid control over all important sources of power. It will do so sequentially through rule by military decree (which was the pattern between 1962 and 1974 and as it has done since 1988) and then through a civilianized regime essentially hostage to the *tatmadaw* under a constitution being interminably drafted by a subservient National Convention [18]; it will mandate military control over a unitary state. The model clearly has been Indonesia in the Suharto era, where military authority persisted.[19] The problem with the Indonesia model is not only the obvious one about its collapse, but rather more fundamentally that the institutional basis on which the Suharto regime was able to continue for as long as it did was predicated on two factors lacking in Myanmar. These are the willingness to use sound economic and apolitical advice from qualified staff (and foreigners where appropriate) in the formation of policies, and adequate institutions by which to translate policies, should they be formulated, into action and administrative capacity. Any premilitary administrative mechanisms of competence were intentionally subverted in the interests of ideological loyalty to the *tatmadaw* and its policies. Whenever any regime determines that it will opt for reform, it must first rebuild its institutions, giving them the authority needed to manage their responsibilities. But to do so, if previous experience is relevant, means the climate of fear must be broken to allow authority to be delegated.

Since the military hierarchy has evolved into one essentially ethnically Burman, any local autonomy or self-administration that may be granted to marginal ethnic groups is tactical largesse to provide both internal and external fig leaves of cover for a unitary state in which the military will reign supreme. The military, distrustful of any form of pluralism, has controlled and coopted civil society: only approved private organizations can function and then within prescribed boundaries. It has created its own "civil society" in the USDA. "Civil society" is thus alive and well and run by the government.[20] All forms of internal media are under strict state control and censorship, and external information is suppressed or only judiciously distributed. Political and civil rights are effectively restricted or stifled. Rule by law is rule by arbitrarily formulated and administered edicts promulgated by the state to support its perceived interests at the expense of abstracted rights.

Yet there have been important changes in the *tatmadaw* and in Burma since 1988 in spite of the apparent stasis that reduces foreign interest and press coverage on that country. As noted, the army is more powerful than it has ever been in Burma's modern history. At the same time, it has quelled (at least temporarily) many of the rebellions and thus is more free to deal with internal control and external contingencies. According to Andrew Selth,

> The armed forces' increased strength permits the regime to enforce its will over the country in a way never before possible. Indeed, the *Tatmadaw*'s greater size and military capabilities, combined with the shrewd management of various ethnic and narcotics-based insurgent groups, means that (formally, at least) the central government's writ runs over more of Burma than at any time since it regained its independence from the United Kingdom in 1948. . . . Similarly, any

lasting solution to Burma's complex ethnic problems will depend to a large degree on the willingness and the ability of the Tatmadaw to countenance some sort of political compromise. The continuing insistence by the regime on a strong central government in Rangoon dominated by ethnic Burmans, at the expense of any power-sharing arrangements with minority racial groups, will inevitably see a return to the bitter and costly fighting of the past.[21]

The military is not only stronger, but also it sees itself "as embodying the state, and what is good for them [the armed forces] is considered *ipso facto* to be good for Burma. . . . The regime has long claimed the right to exercise a monopoly over all aspects of Burma's national security debate." [22]

Two generations ago Burma was potentially the richest Southeast Asian state. However, the promised wealth of the country has been sacrificed first on insurgencies that sapped the vitality of the civilian administration, then on the altar of an ineffective economic ideology and incompetent administration, again on environmentally unsound depletion of forestry and fishery reserves, and finally on the primacy of rigid political power and control. The economy is in parlous condition but is not necessarily on the verge of collapse. The abrupt abandonment of a devout, noncommunist socialism has encouraged the indigenous private sector and some foreign investment (but less than one-third of that in Vietnam, on an approved—but not yet disbursed—basis, which liberalized its economy at about the same time), but the state remains highly suspicious of all private sector activities not directly controlled or authorized by the *tatmadaw,* which has and will continue to maintain a direct financial interest in and domination over large segments of the economy.[23]

The confrontation between the SPDC and the NLD intensified in 1999–2000. There was discussion in the controlled press of forced deportation of Aung San Suu Kyi, which the government denied but which may have been a trial balloon. The SPDC has agreed to discussions with the NLD only if they exclude "the lady," as she is known ("our lady" to some younger dissidents). This the NLD has rejected, saying that each side should be able to designate its representatives in any dialogue that might develop. The military has demanded the abolition of the CRPP before any discussions can take place; this the NLD has refused. This stalemate has prompted some knowledgeable Burmese to blame all parties for the continuing and politically stultifying confrontation that is harmful to the country. "A plague on all of them," as one former senior official said.[24] It has become evident that the NLD has been successful in increasing foreign attention to its plight. But other groups have been dissatisfied with U.S. policy, which calls for recognition of the results of the May 1990 elections and thus a new government. As such, no partial progress is possible. There is the argument in many circles in the United States that unilateral sanctions imposed on a multitude of states have not produced the intended results.[25] And the elimination of sanctions is exceedingly more difficult politically than their imposition.

Some would argue that U.S. policy to honor the results of the May 1990 elections is tantamount to telling the government to get out of power before discussions can take place with it. As noted, the United States has imposed a travel ban on senior regime officials (thus further reducing the possibility of higher-level dialogue at international fora in the United States), although discussions are held in Rangoon with the U.S. Embassy at a lower level. The United States refused to attend an Interpol meeting in Rangoon in February 1999 on narcotics control on the grounds that it would further legitimate the military, but it thus ignored the opportunity to have a dialogue with it on its home turf. This has occurred in spite of the reduction in opium production from an estimated 2,500 metric tons to a present level of 1,750 metric tons. This reduction was in part due to weather but also to increased eradication and crop substitution.[26] It has also had an arms embargo and prevented the appointment of a new American ambassador. There are elements in the Congress that call for the virtual recognition of the NLD as the legal government of Myanmar and want, and have legislated, international programs, such as those sponsored by the UNDP, to have Aung San Suu Kyi's formal consultation, even approval (rather than informal acquiescence as has taken place). This was initially opposed by some in the Department of State. Under legislation passed in November 1998, however, UNDP programs must be subject to prior consultations with both the NLD and the NCGUB, the government in exile in Washington, D.C. Yet the NLD maintains that is has no contact with the NCGUB and there is no coordination of activities—the NLD acts internally and the NCGUB externally.[27] By denying contact, the NLD has tried to retain its status as a legal political party. Some expatriate Burmese and human rights groups call for the expulsion of the present regime from the United Nations. Major changes in U.S. policy seem unlikely under present circumstances. Prospects look exceedingly gloomy, and the picture is not a pretty one; if analysis of Myanmar is an art, we may be looking at what might be called the "ashcan art" school of politics.

Assumptions and Constraints

The NLD has called for negotiations, and the SPDC has said that it would not negotiate as long as Aung San Suu Kyi and Tin Oo are involved, and it wants the NLD to eliminate the CRPP. It may also be that the NLD is somewhat fearful that some members of its leadership, who are former military officers, might be willing to compromise with the SPDC to some unacceptable degree. This impasse may continue, but it is prudent to prepare for the contingency of dialogue and negotiations. To do so, however, requires a realistic assessment of priorities and issues. If one is to consider the effectiveness of policies, present or proposed, and be prepared to understand a society so as to negotiate any of the issues, it is imperative to consider not only the objective conditions at the time, but also the assumptions and perceived constraints under which any party to such negotiations operates. All parties must also objectively consider their own negotiating constraints, and distinguish between hopes and possibilities.[28]

Most important are the core values that parties maintain beyond the cant, propaganda, and public relations statements that are associated with staged announcements made to assuage international opinions and mobilize internal support. These beliefs often are ignored or denigrated by outside critics, who also doubt their existence or find them illogical, but it is important to differentiate between views that are strongly held but may be completely incorrect (however tenaciously they are promulgated and repeated) and those that are simply propaganda. Of course, we assume here that there are such views; although some might disagree and dismiss all official statements with which one disagrees as mere propaganda, the case may be made that any party to any negotiations comes to the table with some almost primordial conceptions.

An important caveat should first be stated. Although we speak of the military in the singular, we do this as a rhetorical convenience (and as a result of a considerable measure of ignorance, for much of the military leadership is effectively off limits to foreign dialogue) that reflects the unified public image and corporate decisions of the elite leadership. But it is highly probable that there are significant differences within this elite, not to mention other elements of the military.[29] According to one writer, "There is today no hidden element within the armed forces that could emerge from a kernel of opposition into an element capable of opposing the will of the senior leadership." [30] In spite of these differences, which may reflect policy debates, personal rivalries, and factional groupings, most probably share the views below to a significant degree, and the differences may be more apparent in tactical responses toward reaching agreed goals than in disagreement about the goals themselves. There are contending views concerning potential splits within the military. One is that the loyalty and unity of the *tatmadaw* have been ensured through promotions and expanding the military's role in government and business. This is important because the military pension system is lacking and because of recent pay raises. A differing view is that the augmentation of the military and its changed role from defense to administration will cause future internal problems. If the military has potential fissures, it would be well to remember that the NLD and the minorities, separately and together, have potential splits as well.[31] Tensions within the beleaguered NLD have become evident. Power is highly personalized. As a result, factionalism has been an important characteristic of Burmese politics, as it has since at least 1937.

The strongly held military views that affect negotiations may be divided into those internally and externally focused.

Burmese Military Views—Internal

- The military believes that it is the only present and future institution capable of keeping Myanmar united and that pluralism is destructive of national unity. This assumption is true at present because the military has effectively destroyed every other institution that might have played a unifying role. It will be true in the future insofar as the military prevents the rise of pluralism and the growth of civil society. This is why it has essentially replaced earlier state ideologies with an ideology that effectively focuses on the military itself, its comprehensive societal role, and, in part, its mythic history. "In Myanmar conception, the security of the state, regime, and the military are conflated. A threat to any one institution is seen as a threat to all. . . . In summary, the values included under the label of security are the unity of the military and its domestic political role; domestic order and stability; national unity; and the territorial integrity of the state." [32]

- The *tatmadaw* considers past political leaders venal, corrupt, ineffective, and incapable of running the state and assuring its unity.
- The military believes that the minorities are inherently inferior (culturally/ socially) and would split from Burman authority if given the chance. It also believes the minorities are distrustful of the Burman majority (including the military) and fear Burman domination. It provides only lip-service respect for minority culture through ritualized holidays and propaganda efforts. It equates Burman Buddhist culture with the state and wants some form of central (Burman) control. Advocacy of Buddhism, association with the *sangha,* building or repairing of Buddhist shrines (including adding one ton of gold to the Shwedagon Pagoda in 1999) are part of the search for both political legitimacy and personal religious merit. The state goes to great lengths to demonstrate its reverence for the *sangha,* and the leadership is continuously depicted in the media as supportive of Buddhism. Buddhism is intimately associated with political legitimacy.[33]
- The military views economic progress, reform, or liberalization as secondary to maintenance of political control, or indeed as a means to such control. The primary function of an improved economy is greater military power, general political acquiescence of the population to military control through military delivery of greater economic rewards for loyalty, and improved political legitimacy. To this end, the military believes it must control the economy and has set up direct and many indirect mechanisms to do so.
- The military views any form of pluralism within the administration at any level, in the dissemination of information, and among NGOs as a threat to the state and military control.
- The military has no intention of giving up essential power even though a civilian facade for its control might be established.
- The military has no intention of granting to minority groups any significant degree of power at the national level, although some modest local self-government will be given to some groups with which cease-fires have been arranged.

Burmese Military Views—External

- The Burmese regime believes that the country is surrounded by enemies— real and potential. Threats no longer take the form of territorial aggrandizement but rather economic domination and the encouragement of minority separatism. These fears are based on a reality once extant but now completely outmoded. Past instances of foreign support are well documented and include American assistance to Kuomintang forces in Burma, Pakistani–Bangladeshi support for Muslim insurgents, Thai help to a variety of insurgent groups (both ethnic and Burman), Indian backing of anti-SLORC groups, some British support for the Karen, Chinese aid to the BCP, the inclusion of northen Burma in early Kuomintang and PRC maps, and a general perception that Christian minorities have more support and contact with foreigners than do the Burman Buddhists.

- It is feared that China potentially will have (or perhaps even presently has) undue influence in Burma.
- The military regards the United States as highly significant because of its international influence but distrusts the U.S., believing that if sufficiently provoked, it might intervene militarily in Burma.[34] The military also believes that the United States wants a different regime in Myanmar—one that would support a U.S. "containment" policy toward China.
- Foreign public criticism of the SPDC simply forces a nationalistic response, foreign pressures for reform are viewed as infringements of Burmese sovereignty, and foreign support for the NLD undercuts the NLD's potential legitimacy (in the military's view).

NLD Assumptions

- The military is out to destroy the NLD.
- The military is intent on splitting Aung San Suu Kyi from the party.
- There is a potential role for the military under a truly civilian (NLD) government, but one under civilian control and review.
- The immediate needs are to maintain the NLD as an entity and seek to continue international support, including sanctions.
- It is necessary to deny the military any possible avenues that would increase its public legitimacy internally or externally. This includes opposing any humanitarian assistance that benefits the SPDC or its agencies (e.g., USDA) and the operations of foreign NGOs in Myanmar, as well as denying to the government the foreign exchange generated by business, investment, or tourism.

U.S. Assumptions on U.S. Policies toward Burma

- Burma is low on the list of U.S. foreign policy concerns, even though Secretary of State Albright has taken a personal interest in the human rights and political problems in that society.
- The United States has residual antinarcotics interests that are important but not sufficient alone to drive policy change. Although antinarcotics activities were more important to the United States in the BSPP period, when it provided considerable assistance, since the SLORC/SPDC period, and largely in response to internal U.S. public pressures, human rights have become more significant in policy formulation.
- There is a significant lobby within the Congress and in the U.S./international NGO community insisting (minimally) on greater political and civil rights—more comprehensively that the military relinquish its authority as a result of the May 1990 elections and for Aung San Suu Kyi to assume the reins of government.
- The United States is preoccupied with the Balkans, the Middle East, China, North Korea, India–Pakistan nuclear issues and Kashmir, and Japan. Little attention will be paid to Myanmar.
- Although the executive and legislative branches are in formal agreement at this juncture, should the administration desire to shift its present policies, it will not be prepared to use up any political capital on confronting the Congress or individual legislators on Burma issues.
- Considerable changes in U.S. policy—including lifting sanctions and the reinstatement of a U.S. ambassador in Rangoon—are unlikely without major internal reforms in Burma because they would be seen as rewards and would be politically indefensible within the United States.
- Current U.S. policy will limit the capacity of any U.S. administration in the near future to agree to multilateral donor assistance to Burma without clear quid pro quos.
- If amelioration were to take place in the near term, it would be opposed by Aung San Suu Kyi unless it were accompanied by the release of political prisoners and the freedom of the NLD to operate as a real political party.
- Other, more important U.S. policy issues with China (trade, human rights, influence on North Korea, etc.) mean that Myanmar is low on the priority list for bilateral discussions. The same is true for Japan. Yet both the United States and Japan are important for Myanmar dialogue.

- Individual members of Congress believe they cannot be seen to support a pariah regime and thus will follow a minority strongly opposed to easing present U.S. policies.
- At the same time, there is a significant body of businessmen or women who, perhaps for either intellectual or financial reasons, believe that private sector activity will bring (perhaps eventually) democracy.[35]
- Japan desires to resume major foreign assistance and has been prevented from doing so only by U.S. pressure. It is likely that it will restart at least a portion of its program. Japanese assistance is important to the country. Its past role has been essential to the survival of previous Burmese governments, and it has strongly influenced positive change (the shift to the private sector).
- China could be influential in effecting change if it were convinced to play such a role, in spite of Burmese concerns about Burma's already considerably exposed position.
- China believes that a stable, friendly, pliant regime in Rangoon is in its national interests, and it would support the present government in the face of induced change. China is, however, concerned about increased narcotics activities emanating from Myanmar and raising AIDS/HIV rates in Yunnan.

Although Indian relations with the Burmese regime have improved since Rajiv Gandhi, India views with suspicion a Chinese presence and influence on its undemarcated northeast frontier (the scene of fighting in the Sino-Indian War of 1962) and is concerned about Chinese access to the Bay of Bengal.

The Changed International Milieu

After years of international neglect, foreign attention and sympathy have focused on Myanmar since 1988 because of seven new factors:

- The opening to the private sector and the lure of quick profits for investors using a cowed, unorganized, and underpaid labor force and Myanmar's inherent natural resources;
- The massacres of 1988 (a year before Tienanmen);
- The government's blatant ignoring of the results of the May 1990 elections;
- The increased international attention on human rights and the creation and/

or strengthening of mechanisms for monitoring and responding to violations (in spite of the fact that the Universal Declaration on Human Rights dates from 1948 and Amnesty International has been around a long time);

- The personal magnetism and strength of Aung San Suu Kyi and her internal and external support;
- The forces of globalization; and
- The growing articulate and educated expatriate Burmese community, which has effectively organized itself and other supporters in antimilitary activities through the new technology of the Internet and e-mail.

Polarization on Burma/Myanmar has been intensified by two constraints: first, the unwillingness of foreign observers or governments interested in democracy or liberalization to criticize any of the policies of the NLD or Aung San Suu Kyi because this would provide propaganda ammunition to the SPDC and be used against the liberal movement and would strengthen the regime; second, conscious decisions by foreign observers not to compliment the SPDC on any actions that might be considered "right" or appropriate because it would serve the regime's interests and increase its legitimacy. Thus virtual prohibition of outside criticism of the NLD on the one hand, and, on the other, prohibition of complimentary remarks about the SPDC have become political weapons against those working for reform and/or compromise.

Future Prospects

As of January 2001, political stagnation continues. But change will eventually come to Myanmar; societies do not forever remain in aspic, although change does not necessarily mean either progress or that it will come quickly. If change were to occur suddenly, there would seem to be little that foreigners might do to assist the course of events in some positive manner for the benefit of the people of the country. Gradual or incremental change, however, might enable some elements of the foreign community to play some appropriate role under various conditions.

If change were to occur in the next two years, it could well be traumatic. The possibility of political stasis continues, with the NLD making every effort to force confrontations that attract foreign press and sympathy; the more this is effective, the more the SPDC will charge that the NLD is controlled by foreigners and use this as an internal weapon against it. It will invoke nationalism against the NLD, charging that Aung San Suu Kyi and the NLD are "axe-handles" supporting destructive elements. The military is more powerful than it ever has been. It has indicated no interest in compromising with Aung San Suu Kyi or sharing power with the opposition. But the cease-fires with the minorities will hold only insofar as their well-being improves through services provided by the center. To reform the economy, the SPDC wants and needs large infusions of international assistance, which will not be forthcoming without substantial political reform and cessation of human rights violations. But the SPDC has specifically indicated that no strings should be attached to aid. Foreign assistance is also needed in the minority regions as an element to maintain the fragile cease-fires. The SPDC has dealt with international NGOs on a piecemeal basis, approving each operation or program separately.[36] It has exacerbated its difficulties by defaulting on repayments to the World Bank in early 1998, using the circular argument that if the bank supports the SPDC, then the SPDC will repay old loans; this is contrary to bank policy. The SPDC altered its stand in the fall of 1998. Political stasis thus affects economic progress.

The *tatmadaw* leaders, now held together because they need each other to survive and to retain the perquisites of their commanding position, have shown signs of potential fissures—essentially between the line command and the military intelligence community. The formation of a sixteen-man "political committee" in September 1998 is significant because it is chaired by Khin Nyunt of military intelligence and is composed of many of his associates.[37] It may signal the formation of a government-related political party, a possible link to the USDA, or even a first sign of challenge to Maung Aye and the regional line commanders, who increased their role in the leadership in the November 1997 transformation from the SLORC to the SPDC. But Maung Aye is chairman of an industrial committee that gives him a major voice in economic policy. Because of traditional concepts of personalized power, factionalism and entourage formation have been characteristic of Burmese politics, and the military is not immune. The possibility of overt tension is ever present. A retired senior military officer remarked, "Than Shwe is riding a bullock cart with a pair of bulls [Khin Nyunt and Maung Aye]."[38] But Than Shwe is reported (summer 2000) as being ill and wanting to retire.

The additional glue that holds the military together is the oversight, fragile though it may now be, of Ne Win.[39] At age eighty-nine in 2000, he may soon go to his karmic reward. This may induce more overt splits and jockeying for position that could even lead one military group to seek alliances and compromises with the opposition (Ne Win is said to have a special antipathy to Aung San Suu Kyi and even to her father, to whom he was subordinate) and/or with some of the more powerful minorities. At worst, factionalism could dissolve into civil war, although this seems less probable at this stage. At best, it could offer hope for the easing of regime rigidity. Latent political and social unrest will continue to fester, restrained beneath an exterior made placid only through implicit force. As a senior former military officer said, "The government will not collapse as long as it holds the bayonet." [40] There is also the fear among the military leaders that if they divide, the consequences could be dire for all of them; and this certainly is one important pressure for unity, although personal ambition or other factors may intercede.

A regime misstep, even one produced by a low-level bureaucrat, or blunder or skyrocketing urban inflation of essential foodstuffs, such as rice and cooking oil, could engender riots reminiscent of 1988.[41] Continued deterioration of the economy might prompt the search for scapegoats, both spontaneous and officially induced; the Chinese community is the most obvious target because of its increasing presence and affluence. The precedent occurred in 1967. The potential for chaos is there, but rather than averting chaos, the *tatmadaw* could in large part cause it by its own actions.

The government and its leaders may shift (based on tactical or personal considerations—e.g., Than Shwe for Saw Maung),[42] but a regime change would be more basic, involving removal of the military from essential state control, and thus would be far more difficult. Although the immediate prospects are dim and the future in the short term uncertain, unbounded pessimism is not completely warranted. The military will likely continue as the determining power and influence in the society, but it should not be thought of as singular but potentially plural.

There are individuals among the *tatmadaw* who have more expansive visions. Many military officers have now been exposed to the external world and have access to more international information.[43] Moderate elements exist and could play a more significant role. The opposition is not without some power and moral authority. Aung San Suu Kyi is a very strong person with charismatic appeal, not only to foreigners. Should anything untoward happen to her, it could easily spark an antimilitary revolution, for whoever might be responsible, the military knows it would be blamed. A coup of dissatisfied younger officers who believe that the reputation of the military is being sullied by corruption or political power might occur, or the refusal of troops to fire on rioting civilians (as has happened in a number of countries) could also prompt political transition.[44] The cries for change seem widespread. However, should the NLD be propelled to a position of power, it also would not be immune to the factionalism so prevalent elsewhere. As the military is held together to retain power, so the opposition is united to achieve it.

About one percent of the population of Myanmar/Burma has emigrated (in addition to the refugees along the periphery in Bangladesh and Thailand—some 110,000–120,000—and unskilled labor—about 700,000 before the economic crisis in Thailand), and it is a highly educated group, many of whom would return under more favorable conditions. They may be a force for the future, even under a liberalized, military-dominated government, and not only should the NLD come to power. They are inclined toward the opposition but might be induced to contribute to a regime bent on reform and liberalization—one that had pluralistic centers of power. This was true in Cambodia. It may be idealistic to talk now about democracy in terms that would allow international comparisons, but pluralism would be feasible as an intermediate stage on this road.

First Steps

The growing sense of frustration among the diverse members of the donor community has been reflected in bilateral conversations between some of them and in more structured, although informal, general meetings. As noted above, the first of these occurred in October 1998 in Chiltson Park, England, and ended with a prematurely leaked statement to the press that prompted a negative response from the SPDC. A second meeting took place in Seoul in March 2000, hosted by the Korean Ministry of Foreign Affairs and Trade and sponsored by the United Nations. Its purpose was not to develop a blueprint for action but to air views. No specific changes to any policies of any potential donor or observer seemed to occur.

The dilemmas of foreign policy toward Myanmar are both internal and international. Human rights and humanitarian interests are domestic to that country and of worldwide interest. Security related to regional rivalries is of importance, as are relations with China and Japan, each of which may have different interests in furthering its good relations with the administration in power. International narcotics distribution is also a worldwide U.S. priority.

It is evident that international credibility can suffer from inconsistent policies (however much they may reflect American interests).[45] The United States can continue to occupy the moral high ground on Myanmar—in contrast to its policy in China—because it has only marginal interests in Myanmar. However, this highly moral position is seriously compromised because it is clearly inconsistent not only worldwide, but also in Asia itself (e.g., China, Vietnam, Indonesia, etc.). It is true that the United States wants to see narcotics trafficking eliminated, and it would be seriously concerned should regional rivalries among China, India, and Thailand center on Myanmar, on Chinese access to the Andaman Sea, or on Chinese economic hegemony. Yet the influence that it can exert on these three countries is limited because among the issues with which it is concerned in the region, Myanmar is not of first priority. Yet it could be drawn into confrontations over Myanmar because it has a defense treaty with Thailand, although admittedly this would be a remote possibility.

The U.S. position is rigid and unlikely to move any group forward. It has, in effect, said to the SPDC to honor the results of the May 1990 elections before it will talk about eliminating sanctions, approving multilateral economic assistance, or the like. This is not the basis for negotiation—rather, it is an obvious formula for stalemate. As in a number of other countries, the United States also has personalized foreign policy by relying on a single individual and by assuming that there is a mutuality of both tactics and goals. U.S. and NLD long-term interests may be compatible, but their shorter-term objectives may be somewhat different, although neither may be inappropriate for its proponent. It also should be noted that the United States is plural. The State Department watered down a congressional motion for sanctions (from retroactive investments to future ones), and there may be differences within the State Department on Burma policy rather than consensus. As always, any major change in policy would require congressional as well as administration concurrence.

Even if one assumes that the above scenario related to the passing of Ne Win to his karmic reward is erroneous—and there are those in Rangoon who so say—then what are the next steps? Stasis is evident, with the military attempting to marginalize the NLD or split it from Aung San Suu Kyi or expel her from the country, and she determined to garner foreign support to hold on to her tenuous position. We admire her pluck and determination, and her stated objectives are certainly compatible with U.S. conceptions of good governance, however problematic they might be should she and the NLD come to power. It is far easier to formulate theoretical policies while in opposition than it is to execute them while in office. Is it U.S. policy, as in Iraq, to foster revolution to overthrow the regime? Is the United States prepared to see blood in the streets if there should be a popular revolt? And would it intervene? These are highly unlikely. The NLD has publicly eschewed violence (to advocate it would make it illegal). We might remember Hungary in 1957—far closer to U.S. national interests—when the United States did not intervene. The U.S. military would likely be strongly opposed to an intervention that could put the United States in an ambiguous, perhaps confrontational, position with China.

By insisting on "democracy" and essentially defining it simplistically in terms of free elections, the United States may be creating problems for itself in terms of the credibility of the results when such elections take place. Although the campaigning for the 1990 election was circumscribed, the balloting seems to have been free and fair. Whether there is a sufficient heritage or experience of relative freedom in Burma/Myanmar to make it meaningful among a significant percentage of the population is the subject of intense debate among academicians who study the country. This is not to espouse what have euphemistically been called "Asian values," which often are a justification for political repression and have been so used by the military. Rather, there are other aspects of democratic governance (concepts of power and authority, for example) that are critical. In addition, the concept of gradual change in regime ideology through liberalization seems not to have been an alternative carefully considered. This means discussing how civil society might be built, how pluralism could be expanded, and how political rights could gradually be restored. It is a frustrating approach, however, because it is incremental and lacks the clear and distinct decisiveness of the strategy that the absolutism of demanding democracy provides and that Americans seem to prefer, but it is likely to be far more effective than the absolutist one now in operation.[46] As is often remarked, democracy is process, not product.

The United States has backed itself into a corner from which escape is difficult. The U.S. position will not change without change inside Myanmar, and yet to pursue the Japanese option, which is to seek solace in transparently superficial accommodations, does not get to the heart of the matter. As in many negotiations, the United States is often accused of "moving the goal posts," making more demands over time as earlier ones are met.[47] And there is currently a rule of thumb that the less national interest the United States has in a country, the more human rights loom large in policy.[48]

If the goal is to motivate the military to move from the center of political power, a study of how this has occurred in other states might be useful. What legitimate opportunities for the military exist in any society, assuming that the national goal of unity is met? Access to some levels of power through control of some economic assets and through the representative political processes seem to have been important in some countries, such as Thailand. These have provided avenues of mobility for the military leadership, both on active duty and in retirement. Should there be change, how will retribution for previous military excesses be treated? The NLD has said there will be no retribution, but the people may disagree, and there could be pressures for some sort of international tribunal. The problem of Chile's Pinochet may not have gone unnoticed by the military.

This bleak situation is a cause for pessimism, but it need not be a prescription for inaction. The United States, through quiet, high-level private discussions in some third country, should begin to offer positive inducements to the military. These might be staged sequential or parallel benchmarks, after the completion of each of which a new action would be initiated; if no action took place, a reversion to a more rigorous policy would follow. This might be called a "road map," but in fact that would be a misnomer because normally a road map leads to a destination, and here we are predicating actions that, while important, move a process toward unknown but one hopes more liberal ends. It is, as Graham Greene once wrote about Africa, a "journey without maps."

Common Goals?

To negotiate requires commonalities. Are there any? Are those concerned, as the Chinese and Koreans say, in the same bed but with different dreams? With the NLD, the United States has the same dream, but perhaps we are in different beds. The goals may be shared, but the process to reach such goals, although ideally dovetailed, may not succeed. The United States has shared goals, and perhaps processes, with the Japanese, but the conditions for implementing actions and the pace of change might be quite different. The Japanese are prepared to move with (from this viewpoint) too great alacrity toward accommodation. With the SPDC, on the surface we start from different premises and, if analysis is accurate, work toward different ends. It may be possible to explain to the SPDC that it could accomplish some (if not all) of its most important goals (such as a regime of national solidarity, sovereignty, security, and development) through a different path that would benefit the people, consolidate the state, protect the integrity of the armed forces, and reduce foreign opprobrium. Compromise could result in the achievement of some (but not all) U.S. goals. And some of the goals of the opposition could also be furthered. The importance of maintaining the dignity and prestige of all parties to negotiations cannot be underestimated. Face must be saved, but face is as much a Western as an Eastern requirement in this instance.

About five years ago, this author suggested a compromise to some of the SLORC authorities that he felt might move the process forward. Under that proposed scenario, the SLORC would have called into session the National Assembly voted into office in the May 1990 elections just before its term was to expire, although that term was never made clear. Under a previous agreement, the Assembly would have voted to allow the military to govern (with civil liberties to be promulgated and political organizing to take place) for a specified period of time, perhaps to write a new constitution, after which there would be a new election. The precedent for this would have been the military Caretaker Government (1958–60), which was constitutionally voted into power by Nu's civilian government and which has been regarded by both military and foreign observers as quite successful. This would have been a "Burmese" solution on Burmese precedent. Under this suggestion, the 1990 elections would have been titularly honored, the military assuaged, and political stasis avoided and perhaps foreign aid and economic development furthered, governance liberalized, and the opposition allowed to organize for a new election. This idea was ignored. Could it be resuscitated?

In any plan, it is important to remember the lessons from foreign assistance in the 1970s and 1980s. During that period, economic aid flowed too easily; as a result, the BSPP regarded assistance as its due, and the modest reforms that were allowed were slow to be approved and haphazardly implemented, while fundamental reforms were ignored. Assistance of any sort, including humanitarian activities, should have carefully constructed and defined benchmarks of mutual action, the violation of which would prompt cessation of programs. Open-ended assistance, if experience has meaning, will not produce the expected results.

If a commonality of goals may be difficult to achieve, there may be commonalities of limited agendas. For example, stripped of propaganda, it may be that the SPDC is really interested in reducing or eliminating the drug trade, as the drop in opium production has indicated. (It is not interested, however, in eliminating the money laundering from past activities of such dealers as Khun Sa and their investments in business and industry, although this is a U.S. concern.) As noted, there seems to be no direct evidence that the SPDC or central state entities (as opposed to local military commanders or civilian officials) directly benefit from the trade, although some argue there is circumstantial evidence to this effect because of the continuing ability of the government to buy foreign arms without clear sources of foreign exchange. Are there limited common interests in working on programs in this field? What about humanitarian assistance or endemic disease controls? Controlling environmental degradation? Is there mutual interest in alleviating poverty and/or assisting the peripheral peoples to improve their condition and thus control centrifugal tendencies? There are a variety of issues that might contribute to some of the ends of a number of the participants in any future dialogue. Only dialogue will tell, but such dialogue seems lacking.

Perhaps, as the military is wont to say, confidence-building measures might be induced between the SPDC and the NLD. These might start with simple, rather obvious actions: the NLD might accept the three principles of the military (national unity, sovereignty, etc.), since in the abstract it would mean that the military is not the sole proprietor of these goals, which, aside from their advocacy by the military, are likely to be widely accepted. In turn, the SPDC would lift some repressive measures, such as the vitriolic press comments on the NLD and Aung San Suu Kyi and limitations on assembly by more than five people without government approval. A series of small movements might lead to sequenced easing of the confrontations now in effect.[49]

Specific Actions

Complaining about stasis and stalemate accomplishes little except to increase general frustration. Some positive tentative steps might include the following:

Because of the potential influence of both Japan and the United States on Burmese development, setting up a Track II dialogue between Japan and the United States would provide for a sustained discussion of both policies and facts as they exist in Myanmar. As agreement or confluence of views is articulated, subsequent meetings with appropriate Burmese in a quiet and apolitical atmosphere would be arranged. There are no unofficial channels in Myanmar except the opposition, but since an even-handed approach of working with the regime and the opposition (and minority groups as appropriate) is required for credibility of intentions and efficacy of results, foreign parties might first reach consensus on approaches. Japan and the United States should reach unofficial agreement on some plan or benchmark, and then bring it to the attention of the official communities, after which informal discussions might take place with various groups, government and opposition, in Myanmar. Coordinated but unofficial relationships at the beginning might be more fruitful. Any U.S. administration would have to carry out quiet discussions on these issues with congressional leaders.

Another approach has already been attempted with external actors. As noted, the informal and quiet meeting of potential donors and others in August 1998 at Chilston Park in the United Kingdom assessed current conditions in Myanmar. Although the discussions were private, an offhand estimate of $1 billion was suggested as the amount that might be needed to move the Burmese economy forward. This figure was based on the Vietnam experience in reform, which was $2 billion (with a population approximately double that of Myanmar). This figure was leaked to the press, and the Burmese responded angrily that they could not be bought. The initiative seemed to end, but a smaller meeting was held in Seoul to air problems, although it seemed to produce no new concensus to ameliorate a deplorable situation.

If informal and unpublicized discussions were to be held with the SPDC, then other actions might be considered such as the following (not listed in sequence):

1. Guarantees by the ARF (including the United States, along with China and India) of the territorial integrity of Burma/Myanmar to assuage fears of national dismemberment. This simply reaffirms the status quo.
2. Agreement to withhold UN voting on human rights issues in Myanmar for a specified time (one or two years) in return for easing political repression.
3. Encouragement of international NGOs to expand humanitarian activities inside Burma.
4. Agreement, subject to multilateral donor economic criteria, to restart foreign assistance from the World Bank and the ADB for poverty alleviation activities.

5.   Appointment of a U.S. ambassador in Rangoon.
6.   Gradual lifting of sanctions.
7.   U.S. support for environmental projects in cooperation with ASEAN.
8.   A study/action plan for addressing some systemic issues related to poverty and humanitarian assistance (including HIV/AIDS) with foreign partici-pation building on the 1999 World Bank report.

These would be contingent on the SPDC taking the following actions (not in sequential order or priority listing and staged in relation to the inducements noted above):

1.   Ceasing harassment of the opposition, including (but not limited to) Aung San Suu Kyi, and release of political prisoners.
2.   Presenting a timetable for completion of a constitution that would ensure political and civil pluralism, perhaps staged over some discrete period. Agreement would have to be reached on articles that were deemed accept-able to all parties. (It is unlikely that the SPDC would agree to scrap the effort to date, for that would be humiliating.)
3.   Presenting a timetable for more freedom of information through the de-velopment of a private press, as existed before 1962.
4.   Making macroeconomic reforms (exchange rate, money supply, central banking autonomy, etc.), as suggested by the World Bank and the IMF.
5.   Establishing reasonable and standardized guidelines for the operation of foreign NGOs in Burma (e.g., on registration, visas, residence permits, import of supplies and relief or educational materials, customs clearances, and reporting mechanisms).
6.   Setting a date for a new election that would be free.
7.   Negotiating with the minorities on some form of power sharing but with stipulations of national unity.[50]
8.   Determining a system to protect the integrity and legitimate interests of the *tatmadaw,* and defining what those interests are.

In effect, the United States would be tacitly admitting that the military will continue to play an important role in Burmese society, retaining an ultimate veto over actions potentially leading to the breakup of the state. This admit-tedly will be unacceptable to many in the United States and to many Burmese expatriates. It may be unacceptable to the Burmese military as well. Yet without specific suggestions for moving the process forward, it is the Burmese people who will continue to suffer.

Conclusion

Although there are a number of possible approaches to Burmese issues, there are no answers that will satisfy all parties, primarily internal and secondarily external. While any progress toward resolving internal problems must come from the Burmese, the role of foreign negotiators may be to suggest avenues of discussion while carefully avoiding identification with specific internal political entities and upholding political ideals and goals.[51] It is, after all, the betterment of the futures of the peoples as a whole that is our concern. What is listed above is one of a multitude of potential paths toward progress.

To follow any such path would in effect recognize that the immediate (not longer-term) objectives of Aung San Suu Kyi and the United States regrettably are not identical. This would be interpreted in some circles as an abandonment of her and U.S. democracy objectives. This is only partly correct. U.S. democratic strategic objectives remain intact, but tactics shift to gradual liberalization, which has more chance of success. It would not be abandonment of the NLD but a type of separation, for Aung San Suu Kyi would be free to pursue her political objectives inside the country (but without having articulated U.S. support) and perhaps assume political leadership at a later date. Would this be an unpleasant shift from idealism to pragmatism? Yes. Is it a possible scenario—yes, although unlikely. Are there alternative avenues that might in the longer term move Myanmar toward pluralism? Perhaps, but if so, they have not been articulated or essayed. These suggestions are simply an attempt to move the process forward, and if it encourages others to consider other, perhaps more realistic, alternatives, it will have been successful.

It is not appropriate simply to wait (as if for Godot) for change that seems unlikely to come without effort or to call for bloodshed in the streets of Rangoon and Mandalay. We are seeing a concerted plan to marginalize the opposition in Myanmar, and it is likely to succeed over time through intimidation and sheer attrition. It is true that latent fissures in the *tatmadaw* might become active and evident, and the results might change predictions. But over the next few years time is in favor of the military, even if over a decade or two it will likely be on the side of liberalization. If this is true, then the present stasis is destructive of the liberal goals for which observers would hope, and it should be ended if possible. If our purpose is to concentrate on the well-being of the Burmese people as a whole, to assist them out of the poverty so evident in the urban slums and in much of the rural sector, and to avoid bloodshed and begin the process of liberalization, then a compromise that honors the core interests of all parties should be proposed. This may not be our Panglossian best of all possible worlds, nor even what we might like, but it may be enough to move the people forward, and that would be a major improvement. It is difficult to write prescriptions that one knows will satisfy no one. Yet if compromises are not proposed—compromises that necessarily do not fulfill one's aspirations simply because they are compromises—then the ensuing stasis is worse. Not proposing avenues of compromise is tantamount to making decisions that are likely to result in even more onerous situations.

The possibility for cooperation between the military and the opposition is there, but the probability is more remote. One Burmese observer speculated that the military would have been willing to share power with a coalition of opposition parties had the May 1990 election results been more ambiguous (perhaps because it could control power), but it was shocked when the NLD swept the election. According to this observer, the military is adamantly opposed to Aung San Suu Kyi and is unwilling to see her assume the reins of government. The release of political prisoners and security issues can be compromised, he continued, but the NLD wants the National Convention to be rescinded, an issue on which the military will not compromise.[52] A falling out among some military might prompt at least partial collaboration with the NLD. There is another, remote possibility: Perhaps there is an influential person outside the two opposing camps who could bring the sides together for modest cooperation in spite of the mistrust. For example, the HIV/AIDS epidemic that is sweeping Myanmar, with estimates of the infected population at least 2 percent, is a national emergency. It affects all groups, including the minorities and the military, and is of such a scale that the country under any circumstances will long suffer from it. This is a disaster that the regime has yet to recognize, but it has insufficient funds or trained personnel to begin to deal with the issue should it do so. Foreign donors could provide the hundreds of millions of dollars required to stem this tide, but they are reluctant to engage the country because of internal problems. If some appropriate person were to suggest to the military and NLD that collaboration was required in an educational campaign, would they agree? Each would say that such a campaign would strengthen the other, and this would be true to a degree. But the good will generated might offset the value added to either group. Rather than start with the fundamental issues of governance, would this small but critical step be possible?

There seems to be no one in Myanmar who stands above the political fray, such as the king in Thailand. In the past there have been venerable Buddhist *sayadaws* (abbots) who have led the public. Perhaps in some monastery there is one who, through his own religious stature and recognized benevolence and with a sense of social courage, can impress upon both the public and contending parties that some form of reconciliation is necessary for the good of the people. Burma/Myanmar celebrates Martyr's Day, the anniversary of the assassination of Aung San and his colleagues in 1947; Aung San Suu Kyi has been portrayed as a martyr to the cause of democracy, and indeed she has egregiously suffered. Yet it is the people who are the real martyrs, who have no say in their future, and whose economic, social, educational, and health standards have deteriorated.

These factors prompt this observer to be pessimistic about the near future of Myanmar in spite of the obvious wealth and potential of its people and land. It is a society so torn that the healing process will have to be long and will likely be tortuous. The present political impasse is unlikely to be resolved to the reasonable satisfaction of any of the contending groups.

The evolution of political attitudes, including those deeply rooted, is both inevitable and perhaps may come more quickly than many suppose. Democracy, however defined, is not denied societies simply because of traditional views—the "Asian values" argument is a self-serving rationale for authoritarian regimes. Political cultures differ in important aspects, as we have attempted to show, but they also evolve. "Social capital" can be accumulated and social norms change, in some societies faster than one might imagine. There is no reason why pluralism and democratic governance may not emerge over time in Burmese society. The issue for the Burmese is over what period, and for the foreigners it is what role they might play to assist the process.

If diplomats usually characterize their attitudes toward crises as "cautiously optimistic," in the Myanmar case it would be more accurate to portray our views as "pessimistic." Perhaps some new initiatives might move the categorization to "cautiously pessimistic." That, in any case, might be called progress. "The essential issue is not how foreigners, however well-wishing, may regard Burma, nor how theoretically sound their analyses. Rather, it is how well these foreign perspectives conform to Burmese conceptions of their own society. Whatever road Burma/Myanmar chooses, and whatever the results, action will be taken *bama-lo,* in the Burmese manner." [53]

Notes

1. A Burmese intellectual on the prospects for the future.

2. U Kyaw Tint Swe (Director General, International Organizations and Economics Department, Ministry of Foreign Affairs) and U Aung Htoo, "Myanmar in ASEAN: Cooperation for Development," Proceeding of the Symposium on "Interaction for Progress: Myanmar in ASEAN (Yangon: Office of Strategic Studies, Ministry of Defense, October 23–24, 1998), p. 232.

3. Aung San, "Blueprint for Burma," in *The Political Heritage of Aung San,* ed. Josef Silverstein (Ithaca: Cornell University, Southeast Asia Program Series 11, 1993), p. 61.

4. Mary P. Callahan, "Democracy in Burma: The Lessons of History," *Analysis* (National Bureau of Asian Research) 9, 3 (1998).

5. Khin Nyunt, Opening Address, Proceeding of the Symposium on "Interaction for Progress: Myanmar in ASEAN (Yangon: Office of Strategic Studies, Ministry of Defense, October 23–24, 1998), p. 10.

6. For a discussion of the role of foreign observers in Burma/Myanmar, see the introduction to this volume and David I. Steinberg, "The Road to Political Recovery: The Salience of Politics in Economics," in *Burma: Prospects for a Democratic Future,* ed. Robert Rotberg (Washington, D.C.: Brookings Institution, 1998).

7. On ASEAN membership, see chapter 8 and David I. Steinberg, "Myanmar: Regional Relationships and Internal Concerns," in *Southeast Asian Affairs 1998* (Singapore: Institute of Southeast Asian Studies, 1998).

8. In May 1999 the United States extended the sanctions for another year.

9. The SPDC has used the 1961 Habitual Criminal Offenders Act against NLD members; it places repeat offenders under permanent bail. AsiaWatch, "Burma," *World Report 1999,* pp. 165–70.

10. As reported by Reuters on Internet (Burmanet), December 3, 1999.

11. Aung San Suu Kyi has specifically denied that the NLD has fomented confrontations with the government and has claimed that it is simply pursuing its legal political activities.

12. Aung San Suu Kyi agreed to accept lower-level dialogue between the SPDC and the NLD, but one of the conditions of the SPDC for dialogue is the elimination of

the CRPP, which the military clearly deems to be an affront to its leadership and illegal under its laws. The NLD has refused. AsiaWatch, "Burma," *World Report 2000,* pp. 169–73.

13. The government claimed it denied the visa because it would place an undue burden on its limited health facilities, but this attempt to garner humanitarian sympathy was patently absurd. Foreign observers, including the Japanese, it is reported, requested the authorities to grant Aris a visa.

14. Ironically, nine is said to be Ne Win's lucky number, but the juxtaposition of dates offered an opportunity for action.

15. It has since amended this position, stating that if the NGOs or humanitarian assistance benefits the people and not the government, it would not disapprove. It wants to vet all such assistance. Maintaining a strict dichotomy that would exclude the vast state-sponsored network of organizations and individuals would be exceedingly difficult.

16. As noted, although military intelligence may be more extensive and surveillance more strict, the proliferation of new technologies and their increased availability in Myanmar (from simple copying machines to short wave radios, videos, television, and the Internet) has meant that there is less control over the internal leakage of foreign news and opinions. The encouragement of tourism and business also furthers this leakage.

17. Universities have only been open about thirty months since the coup of 1988. On January 5, 1999, the state announced the reopening of four medical schools in May of that year. In June 2000 all universities reopened.

18. The government claims that as of April 1999 six of the fifteen chapters of the new constitution had been written, but it is seeking "consensus" (among what it claims as 135 ethnic groups) on the sharing of power, and this is the most difficult of issues. This is the cardinal point and the excuse for delays, but the military obviously wants to ensure that the document is approved, and thus it will not be subject to any form of referendum or public discussion until it has its mass mobilization organizations in place and supportive of its aims.

19. The lesson from the Suharto resignation may not be what outsiders expect. The Burmese regime may believe that Suharto fell because he did not crack down on the students early and hard enough. At the exact moment of Suharto's resignation, military intelligence figures, who had telephoned the author, were watching the events on CNN. See David I. Steinberg, "A Whimper in Rangoon," *Bangkok Post,* June 6, 1998.

20. For a discussion of the USDA, see chapter 4 and David I. Steinberg, "Myanmar and the Requirements of Mobilization and Orthodoxy: The Union Solidarity and Development Association," *Burma Debate,* February 1997. Minoru Kiyru, in his "The Political Structure of Myanmar" (Research Institute for Peace and Security), advocates the USDA becoming a political party challenging the NLD. If so, this would represent the interests of the military in mufti. There are rumors that this is a likely possibility and could mirror the Indonesian change of GOLKAR into a political party.

21. Andrew Selth, "The Burmese Armed Forces Next Century: Continuity or Change?" (Canberra: Australia National University, Strategic and Defence Studies Centre, September 1999), p. 11; Working Paper No. 338.

22. Ibid, pp. 2–3.

23. See Appendix I.

24. Personal communication, 1997.

25. Human Rights Watch/Asia has called for a reassessment of policy; the Center for Strategic and International Studies (CSIS, Washington, D.C.) and the Cato Institute, among other groups, have written against the sanctions policy on both ideological and business grounds.

26. Personal communication, U.S. Embassy, Rangoon, 1999.

27. Personal interview, Rangoon, April 1999. Section 1106 of the November 1998 legislation states that all UNDP programs are to be certified by the president to be "focused on elimination of human suffering and addressing the needs of the poor . . . are undertaken only through international or private voluntary organizations that have been deemed independent of the SLORC [*sic*], after consultations with the leadership of the National League for Democracy and the leadership of the National Coalition Government of the Union of Burma."

28. The author here subordinates his hopes to his perception of the realities.

29. The differences are apparent in the rapid shifts in policy related to external relations—e.g., inviting in the press and then excluding it, etc.

30. John B. Haseman, "The Burmese Army's Role in Ethnic Burma: Obstacles and Opportunities for Advancing National Unity and Drug Control," conference, "Towards a Twenty-First Century Burma," Department of State, Intelligence and Research Bureau, May 28, 1998.

31. It is significant that Aung San Suu Kyi was charged with trying to split the military, a heinous crime and one to which the military seems particularly sensitive, perhaps because it recognizes the potential for this to occur.

32. Tin Maung Maung Than, "Myanmar: Preoccupation with Regime Survival, National Unity, and Stability," in *Asian Security Practices: Material and Ideational Influences,* ed. Muthiah Alagappa (Stanford: Stanford University Press, 1998), p. 415.

33. Yet in 1990, the military entered monasteries and pagodas in Mandalay and suppressed dissident Buddhist monks. In part, the *tatmadaw* may be attempting to assuage the anger generated by this poor and politically disastrous image.

34. However farfetched this may sound to Americans, it was viewed as a real possibility in 1988, when a U.S. aircraft carrier was reported to have been stationed off the coast of Burma to enable the evacuation of U.S. personnel. Later, the SLORC conducted an informal survey among key individuals to ascertain their reaction if the United States were to intervene. (This was after the U.S. invasion in Haiti.) A senior military official said that the government had no faith in official statistics on U.S. congressional aid levels related to Burmese refugees: "They say it is five million [dollars] but it could be fifty." Personal interview.

35. The evidence for this in Asia alone over any reasonable time is highly suspect—e.g., Korea (1961–87), Taiwan (1949–92), China, Vietnam, Singapore, Malaysia.

36. In 1994, the author tried to persuade the SLORC that transparent and consistent rules of international NGO operation in Myanmar should be formulated in consultation with the NGOs; although there was some interest, the SLORC made a decision to deal with each NGO separately. In June 2000, a number of international NGOs in Myanmar formulated a code of conduct to ensure transparency of operations and to reassure the military of their apolitical programs.

37. SPDC decree #25/98 of September 18, 1998.

38. Personal communication.

39. As noted in chapter 2, whether Ne Win still maintains influence is heatedly debated. As long as he retains his intellectual faculties, he probably influences major decisions, and his mere presence may be a source of both fear and respect. He is said to be briefed on current events, and he seems to remain in reasonable health for his age. How his departure will affect the active military closely associated with him (e.g., Khin Nyunt) is an important but now unanswerable question.

40. Personal communication.

41. Senior officials indicated that one of the mistakes that led to Suharto's downfall in Indonesia was not having sufficient stores of rice in hand (although distribution of rice may have been the problem). The SPDC is intent on not letting this happen in Myanmar.

42. Than Shwe (born 1933) is beyond retirement age, as is Tin Oo (Secretary-2).

43. One of the policy disputes that is evident in Myanmar, although it has been common in a number of countries, such as Indonesia, is whether all training and exchange with the military should cease or whether it is better to try to influence military leaders by exposure to external ideas through travel and training in democratic countries. Constant military training in and travel to China could negatively (from a liberalization perspective) influence future actions. On the other hand, foreign association with a repressive government and assistance that would in some quarters be interpreted as furthering an undemocratic regime would be indefensible.

44. In the May 1990 elections, some districts with large percentages of military voters opted for the opposition candidates.

45. Since the United States is the leader of states opposed to the SLORC/SPDC, the discussion that follows focuses on that country's position. It should not be inferred that all democracies hold to the same position, but the U.S. stance is the most rigid of the developed countries and thus concentration on its policies provides contrast for analysis.

46. For an analysis, see Catherin Dalpino, *Opening Windows: Letting Liberalization Lead* (Washington, D.C.: Brookings Institution, 2000). Dalpino questions the concentration on democracy rather than incremental change through liberalization.

47. So a senior North Korean negotiator told the author some years ago.

48. This was suggested by Marvin Ott of the National Defense University and should be designated as "Ott's Law."

49. The problem is reminiscent of negotiations between South and North Korea. The former believed that small incremental steps should first be taken, and these will lead to better relations and more fundamental agreements; the latter maintained that first the major issues should be resolved, after which the smaller differences could be sorted out. The June 2000 summit meeting by the leaders of both countries did not address this issue.

50. One of the problems with the planned constitution is that on its approval, the minorities with which the military has cease-fires would be expected to surrender their arms. This is likely to be a major issue unless the minorities perceive the sharing of power and authority as just, fair, and certain. It seems unlikely that there will be effective implementation of this provision; if forced, it could result in a recurrence of fighting. The dangers for the future are apparent.

51. One senior Burmese official specifically called for the intervention of foreign negotiators in the stasis between the SPDC and the NLD; it seems likely he expected the latter to change, not the former. Personal communication.

52. Personal communication.

53. David I. Steinberg, *The Future of Burma: Crisis and Choice in Myanmar* (Lanham: University Press of America and The Asia Society, 1990), p. 98; Asia Agenda Report 14. The official denigration of foreigners has continued. *Myanmar Alin* commented, "What are the development and betterment plans for the country and the people that her ["democracy princess"—Aung San Suu Kyi] Oxford brain has worked out? Does she plan to build the country with ideas of those long-nosed great foreign experts?" (November 30, 1999; reported in *Burmanet News,* December 14, 1999).

Economic Reform in Burma: Problems and Priority Needs. 1988

Note: This memorandum, dated November 5, 1988, was written by the author to the World Bank. The continuity of problems illustrates some enduring problems of the Burmese economy.

1. Problems in the Burmese Economy

1.1 Some of the problems facing the Burmese economy are generic to all past governments in Burma, and some a result of the practices of the last twenty-six years. Those that have been endemic in each government include:

- The inseparability of politics and economics, so that political decisions have prevailed over economic rationality. This has been true of each government, but most acute under the past regime. This has affected both urban and rural sectors.

- Attempts at reform have been piecemeal and (as a result) have not worked. Burma's problems have not been able to have been treated as superficial wounds; they have required major surgery.

- A deep-seated (and historically understandable) mistrust of the private sector, including those ethnic minorities active in trade, and indeed the need for and importance of trade itself. There has also been a belated recognition that the private sector is essential both for production and employment. This was recognized in 1955, 1971, and again in 1988. Little practical has been accomplished at any time.

- A relatively weak and politicized bureaucracy that had difficulty in administering a highly centralized, planned economy.
- Unrealistic exchange rates from the 1950s that have made rational operation of the economy in both the public and private sectors virtually impossible at the official rates.
- Heavy expense expenditures (one-third of the budget in the 1960s, admittedly 20–25 percent today, but more likely to be 40 percent) that detracts funds from development.
- Official salary levels that have been impossible since the 1950s, and today are both anachronistic and counter-productive, giving rise to pervasive and, indeed, necessary corruption at all levels.
- An ideological reliance on the public sector to produce the requirements of daily living, a reliance that has been ill-placed.
- In spite of attempted but partial reforms in the 1970s, a continuing, underlying lack of dedication to making the public sector both economic and efficient.

1.2   Among the problems most acute since 1962 have been:
- A brain drain, forcing for political, economic and policy reasons some of the most talented Burmese individuals outside of Burma, to the detriment of economic planning and implementation, teaching and scholarship, and effective administration.
- An increase in smuggling so that the Burmese economy has become dependent on smuggled, foreign goods for daily necessities.
- A tendency to micro-manage the economy in a hierarchical (and military) manner, forcing all decisions to the top, thus eliminating the possibility of flexibility that the state has on occasion indicated that it wanted, but that it cannot attain.
- Reliance on a hierarchical series of retail stores that allow the authorities at various levels to receive tax-free, unrecorded income through resale of those items in short supply in the local bazaars.
- A policy toward the minorities that has forced more military action against them, made more go into revolt, indirectly encouraged the spread of opium production and trade (as well as general smuggling) to finance

some of these rebellions, and denied vast geographic areas to the government that could be used for national economic development.

- The destruction of local autonomy and initiative by too great a reliance on central decision-making.
- A lack of a sense of economic predictability, and thus confidence, in government, and a feeling that economic policy is erratic and whimsically determined.

2. General Principles of Economic Reform in Burma

2.1 The following general principles are important to Burma at this stage in its economic crisis:

- No fragmented reform effort is possible. Reform must be comprehensive, and planned as such from the beginning, even if it is sequentially implemented. The population must understand the nature of the planned reforms and the government will have to regain the confidence of the people.
- There must be early and visible improvements in the economy if public confidence in a new economic system is to take place, and these improvements must affect a broad spectrum of the populace.
- Although any Burmese government may not wish to rely on foreign economic support, it will be required to do so for an interim period. With such support will come advice on policy formulation.
- Since Burma must export to survive economically, and must import much of its intermediate goods and raw materials as well as consumer items (either legally or illegally), Burma must be prepared to open itself to the outside world. This is not simply a matter of new, foreign technology (essential for such industries as petroleum), but more fundamentally increased access to international economic (and other) information, training, and ideas. This may be a painful process, as increased international economic exposure cannot be contained, and will affect other areas as well.
- The public sector has proven to be inefficient, and subject to political whims. It must be thoroughly studied on an individual enterprise level, and rationalized on economic grounds. This may create short-term employment problems.

- An effort should begin immediately to increase short-term but productive urban employment (perhaps through efforts such as food-for-work), until private employment possibilities are sufficient to absorb new entrants into the labor force.
- The private sector must be encouraged, but the economy should not be allowed once again to be dominated by foreigners; it must essentially be Burman controlled, even if there is an enhanced role for minorities.
- The agricultural reform begun on 1 September 1987 should be continued, with freedom to trade internally and externally.
- The political process must be kept at a distance from the economic process, or economics once again will be prey to political subversion. This is another reason for dismantling or reducing the state economic enterprise system.

3. Specific Economic Reform Measures

[Note: The following reforms cannot be undertaken without comprehensive donor support, which in the aggregate would probably require some $500 million per year for several years. The purpose of such support would not only be to help finance development, but to protect the economy from hyperinflation.]

- **Exchange Rate Reform:** A major depreciation of the exchange rate to a point where it becomes economically profitable to export, and where confidence in such a rate becomes established. It should probably be allowed to float within modest limits. This devaluation probably would be in the range of several times the current rate. Although it will increase foreign debt, it could be enhanced by exports.
- **Public Sector Salary Reform:** Raising of public sector salaries to levels that will ensure a living wage at the bottom, and a level so that corruption becomes a crime, not a necessity, at the top.
- **Financial Institution Reform:** Rather than the state's maintaining a monopoly of the banking institutions, there is a need to establish the central bank as autonomous from the executive branch, and there is an urgent need to ensure that an autonomous development bank be established (separate from government) to provide funds for indigenous and foreign–domestic collaborative private investment activities. No such

mechanism now exists to lend legally to the private sector, except to farmers. If such an institution is not established, the private sector will revert to Indian and Chinese control, raising a past political spectre best avoided. The entry of foreign banking should probably proceed slowly.

- **Private Sector Development:** Encouragement of private sector activities in all fields through joint ventures with public and private sectors with guarantees against nationalization for a sufficiently long period to make the investment profitable, and with reasonable regulations for the repatriation of profits and capital.

- **State Economic Enterprises:** Studies of each state economic enterprise to determine the causes of debt and inefficiencies, and the economies of scale and other factors of foreign, related industries, whose goods are currently smuggled into Burma; and the leasing, contracting, or selling of those enterprises that do not meet appropriate guidelines for profitability. Also required would be the restaffing of state enterprise management on conditions of economic rationality and profitability. Where the state perceives a need for critical industries that are in the national security or social interests and thus where profitability is not the primary issue, then the development of some competitive measures and standards by which to judge the efficient operation of such firms.

- **Regional Industrial and Economic Development Diversification:** The formation of plans by which (through tax or other appropriate incentives) economic development activities are encouraged to be regionally located, thus providing employment and economic progress to certain geographic regions of the country.

- **Economic Planning and Technical Institutions:** The setting up of administrative mechanisms to invite back into Burma those who could contribute to the economic development of the nation through the formation of autonomous, quasi-governmental (with separate salary scales) institutions but with intimate ties to the formation of policy or programs for Burmese now abroad to assist in rational economic and technical and professional planning (Korea and Thailand have both used these models).

- **Establishment of an Autonomous Board of Audit:** The formation of some type of independent watchdog group to audit corruption and political misuse of administrative influence or power.

- **Increase in Foreign Exchange Earnings:** The encouragement of tourism and service industries (hotels, etc.) within social and environmental guidelines to bring in immediate foreign exchange. This would require an increase in air traffic, ground transportation, and hotel space, and in liberalizing visa limitations.

- **Agriculture and Rural Development:** Improving security of farmers to their land, and encouragement of the diversification and production of crops for export.

- **Statistical Base:** The development of an autonomous unit not subject to political manipulation or influence to collect statistical information for planning purposes. Such information should be internationally comparative.

- **Foreign Economic Coordination:** Strengthening the unit coordinating foreign assistance, together with assuring that it has the authority and staff to manage increased assistance levels.

- **Urban Employment:** To ensure domestic tranquility and to repair badly neglected infrastructure, the development of short-term urban work programs that would enhance development potential, provide employment for the urban population, and visibly demonstrate to the populace the beginning positive effects of economic reform.

- **Enhanced Revenue Collection:** Rational customs duties imposed on all land borders that would increase revenue and channel imports through legal markets; the development of a new, fair, graduated income tax capturing incomes now presently unreported (such as food and other rations).

Further Reading

There is a wide spectrum of writing on Burmese history that provides the necessary background for discussion of the period since 1988. These writings have not been listed in this bibliography because it would be redundant with other bibliographies, although they have provided the basis for much of this study of Burma/Myanmar. These works may be found as standard references to any study of the country. In addition to the works listed below, there are travel volumes and personal memoirs that add color to the landscape. In addition, there are periodicals and electronic media that carry important information on contemporary issues. Among the publications are *Asian Survey, Pacific Affairs, Contemporary Southeast Asia,* and *Burma Debate* (Washington, D.C.). The annual volume on *Southeast Asian Affairs* (Institute of Southeast Asian Studies, Singapore) often has helpful articles, as does the *Far Eastern Economic Review Yearbook.* That publication and *Asiaweek* also have articles on immediate issues. The *Asian Wall Street Journal* is an important source as well. There is considerable coverage on Burma/Myanmar in the *Bangkok Post, The Nation* (Bangkok), and the *South China Morning Post* (Hong Kong). For a government view, consult the controlled *New Light of Myanmar,* formally called the *Working People's Daily* (Yangon), and the weekly launched in February 2000, the *Myanmar Times and Business Weekly* (Yangon).

Myanmar publications also include annual reports on the social and economic conditions of the country, and some statistical and trade publications appear in English. Assessments of economic conditions can be found in World Bank and ADB publications (and on their web sites).

The Burmese government distributes electronically a newsletter, and further information from a broader perspective may be found on the Burma Fund web site and on that of the Soros Foundation.

There are publications of a wide variety of groups in opposition to the government, such as *Irrawaddy* (Bangkok), and various publications of diverse ethnic groups as well. The Burma Fund and Soros web sites provide additional information.

The Burma Studies Center of Northern Illinois University (DeKalb) publishes a journal on the full range of Burmese topics, and the Burma Studies Group of the Association for Asian Studies (Ann Arbor, Michigan) is an organization of scholars on Burma worldwide.

Although the current problems of Myanmar have attracted wide journalistic and popular and partisan interest, there are relatively few volumes that deal specifically with the contemporary period there. Some are conference volumes in which chapters vary by subject and quality. Important articles are often found in journals and volumes that cover the region and not only Burma/Myanmar. Some are cited in the volume. Below are listed some of the more important works devoted to this country that deal with the period since 1988.

Aung San Suu Kyi. *Freedom from Fear and Other Writings.* London: Penguin, 1991.

Ball, Desmond. *Burma's Military Secrets: Signals Intelligence (SIGINT) from 1941 to Cyber Warfare.* Bangkok: White Lotus, 1998.

Brandon, John, ed. *Burma: Myanmar in the Twenty-First Century: Dynamics of Continuity and Change.* New York: Open Society Institute, 1997.

Carey, Peter, ed. *Burma: The Challenge of Change in a Divided Society.* London: Macmillan, 1997.

Houtman, Gustaaf. *Mental Culture in Burmese Crisis Politics: Aung San Suu Kyi and the National League for Democracy.* Tokyo: Tokyo University of Foreign Studies, Institute for the Study of Languages and Cultures of Asia and Africa, 1999. Monograph No. 33.

Khin Maung Kyi, Ronald Findlay, R.M. Sundrum, Mya Maung, Myo Nyunt, Zaw Oo, et. al. *Economic Development of Burma: A Vision and a Strategy.* Singapore: Singapore University Press and Olof Palme International Center, Stockholm, 2000.

Lintner, Bertil. *Burma in Revolt: Opium and Insurgency since 1948.* Boulder: Westview Press, 1994.

———. *Outrage: Burma's Struggle for Democracy.* Hong Kong: Review Publishing, 1989.

Maung Maung. *The 1988 Uprising in Burma.* New Haven: Yale Southeast Asia Studies, 1999. Monograph 49.

Mya Maung. *The Burma Road to Poverty.* (Westport: Praeger, 1991).

Mya Maung. *The Burma Road to Capitalism: Economic Growth versus Democracy.* Westport: Praeger, 1998.

Mya Than and Joseph L.H. Tan. *Myanmar Dilemmas and Options.* Singapore: Institute of Southeast Asian Studies, 1990.

Mya Than and Myat Thein, eds. *Financial Resources for Development in Myanmar: Lessons from Asia.* Singapore: Institute for Southeast Asian Studies, 2000.

Pedersen, Morten B., Emily Kudland, and R.J. May, eds. *Burma-Myanmar: Strong Regime, Weak State?* Adelaide: Crawford House, 2000.

Renard, Ronald D., *The Burmese Connection: Illegal Drugs and the Making of the Golden Triangle.* Boulder: Lynne Rienner, 1996.

Rotberg, Robert I., ed. *Burma: Prospects for a Democratic Future.* Washington, D.C.: Brookings Institution, 1998.

Seekins, Donald M. *The Disorder in Order: A Political History of Modern Burma.* Bangkok: White Lotus, 2000.

Selth, Andrew. *Transforming the* Tatmadaw: *The Burmese Armed Forces since 1988.* Canberra: Australia National University, Strategic and Defence Studies Centre, 1996.

Silverstein, Josef. *Burmese Politics: The Dilemma of National Unity.* New Brunswick: Rutgers University Press, 1980.

Smith, Martin. *Burma: Insurgency and the Politics of Ethnicity,* 2d ed. London: Zed Books, 1999.

Steinberg, David I. *The Future of Burma: Crisis and Choice in Myanmar.* Lanham: University Press of America and The Asia Society, 1990.

Taylor, Robert. *The State in Burma.* Honolulu: University of Hawaii Press, 1987.

Taylor, Robert, ed. *Political Economy under Military Rule.* London: Hurst; New York: St. Martin's Press, 2000.

Victor, Barbara. *The Lady: Aung San Suu Kyi, Nobel Laureate and Burma's Prisoner.* Boston: Faber and Faber, 1998.

Postscript

Since this book went to press in December 2000, the political state of Myanmar has remained in a military-woven shroud that, although there is new evidence that it may become partly opened, still obstructs a holistic view of the political economy and society. In the almost fourteen years since the coup of September 1988, political stasis has continued, yet there have been signs that some type of political accommodation is under serious consideration. It may not completely satisfy the aspirations of either the military junta or the opposition, but it could mollify the impasse that has been all too apparent for over a decade.

In January 2001 it was revealed that secret talks had been going on since October 2000 between members of the State Peace and Development Council (SPDC) and Daw Aung San Suu Kyi, Nobel Peace Laureate and effective leader of the opposition National League for Democracy (NLD). There have been five trips to Yangon by the United Nations Secretary General's special envoy, Ambassador Razali Ismail of Malaysia, as recently as September 2000. These trips were supported by the visit in January 2001 of Malaysian Prime Minister Mahathir, who is said to have encouraged the military to compromise with the opposition in some manner.

As of this writing, almost 200 political prisoners have been released in small batches, and some NLD local offices been allowed to reopen, giving credence to the view that this confidence-building measure, without which Daw Suu Kyi would lose credibility among her own supporters, is a prelude to more accommodations from both sides. Vitriolic attacks against the opposition and its leaders in the controlled press have been reduced.

The specific details of the talks have, however, been closely held by both sides, which has caused concern among many Burmese and other observers—and this concern has increased as the talks appear to continue without any pub-

lic resolution. Foreign observers, however, have indicated a modest amelioration in the dire pessimism that seems to pervade thinking about the political
future of the country. The usual "cautious optimism" statement that often ac-
companies diplomatic parlays would be too strong a term for the present mood,
but some modest modification of the utter despair that has characterized so
much of the past seems evident. Yet, "nice and tidy" endings, as Berthold
Brecht once wrote in the *Threepenny Opera*, are unlikely.

The welcome dialogue has not included the third critical component of any
real solution of the ills of the state: The minorities have been excluded, and the
NLD remains a Burman party, although Ambassador Razali has talked with
minority representatives. Minority issues, the sharing of power to some degree
acceptable to the multiple ethnic entities, remains the most intractable issue
facing the state. The military is also unlikely to give up essential control over
its future autonomy and what it regards as the protection of the unity of the
state, which it feels uniquely qualified to maintain. The military believes it is
the only institution that is capable of holding together the disparate elements
of the complex set of societies known as Myanmar/Burma. The *tatmadaw* is
also likely to protect its extensive economic assets and social position. The
talks have been held under the auspices of General Khin Nyunt, Secretary-1,
but his authority, though highly significant, is not completely pervasive; he
must deal with others on the SPDC. Should the talks linger beyond early 2002
without resolution, pessimism is likely to return.

The reaction of foreign states to Myanmar's situation continues to be
mixed. Although the United States has remained adamant that democracy (i.e.,
the NLD sweep of the May 1990 election) must be honored, the Japanese,
based on the dialogue already underway, have provided significant new assistance to the current regime, including renovation of a major hydroelectric project, under the guise of an expanded definition of humanitarian aid. Sanctions
on new investment by the United States continue, and there have been congressional efforts to limit or eliminate the growing textile and garment imports
from Myanmar to the U.S. Yet, such factories employ some 100,000–200,000
workers who would otherwise be destitute.

In the summer of 2001, the United Nations agencies operating in Myanmar
petitioned to eliminate sanctions and requested increases in foreign aid on humanitarian grounds for the unadmitted but widespread prevalence of HIV/
AIDS, for malnutrition, and for poverty. The government has rejected this

characterization of internal conditions. Relations with the other Association for Southeast Asian Nations (ASEAN) states remains mixed. Internal political and economic crises have prevented Indonesia, the past preeminent nation of that group, from exhibiting leadership in spite of the visits of its two recent presidents.

The Thai situation has markedly shifted. A number of relatively minor military confrontations between the Thai and Burmese militaries have occurred, resulting in border tensions and temporary closures of trading posts. The Thai administration, worried over the massive influx of methamphetamines from Myanmar, have been clandestinely arming the insurgent Shan State Army to fight against the minority Wa group, said to be the leading dealer of this narcotic. In essence, surrogate warfare between the Thai and the Burmese have been carried out through minorities on either side of the political fence, although questions remain as to the degree of Burmese control over the Wa. The basically liberal former Thai foreign minister and deputy foreign minister (both of whom advocated greater democratization in Myanmar) were replaced after the January 2000 Thai election, and the new government has improved relations with the Burmese through the visit in July 2001 by Thai Prime Minister Thaksin Shinawatra and, later, his Minister of Defense, General Chavalit Yongchaiyudh (who was the first senior foreign visitor to Burma in late 1988 following the coup and who arranged teak and other concessions for the Thai). General Khin Nyunt, Secretary-1 of the SPDC, visited Thailand under high security the first week of September 2001. General Than Shwe visited Malaysia the end of September 2001. As the Indonesian leadership of ASEAN has waned, Malaysia has played a more important role in Burmese relations.

Economic conditions remain extremely poor. The Burmese currency, the *kyat,* has deteriorated in value, ranging from K.700 to 800 to the U.S. dollar, while the official rate remains about K.6 to the dollar. Foreign-exchange certificates, adopted on a Chinese model and originally calculated at par with the dollar, have dropped by 20 to 25 percent, indicating a serious lack of confidence in the currency and the fiscal policies of the state. The price of rice, a critical indicator of economic well-being and political stability, has doubled since 1999. Cooking oil, the second most important commodity, is increasingly expensive and in short supply.

The military continues to attempt to justify its position but has taken the criticisms of the International Labor Organization (ILO) most seriously and has tried, at least on the surface, to accommodate to their concerns on forced (or corvée) labor. A high-level ILO inspection team arrived in the country in September 2001 and have been given free access.

Myanmar essentially remains "plus ça change . . .", but the stasis may still be broken by current negotiations, which may alleviate more fundamental problems but are unlikely to resolve them. The purported leak of minutes of the dialogue in late September indicates that some sort of a "political consultation committee" and a military-civilian-ethnic-interest group "coalition government" (on the precedent of the Caretaker Government of 1958–60) might be formed. The group would allow the reformation of the National Convention on the constitution and call for new elections thereafter. The American administration, influenced by a vocal congressional minority that it believes it cannot alienate, remains adamant in its resolution for democratic change. But, if sanctified by Aung San Suu Kyi, some political accommodation that would bring the NLD back into the National Convention and resuscitate the process of formulating a new constitution, with the prospect of future new elections, would revitalize the international nongovernmental aid organizations and perhaps attract foreign investment again should the ILO findings be less adverse than in the past. The U.S. has abrogated its potential leadership role in the resolution of the Burmese political conundrum by its adamant stand; the European Union, led by the British and supported by the Japanese, may be more pliant.

It is unlikely, however, that the more basic issues facing the society will be resolved by any immediate rapprochement between the disputants, although amelioration of the present impasse would be most welcome. Power is still personalized, internal chauvinism is pervasive, law remains whimsical, the military is stronger than it has ever been and its sense of mission is undiminished, and the minorities are unassuaged. The ultimate national and continuing tragedy is that a state with so great a human and material potential and so rich a heritage should remain mired in a deteriorated present and a clouded future.

Bethesda, Maryland
September 2001

About the Author

David I. Steinberg is Director of Asian Studies, Georgetown University, and a Senior Consultant to The Asia Foundation. He has been Distinguished Professor of Korean Studies at Georgetown and President of the Mansfield Center for Pacific Affairs. Prior to these positions, he was a member of the Senior Foreign Service in the Department of State, Agency for International Development, where at various times he was Director of Technical Assistance for Asia, the Near East and South Asia, and the Middle East. As Director for Philippines, Thailand, and Burma Affairs, he negotiated the reentry of USAID into Burma in 1978. In USAID, he also spent three years in its Regional Mission in Bangkok and in the Office of Evaluation in Washington, where he wrote a number of the evaluation studies published by that office. He was also a representative of The Asia Foundation in Burma (1958–62), Hong Kong, Korea, and Washington, D.C.

He is the author of ten books and monographs, including *The Future of Burma: Crisis and Choice in Myanmar* (University Press of America, 1990); *Burma A Socialist Nation of Southeast Asia* (Westview Press, 1982); and *Burma's Road toward Development: Growth and Ideology under Military Rule* (Westview Press, 1981). He is also the author of a variety of works on Korea, including *The Republic of Korea: Economic Development and Social Change* (Westview Press, 1989), as well as some 80 articles and volume chapters. He is a frequent writer for the press and has published over 200 columns, called the "Stone Mirror," in the *Korea Times* (Seoul).

David Steinberg was educated at Dartmouth College, Lingnan University (Canton, China), Harvard University, and the School of Oriental and African Studies, University of London, where he studied Burmese and Southeast Asian history. He has lived over seventeen years in Asia, including four years in Burma. He is a native of Boston, Massachusetts.

Index